TECONOMICS of Infrastructures

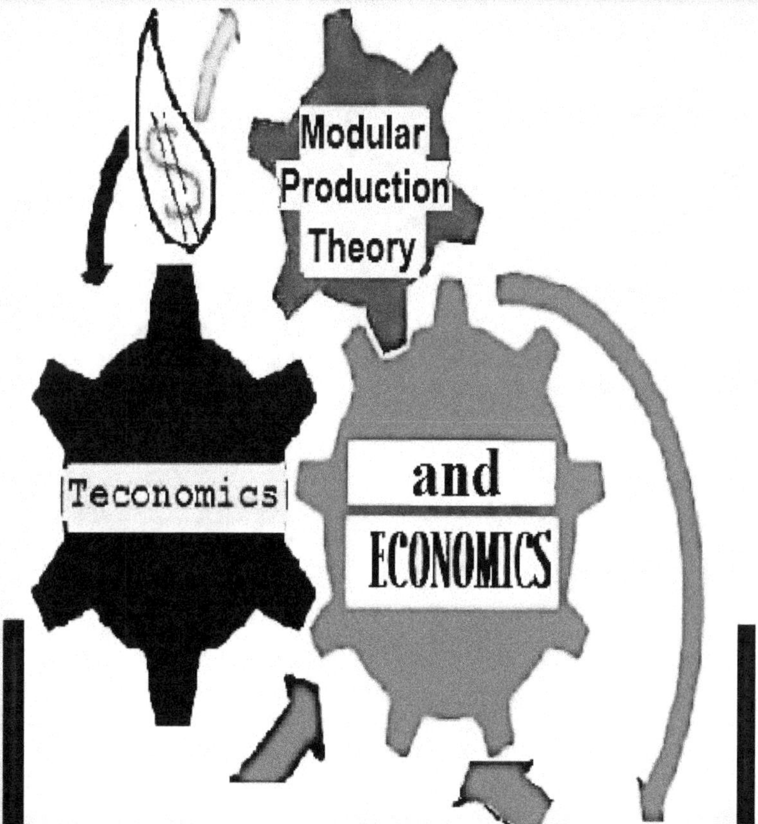

Bahman Fakhraie, Ph.D.

TECONOMICS OF INFRASTRUCTURES

[Original Work]

Teconomic of Infrastructures as Holistic Foundations And Integral Part of Dynamic Productive Modern Economics

BY

Bahman Fakhraie, PhD

April 7, 2016

Library of Congress
Copyright certificate # 13278220881
ISBN-10: 0-9894539-8-7
ISBN-13: 978-0-9894539-8-1
$125.00
ISBN 978-0-9894539-8-1
59999>
9 780989 453981

ABSTRACT

This book of original work advances the constructive implications in the teconomics of infrastructures that studies infrastructures foundations as integral parts of productive and dynamic modern economics, which have deterministic result in today economies. The infrastructural maintenance, updating, and dynamic modernization are important part of the technological injections and comprehensions of holistic infrastructures in productive and functional economics advancements.

Scientific Synthesis of Political Economics, Microeconomics, Macroeconomics, Mathematics, and Statistical Methodologies, Technological Parameters in Production Theory, and Political Teconomics of technological injections of dynamic variables in production and microeconomic theory contribute to the societal benefits, which combined with constructive creation in good governance will advance humanity level of wellbeing. This study follows author's previous four-works and studies since 1975, including Dr. Bahman Fakhraie's dissertation.

DEDICATION

To Kay Davis, Lara Fatemeh, Anayat Wayne Fakhraie and my family at large, I am grateful to my family Kay Davis Fakhraie, Lara Fatemeh Fakhraie and Anayat Wayne Fakhraie. They were great help in my recovery. I also appreciate my extended family in Dezful Iran, which has expanded globally and they shared their concerns, in memorial to Sied Mehdi Fakhraie, PhD. I especially thank Dr. Hamid Fakhraie that took some times out of his busy schedule to visit and help with his skills. In addition, I thank many helpful friends here in United States.

The book is dedicated to all hospitable and free people that are so sprinkled frugally among humanity, globally. They deserve to live with freedom, prosperity, and in peace.

CONTENTS

LIST OF TABLES

Table Page

LIST OF FIGURES

Figure Page

PREFACE

In process of finishing this work, our parents and some family members and great teachers have passed away. In memoriun, they remain in our thoughts.

I have been the beneficiary of education systems, medical technologies and infrastructures, roads, in planes, trains, and vehicles mainly in two countries and substantially globally, and I agree that nothing will substitute for great educated and skill professionals, good educational institutions, and genuinely concerned educators, and parents internationally. Each child miss undereducated, or ignored is a lost chance to improve all human lives. It will take extra resources to balance each event of abandonment or partial or complete neglect. It is only noticeable to our determents that insufficient investment in infrastructures affects our limbs or lives greatly.

When we are in a new place or new situations that they have under invested in such infrastructures, our operational and sometime survival risks are much greater palpably, including financially. All nations can be as kind and generous as the best of their people, and as inhospitable and inhumane as the worst of their political leaders make it so, and their funding choices are telling.

This research is an accumulation of many years of analytical empiricism and academic studies. It is the accumulated experiences in enumerated research papers, oversea studies, experiences, travels, and written and published more than fifteen books, and e-books. The economic scholarly focus here in national wealth creation does not advance personal greed, hubris of wealth concentration, monopolistic profiteering, but by job creation, livable wages, flow and rates of circularity of money that supports economic growth in both arenas of demand and supply expansively, inclusively, and globally.

It is the endeavors of good scholarship to enhance lives and survival expansively and positively. I hope this book accomplishes a small gesture of good will toward those endowers of good scholarship.

Bahman Fakhraie PhD, 2014

CHAPTER 1

INTRODUCTION

In the new Paradigm of Teconomics, constructions, and deconstructions of infrastructures have consequential impacts on civil society, in economic, and in sociopolitical sphere of human endeavors. The past minimalist definitions of infrastructures have failed current events substantially. Humanity cannot ignore the road, bridges, internet digital highways, and organizational infrastructures aspects of modernity that link all limbs constructively, to chance events and incidental divestment of history.

The Ebola epidemic of Africa n modern economy went unnoticed, devastating village to villages, but soon it was a global pandemic. It was controlled finally by injection of modern medicine and technologies, and regional healthcare centers, and international skilled physicians to stop its devastating expansion. The ages and epochs of caravan sojourns for commerce of spices and trinkets have long past to modern but civil and constructive infrastructures complexities. In this book, that eventuality is studies.

Bahman Fakhraie, PhD. © 2015

Can we reconstruct the bonds among humanity that congeals all of humanity, against the hours of madness unleashed upon us by too many odd events, and odder hate groups, endogenous or exogenous? That is the hour of contemplative reconstruction and uplifting of prized cultural values, modern infrastructures of constructive coexistence, and about freedom of speech, free press, freedom of thoughts, trade, commerce, peaceful and long lasting tolerance, more employments, and uplifting of others, rather than momentary and dangerous hate speech and perpetuation of group hate. That would be the constructive infrastructures, which will endure as a legacy of cultural sustainability against terror and terrorisms for all of humanity, and more deconstructive power struggles globally.

This study introduces the definitions and establishments of known and studied economic variables in the contexts of this research in the infrastructures as holistic foundations of dynamic modern economics.[1] This will establish the criteria and frame for microeconomic comprehension of technological progress and economic history and economic thought.

This study uses the endogenous nature of technological advancement in production theory of microeconomics in political economics. Statistical study of

United States economy 1950-80, will measure the specific inputs and for the impacts of comparative data on the overall production. Furthermore, graphical presentation, game theory, set theory, economic history, and economic welfare theory will support the constructive arguments for developing nations, which would like to adopt positive and constructive economic strategies for global beneficial adoptions.

The supply and demand aspect of technological advancement only partly allow for sustainable economic success, however, the essentials and systems conditionality requires detailed scrutiny and scholarly study. When free perfectly competitive markets in democratic systems are the last strategic hopes for sustainable economic advancement, often-derailing details are missing from these complex strategies for global sustainable survival. Ignorance of such details does not enhance global security and stability, but endanger it. An expanding global population needs to employ diminishing global resources to meet demands, which without education will implode all systems, as the rate of pollution growth far exceed the capacity of detoxification, either natural or manufactured. Other issues of health, food, and wellbeing complicate realities, these without prioritization of needs, wants, and without appropriate pricing remain problematic. In this paper, we study that even segmental corrections can yield promising results for the economic welfare of the globe.

Sooner than later, outside the academic world, there will be a realization beyond the familiarity of buzzword like "technology" that the fields of statistical economic analysis has evolved into econometrics, and the newly advances in the technological studies, econometrics, and modular economic production theory, economic welfare theory, and political economic studies. This compendious volume is presented in this study for interested readers, scholars, and future economists of our time, in Politeconomics book as an innovation study, which evolved into the new paradigm field of teconometrics. However, we can grow knowledge at the biological, organizational, and institutional capabilities of societal rate of comprehension.

The last few volumes of works in production and technological injection, and capital formation and economic systems expansively explain the complexities of economic systems that motivate advanced economies needs to remain sustainably in productive and distributive capacity, functionality, and system stabilities.

Occasionally, certain class, feudalist of the middle ages Europe, Cooperates' Chief executive officers of modern cooperation, government functionaries of totalitarian, dictatorial, even socialists and democratic system can bend and twist the rules and conducts of economics systems into absolute wealth concentration mechanism, often without transparency for certain given periods. That period can get shorter historically. Alternatively, if transparency exists in none democratic systems or it is forced by technological paradigm shifts, then the systems may tend to relay more on brutality, militaristic means, revolving door military industrial complexes, and on militarized police forces. A better more strategic democratic development path will contain these new modular production factors will meet three fundamental conditions. Lemma 1, is it necessary? Lemma 2, is it sufficient? Lemma 3, is it sustainable? Since the advancement of the second best theorem, in complex optimization formulation in welfare economic theory, this is the first prominent study that advances the economic science toward sustainability condition. The difficulties arise as economic cyclical system develop and progress, even with technological injections, they can ran into the governmental counter cyclical developments, civil unrest, and even revolutionary deconstructive phases. That is why the final chapters detail and specify case studies in such ubiquitously unpalatable subject matters.

Modern societies have been the beneficiary of education systems, medical technologies and infrastructures, roads, in planes, trains, and vehicles mainly in two countries and substantially globally, and I agree that nothing will substitute for great educated and skill professionals, good educational institutions, and genuinely concerned educators, and parents internationally. Each child miss undereducated, or ignored is a lost chance to improve all human lives. It will take extra resources to balance each event of abandonment or partial or complete neglect. It is only noticeable to our determents that insufficient investment in infrastructures affects our limbs or lives greatly. When we are in a new place or new situations that they have under invested in such infrastructures, our operational and sometime survival risks are much greater palpably, including finically. All nations can be as kind and generous as the best of their people, and as inhospitable and inhumane as the worst of their political leaders make it so, and their funding choices are telling.

This research is an accumulation of many years of analytical empiricism and academic studies. It is the accumulated experiences in enumerated research papers, oversea studies, experiences, travels, and written and published more than fifteen books, and e-books. The economic scholarly focus here in national wealth creation does not advance personal greed, hubris of wealth concentration, monopolistic profiteering, but by job creation, livable wages, flow and rates of circularity of money that supports economic growth in both arenas of demand and supply expansively, inclusively, and globally.

These are not mutually exclusive processes subject to partisans' entertainment, but they are balancing, and yes, dynamically balancing-recursive equations with negative externalities.

It is a common mistake that animal spirit and competition will naturally encourage comparative perception of doing well relative to others miseries. However, in flow and circulation of monetary theory, and appropriate exchange theory the more agents and organizational factors are employed in economic activities, the better off the entire economy will benefit, and the higher redistributive influences of economic wellbeing will carry. The book will hope to demonstrate that as much as possible.

It is the endeavors of good scholarship to enhance lives and survival expansively and positively. I hope this book accomplishes a small gesture of good will toward those endowers of good scholarship.

Advancement of modern society is not a one-dimensional progress, often group thought persuades masses toward the wrong idols. Parsimony, penny pinching, and under funding of resources can harm growth orientation of an advanced economy as well as, too much regulation, too much taxation of embryonic small businesses, and the micromanagement of people endeavors. Adam Smith example of villagers with a small load of produce, can bribe each bridge toll and have very little to sell in town, and have even less saved to pay taxes to the government. Nevertheless, he or she will have a lot more produce for the town and more income to pay taxes without the bridge tolls. We tend to forget that. We favor scale and large size industries, while small business advances our national wealth, create jobs, and circulate money.

Sooner than later, outside the academic world, there will be a realization beyond the familiarity of buzzword like "technology" that the fields of statistical economic analysis has evolved into econometrics, and the newly advances in the technological studies, econometrics, economic production theory, and economic welfare theory have had innovational-evolution into teconometrics. However, we cannot hurry or push knowledge beyond the biological, organizational, and institutional capabilities.[2] Besides, the magnitude and speed of advancement in knowledge is a source of job security for sharp librarians, new PhDs, and sharp academics, among others.

Furthermore, if functionalities of appropriate government prevail, wealth of nations can expand substantially in light of such technological advancements. Each child miss educated or ignored is a lost chance to improve all human lives, each group, gender, victimized domestically and blocked in progressive mobility globally, is another resource underutilized. Humanity is that interconnected, economically and globally.

Teconomicalogy is the scientific study and recognition of the ubiquity of technology in all economic endeavors, but specifically as a new production variable in Teconomics (Tekonomics). This is the addition of the variable, which is affecting other variables of production labor and capital. But it must exists, before any combination of variables and resources could be applied, as the methodology of production, also it exist in each labor as skill to use and function with the capital in each production activity, and in capital item used, and its replacement as it is being developed.[3]

Since economic is a scientific advancement, which did not exist until capital and labor got detached from their traditional and social status and become economic agents exchangeable in newly created innovation called markets, borrowed from old Bazaars of Persia, around 1300-15000 century BC. It is fitting that we now add another recognized elements of production, which attributes greatly to functionality and multiplies the effects of both labor and capital, and creates capital (human and physical). It is recognized to enhance production often endogenously to the process of production. Techno-economic-logy is to represent technology, economics, and science. Techeconomics is used as a shorter form for the economy of entomology. These definitions are to avoid other potential misrepresentations of, which science popular words may carry with them. Therefore, tekonomology and tekonomics are used to mean the same in this study. This chapter studies the general presentation of this research.

The impacts of different measurements of capital stocks on embodied and disembodied technological variables, on productively, and economic growth of national social products are tested. The role of a new capital stock measure introduced in writing of Friedrich August Von Hayek, John Maynard Keynes and further developed by Evsey D. Domar and ignored by most modern economist are examined. Therefore, we focus on the demand and supply side of technological embodied in capital both human skill and produced goods and services and the economy.

On the demand side of technological injection, it is

important to establish that what 75-78 percent of the economy wants they will have, and the reverse is also true, what majority of the consumer reject will vanish in the market place. The implications of global consumers' demand have universal impacts as well. That is, what the consumer reject from their producers at home, they also reject in global market. However, the most telling aspect of demand side is the related to the income of local consumers, with a decreasing disposable income, the demand of all product declines, more so for experimental, newer technology embodied products, which often may have the higher prices. Therefore, the demand of producers for new technologies will inevitably reflect the demand of consumer for their new products. It is inevitably significant to realize the consumers will seek the bundles of goods and services which lands them on the highest utility curve they budget constraint allows.

The supply side of technology analysis is a more extensive study of the long strings of events, which in full fruition produce a saleable, useful item. Moreover, in the process of supplying, properly paid workers are employed. The wages as value in products require meeting modern formulation, within the standard of civil society in a manner that accommodates a family life, and functionality in an ever more complex and demanding societal complexity, and remain relevant to the value of final product sold.

On the supply side, the transformation of relevant insights on innovation is presented. The analysis reflects the evolution of ideas about discovery and invention, via Abbott Payson Usher cumulative synthesis process is newly advanced, in the process of supply side of technological injection in the economy.

If the same theoretical frameworks are abused in injecting decay in developing nation, or the technological advancement made the same frameworks under new assumptive conditions useful, would the developing nation adopt the new skills, and use them under the restrictive assumptions imposed? Global trade, freer-trade, democratic governance with decentralizations, relatively freer market pricing, improvements in capital markets are among some of these principles, which have been expensively miss appropriated and miss applied by some of the worst political and economic charlatans in modern times. It is important to start with perfect-competition assumptive conditions and clear explanations, but introduce economic success or corrective strategies, when possible.

Perfectly Competitive Markets and Democracies

Aimless revolutions and capital destructions, without

developing or adopting and modifying political and institutional technologies to encourage democratic functionality is too costly for human and tangible capitals to sustain. During 1970s, some South American countries had a revolution per year. Simply putting out laws like a broken-down sausage machine using bad meat using faster better technologically more superior machine will only compound the problems and costs faster. It is not only bad governance, which is misusing bad technologies and inappropriate inputs. It is unstable governance. Unless quickly, democratically, and internally the unstable governance is replaced by the governed, nothing less will do. Fundamental realization is that consumers, producers, employers, and employees, all members of society and global societies will gain or lose at either the margins, but greatly en mass from arrows and slings of global economic and technological activities.

Here the newest tools of economic science explain the impact of technological alteration on the economy. Game theory, set theory, mathematic economy, econometrics, and Bayesian statistical theory of decision-making, and the production theory at advanced economic levels are newly utilized. A fundamental aspect of experimental economic technological advancement is that it remains scientifically experimental in nature, and not dogmatic. To that extend, this study will be timely.

It is an expansion and inclusion of ancient and modern elements of economic studies that enlightened us to the origin and complementation of modern studies in this field.[4] The thesis states that the dynamic influences of technology and elemental factors of production --defined and measured in this study-- are greater than commonly have been calculated or expected, and the production optimization processes must meet necessary, sufficient, and sustainability conditions in order to assist in sustainable development path for economic advancement.

Foundational Definitions For Political-Teconomics

The narratives developed here parallels perfect competition analysis of market with functional democracies, which will serve those markets and the future sustainability in the market.

Sustainability is defined as balanced but functional political and economic institutions, which allow longer-term (dynamic) adoptive changes to materialize, without major melee, civil wars, and capital destructions.

Therefore, we have presented competitive assumptions of perfectly competitive free markets, as required apolitical conditions to allow democratic changes to function. The explanation for the conditionality is not too difficult to present. Imperfect competitions in market allows wealth accumulation, rather than functional distribution of income, normal with proportional wage setting and majority benefits from slow but sustainable wealth accumulation. The wealth concentration, and the power of market manipulations of market place of ideas and decision-making, the political arena, both create misrepresentation, which are not healthy for the dynamic economy or democracy. A monopoly will manage production in such a way to keep profits maximum, aside from resources, jobs, and production are kept to a minimum. Wealth concentration allows political monopoly arrangement, to generate laws, which keep maximum benefit of the source, rather than social benefit of the community. The operation of the economics activities are managed in order to advantage the short-term massive and historical gains of the few only, leaving extensive unemployed resources. Versus, economic resources are operationally managed to employ most resources optimally, and sustainably.[5] In such a way, that it will advantage the longer-term or sustained gains of the group, or even the society, including the few.

Investment or Divestment In Infrastructures

Teconomics of infrastructures-rebuild studies the beyond the additions of physical and structural systems.

The investment or divestments in infrastructures have important affect in the functionality and advancement of economics systems, which are not properly understood. It is important to understand that roads, tunnels, bridges, and the new internet digital highways connect markets, systems, and subsystems, between economic and sociopolitical systems.

Hate groups and political parties divided loyalties were not deconstructive strategies just in the past. The recent advertent vehemence anti-immigrant political rhetorical-attacks have deep hooded hate-robe-roots. Some scream about dual citizenship, and minor immigrants, and avoid allowing people to vote, using divided loyalty to hide xenophobic bigoted cultural history. The biggest bugaboo is their divided loyalty for public good versus the big banks' monopolistic political controls, and overt law makings that are deconstructive.

That infrastructures deconstructions and divided loyalty runs between their shoes and they are very quiet about it. That lack of acquiescence must be important to their check accounts economics and their political bookkeeping, but not to the middle class minority accounts. We are all at risk as early as next year, as the house turns, and the big banks dream of wild and free good-old derivative-days spring eternal again. Therefore, financial security can be vaporous, but what about the other securities that were charged to the taxpayers in full. Despite the super human hard work of all patriots in the fields, has that flame- proofed our celestial garment? The wild militaristic and dispersed focus has diminished our attention zones, while they have narrowed our dangerous-groups vision-scopes to anything and everything Muslim.

Who caused France, Australia, and Other Tragedies! Condolences to all family members of large group of people already dead, martyred, and newly killed by ISIS, ISIL, and "Al-Quad-eh Inc. Intl," more recently in France. Those victims include Shia, Sunni, other Muslims, and some none Islamic religions in Iraq, Africa, and Middle East, too.[6] Unfortunately, some cheapen the importance of each moment, and the concepts of free press and freedom of thought and expressions in the Popperian "Open Society."[7] They pass on their own libel, ignorance, group hate speech, and cheapened Islamophobia insults in disguise as important cultural and security statements, and impose and dictate some delusional nonexistence cultural and racial purity tests. That imposed on any one religion is foolish and dangerous.[8] In such state of delusional hyperactive security, a population minority of 7 percent yields 70 percent of jailed population unquestioned, by the free press in that same country. This is easily a discriminatory misapplication and destabilizing illusion of justice systems. It preposterously increased orphaned and free radical population for extremism foreign or domestic, national or international exponentially. Where is the free press? Who can deconstructive domestic national infrastructures t that extend? Is it some external monastic theology, or divestments in infrastructures due to bigoted, xenophobic, and past colonial history? Rightwing nuts' blame-game politics against minorities and by abusive politics of self- flagellating laws, alienating and segregating immigration policies, commands, and deconstructive ideologies have long lost their lusters.[9] Those losing propositions have created self-defeating socioeconomic conflicts and mass joblessness, and diminishing endogenous and exogenous benefits. They never had intellectual, logical, or holistic socio-economic foundations. That is why they needed and used maximum anti-social forces, and the incredible and massive abuse of national security privileges and laws.

It is time for minimal-evolving to run the governments, in USA, EU, Israel, and anywhere and everywhere. All governments and especially democratic republic governments need to relay on their maturity and informed publics, instead of spin politics of Neo-Nazis extremism, colonial privileges, and slavery epochs' mandates, or overt xenophobic hate mongering to gain legitimate respect and leadership positions.

Educated people in Islam and out of that multi-varied cultures already understand the difference between xenophobic hate speech passed on by political hate groups, Western and Eastern rightwing extremists hate groups to encourage and induce divisive hate against Islam and other religions, Muslims, Jews, Christians, Immigrants, other minorities, and cultural and political groups.[10] They do this at times to perpetuate wars, or self-help their dying political legacies, and failed careers, and extremist political and theological movements, if they are sophisticated enough.[11] Otherwise, they are manipulated mercilessly to such ends. Why should any open society help them to divest in the constructive and functional infrastructures of modern and tolerant economic systems? They also block and stop voting and they perpetuate disorder and propagate terrorism, while wasting needed reconstruction resources, often on military equipment, frequently badly advised by advance economies or industrial nations.

Very few people will confuse xenophobic hate speech by rightwing para military hate groups with respectable free journalism, scholarly work, or good cartoons with sophisticated ideas and some new information, not just insults and verbal trash aimed at the other cultures, minorities, Jews, Muslims, women, gays, increasingly Middle Easterners, Arabs, and African people, or liberals.

No one advocates a fearful-pass or blind eye on all the ills and cultural violence against humanity by any religion, society, dictatorships, nations, or culture. Since we already have had enough funny and biased political media, we still need that other democratic principle in good media. That media is good enough to die for, if it is free press. That contributes to the society in constructing, maintaining, and advancing political infrastructures.

Free presses are part of those important infrastructures. They are part of functionally good democratic republics that help honest governments be functional, stable, and sustainable. Moreover, good journalists are targeted by all cultures, nations, and government, and none government entities. If media is only targeting a religion, or journalists, in the middle of implosive socioeconomic and jobless conditions are not doing the job. They are divesting in the infrastructures of those societies.

Free and independent, journalism is the third leg of any good, functioning, and democratic governments. It remains indispensable infrastructure of a free society. It is a cherished democratic value, which the right-wing-nuts hate among all the other things; they enumerate in their vociferous hate speeches. In cultural unification and solidarity, we easily defeat their global terroristic purposes here, there, and everywhere.

Are we there yet? The process of giving up some of your rights for some security is not a finished dogmatic entity or notion, as Benjamin Franklin had always suspected it. It is still in developing and metastasizing state of dynamic flex. The separation of powers as exogenous and endogenous entities have dissolved as well, for more security reasons but not strictly or successfully, it seems, as at least some of American representatives had noticed and were under attacked for red lining criminal misadventures in the darker corners.[12] It will prove counterproductive if the so-called sand-cave dwellers were another assigned code name for American citizens or bunch of dear old church people at large, again.[13] Just a few degrees worse than the same cave dwellers dictating fear-policy, or generating group hate against Jews, other Muslims, or minorities by their overt criminal misconducts individually or in groups.

Why, do the modern societies doubt we have mastered some cultural maturity to handle all of our cultural diversities? The kind of misguided and costly preoccupations, which would disguise tectonic growth of say the ISIL types totally undetected, and after taxpayers spent treasures is still an issue. The security-incarcerations industrial profiteering complexes and the misapplication of resources are divestment in the infrastructures issues, when even after the facts, they try desperately to refocus effort in targeting mass and general data collections, instead the rifling-focus should have filtered preselected-data for use of national resources. That somewhat operationally and economically wasteful failure should not continue. Are the citizens-doubts permitted under the newer national security greed-machines laws? Is thinking, writing, expressions of all doubts or all humor permissible? On the other hand, are the ever so rarified intellectual thoughts parts of those permissible sins these days? Why do we see the new conjecturers' constructs alienate and isolate too many minorities, races, and religions, and feed the fires of joblessness and extremists, and make more shadows for corruption commerce, and thriving terrorism? Should we use every occasions of murderous rampage as an occasion to denigrate theological masses of others, engage in-group guilt, and spread group hate on top of alienations, infrastructure divestments, and joblessness. Can we reconstruct the bonds among humanity that congeals all of humanity, against the hours of madness unleashed upon us by too many odd events, and odder hate groups, endogenous or exogenous?

That is the hour of contemplative reconstruction and uplifting of prized cultural values, modern infrastructures of constructive coexistence, and about freedom of speech, free press, freedom of thoughts, trade, commerce, peaceful and long lasting tolerance, more employments, and uplifting of others, rather than momentary and dangerous hate speech and perpetuation of group hate. That would be the constructive infrastructures, which will endure as a legacy of cultural sustainability against terror and terrorisms for all of humanity.

Teconomics of the Infrastructures

The policies of deconstructions of American infrastructures and economy have not been good for American middle class, or American economy. Why should we sugar code them now, if we are at the beginning of rebuilding of America agenda? Let us beware of anti-immigrant xenophobia, anti-minority racisms, anti-elderly ageism, and anti-women sexism, anti-democrat, anti-science, and anti-liberals deliberate bad-news-clustering by monopolists media (YNN, Fixed News, others). They use bad news clustering, and planted attack news, as political agenda. For example, the xenophobic, bigoted southern strategists, fake rented-intellectuals, and token purchased-

GOP energy experts are taking advantage of fake Democrats and dumping news on American viewers, while they insist on American deconstruction policies. They think you are on their side, like the 1/4 they allow to vote for them. The rest they try to block the citizens' votes. Continuations of such bad policies will be bad foundations for solid formations of sustainable democratic political infrastructures.

Even a quick overview will tell a lot. That it is time to think about reconstruction policies for American economy. Somehow a pipeline to export Canadian very dirty and polluted oil to other international markets, which will pump and dump that toxic pollution in the California, Oregon, Seattle and Alaskan air initially, and the rest of America later, has become the end of all policy mantels of the vocal village idiots for cash. It is important that proper expert-studies that would measure the huge and increasing negative externality costs of toxic pollution went ignored, unpaid, and unstudied. However, those less than about 100 permanent USA jobs are job creation, but the multimillion jobs for needed infrastructures-projects were not, and they were not job-creation.

All these years the American infrastructures were to be ignored, because they help employ Americans, but tangentially they may help a black minority president. The other ballyhoo screams these days has been that immigrants take jobs away. These incompetent anti-science-jerks, sexists, xenophobic bigots refuse to acknowledge that they have obstructed job creation, for all these year that they have illegally derailed, usurped, tricked and cowed administrative enforcements, and blocked ethical, moral, or functional comprehensive immigration laws, while they are calling the waiting victims of their institutional legalese inactions, abusive, and plunders, illegals. These are divestment in infrastructures of a functioning democratic economy.

Let us read the first sentence of Amendment XIV Section 1, "All persons born or naturalized in United States and subject to jurisdiction therefore, are citizen of United States and the state wherein they reside." any of the three conditions are qualifiers despite the xenophobes' exclusionary interpretation. Abraham Lincoln was the 16th president of the United States. He found the intellectual root and the immigration links to Declaration of Independence. John F. Kennedy another great president of the other political party before President Obama thought the subject of such importance that he wrote a book on immigration.[14] Therefore, no president has left his or her constitutional purgative unexercised in fear of mouthy xenophobic bullies.[15] So, going big and flying high and bold for America, easing and unclogging naturalization regulations maize and costs, is the only legal way to stop the odoriferous and odiously anti-constitutional intellectual-constipation of the GOP-anti Reagan and anti-immigrants' un-American-agenda. Moreover, presidents expand the dwindling election fortunes of his or her political party, especially after the gerrymandering and vote blockages.

The ill impacts of wealth concentrations versus wealth-jobs-creation have been enumerated in multiple scholarly studies and books. The negative externalities of declining real disposable income and middle class Americans had been demonstrated as well. All of these occurred as they blocked immigrations, but followed bad policies of deconstruction of American infrastructures, and economy among their own selves.

Global Embarrassments

[Grâce et Mondial Embarras], Global-Embarrassments are poor substitute for international commerce and smart free trades policies. For example, EU is offended not by the democratic American administration preoccupation with the scheduled international leaders and guests at home, but war mongering and profiteering political and media moochers, and the right wing-nuts' spin machine and their fixed news giving it to EU_ minorities, while they were going to their funerals.[16]

These global embarrassments forget their recent shameful human right records and over-reaches at home, and their war on immigrants' children and refugee victims, and of course, the 20 years broken legal immigration laws, and their unconstitutional toll-road to none-citizenship, the laws they wrecked. Know-nothing and do-nothing rightists do not travel in grace or well globally.[17] They are international embarrassments now. EU, UK, Dutch, and France do not let international extremists' embarrassments denigrate their style or panache for too long, even when they are under fire. However, like the plot of Oscar list movie "The Budapest Hotel" the outdated even pleasant traditional institutions await current events to introduce them to unsustainable current realities, sometime with unpalatable results, which "SELMA" another Oscar list movie tried to explain, and it was eased out. While maturity, decency (morally or ethically), cooperate coexistence, ample assimilation, employment, and educational dynamics can substantially alter even intentional bad faiths, occasionally.

Those constructive infrastructures go unseen. Although, the Europeans already are teaching American rightwing anti-immigrations-gangs, they can mend fences, and bring their immigrants in the fold from the cold and script victories, just like the inclusive American model has done for a long time. They think they do better, than the Americans do, while American rightists' extremists have been breaking laws, fumbling around with the legal immigration laws for 20 years, making functional self-improving tools for individuals, for families, for USA economy, for young students, for elderly citizens, and for the nation holistically nonfunctional. Their unconstitutional law manipulations have created only petty cash but punitive long shadows for bad international criminal actors (drug cartels, human and drug traffickers, organized crimes and terrorists) to fish souls, to shark victims, and cause mayhem. At some point, the urgency of political hate groups may overwhelm Europe as well. At height of hypocrisy, then self-deceptively ignorant politicians blame the victims of their political ineptitudes, and callus tardiness. When a political party leaves the higher grounds and the brighten path, for corporate citizen' greed, rightists' intellectual self-dilutions, and the spin-falsehoods militarists' corporatism, all kinds of unconstructive things and backlashes happen along that dark path.

The ideological blinders are hard to discard, until the hard knocks on the noggins.[18] When it is time to fix a broken toll bridge, you fix it, or it will cave in on you.[19] That simple lesson of "Infrastructures Teconomics" was not hard for Presidents Franklin D. Roosevelt and Eisenhower. Nevertheless, many new rightists' politicians are happier to be simpleton Barn-Kickers than barn builders, or humbler more constructive traditional American barn raisers.

Historical Amnesia

The rightists' dangerous delusions are malformed some by miss read of the history, partly by self-leaking security-industrial- complex and the foreign land-grab-embezzlement political machines, since juxtaposing terror and others have a media center and a foreign military political machine in common.

Those worshiping failures 50, 30, 20 years old debunked and failed models are not bringing success to the arena of American or global politics. They are eating caviar and feeding the masses old cheese wiz, they know they are buying an expensive public puking as in the past, except the American taxpayers, and the middle class, are tagged for the whole bill. Misplaced hero worship is allowed in any free society, it is fine for some to live on it and off it. Yet, some of the real heroes in America are the USA war veterans. They have been dying in hospital queues and in the inefficient healthcare that the right wing nuts are promising not to fix but to dismantle for the middle class. An issue my father in law a WWII veteran, Korea, Vietnam era, and many new Iraq-war veterans have had to harangue with in their deathbeds.

There are a few politicians sneaking by their constitutional duties and responsibilities to poke a minority eye in the White House, and they declare others illegals, foolishly. Their own assigned duty, their service that gives them their taxpayers' paychecks, creating domestic jobs, infrastructure-rebuilding policies are all ignored.

Some political actors have tried to forget, ignore, or miss-spin the post-Vietnam blood-earned hard education at everyone else's expense. The real American victims of more than fifty thousands dead Americans and years of wrongheaded war monopolists and their media profiteers is for not, in the land of no-historical memory. The statistical bulge in population of Iraq and Afghanistan returned veterans on suicide watch and hospital queues that dropped dead did not bring out the well-groomed spin media, nor the well-funded financed political enchanters, except for one lone Arizona hoofer that politically paid for it in the last presidential election. We have forgotten that after President Kennedy assassination, the snipers crimes were uplifted to international human-right crimes and indecencies.[20] It was considered a heinous crime unanimously and ubiquitously. Do I need to remind these buckaroos, the media rightists, their military complex head-bobbers, the political right wing extremists, and some of their foreign allies and propagandists that they are all still responsible for John F. Kennedy's shortened presidency? Even if, they call people lefty, the history wrote a different movie script, truthfully.

However, we cannot blame the movies for political missteps and the do-nothing present realities, and their narrowed and small global intellectual visions. Nor can people logically, rationally, or even sanely blame the theological inclinations or readings for serial pedophilia abuses of little girls and boys, murderous criminality, and genocidal killings. That is the doings of global village idiots under false flags and self-chosen labels, using excuses that a viral media propagates swallow hook and sinkers, and spin-fully.

At the same time, the right wing political leadership plays blame games, tag the minorities, and load up malarkey laws, while the Ukraine burns. They are helping their left-uncle and the terrorists, when they unhinge. They and the terrorists like to attach Islam or anything (Iran, Saud, Shia, Sunni) to their every misdeed, one for juvenile recruits, cash, genocidal and criminal mass murders, and the others for self-glorification, new wars, wealth concentration, xenophobic bigotry laws, joblessness, torture, and war crimes. What motivate the rest of media mimickers, I am sure they will explain fully. They hold in common the shared abundance of ignorance. Perhaps those explain better, why moderates of any religion or many political creeds do not want to be close to their media manure spreaders in full operation.

They have been the most dangerous direct dismantlers of American infrastructures, heath, education, and jobs of the recent history. For the most parts, we are all willing to give the Hollywood creative licenses. Nevertheless, when they glorify war-failures instead of helping the real veterans, or Americans, or American minorities, the empty chair will talk back, and tell them where to get off. You can also use some of the worst expletives from their many movies. Nevertheless, the controversies seem to boost the ticket sales, until they and their plutocratic political machine put that part of the economy out of its misery and create more and newer joblessness, again. It mostly explains the average age of the moviegoers, not the moviemakers. It does not reflect the moviegoers knowledge, nor their sociopolitical and historical prospective. That discovery explains the shock, revulsion, and social unrest of anti-Vietnam-war youth at tale end of that war in 1960s and 1970s, which were bleeding both in the rice fields and on the American campuses. Then our American securities wonks were shooting white students on American campus colleges, with harsh backlash responses. Did we learn any hard lesson from the unrest, the discords, and the divestments in the political infrastructures? Regardless, how much and whom want to desperately exploit and blame old stories for their newer spins, and their long-war strategic implosions. It is not surprising that they are casting a long net to fish new more-war-propagandists foreign leaders that do not uphold American values, but violate them.

Infrastructures Reconstructions Efforts,

Those past examples vividly affirm the societal need for reinforcement and funding of technologically upgraded educational infrastructures. They prescribed rebuilding of public education systems, rather than dismantling it for petty cash, regional profiteering, promised votes, or reflective prejudicial incarcerations strategies. These are a few examples of costly failed free-market experiments of tinkle down economics mostly on the tax money from the middle class and the 90 percent, rather than the new middle class rebuilding plans. It is true that congress and they are in control of the agenda; however, they have not left many sound economic or infrastructure foundations for their new miss-steps. Just in case, their normal pro-CEOs, pro the one percent richest, plutocratic tinkle-down economics fails the global economy, again. While their government paid plutocrats cash upfront for the disaster they caused (in the crony capitalism).[21] The middle class and the poor never were refunded, their bank foreclosures and credit dents in their permanent records, but their services were sequestered, and their taxes increased, in crude phraseology of modern street scholars, they were screwed.

Plutocratic Agendas

Those twisted plans for hording cash for the 1 percent plutocrats in the name of job creation are numbered for many reasons. Therefore, you either come up with your new Middle Class economic development plan or adopt one. Those days of dancing about killing people or hateful deconstructive immigration policies unconstitutionally are dubious, since they have yielded better distasteful and murderous fruits, and because theoretically the congress both houses are now the responsible adults in charge of constructive policies for all human lives and all foibles. It is a free country; we can dream positive dreams, too. It is long past time the houses advance with the constructions of infrastructures policies, especially domestically, instead of feeding the war-moochers for new tricks, with middle class taxpayers' hard-earned cash. Otherwise, their constituency will remind both houses by their purses and ballots.

Teconomics of Infrastructures

The American people expect a fixed humane immigration law-machine that helps people long in the queues, not the unconstitutional-savage incarcerations-complex for the profiteers and xenophobes' employment guarantee and the failed intellects of southern strategists.

If you live in total ignorance and in oblivion,
Of all others' misery you caused,
You make it impossible to name you,
Among the ranks of humanity,
Regardless of whom you blame,
For all of the pains you've caused.
Saadi, a Persian poet 1200,[22]
Dr. Bahman Fakhraie © 2015

American-taxpayers are still hopeful both houses will do the jobs on their behests respectfully. Moreover, they expect them to help the middle class economy, since the Middle Class paid for their global moves, self-dealings, the big bad bankers, and the one percent laws twisting and twerking, and the perpetual failing war machines.

The Jobs Infrastructures

All these years job creation has declined and data shows job per population ration and trend lines have structurally declined, and unemployment rates have increased not because of immigration, but because of insufficient flow of immigration, human and other capital constructions.

They have been the job killers, since data shows the rate of unemployment has increase for all those years that they blocked comprehensive immigration, a fact that presidents after president understood and said so, President Reagan expressed it. Those presidents used administrative enforcements to countermand xenophobic self-flagellations of grand wizards of temporary success, and short-term shenanigans, which victimized American job creation for all these years.

Talking about important presidents, that is why we have reached that point of constitutional and constructional-crisis, which a president can rightly tell the know-nothing and do-nothings: you have failed to do your constitutional duty for too long. Therefore, we will give you a full meal in form of a comprehensive immigration laws, and for teconomic of infrastructures reconstructions, and the middle class economic rebuild. Moreover, you can tell Americans, why you cannot tie your shoes running to cash your taxpayers paid big congressional checks for all of these years that you have done nothing, but obstruction.

The epoch of political mantras are past, the focus will have to be forward looking to 2016 and way past the election. Because mostly stopping deconstruction of United States economy and meaningful job-creations cannot wait for another election and a republican president. These were studied and recommended in the rebuilding of American infrastructures in three out of my last eighteen economic books and e-books, and even under graduate papers, since 1970s. The construction should be dynamic regardless of peculiar politics of the unread, or the un-informed.

Notes

[1] This is a continuation of previous work author has finished and some work in progress in this field.

[2] There are more explanations in this study, the book-link is as follows, https://order.proquest.com/OA_HTML/pqdtibeCCtpItmDspRte.jsp .

[3] For long time, it has been assumed that certain variable must exists along labor and capital for modern production theory, this study extends that on the shoulder and work of economic giants into a mathematical and new econometric formulations and framework, into modern thought and economic theory.

[4] Sometimes, we forget that human advancement has very long multicultural roots. In studies, those roots are sometime neglected, or the historical progressions are missed or misrepresented. Such scientific conducts subtracts from human knowledge unnecessarily. The intention of this research is to clarify and expand our human knowledge and not to subtract from it, or assign fault and guilt.

[5] Dr. Bahman Fakhraie books are on internet for all interested readers regardless of their intellectual leanings, or creeds, http://drbahfecon.wix.com/teconomics

[6] This is not just one religion; Buddhists in Asian villages did the same thing a few month back! Sudarsan Raghavan, Tens of thousands of Muslims flee Christian militias in Central African Republic, February 7, 2014

[7] Karl R. Popper, The Open Society and Its Enemies, Princeton University Press, 1950

[8] Scott Kaufman, Reza Aslan: Anyone who asks why Muslims have not condemned terrorism can't use Google, 11 Jan 2015 at 13:09 ET, http://www.rawstory.com/rs/2015/01/reza-aslan-anyone-who-asks-why-muslims-have-not-condemned-terrorism-cant-use-google/

[9] Updated by Max Fisher, This map shows every attack on French Muslims since Charlie Hebdo, January 10, 2015, 11:30 a.m. ET, http://www.vox.com/2015/1/10/7524731/french-muslims-attacks-charlie-hebdo

[10] http://www.rawstory.com/rs/2015/01/46-examples-of-muslim-outrage-about-paris-shooting-that-fox-news-cant-seem-to-find/

[11] Ku Klux Klan reemerged in the U.S. http://www.pbs.org/wgbh/americanexperience/films/klansville/

[12] Gregory Fouladi, The Federal Government's Phishing Expedition, JURIST - Student Commentary, Dec. 19, 2014, http://jurist.org/student/2014/12/gregory-fouladi-government-phishing.php.

[13] JURIST Guest Columnist Tung Yin of the Lewis & Clark Law School argues that the Privacy and Civil Liberties Oversight Board's report on the NSA's telephone records program is likely best directed toward statutory changes in the Foreign Intelligence Surveillance Act rather than influencing decisions of the Foreign Intelligence Surveillance Court..."
Tung Yin, "Oversight Board Report May Lead to Surveillance Changes, http://jurist.org/forum/2014/02/tung-

yin-nsa-pclob.php

[14] Political Deconstructions of Infrastructures, Immigration Law, and American Economy, 2014

[15] Lawrence Downes, Behold the Republican Immigration Strategy: Mass Deportation, January 9, 2015 3:05 pmhttp://takingnote.blogs.nytimes.com/2015/01/09/behold-the-republican-immigration-strategy-mass-deportation/?_r=2

[16] http://www.thelocal.fr/…/hostage-hero-set-to-receive-french…
*-http://www.telegraph.co.uk/…/Paris-mayor-Well-sue-Fox-News-…

[17] -Patrick Young Esq., Lincoln, the Know Nothings and Immigrant America, http://www.longislandwins.com/…/lincoln_the_know_nothings_a

[18] Elemental aspects of some cultural changes: http://www.dutchnews.nl/…/expat-is-meaningless-its-time-to…/

[19] Just listen to them! Sadly, you will know what I mean. http://www.thelocal.fr/…/hostage-hero-set-to-receive-french…

[20] Clint Eastwood: 'American Sniper' is anti-war, 01/25/15 05:40 PM, http://www.msnbc.com/…/clint-eastwood-american-sniper-anti-…
*- http://www.washingtonpost.com/…/how-clint-eastwoods-ameri…/…

[21] Bahman Fakhraie, PhD, Analytical Remedies For The Millennial Cascading Economic Declines: Teconomic Analysis of Modern Political Economic..., Ferdat Publishing, Mar 1, 2013
http://www.amazon.com/Analytical-Remedies-Millennial-Cascading-Economic/dp/0985295864/ref=la_B00IKAR1CM_1_2?s=books&ie=UTF8&qid=1458577176&sr=1-2

[22] An interpretive translation of Saadi poem
For more in English check the following link on Saadi, http://www.payvand.com/news/05/oct/1083.html

CHAPTER 2

SELECTED DEFINITIONS OF TECHNOLOGY

This chapter examines the definitions and establishments of known and studied economic variables in the contexts of this research. This will establish the criteria and frame work for some future research and application of the same academic work, as it is required of all scientific research.[1] The evolution of ideas into the dynamic influences of technology and elemental factors of production --defined and measured in this study-- are greater than commonly have been calculated or expected, and the production optimization processes must meet necessary, sufficient, and sustainability conditions. The thesis is a quantitative econometric and macroeconomic study of microeconomic concepts aiding the production function, to test the impacts of different measurement of technological variables reflected in national accounts data. The imperial work combined with analysis of Usher-Schumpeter model in a new synthetic formulation of technological change creations and adaptations in this production function, with extra care taken to select least distorted data. The data and study will use real economic data to factor out money delusions as much as possible. This is to take out the cross-impacts of more relative nominal fluctuations to avoid over and under estimations of data. The real economic data become more important when dynamic studies are carried out and variables are studied over an extended periods. The econometrics analysis studies the aggregated data relative each period.

Human behavior inevitably determines how economic variables interact. The main challenge to economists often is to correctly define and then predict events as the causal result of flex human behaviors. Two major economic variables with varied definitions and uses are theories of value and capital. They influence technological changes and production functions. What is capital, what measures as capital? How do depreciation and replacement affect aggregation of capital and technological parameters?

Human Behavior

Most economists make assumptions about some aspects of human behavior to formulate their economic models. While dynamic economic models, economic forecasters, long-term economic planners, and all of their political dependents know how quickly human behavior tends to change. The use of economic models is a scientific aspect of academic economics, which will remain useful as long as we need some prediction with some degree of certainty. J. A. Schumpeter formulated motives of the entrepreneurs. Schumpeter enumeration of reasons for entrepreneurial activities went beyond what he called the "an insatiable craving for hedonistic satisfactions." The entrepreneurs struggled because,

1. One, they are seeking "private kingdoms."
2. Two, they have "the will to conquer."
3. Three, they engaged in "joy of creation."[2]

These may very well be in the psychic of entrepreneurs or part of their characteristics and beliefs system that affects their complex choice-decision makings, as we will study later.

J. M. Keynes in explaining motives for saving he noted more complexities involved.[3] Those motives differentiate with "the institutions and organization of the economy society." Those habits vary by "race, education, convention, religion, and current morals." "Present hopes and past experiences," by "scale and technique of capital equipment, and the prevailing distribution of wealth and the established standard of life reflect those motives. Further studies have further evolved beyond Keynes work.

Recently, inflationary psychology is under study on expected elements effecting economic behaviors. It is important to start with a general idea about what forms human behaviors.

There are two major divisions here, inherited (genetically pre-formed) or environmentally formed (learned) backgrounds, from the union of social, political, and economical subsets and degrees of education and the complexity of our understandings. These two wise subjects, with the more general background experiences, educations, will determine the way we form our thoughts, opinions, beliefs, and convictions. These serve the bases on, which we act and react, or plan to act in and upon our environments to acquire, reach, and overcome our equally complex goals out of our formulated needs and wants, as our desires.

Our genetic mix, 50 percent from our parents and 25 percent from each of our grandparents and on (DNA, deoxyribonucleic acids in the chromosomes of each cell nucleus) form us with inner biochemical mechanisms, neuromuscular thought-action modus operandi, contribute to these processes of production, with all capabilities and limitations in case of genetic diseases. Part of our genetic makeup is fixed. We cannot grow wings and fly, but behaviorally with other peoples and skills, we can learn to make planes and fly in them. Some limitations we can modify, cure, or overcome.[4] In case of some genetic illnesses, such as Down's syndrome, individuals may overcome handicaps by behavior modification and in the near future by genetic reconstructive medicine.

Environmental factors seem more important because they are all the factors we can change and can change our decision-makings around ourselves. They are nutritional factors, social factors, familial, religious, educational, societal (economic, political, legal, and regulatory) factors that shape human behaviors in one way or another. These are the gestalt, the whole, which are incremental advancements, expansions, and learned skills.

In modern times, television (technologically computer-chips enhanced multimedia screens and mediums), family, and educational factors all have potential of affecting us short term and long term. What we eat nutritionally can affect how much we grow physically and mentally as well as how we feel and how well we can perform tasks. Are there positive human models in our lives to teach us to study, work, and play, take constructive risks, avoid unproductive adventures? Some of the damages are reparable later, with added expenses to society, but the least costly way historically has been for the society to do its best with the education of family units, which has the most far-reaching effects on children at the lowest cost.

The Political Teconomic Forces

Educational, economical, and political systems and

institutions exact their influences upon us, too. Thereafter, we become optimally educated. Alternatively, individuals have formed a methodology to pick best alternatives techniques to achieve goals. However, these systems can formulate our attitude and approaches to life and risk-taking, and establish barriers to our progress by modification of our actions, or others around us in neutral, productive, and or counter-productive ways.

The genetic mix, with environmental factors, combines to create a naturally diverse range of behaviors, which can allow for a variety of successful experiences under different circumstances. If we all are educated and trained to behave and react in the same way to events, fallacy of composition would make most experiments failures. Extreme mass uniformity and centralism forced by institutions, and exogenous forces (i.e. Hegelian dialectics and historical studies) over individual market decision-makings are fighting economic theories, market laws, and motivational forces of self-interest of the producers. Human ingenuity in fighting external forces has a long evolutionary reservoir. None of those skills is useful or often suppressed by free will, when producers are self-motivated, or self-interested in producing more for market place demands and private profit. There is room for some uniformity for smooth functionality of modern society.

Educations, among other social variables, ethical and civil laws, are some factors used for mass-uniformity. Beyond certain limits, state administrators inflect economic wounds, expand unemployment of resources, and even increase instabilities, by pushing the uniformity snowball up the hill. While market individualism beyond its limits will lead to inefficiencies as well, for example specializations of tasks and benefits of mass production and scale savings will not occur. In addition, market (price)-mechanism, which sustain market individualism does not always determine prices efficiently, which could also become inhumane to marginal members of society with outrageous raised social costs. In both examples, price distortions, can make operational costs terminal.

All stockholders reacted to surprising set of market signals by selling (shorting); a crash would soon halt trading. This is another example of fallacy of composition at work. Long term versus short term goals, high risk-reward versus lower risk-lesser reward goals of different segments of public in different phase of their life-cycles (younger, mid-life, and older) insure an orderly exchange and survival of an exchange market (capital) system in different economy cycles (up or down). Yet, if we have retraining for dislocated unemployed workers, we induce smooth operation of industries with less labor-management conflict costs and less anti-societal costs to the nation as a whole. Thus, a productive society (in capitalist societies, this implies with sufficient disposable real income, and demand via sufficient employment) accommodates individuals to take care of their most immediate needs (shelter, food, and protection) and plan to allocate and meet some of their present and future needs and wants.[5]

Abram Maslow, an innovator in the field of humanistic psychology developed a “hierarchy of motives,” which explained an ordinal classification of human behavior. This is observable both in urban industrial areas in need of development, as well as in most developing economies. Maslow’s’ hierarchies from low to high levels are as follows. One is the physiological needs (hunger, etc.). Two, is the security needs (to feel safe, or out of danger). Three, is belonging needs (to be affiliated, accepted, and loved). Four, is approval needs (esteem, competent, and recognition). Five, is cognitive needs (study, explore, understand). Six, is aestatic needs (for beauty, art, peace, order). Seven, is self-actualization needs (to seek and realize own potential, to grow, self-fulfillment).[6] While exceptional individuals can readily break through most barriers to their advancements, the common observations are supportive of these ordinal forms of human behaviors.

Then the productive members (hypothetically all members at the productive levels) of the society can increase knowledge and expand the positive experiences in that society, also increasing capital, and expanding production processes, employing more in the society. That is, to influence both the supply and demand factors. That is not a detached social contract between education institutions and individuals, but societal social contracts, involving all producers and consumers.

The economic factors, which interplay with psychological variables, influence our lives regularly. A study of Maslow can explain workers and entrepreneurs' motivations. The "hierarchy of needs" states that low priority needs must be met (even partially), before higher priority needs can become the motivators. The socio-pathology of slaves and slave-owners are in keeping the slaves in levels one and two of the "needs hierarchy," thus insuring minimal productiveness, yet, nothing close to efficiency of the existing inputs. In cases of vanquished and victors, victimized and victimizers, conquered and imperialists, occupied and occupiers the same social pathology develops and can linger on. The moral of the story is that full productivities and resource employments remain subverted and dwarfed. These Scio-political pathologies have an important influence on thwarting technological development.

Allport defined prejudice as "an aversive or hostile attitude toward a person who belongs to a group, and is therefore presumed to have the objectionable qualities ascribed to the group."[7] The socio-pathology of modern discriminatory, racist, and xenophobic behaviors against women based on sex, blacks, Native Americans, Asians, and Arabs and other immigrants based on race, Jews and Muslims based on religion, Iranians based on national origin and religions subvert market efficiencies, productivities, defined under levels one to five. That is, the basic needs, from employment to safety, to institutional discrimination in education, jobs, loan procurements for mortgage and businesses. Individuals face de-motivators, which beside the personal damages they affect societal inefficiencies and economic damages.[8] They substantially reduce group and national productivities. The empirical studies of economic losses of the minorities and society have been studied and explained.[9] Aside the periodical political ploys to pacify the ignorant and political fringes, some free societies deserve credited for legislative and cultural abolishment and vigilance against such bigotry, xenophobia, and discriminatory practices.

They have expedited the political and historical implosions of other systems that cultivated the pathologies (neo-fascism, communism, dictatorships, oligopolistic financial plutocracy, and monopolistic political elitism). The history should be a good reminder to the thinkers of our time, to be on guard against present or future Scio-political pathologies mimicking quasi-democracies, and worse, semi mature democracies deluding themselves into nonsensical self-destructive economic and sociopolitical miss arrangements.

Entrepreneur's actions are at level seven-motivation level is for self-actualization (also Schumpeterian motives), thus, the individual entrepreneurs must meet their other needs as well. There have been more than casual observations made that Islamic or Calvinistic ownerships have had productive motivational forces on small farm production of the old Soviet Union, comparative to state agro-production units. Keynes recognizes as much when he stated, "There are valuable human activities, which require the motive of money-making and the environment of private wealth-ownership for their full fruition." His further recognition of harmful effects of political and legislative misadventures is rare. He wrote,

> " it is better that a man should tyrannise over his bank balance than over his fellow citizen ... it may still be wise and prudent statesmanship to allow the game to be played, subject to rules and limitation, so long as the average man, or even significant section of community, is in fact strongly addicted to money making passion". [10]

It is unrealistic to expect people, which have not met their level one and two needs (due to exogenous or endogenous socio-political and economic reasons) to become entrepreneurs, even if they are well trained. Despite the performances of out layers, progress can require exogenous injection of resources for initial development. It also is counter-productive to overload human learning, adjusting, and adopting by excessive regulations, or abject alienations. Alternatively, these create socio-political environments that lead to unproductive behaviors, capital destruction, and environmental and toxic sicknesses. For example, if consumers have to spend all day hunting for water and food (or at two jobs with bellow poverty real disposable incomes), there will be no more time or resources left to apply to other endeavors for present or future alternatives. Especially, if transformative education and job retraining and creations are required, any promise of self-advancements or free market initiatives will be vacuous.

Hence, it is usual to find the rest of societal productions lag behind at bellow optimum levels. Two issues must then become clear, one, a group of people, or a large segment of the economy will be unable to exercise the more usual services of entrepreneurs, two, beyond a certain limit of socio-political bureaucracies and market interventions, and no other entity remains able to exercise the special entrepreneurial services beneficial to production in a dynamic economy. Then, the state will intervene to remedy in-efficiencies caused by prior state interventions, or the relative free market reluctance to do the dynamic job-creations.

In term of this paper, capital, labor, education, and entrepreneur production combinations determined in a free market are supplemented by judgments of third parties, detached from the forces of market for all economic activities. All in the name of improving the efficiency of response to the market, an input and balancing forces vanish from the production process. Each step further away from the free competitive market will multiply the probability of the decision errors, and failure of such experiments. Needing a reservoir of funds to pay for such failures, but soon oil reserves, foreign aids and such sources dry up, and an economy is left with choosing only the most productive, efficiency means of productions and distributions, which optimally equates supplies and demands in that economy. All other arrangements are dependent on wealth creations of the previous economic endowers create in surplus above current consumption at each period. Thus, a dynamic system requires the injection of new ideas, knowledge, and technologies in all variables of production to maintain or sustain such arrangements and surpluses, in a dynamic optimum demand and supply system with sustainable real growth.

From ideas to beliefs, from desires for choices among needs and wants, from rational choices to expectation of gains, these factors determine actions. The rational choices of individuals among present goods, services (forgoing some current consumption for saving), and for future wants subject to their disposable income constraints constitute the demand side. The rational choices of individuals and economic entities subject to their financial constraints and loans, formulating alternatives to invest and produce to achieve better rewards and goals, based on observations and experimentation of successful and failed alternatives under different circumstances constitute the supply side. That is, the appropriate investment in alternative means (methods, technologies) with inherent risks and rewards for each goal can sum up the basic choices of suppliers or producers. The dynamic demand and supply side-behaviors in balance sum up the economic activities of modern economic entities. A market-choice decision-making model allows entities to make strategic rational choices given their beliefs, and level of information and background subject to limitations of resources and constraints, for reasonable probability of successfully reaching their economic goals (bundles of goods and services).

From Ideas to Inventions and capital formations

Abbott Payson Usher studied innovation of mechanical products (the original manuscript is dated back to 1929), from "acts of insight" and "novelty in thought and action" to "emergence of new mechanical product."[11] While the synthesis and cumulative synthesis are defined, the microeconomic aspects and behavioral aspects, and the macroeconomic aspects and synchronization are left unexplained. The product of this kind on innovation process may become a new technology or capital, and may become financially productive. Market can deselect non-functional or non-useful ideas. There is an assumption about ideas being readily available everywhere on demand. That is, too many ideas-on the shelves (as technologies on the shelves) are available to everyone on demand, they only need to put a request form for them. That is a myth.

Most organizations learn quickly without appropriate

cultivation of creativity, and credible (ahead of the curve) policies, and proportional remunerations, and reward-packages to encourage individuals' innovational and technological progress, in their businesses (instead of the executive pay-packages mimicking it) they fall behind their competition quickly. These monopolies, oligopolies, and plutocracies relay on too big to fail and corrupted-political systems for socialized-subsidies from taxpayers to pay for their private gains, profits and their risk taking private market endeavors. They compete and deplete infrastructures' funds, education, roads, and defense and security budgets. If an organization is reacting to its competitor, they already know they are, at least, second behind the same competitor.

The microeconomic concept of supplying new technologies is the least understood and most modified aspect of technological change in developing nations. There is a misconception that products, rather than new processes yield new products. Often, industries or modifications that require the least capital, with reasonable linearization and training costs to create global products go ignored. Cultural and educational products, music, art, filmic industries, theatrical works, and tourist-oriented programs followed by international investments are often the victims of such shortsightedness.

Most job creation of modern service economies, financial and money-printing industries among others are human manufactured and trust-dependent institutions. Isolated, closed economies, risk and global averse regions or nations seem to take negative impacts and shocks much harder, and repair themselves more sluggishly in such non-corrective economies, unlike more modern economies. Most industrial economies are not as immune to this self-delusional impulsive phenomenon, as they think.

In business cycles, the macroeconomic forces created demand for the available technologies, the lack of synchronization can easily explain lack of sustainable growth, and development strategies.

Conversion of ideas to inventions

Most modern ideas journey through the synchronizations of Inventions by Individuals and Worker-Manager Teams, and they are the final product of the dynamic complex syntheses process, during expanded periods of trail and errors, and developmental phases. There are certain financial, regulatory and knowledge constraints, too.

This study redesigned the evolution of complex ideas to inventions, in numbers of small dynamic steps (Figure 1). The first four clockwise steps are (I to IV). At this level, the process is internal and individualistic, the new ideas or "occasional acts of insights" come from varied sources as diverse as daydreamers and scientists, but mostly from the immediate environment and work or study patterns of researchers or workers. They are shown by (±). The direct-stages point to the next stage for endogenous innovations. The donut with wave-patterns is formed out of initial fragments. A second dot and arrow shows economic factors become relevant, shown by (checkered) half-donut patterns. A third jagged poly-line with dot and arrow shows regulatory and governmental factors are becoming relevant and important, shown also with break half-donut patterns (IV to VII phases). However, the last two can dominate and subvert the process of innovation. The second phase is the phase that most cooperation and multinationals adopt in developments of new products. The double arrowhead and the jagged poly-line show dynamic continuity of the process. This is the dynamic process newly define in this research. The process is also used in academic research studies, or the development of ideas to products, to re-modified products to new specifications, including government, regulatory, and economic specifications. The process is not only prescribed to a mechanical invention or product, it could be a copy righted study, a book, a movie script, and apt, or computer program, etc. Figure1 shows the stochastic dynamic innovation model. The dynamic process can start over with a new pattern, or sets of specifications.

In most advanced economies, with the supply side generation of technologies, some older static version of this process has been institutionalized. The byproducts of engineering departments or internalized institutions under research and development, or product development branches in some successful industries use the static versions of this model.

This is the dynamic process newly define in this research, which is also used in academic research studies, or the development of ideas to products, to re-modified products to new specifications, including Governmental, regulatory, and economic specifications, no longer, only a mechanical invention or product, it could be a copy righted study, a book, a movie script, etc.

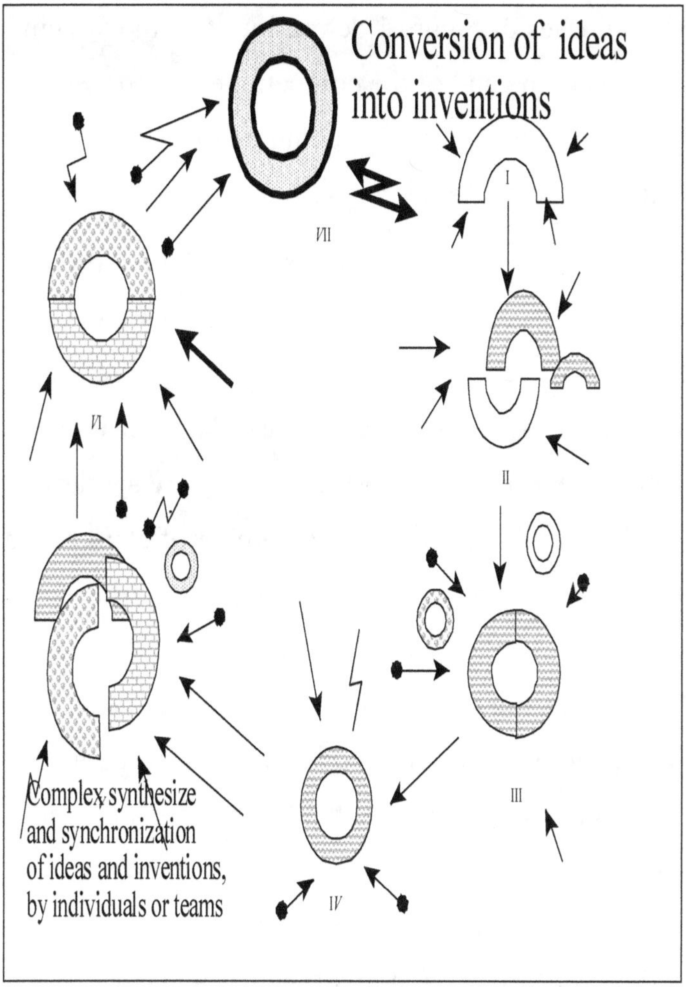

Figure 1. Shows a stochastic dynamic invention-innovation model.

The important innovative acts of individuals are discouraged only in the most lethargic and non-progressive of economic systems with harsh Scio-political and economic consequences, which include total system implosions. So take it as lightly as you wish, the first of these two phases of Figure 1 determines that the system lives or dies in the end of the competitive period. So making it all functional, and accommodating it to their survival needs is self-evidently rational.

The second more complex phase is where more of a modern society's resources are spent, or sometime are wasted, if they ever become alert to anything other than military technologies. In this complex phase, insightful ideas and inventions are reinvented. They are synthesized and synchronized to fit, by a large number of elements in each economy. In this phase all incomplete, partially completed, or even useless ideas, inventions, products, organization arrangements, and suggested on the shelf, old, or new technologies are filtered and picked over very carefully as to usefulness or extend of modification, and their economic viability. At the later end of the phase governments' regulations and barriers are often studied and injected, as they often need modification and corrections. While we build universities, the individual academician carries out the first phase on inventions. While funneled tax money goes to the research and development section, it is the team members, which do the initial or multiple-phase discoveries. When our State businesses get the contracts and funding, the small business needs to produce the goods and services. They employ the most, and produce the most in the economies. They will pull the states out of their economic funks. When the Soviet Union state economy imploded by military over spending, the United Stated economy was pull up by the employments of electronic discoveries. Recently, multiple wars' spending, mortgage securitization, and regulatory manipulations overwhelmed The American economy, causing economic downturn and up to 17 percent sustained unemployment, the multinational mega businesses left the country for cheapest employees, and they run to violate reasonable pollution and humane laws. The small businesses, their employees and middle class America and immigrants had to survive, innovate, employ, and build up American economy here.

Cropping New Ideas

The misinformed assumptions are that ideas are plentiful, and all you have to do have a brainstorming session and you will be flooded with ideas. The realty is different. It depends on what kind of ideas we are cultivating. People and organization recoil at the costs and notion of change, which new ideas entail. Often, the immigrants are the most potent sources of new ideas in modern time. Table 1, lists creative and critical thinking in synthetic conversion of choice ideas into practical and applicable technologies.

Table 1. Creative and critical thinking, in conversion of choice ideas to technologies.

Thinking Creative, Intuitive	Thinking Analytical, Logical, Critical
Shot-gunning, Scanning, wide angle	Rifling, Aiming, telescopic
Generative	Selective
Possibilities	Probabilities
Free thoughts	Judgmental, Rational
Diffused Brain Storming, free association	Focused Analysis
Subjective	Objective
All, or any answers, maximum responses	Best answers, optimal response
Associative	Linear, Functional, numeral
Yes and (what else, what more)	Yes but (what, when, where, why, & how)
Novelty, modus imagenium <alam khyal>	Reasoning, modus oprendi Scientific Methodology <alam alm>
Divergent	Convergent

Teconomics of Infrastructures

Large members of so-called civil societies attack emigration and emigrants openly and vociferously, even those who enslave and profit from their toils the most, that also includes governmental departments, which are set seemingly to benefit them or ease their plights, but mostly to regulate their lives as humanely and speedily as possible. (Bureau of the American Indian Affairs and Immigration and Naturalization Service are just two older examples), incarcerations industrial complex is a newer example. It is important to realize that all or nothing regulatory propositions regarding any involuntary groups are loaded with fallacious abuses.

American corporations only in the last decades of the last millennium have realized the potential of new and innovative ideas in the work place as foreign notion to them, even though the United States perfected scientific methodologies. The competitive success of Japanese initially low quality products to high quality replacement goods shocked United States operations by losing them their customers. Auto-industries machinations during recent history 1970s to 2010 are just one of the richer examples.

The appropriate uses of creative thinking, and critical thinking, intuitive and logical thinking, will lead to constructive concept idea creation. Moreover, the innovational uses of choice inventions. Importantly, it contributes to the process of synthetic-conversion of choice ideas to practical products and technologies applicable in the production processes.

The new millennium challenges have not yielded to easy adoption of technologies. It is documented the scientific methodologies and appropriate scientists, which are to solve these problems have been effectively discouraged rather than sought. The accumulated costs are already astonishingly too high.

Ways to encourage new useful (innovational) ideas,

1. Question critically all aspects of the Status Que.
2. In addition, how it could be improved. You need not share it with the world initially.
2. Set aside thinking time.
3. Let yourself to have, a- general open thinking time, b- More targeted or focused thinking time, c- eventually critically reality checks off each idea.
4. Write down any ideas that come to you as soon as possible.
5. Carry an idea note-pad (on cell phones). Categorize and classify idea-files periodically.
6. Write down associative ideas that branch out main ideas, too.
7. Find where you can get good ideas, books, trade papers, research labs, the internet, library, seminars, university, and your idea files. Be mindful of true copyright and other legal restrictions and required permits.

8. Maintain a general file for initial generated ideas, and a specific files for more processed, complex, productive, profitable, and filtered ideas.
9. Obtain the prerequisite education and training for more scientific ideas, or call friends, scholars in the related field.
10. Use the Combination of intuitive, formal (or scientific), and mix approaches in generating and adopting new ideas.
11. Study each idea from different perspectives, the competitions, the workers, the Production processes, marketing, finance, laws, as far as your time and knowledge allows.
12. Reject but save and file the rejected ideas, for future reassessments.
13. Maintain cross references of these ideas, where they have potentials.
14. Make thinking creatively a regular work habit.
15. Cultivate friends and co-workers, who have worked in innovative environments.
16. Set aside time to practice your productive techniques in generating innovative new ideas.

How research and development departments can encourage organizational creativity? They can do this by changing old procedures, and adapting new procedures. These could also apply in cases of new products, procedures, and processes (innovative methodologies). The following lists is how to assist organizational adoptions of new appropriate technologies,

1. Introduce the current procedure to all in research

and development, or the factory if possible.

Invite initial everything goes, and nothing is sacred approach in generating initial new ideas.

2. Undo fearful anxieties and notions as often as possible.
3. Lay out a Fish-Bone graph for generating idea inputs (the idea generation phase), of all available elements of the procedure on mapping paper, or computer graph.
4. Invite post-it and idea-notes, and comments from everyone and the experts.
5. Leave it out a few weeks for ideas to come in.
6. Reward your more productive and enthusiastic help in the process often.
7. Assign a team to pick few best ideas on each item. Moreover, share that with everyone.
8. Establish testing or measuring methods for the new procedure.
9. Lay out the new procedure as fish-bone graph for farming new ideas. In addition, allow time for inputs.
10. Adopt the new procedure and tests.
11. Assign team members from all related departments to work the new procedure.
12. Train and allow for education of the teams involved with the new procedures.
13. Invite post-it ideas, and comments from everyone and experts.
14. Have team leaders report the test results, positives and the negatives associated with the new procedures.
15. When the new ideas about the new procedure are enough to form a new fish-bone graph for cropping related ideas (the complex synthesis phase). Start the process all

over again.

16. In case of new products accommodate for more complex issues of costs, appropriate methodologies and machinery as well.
17. Cultivate the innovative process, as regular part of the operation process.
18. Maintain and pay to keep your research and development teams. The firm pays (sometime with loss of jobs) much more when they work for the competition.

Figure 2 shows the fishbone graphic in developments of

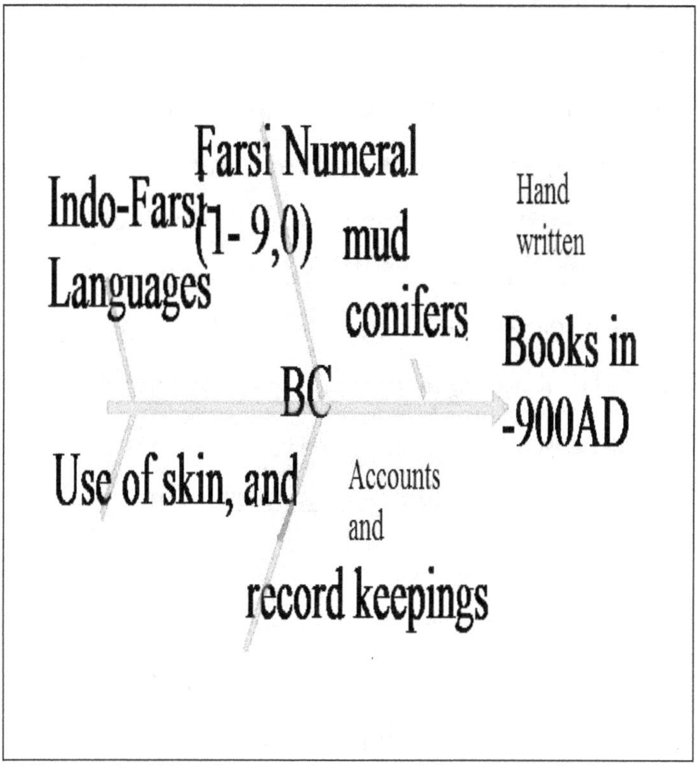

Figure 2. Words, numbers, and hand-copied books.

Words, numbers, and Hand-copied books. A process that may have started as early as humanoid decided to save records, as in allegory, by storytelling, and later in different form of writings.

Ancient redemptory formal education was mostly learning by doing, and in the higher up classes and government, reading a few selected hand-copied books in algebra, mathematic, philosophy, theology, astronomy, poetry were treasured and Passed on. Hand written books, were more commonly distributed, and kept within familial libraries, as a grantee against common war raids, which tended to loot tangibles and burned the sources of knowledge, the hand copied books. By the time of Alexander of Greece raids into Persepolis of Persia, the intends and defense against them were common knowledge, and practiced religiously.

Competitive Technology Changes in Production

Internalization of innovation process leading to technological changes occurs if the management of the production organization attaches importance to them. The management can logically link the adaptations of the technological changes to profitability, continuation of employments, higher wages, and rewards for skill improvements, and adopt other reward-mechanisms in a successful production operation. Then, the production organization and process adopt the process of technological advancement internally.

Continual, gradual, and incremental technological changes are adopted in the day-to-day operations. One organization can advance ahead of another competitive organization for the same services, products, and customers, by use the following list, organizing tools, reformulating, order forms, conceding demand and inventory reordering, and thousands of small but helpful changes that can put.

Larger technological changes in function and methodologies, organizational structure, main product lines changes, product life cycle strategies are also very important in the continual dynamic success of the operation.

<u>Building Technology Adoptive Production Process</u>

Building the production organization around the concept of competitive technological changes requires some organizational deliberative steps. From the initial few steps, all members of your organization need to realize what entails to be an innovative production organization. If you have, a mission-statement you need to enumerates and clearly describes how the production process needs to accommodate the adaptations of technological changes in the process. Moreover, how workers-manger teams need to contribute to it continually.

In the innovational development of knowledge about writing, to block book printing and publishing, the process took more than 14 centuries to evolve, mostly naturally. There were mutually exclusivity among, development of ink, paper, record keeping, diffusion of bookkeeping, and wine press and clock making of Asia and Europe. Yet, the final process could have not happen, without the initial steps.

However, in modern time, systematic instructionally induced technological innovations for commercial products have a faster development lifecycles. Centuries, even years, or a few months will be too late for survivals of a technology-industries leader.

Figure 3 shows the diffusion of global skills leading to book publishing. Use of record keeping found in Persian mud cylinders. Tracing linen paper development from china to Africa and then to Europe. Where, the Monks had already transferred the hand-duplication and the recopying of books from Persia. The Use of wine press and clock making in Europe, are more technologies steps in place, which yielded the book printings.

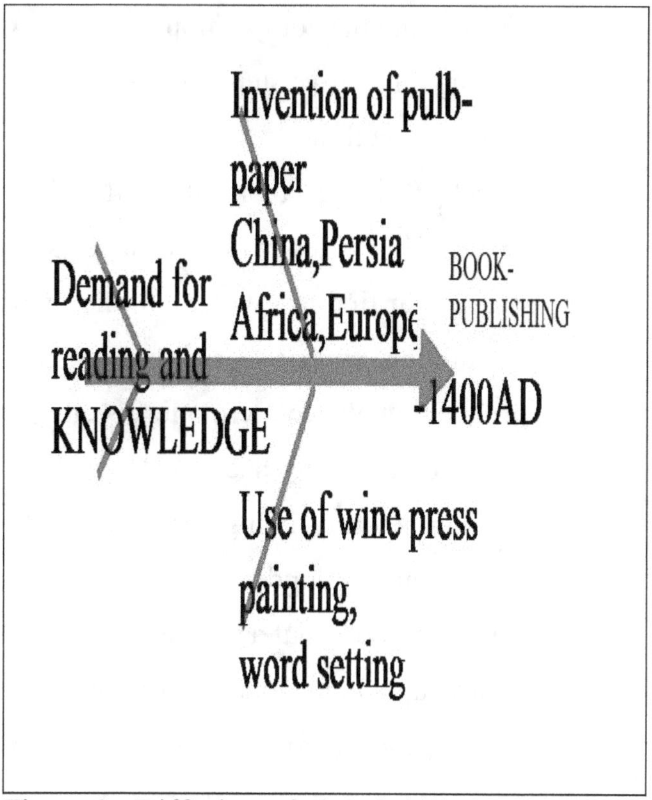

Figure 3. Diffusion of global skills leading to book publishing.

The followings are some of these important steps,

1 Arrangement of the right ideas' incubations, visions and environments.

2 Focusing the workers-mangers teams with clearly worded goals.

3 Setting stepping-stones or marker posts along each goal.

4 Involve all elements of production units in scanning the competition and finding innovative steps to stay ahead of the competition.

5 Check customers, their satisfaction, and shifting tastes, with a reward system.

6 Share your findings with all of the teams. In addition, replace fear with rewards for progress, at all production levels, not just by executives' pay-packages.

7 Encourage idea sharing and flood of ideas as preliminary condition of innovativeness, but assign teams to evaluate follow-up and profitability values of the better ideas, for an implementation priority list. Moreover, rewards successful teams accordingly.

8 Make sure teams are not self-promoting ideas. Make all other teams share the vision of profitability and success of the selected ideas.

9 Assign and increases finance team members as they are needed, like from finance, marketing, and engineering to ensure success of good ideas.

10 Establish quality control in quantified measures to accept or reject profitable ideas, in addition, re-assess the rejected ideas as time and circumstances change.

11 Make sure inventors, and innovators of ideas are assigned team members who are good advocates and can present and sell the ideas in the organization. Also, assign upper managers to related fields as part of their idea-support teams. Therefore, make certain all-profitable, doable ideas get proper hearing from more than one level of the organization.

12 Establish strategy team to sell the concept to capital market.

Operational Managements, refers to art and science of production. It is where the central processing of all data regarding the production of goods and services and skills are synthesized. It is the ultimate central point, where consumers like and dislikes translate into products, or in termination of production of the products. If marketing, sales finance, promotional (and advertising) departments keep such data, they must relay it almost immediately to operational managers. In smaller production units, the same teams may handle all of these decisions. Operational managers need to have a clear understanding about the following areas.

1. Consumers' likes, and dislikes for the products.
2. Least costly best ideas in initial production methodologies.
3. Most optimum Input ratios.
4. Workers, and updating workers' job and production skills.
5. Quality, timeliness, and costs of partially process inputs and dependability of their sources.
6. Technologies and methodology of all choices, and their continual updating.
7. Access to capital market and most updated capital inputs.
8. Continual updating production procedures, via TQC (Total Quality control), SPC, SO, CQC.
9. Constant communications among creative and innovative production teams at all levels.
10. Consumers ultimately determine if or what products are produce. Their income, moreover, their demands determine and motivates supplier to produce and supply

the market places. It is with good reason to question wage earners inside the production most optimum Input ratios. Internalize the process to improve what they eventually may consume themselves.

The importance of aggregated demand for products depends on what the consumers are willing to purchase. Some of these consumers' issues are,

1. Income and demand elasticity for the products.
   Price.
2. Useful lifespan, longevity of service.
3. Quality.
4. Trust in the producer or product.
5. Terms of replacements.
6. Terms of credit if applies.
7. Access to repairs.
   Skill of repairers.
   Quality and Speed of repair.
10. Speed of replacement.
11. Costs of repair
12. Preoccupation with each consumer, in contacts.
13. Fashion, Brand, and Reputation.

The profit motives, or cost cutting misadventures can mislead industry to ignore these steps. Successful operations follow these steps, they train their employees, and management teams to follow the steps, and attain sustainable operation or parish. There are many examples. One is the globally known example of oilrig explosion of 2010. The operation produced the drilling oilrig disaster south of the United States. Another example is the automobile recalls of some major auto producers, and auto-industries with their major restructuring, it occurred in 2009-2010. These came after, overt attempts to reduce dynamic-sigma criteria. These misadventures came out of a political arithmetic of modern day mismanagement for short-term gains and profit maximization conditioning, both cultivated in certain academic and financial circles, with selective statistical analysis.

These miss educations are often evolve out of knowing too little, but not enough to avoid the disasters. There are at least three mathematic theorems, which simple profit-maximization will tend to under estimate. One is necessary condition. Second is the sufficiency condition, and the third is sustainability condition.[12] The second and the third conditions are longer term. Auto industry giants have fallen on their own swords, while they fall in short term focus on modus oprendi. Unfortunately, other manufacturing operations have followed blindly. The statistical sciences are applied to shorten life of the products, rather than to remedy errors. Then, parts-failures explode costs, first to the consumers, then to the producers and supplier as well. The energy usages and service-costs to the consumers only add to the negative externalities. Thus, their consumers become onetime shoppers. Nevertheless, Substantial legal costs, and governmental recognitions of international criminal intend have increased regulatory and punitive costs of operation.

Notes

[1] In one of the oldest form of the language, Dari, Dezfuli, Farsi, the word "KARDON" explains the same terminology. It means individual who is knowledgeable of the work skill. In Sanskrit, "TAKASATI" mean fashioner, or fashioning. Latin uses "TEXERE" that means weavers. Greek most recent of definitions explain it, "TEKTON," which means builder, and carpenter, and the word "TECHNIKOS, or TECHNE" that means art and skillfulness. Finally "TECNOLOGIA" that is the didactic and systemic treatment of an art, and logy, implies the erudition study of the same subject. The epistemological study of the word implies it has been with human cultures for a very long time. www.merriam-webester.com

[2] Joseph A. Schumpeter, *The Theory of Economic Development*, trans. Redvers Opie (London: Oxford UniversityPress,1934), 91-94

[3] John M. Keynes, *The General theory of Employment*, Interest and Money, (London Royal Economic Society)

[4] E .R. Higard, R. L. Atkinson and R. C., *Introduction to Psychology*, 7th ed., (New York: Harcourt Brace Jovanovich, Inc. 1979), 54-75

[5] Ibid, 315

[6] Ibid, 316

[7] G. W. Allport, *The Nature of Prejudice*, (New York: Doubleday and Company, Inc. 1958), 8

[8] These are commonly studied problems from 40-60 percent high school drop outs, to 28-48 percent underperformances in GDP due to luck of minority

inclusions in national output.

[9] G. S. Becker, *The Economic of Discrimination*, 2nd ed.,(Chicago: The University of Chicago Press, 1971)

[10] John M. Keynes, *The General theory of Employment, Interest and Money*, (London Royal Economic Society)

[11] Abbott Payson Usher, *A History of Mechanical Inventions*, (Boston, Beacon Press, 1959), 66,69

[12] I have introduced and reintroduced this concept since 1975. It has not penetrated the guiles of ignorance, short-term profiteering, and simpleton's greed. It is an educational advancement and it will take time

CHAPTER 3

SCIENTIFIC METHODOLOGY AND TECHNOLOGICAL PROGRESS

Scientific methodology used here are the use of econometrics and hypothetical testing. The process used is extensive. However, it is familiar to economists as social and behavior scientists.[1] The doctrine and stepping-stones leading to the process of scientific methodology have had a distinct and extensive history. The theological machinations, and its political-structures, and the birth of scientific methodologies have distinguished their mutual exclusivities, repeatedly.

Competitive Technology Changes in Production Process

Internalization of innovation processes leading to technological changes come with strategic importance, influences, and priorities, which the managements of a production organization attach to them. The logical link these managers make between adaptations of the technological changes and profitability, continuation of employments, skill improvements, and other individualized reward mechanisms lead to successful production operations.

Continual, gradual, and incremental technological changes are adopted in the day-to-day operations. One organization gets ahead of the other competitive organizations for the same services, products, and customers, by reorganizing tools, reformulating order forms, conceding to demand and inventory reordering, and thousands of small but helpful incremental changes.

Larger technological changes in function and methodologies, organizational structures, main product lines changes, product life cycle replacement strategies are also very important in the continual dynamic competitive success of the operation. Such technological advancement do not occur without costs, conflicts, or confrontations

Filippo Bruno, lesser known than Galileo, also attempted to rework the theologically dogmatic power system.[2] He supported the heliocentric theory around the sun, in the one galaxy model of the universe. This was contrary to the theologically backed common belief of flat earth terra centric work of Aristotle, commonly thought as belief in theological centers. Therefore, his first confrontation with the local theological authorities forced him to flee.

Commonly, all men of science used to beg and

borrow from place to place and dispense with words of old knowledge, poetry, day labor for food, and a modest place to live. Alas, what he did not know, it was one thing to dispense Aristotelian terra centric ideas, but to fill heads with new Copernicus solar centric ideas was quiet another thing. He did all of these dispensation of his questionable wisdom, so enthusiastically and vehemently, with a monk's passion, enough that it made others look unscientifically foolish, and outdated. His voice became load enough that threatened the cash-inflow of certain organization. That was too much. Further dealing with these ideas, which further curtailed the aged and somewhat corrupted kingdom of mortals benefitting (profiting) from the name of God, was enough to cast his peculiar faith. The insiders to the Church hierarchy were not served better. Martin Luther is an example of that. This is not unique to only one religion, as long as they have the power and the authority of governance. Thus, the concept of "separation of church and state," in first amendment of the United State Constitution gains international recognition and due prominence, after the British attempt to reinvent their own religion, and manage to duplicate the bureaucracy.

Therefore, the chase was on, the Inquisitors' blood hounds, versus the non-reticent philosopher the science geek of that time. While outsiders to the faith were treated even worst, the theological fervor had less celestial consequences for trade and commerce of the time as well.[3] Every unfolding of new science had another bad omen for the shrinking Theo-financial kingdom, so it added more wood-fuels for the end game of his bonfire. Flippo Bruno had freedom to synthesize thoughts into ideas, but he confused that with the freedom of expression of those ideas. In modern day, that would be like the first amendment of the constitution, without publication option or the courts' protection of "some opinions and speech."

In the philosophy of Freedom, Filippo Bruno coined the phrase "Libertes philosophica." or freedom to make philosophy. The right to think of new ideas and to defend their strength and weaknesses in public came later, without that public jailing, killing, or shaming, and burning for those ideas. The fuller fruitions materialized with the jurist prudence of Magna Carte of United

Kingdom, and later the first amendment and bill of rights of United States' constitution, these legal ideas were formulated much earlier.

Filippo Bruno was born in 1548, in Nola, Italy. He attended The Monastery of Saint Domenico at age thirteen, and became a Dominican Priest in short order. The Monastery was where Thomas Aquinas had lived at and thought there. The name Giordano was given him in the Monastery. He soon became over educated for his hosts. His opinions, his frank and outspoken mannerism, his enthusiasms for new ideas, and the acceptance of new ideas, all great attributes for scientists, innovators, intellectuals now, worn out his welcome. His distaste for superstition was set aflame by reading a copy of Copernicus' *De Revolutionibus* in the monastery. Copernicus work was published in 1543, which vindicated the Pythagorean master his times three major fields of study, theology, philosophy, and science of math and Copernicus.

These fields were growing and separating violently apart. In addition, philosophy had parted with dogma (belief) to keep in step with axiomatic experimental and arithmetic sciences, it still does. That is, Bacon-Newtonian work could not explain theoretical physics, or post Newtonian discoveries, without that separation. The unholy marriage of relative scientific discoveries with dogma of theology was a bad idea. The Scientific laws are subject to alterations and upgrades, too. The concept of solar-centric one universe (one galaxy) was not challenged until 1980. The multiple galaxy reality replaced that model, theoretically and by Hubel telescope satellite visual proofs. The Newtonians' law of gravity was modified, because it will not hold the same in space. In Galileo letter to Duchess of Serin, he quoted Copernicus letter of dedication to the Pope,

"If there should chance to be any exegetes ignorant of mathematics who pretend to skill in that discipline, and dare to condemn and censure this hypothesis of mine upon the authority of some scriptural passage twisted to their purpose, I value them not, but disdain their unconsidered judgment. For it is known that Lactantius - a poor mathematician though in other respects a worthy author - writes very childishly about the shape of the earth when he scoffs at those who affirm it to be a globe. Hence, it should not seem strange to the ingenious if people of that sort should in turn deride me. But mathematics is written for mathematicians, by whom, if I am not deceived, these labors of mine will be recognized as contributing something to their domain ..."

What is accepted faithfully, as unchanging truth, as a belief cannot be based on shifting experimental, and true or false hypothetical axioms of scientific methodology. If you do that, you will see your dogma crumbles into falsehood, after the next application of Popper's falsification and verifiability of the scientific assumptive foundations. After all that is what we call it, a scientific idea, a hypothesis, a theory, may be a law, but never a scientific dogma, never a scientific belief. If, evolutionary theorists decide they like the feel of evolutionary dogma as a belief rather than a scientific theory, we will be studying the antithesis, of evolutionary science. There goes evolutionary dogma, there are no missing links or jump species to see or feel. There are axioms, little steps, hypotheses, and the evolutionary theory gains discovery by discovery. If creation-ism, tie their belief to a stone measured 400 years ago, and another new methods says the stone is 200 million years old, there goes the legitimacy of their faith, and their dogma and truth. Eventually a well-placed axiom or logical counter argument can undo the foundations of the misplaced kingdom. No matter who is jailed, what is burned, or who is banished, mortals' kingdom of dogma only goes up in smokes faster and the mortals 'sand castle washes out with each new intellectual waves!

The following from Catholic encyclopedia III, (1908) says that burning of Filippo at the stakes was for his Theo-sophism rather than his philosophy,

"Bruno was not condemned for his defence of the Copernican system of astronomy, nor for his doctrine of the plurality of inhabited worlds, but for his theological errors, among which were the following: that Christ was not God but merely an unusually skilful magician, that the Holy Ghost is the soul of the world, that the Devil will be saved, etc."

A few arguments make those words unfortunate excuses, for another inquisition burning. First, that he was excommunicated after his initial heresy, so when you excommunicate someone, you do not get to burn him for his religious confusions, and call it for the greater good. Two, when you chase and capture and imprison him for seven years, and manage to lose the file on your misdeeds, then you do not get to give unholy excuses about it and have everyone believe you. Three, why if such a shameful proposition is still true, then the same sinners went after Galileo and jailed him for life, for the same philosophies, and were belligerently obvious about their deeds. Four, Post Columbus no one had any problem using public relation and good press in claiming the discovery of America, much to the astonishments of the bloodied endogenous civilizations, and the thriving Indian nations already in America. Aside from the fact that the natives' gold and precious stones were hunted and exported to finance Spain, Portugal and other explorations and expansions of European pre-colonial mercantilists' trades Eastward. Five, it should have been known that attempts to burn progress of freedom of ideas, scientific ideas, and philosophical self-discoveries would not succeed.

However, Galileo restated the following words of St. Augustine.[4]

"It is to be held as an unquestionable truth that whatever the sages of this world have demonstrated concerning physical matters is in no way contrary to our Bibles, hence whatever the sages teach in their books that is contrary to the holy Scriptures may be concluded without any hesitation to be quite false. And according to our ability let us make this evident, and let us keep the faith of our Lord, in whom are hidden all the treasures of wisdom so that we neither become seduced by the verbiage of false philosophy nor frightened by the superstition of counterfeit religion."

Six, by the time Thomas Paine wrote his "common sense," and "The Age of Reason" separation of church and state, followed separation of church and scientific ideas for mutually beneficial advantages. When their modern physicians attend to religious people, they know their life depends on scientific advancements of ideas, and technological evolution of such ideas, based on scientific methodology, apart from the physicians biblical or (Koran, Torah) readings, or other theological teachings or believes.

Therefore, the wise statements of a great Pope, St.

John Paul II put all such misfortunate and past mistakes to rest with a sincere apology, but Filippo Bruno will never die to science, its methodology, and freedom of ideas pass him on.

Leonardo Pisano (Biglo) Fibonacci, 1117-1250 Pisa Italy may have unleashed the power of ideas of Farsi, and Farsi-Arabic-Indian axiomatic applied math in production and profit accounting by learning it in Morocco and teaching "Hesab", but he miss educated Europe about its source, as he wrote in his book " Liber abaci"(1202) ,

"When my father, who had been appointed by his country as public notary in the customs at Bugia acting for the Pisan merchants going there, was in charge, he summoned me to him while I was still a child, and having an eye to usefulness and future convenience, desired me to stay there and receive instruction in the school of accounting. There, when I had been introduced to the art of the Indians' nine symbols through remarkable teaching, knowledge of the art very soon pleased me above all else and I came to understand it, for whatever was studied by the art in Egypt, Syria, Greece, Sicily and Provence, in all its various forms."

Johannes of Palermo used to take mathematic problems out of Khayyam and test Fibonacci. So by that time works of Biruni and Khayyam and other Farsi(Iranian students) of Hesab had translated and hand copied on paper from 700 AD onward , and were widely spread and used in daily applications and commerce back dated to original diffusion routs (-3000 BC) set by primal emigration waves routs (much earlier than that). Soon after, the ice caps relented (at 50000-100000 years cycles) a secondary short cut was established between the Persian Plateau and Eurasia.[5] Later, Silk Road and trades between Persia to Tibet, India, China to East, and Arabia, West costs by way of Syria, and Africa south became common trade caravan roads.

Abbot Payson Usher wrote that discovery and use of paper lingered in China from first to 750 AD. When it arrived at the far eastern edges of Persia, it was transferred on the pre-existing diffusion routs already well-traveled out of Persia. From Persia, it traveled to Baghdad (793), Egypt (900), Morocco (1100), Spain (1150), France (1189), Italy (1276), and Germany (1391). Therefore, Hero of Alexandria and Arab teachers of "Hesab" could hand copy and further transfer their received-knowledge by local modification and innovation added. This was such an established practice that it took the paper invention 700 years to travel in one country to arrive in Persia, but less than 600 years to travel eight countries and three continents.

Therefore, it is not a surprise to read the following. However, what is missing in it, as to other contributors to the ocean of wisdom, is a surprise.

"The second section of *Liber abaci* contains a large collection of problems aimed at merchants. They relate to the price of goods, how to calculate profit on transactions, how to convert between the various currencies in use in Mediterranean countries, and problems that had originated in China."

In addition, Master Biglo was awarded a salaried position by republic of Pisa (1240), under the court of Frederik II, as first king of Germany (1212). Pope (1220) crowned him the Roman emperor. Therefore, uses of such ideas in affair of governments were ubiquitous, that is admitted.

Therefore, when Filippo Bruno was rephrasing or teaching Eastern philosophies, ideas, the matter was not unknown or new to the masters of his time, they were all parroting the same ideas. They were not burning the rich men or women in the bonfires of insanity either.

In the study of the origin of Farsi Hesab (Mathematic, Algebra, Record Keeping) and numerals 1-9 and 0, we learn how easily important issues are ignored, or over looked. Moreover, important contributions to human history vanish from the written pages of history, by dishonest historicism. However, didactic archeology unearths new civilization.[6]

The Farsi Numerals 1 to 9, 0, Hesab, and Accountings Principles

It is true that skirt and India was using numerical symbol by 900 AD.

It is true that some of the symbol have modified. It is true that the numerals also replaced a sideway scratch method of number (account) keeping, -, =, ≡, for 1, 2, 3 used in India at a later dates. In the book of "Ancient Inventions," this issue is stated,

"Two sites in Iran dating to about 8500 B.C. have produced series of clay spheres, semi spheres, cones and disks, incised or punched with dote and lines, it is thought that they were used for simple accounting of animals and crops. Such tokens become common throughout the agricultural belt."[7]

The hypothesis states that this came from Persian or Farsi mathematical numbers and accounting.

1- It matches the predated works in Persian Plateau.

a- The Persian were using scratch up and down method in sheep herd counting later, dating to developing practices 15,000, 25,000 BC, as herds and games were kept inside enclosures. Later, "Xenophon" noted this, in his writing.

b- The Kurdish domestication of wolf Dog, as tribes associated to the original Persian tribes, but among greyhounds, other hunting breeds, other game hens, and herd domestications.[8]

c- Other religious movements before Zardosht (–3000 BC) and Zardosht religion with emphases on learning and animal husbandry (1800-1200 BC) were established in Persian plateau and central mountains.

These developed extensive following and exchanges of ideas all the way to northern India and beyond to China, and southeast back to Africa.[9] Zoroastrianism is a religion founded in ancient times by the prophet Zarathushtra, known to the Greeks as Zoroaster, in central Iran as Zardosht. The religion had defused and established a great following in the known world along other Persian practices, before it was fully adopted as state religion by the Achamanied. It is believed to be the monastic root of Judaism, Christianity, and Islam.

2- The scratch herd-counting method was calculated in block of numbers of 4s, 5s, or 10s, based on the size of the herds.

3- I, II, III, IIII, IIIII, IIIII IIIII, are for 1, 2, 3, 4, 5, 5 5 for 10. The ten is important in herd counts.

4- Large herds are counted in ten at a time units. Therefore, the metric system also shares this origin and tradition.[10]

5- Zero also originated in Persian older languages, as a placeholder used in Farsi language. It is a period (.or ٥). Also predating and leading to the Farsi (pars) and Iran-Indian and Indo-European, along the primal migration routes. Later, it was reclassified to Indo European languages.

6- When in Farsi a period is emphasized, it is

circulated clock wise or counter clockwise, as in modern zero, but much smaller (. or ٥ or o) instead of (0), also Farsi number five, and Farsi letter H (٥, ه) are very close in their shapes to zero. It also looks like a knot. Knot per ten-unit counts, are still common practices in the region, using grass blades, or horse's tail hair strings.

7- It is not a logical pretzel for the intellects, the Farsi symbol for 1, 2 and 3, are a quick or scratch way of I, II, III, Reference to Figure 2, on Sazji (969 AD) copies of Farsi numbers. Biruni 1082 AD shows the corrected Farsi forms.

8- The number ۱, ۲, ۳, ٦, ۷, ۸, ۹ in Farsi (1, 2, 3, 6, 7, 8, 9 in English), have number 1 in their restructures or symbols. In addition, other Farsi symbols (٥, 5), are modified to represent other numbers.

a- (و, ٦,۹) the first symbol is used as "and" in Farsi, the second, and third resemble Farsi numbers are 6 and 9.

b- In addition, check symbols of old Parathion, Old Persian, and Avesta for similarities.

9- Sazji, Figure 3, orientation with Farsi numbers 2, 3, 5, resembles fast copying or writing in errors, the Farsi 2, 3, and 5.

10- Already, in the post-Aristotelian circles, not unlike the pre-Aristotelian times, books and pamphlets, and ideas were being distributed for teaching in Hesab, a Farsi word for mathematics. Therefore, when a monk's copy shows up in Spain (976 AD), in "the *Codex Vigilanus,"* The diffusion and symbol alterations (innovations) of original works are in effects.

11- That languages and mathematics were not the only sciences traveling out of Farsi of Iran. As noted by Machiavelli, and by Xenophon in "CYROPAEDIA," and in John Rae.[11]

12- Contrary to few current propositions claiming pan movements, evidence already exists, that Elamite extended out of Persian Plateau cultures in Central South West Iran already populate since the stone age humanoids and subsequent populations (- 200,000, - 6000, to - 3000 BC). The division in the Plateau yielded from 13 to16 tribes still living in the approximate locals, and some similar cultural practices.

Winter-summer migration to accommodate herds feed availabilities. These human-animal parallel emigrations for seasonal feed supply duplicated pray-predators emigrations observable in nature as well. We can hypothetically assume isolated coexistence and duplication, or a progressive learning curve common to other human activities.

They have had accumulated knowledge and skills in

survivals, trades, wars from prehistoric times, they applied these skills in formulating the known Persian Empires (3000-700 BC). Arabic and Semites (located between Mediterranean, and Persian Gulf), and secondary-Africa and Aryan movements came later to the Persian Plateaus and formulated, emerged into the 13-16 tribes or added to them initially in smaller or marginal force than the outsiders of the region imply.

Table 2 shows the complex and ancient languages develop by some of these tribes. Some of the tribes were also partially returning as the wash-back of the earlier primal waves of people, which left the region as ice cap melted, or as "ice jumpers" for food and new lands. They needed to obtain their survival skills from the region before they left.

Table 2. IRANIAN —> Avesta (--3000-1700 BC) —> Old Persian —>

Iranian Farsi	West	Old Persian	Parthian Middle-Persian	Persian Kurdish Baluchi Tajiki	Persia Iran (Persia) Iran, Iraq, Turkey Iran, West Pakistan, India central Asia
	East	Avestan	Sogdian Khwarezmian Bactrian Old Ossetic	Dezful-Shoshtar Susa KHozestan Lurestan-Ekbatan (Hamadan) Pashto Ossetic	Ancient Persia (South E.& Central) Iran central Asia Afghanistan, West Pakistan, India, Caucasus

14- The diffusion of technologies from Africa to Persia and vice versa, as in movements of hanging looms and return of horizontal looms for rug-cloth making silk, wool, cotton, linen. The other cultural similarity exists between the ceremonial maturity-rites of royal lion-hunts of Persia and central African (Masai) tribe. The diffusion of Lenin-paper from central China (1 to 600 DC) to Persia (700 DC) to Africa (800DC) can have more than one source or causes. The ancient prehistory of the Persian Plateau and coexistence of humanoids (from Homo Erectus to Homo Sapiens) had started at much earlier times, making the region one of few (around six centers) centers of hominoid attainments of survival skills and diffusion. Around 3000-600 BC tribes from Persian Plateau, the Meids and the Elamites gather in expanding units. The Persian Achaemenids "Hakhamanish" dynasties formed them in much larger units. They used to formulate troops in ten thousands bands as Shanhan-shah guards, grouping tribes or families in ten thousand people groupings or larger bands, often under Persian leaders, but later under regional decentralist leaders. These larger "King of kings Guards" were dispatched to different regions, from their tribal roots. They were to hold conquered lands, or acquire new land, or maintain and control. Elamites were in Northeast Russia to Japan, Africans in India, and South East Asia, Greeko-Romans in Africa or India. Some or most of these troops were not slave themselves but had servants or followers or war-captured people (slaves) with them. They sometime vanished, captured, or abandoned in faraway cultures with their technologies and skills. They learnt those skills from their origins, or learned them along the way. They learnt or perfected some skills in Persia plateau.[12]

However, they diffused their knowledge globally.

Iranian dualism is reflected in the digs of Lorestan regions, and intellectual works in the triangle region of Susiana, current Shosh and Dezful, Kurdistan, current Kermanshah, extending through Lurestan and Ekbatan current Hamadan in Iran. Manichaean's dualism expounded the notion of spirits or beings of higher levels, and lower level reflective of choices of the wisdom reintroduces a new source for the origin of thoughtful contemplations. Beyond the Manichaean's source of good (higher, angels) and evil (lower, demons) and Zoroastrianism, contributed to monastic theology. That is the current dominant trend of thoughts, in all modern theology.

In fact, the spread of Manichaean religion by Mani of Persia, in Media where Zurvanite Zoroastrians existed, to Parthia where Mithraism existed to Tibet and India, to China created a universal faith diffusion of thoughts on established pathways of thoughts-technology diffusion already in function. Hence, we cannot dismiss the link of Iranian dualism as a source for dialectics of contemplations, later as the base of hypothetic scientific thoughts, in accepting and rejecting of scientific hypotheses.

15- Some of the main but minor difficulty remains

with the one source hypothesis are,

a- Was the original species mutation took place in the one source region? For example, central Eastern Africa, or few central diffusion centers, in Africa, Persia, Tibet/India, China, and advanced in migration waves back and forth were also additives.

b- Did continents separations (2,000,000 BC) force an initial division in Africa, Asia, Australia, and formulated the locations of original primal waves of; at least, these three humanoid species, out of the same original one-continent gene source, because, there is evidence of hominoid existence (in South Africa), about the same time as continental tectonic separations.[13]

c- Followed by the localized mutations and genetic variations, as small as it is, less than 0.2 percent to 1.5 percent of the gene make up.

The numerals from Sizji's treatise of (969 AD), the numerals appear in the *Codex Vigilanus* copied by a monk in Spain in 976.

Table 3 and Table 4 show the lineage of evolutionary thought development, coexistence, and comingling of different alphabets by 969 AD. Numbers 1, 4, 5, 9 in this table can be easily hand-copies of the

Persian numerals.

However, the Tables 4, 5 further reconfirm this theory, because the repeated appearances and resemblances of original numeral forms in new writings.

Table 3. Sizji' numerals (969 AD).

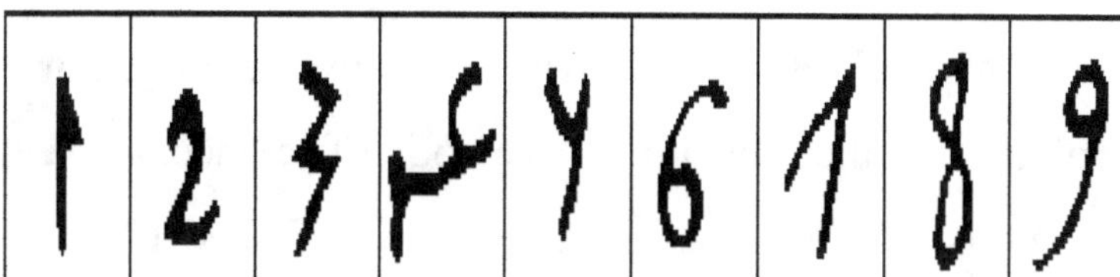

1	2	3	4	5	6	7	8	9

Table 4 is from Morocco, it shows Al-Banna Al-Marrakushi's form of the numerals.[14]

Table 4. Al-Banna Al-Marrakushi's numeral forms.

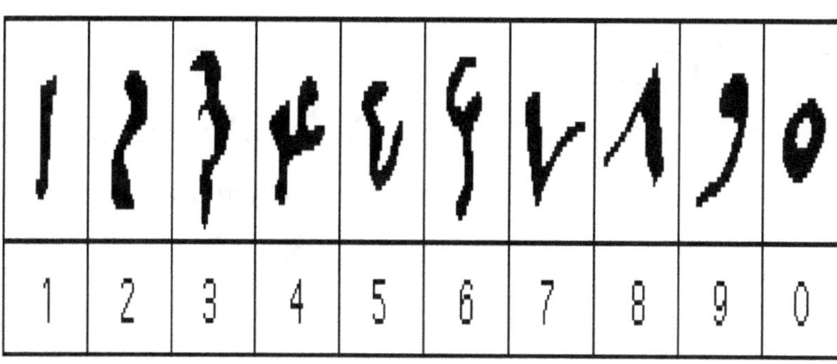

1	2	3	4	5	6	7	8	9	0

16- So Arabic numbers or Indian numbers reflected in Al

Banna Al Marrakushi's numeral forms (Table 4), which with the principle of Hesab he taught to Fibonacci were Farsi, with subsequent addition and diffusion of principles accumulated on to it from regions it traveled after it left Persia, Tibet-India, Arabia, and Africa. In Table 5 Biruni presented the Farsi numbers, which have been in use since before 969 AD. Nevertheless, Fibonacci miss-educated Europe unknowingly or otherwise, to their Farsi origin or contribution to these accumulative body of science, as he wrote in his famous book "*Liber abaci*" published 1202, in Pisa.

Table 5. Biruni's numeral forms (1082 AD)

۱	۲	۳	۴	۵	۶	۷	۸	۹	۰
1	2	3	4	5	6	7	8	9	0

17- The Farsi-Indian-Arabic-African sources of mathematic foundational bases of Western knowledge and civilization was sidelined for the Theo-filtered version in many modern so-called places of higher educations. The one that starts with miracle dialectics appeared in Greece and Europe, they being all good, faithful, and industrious people picked and advanced the technology from there to modern times. Nevertheless, Copernicus and Kepler systems had more to do with data and mathematics and the argumentative conflicts that are more kin and foundational to modern scientific thoughts, and hypothetical advancement of knowledge. The logical source of modern statistics, econometrics, and teconometrics is coming from Italian of (AD) the data collection on conifers and tablets, and linen papers, and hand-duplicated reprinted books coming from Persia, China, Africa (Egypt-Morocco) (BC).

The freed Jewish tribes further introducing it to Iraq and Arabian Peninsula through Babylonia, Mesopotamia, and West to northern Mediterranean and Europe, After the Persian took, lost, and retook the Asia Minor (-1100, -600, -300 BC.) The important point is the diffusion of knowledge, rather than the imperialism and the militarism aspects, which attracts cultish devotion among orientalists' romanticists.

In the field of theology, prophet Mohammad of Islam followed great philosophical pains and advice from his Persian and Arab philosophers, and distinctly forbade attempts to make himself in image of God, considering it a blasphemy, and a cultish untruth, an idolatry, a superstition.[15] The theological teaching dissuades followers from venturing off in the tall elephant grass of sententious theological delusions. The logic of the idea was that mortals of the weaker physical world could not be declared or misrepresented as metaphysical beings, other than by superstitions and blasphemes. This was so powerful of a concept that was used extensively against the advancement of Crusaders (1096), and Inquisitors, and freed the thoughts in the minds of advancing armies.[16] Some deduce that was the reactionary reason -- Moors advanced and held Spain (1187-1492) -- for Inquisitors internal self-destructive vehemence. Others, induced it is a cultural pathological imperfection; because, it has resurfaced in, the Nazis as anti-Hebrew, Klan (KKK) as anti-black and anti-immigrant hate movements, and other xenophobic and bigoted movements. More recently, there is the hypothesis, that open societies have inherent inferiorities and fears, which evolves in pathological anti-social movements in less alert or less educated population. The last notion has a self-remedy asserted in it, which is lost on the ignorant or, anti-educational cultural spasms of the population. Most decent governments and population fight these Scio-pathological tendencies vociferously and rightly so. Judo-Christianity still has issues with the tautology. Which the radical (fanatical) elements will only suppress, seemingly under constrains of manufactured conflicts, violence, or unsanctioned superstitions.

That need not take away from their liberalism, their humanitarians, and peaceful theological works, and true worship of monotheism. That should not encourage any ungodly theological supremacy <fundamentalists' wars> to deteriorate cooperation to improve human conditions.

Scientific Methodology and Technological Injections

Let us see what Filippo wrote, and let state it as this proposition. Should we link Bruno with the history of astronomy, and the "Scientific Revolution"? Looking back to his time his circumstances and education on the run, his degree, his twenty books, and his insightful plays justify we do him better than that. The smokes from his burning corps freed, if not the theology of his time, but science and commerce. He warned his public from the ubiquitous "superstitions ass" that he says in "the Ass of Cyllene," can be found in every place "...not only in the church but in courts of law and even in colleges."

Scientific methodology and injection of technologies, thus industrial revolution may have never bloomed, or jumped the ocean all together. Moreover, perhaps Modernity would have never left the totalitarians of the church and militarists' states narrowed fields of visions. The loathsome threesomes have powerful narratives, which have a death grip on the cultural mindset of nations, and parasitic death leash on national commerce, beyond simple and strong but limited defense.

His views on ideas are in “Cantus Circaeus” questioning the value of traditional knowledge methods and ideas. In his play “Il Canedelajo” Candle maker juxtaposition of knowledge and light and persistence of ideas may be mentally too taxing for some. However, read a translation of it for yourself, and see if that is so,

"Behold in the candle borne by this Chandler, to whom I give birth, that which shall clarify certain shadows of ideas ... I need not instruct you of my belief. Time gives all and takes all away, everything changes but nothing perishes. One only is immutable, eternal and ever endures, one and the same with itself. With this philosophy my spirit grows, my mind expands. Whereof, however obscure the night may be, I await the daybreak, and they who dwell in day look for night ... Rejoice therefore, and keep whole, if you can, and return love for love."

In “The Threefold Leas and Measure of the Three Speculative Sciences and the Principle of Many Practical Arts” John J. Kessler wrote, “we find a discussion on a theme, which was to be handled in a later century by the French philosopher Descartes. In it he says,

"Who so itcheth to Philosophy must set to work by putting all things to the doubt.”

In another of his book, “De la Causa, principio et uno,” (On Cause, Principle, and Unity) he wrote,

"This entire globe, this star, not being subject to death, and dissolution and annihilation being impossible anywhere in Nature, from time to time renews itself by changing and altering all its parts. There is no absolute up or down, as Aristotle taught, no absolute position in space, but the position of a body is relative to that of other bodies. Everywhere there is incessant relative change in position throughout the universe, and the observer is always at the center of things."

This can easily been seen in the light of Albert Einstein attempts to define essence of mater in terms of energy in his version of unifying theory, Stephen Hawking among others are a recent path finder of the subject, working to improve science. The essences of scientific discovery and technological advancements are the stocks of scientific ideas. This formulation explains it,

$$\kappa_i \times \left(\lambda_i + \mathrm{Y}^{\chi}\right) \approx \mathrm{I}_{i+1}$$

Mass of ideas (Ki) are multiplied by circulative learning and teachings (8i) plus innovational injections of new ideas to a variable power (Y^{x}), equating by definition to the current theoretical sum of all science, art, and innovative ideas (I_{i+1}). Circulative (educational recycling, and not tautological) learning and teachings plus innovational injection of new ideas to a variable power, equating by definition to the current theoretical sum of all science, art, and innovative ideas multiply mass of ideas.

What of Astronomy, what did he write relevant to astronomy? His allusion to more galaxies with stars as suns were only confirmed after the telescopic "Hubbell" satellite made the proposition a visual possibility in the second half of twentieth century. The extremes of his allusions and mixing of theology much more theatrical or hypotheticals, like his notion that inhabitants existed everywhere in these galaxies. Nevertheless, these were commonly held opinions, which he held or stated stronger. All the intergalactic show business wags would be bankrupt, if such notion were not still held widely, since they have not let go of their movies about the same subject matter. In other words, he was a theatrical ham, which saw the theatricals of superstition, coveting the methodology of imperialism taking over a universal theology of care, peace, tolerances, and love, and dying in that sin.

He was a scientist and more, and a martyr "a suicide

dead for" science and freedom to form and have ideas, and pass ideas on, if you try to correctly credit the right source, or even a source. He is the start of intellectual investigation for ideas above all else and whatever price it takes, along more systematic inquiries of Nicolas Copernicus and Johannes Kepler and Galileo Galilei. Simply, because he did not give in, perhaps being unmarried or without academic or financial position made it easier for him to do so. Because the smoke of his burning burned enough eyes to allow for independence voices for, academic, commercial, and political ideas, free from frameworks serving the wrong ends. Therefore, the scientific revolution that let to economic studies and philosophical discourses also predates democratization revolutions in governance of nations. One gets the feeling he would rave and rage like the rest of us mortals, he would have had good time in modernity, with multimedia mediums, or even a camcorder and his own web, or blog. He clearly is the beginning of a European phase of "scientific revolution," leading to economic revolution, and mechanical and industrial revolution. Which had its embryonic and infancy in Persia, Africa, Tibet, India, Eurasia (Russia), and China, but, the teenage and early maturity in Europe and maturity in USA, and now globally.

Self-congratulation of humanity or western triumphalism needs to remember the monkey trial involving a real judge and attorneys and juries and the press and few great movies in the United States, others only need to watch their local news attentively. Until 1995, we believed there was only one galaxy. Galaxies were more mythology rather than acceptable science. Verifiable or falsification of hypothesis, or having a hypothesis can still be a hanging offence after nominees are called deviants, spies, terrorists, rather than be gifted with shortcuts to tenure track and grants.

Positivism, empiricism, experimentalism, and scientific methods based on "pure" observations to verify or reject hypothesis have had their gauntlet run through objections and challengers, by design remain open and subject to scientific enquiry. In fact, most scientific statements written on proper model form maintain a form such as,

Hypotheses 1: A —> B; accept iff A=B

Hypotheses 2: A —> B; Reject iff A≠ B,

reject if A is not equal to B

Followers of Bacon and Newtonians insisted on the primacy of ''pure'' observations, as the initial step in the formation of theories. This is misguided, if all observation is selective and theory-laden, there are no pure or theory-free observations. In a way he destabilizes the traditional view that science can be distinguished from non-science because of its inductive methodology, in contradistinction to this, Popper holds that there is no unique methodology specific to science.[17] Science, like virtually every other human and indeed organic activity, consists largely of problem solving and proving then disproving the same hypothesis frequently for better evidence.

Popperian augmentations of verifiability or falsifiabililty came not with enthusiasm or rewards, or governmental contracts, by all the variables we wrote about psychological and behaviors responses and dissent, and social struggle against the comfortable norms. The second phase of invention model can explain industrialization in two periods, one 1300 to1700, when economic ideas, constitutional republics and governments came with jails, beheadings, revolutions (French revolution and U.S. Colonial revolutions), and floods of human blood and lives lost. In addition, a large number of borrowed and new technological equipment and institutions were formulated, experimented with, in the regions. We only write about capital (human skill, physical, and financial), and its economic aspects here, and inventions leading to block books as an example.

In Persia like in Africa, and in China after each stage of ice age cycles, they maintained the centrality in innovation accumulation and application in most of antiquities. However, with each war, new empire builders duplicated Persian Empire's technologies, based on technological skills accumulated from its tribal age to 600 BC. These empire duplications and empire-envy encouraged a bad superiority-inferiority pathology, which led to violent habits of burning libraries, and books, animal skin, and linen paper, and destroying and blowing up signs and symbol of thoughts, or industriousness. Rock and mud tablets did better. Empires wanted to be unique in their triumphalism, after the fact that they already were following others.

There is a modern version of this barbaric culture, in theft and underground trade of antiquities and their cultural icons, implements, and arts. Often dishonest nationalism, nativism misplaced patriotism, replaces scientific methodologies. Figure 4 shows accumulative sources of knowledge, and their proximate historical time line.

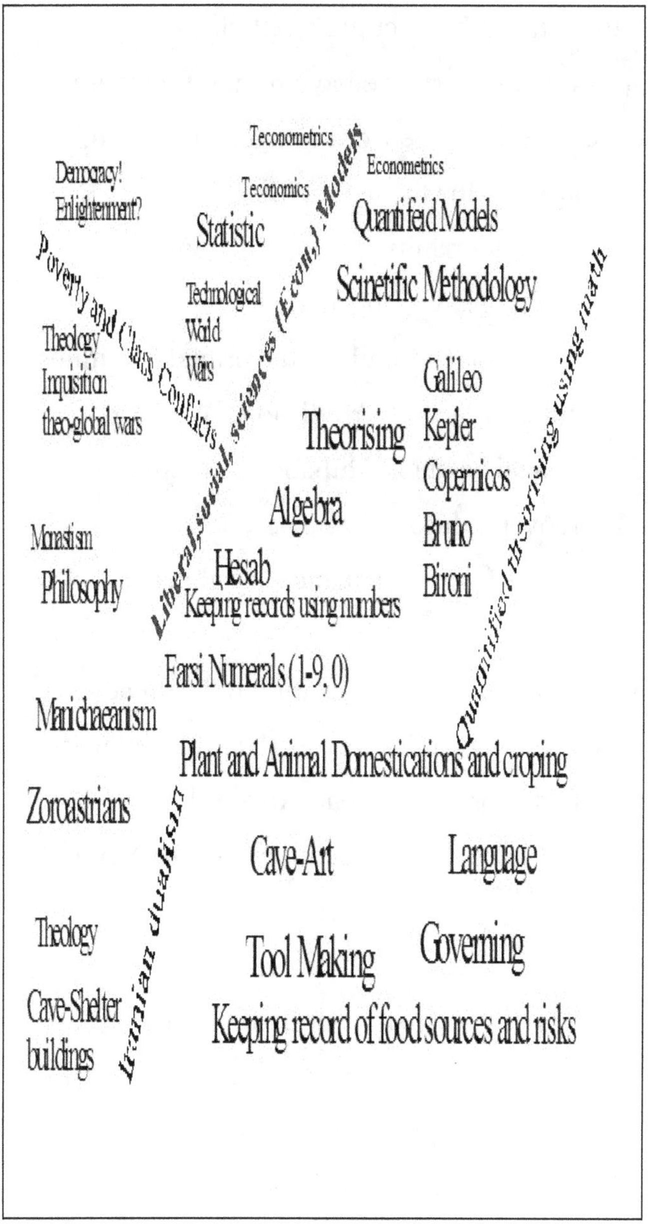

Figure 4. Knowledge sources diagram.

Theological urges changed into pathological phase of seeking and destroying signs of earlier different wisdom and thoughts, others' cultures. Perhaps, in studying of primate we learn, we have been gifted these genetic tendencies to violence from our genetic pool of evolutionary relatives, plus the technological advancement to undo humanity instantly and insanely. Thus, humanity ventures away from the Godly and diplomatic affair of humane minds to the primal hostilities of our primal natures, at least, periodically. We need to constantly dissent against such nihilistic destructive tendencies. Moreover, educate free institutions to encourage humanity to improve chances of global survival.

The human behavior aspect of this study already established complex mechanisms at work at the initial human level in such a process. That explains how difficult and vaporous individual or team efforts become. Specially, if there are institutional counterproductive forces undoing the processes?

Looking only at the final result in the industrial nations befuddles best efforts in creation or transfer to any developing markets, ill prepared to cultivate the process of technological creation or adoptions, let alone growth or sustainable growth.

Cultural inadequacies and theological elements are small compare to governmental and market inadequacies at work, we all need to do better. However, the combined complex counter structures can undo best efforts. All complex matters seem impossible if not understood.

Notes

[1] "The term was coined in 1950s to avoid the identification of social sciences with socialism in the mind of backwoods congressmen... In one sense all sciences study the behavior of something, be it electrons, atoms, molecules, viruses, cells, animals, or people." K. E. Boulding, *Economics As A science*, New York: McGraw-Hill Book Company, 1970, 53

[2] David S. Landes, *The wealth and poverty of nations: Why Some are So Rich and Some are So Poor*, (New York: W.W. Norton & Company, 1998), 189.

[3] Compare the details 0f 1952 with the modern times. David S. Landes, *The wealth and poverty of nations: Why Some are So Rich and Some are So Poor*, (New York: W.W. Norton & Company, 1998), 126

[4] On line," Modern History Source Book Galileo Letter to Grand Duchess.html" (May 2002)

[5] The Ice-age cycles were 50000 to 100000 years cycles.
[6] Signs of earlier civilization emerged from under the dusts.

http://www.youtube.com/watch?v=hD1gFWMTUY8&feature=share

[7] Azilians, in southern Europe, France, and Spain, used less sophisticated tokens by 8000 B.C.
James Peter and Thorpe Nick, *Ancient Inventions*, (new York: Ballantine Books, 1994),476

[8] Dog species diversification is more numerous in China

royal dynasties.

[9]

http://www.youtube.com/watch?v=hD1gFWMTUY8&feature=share

[10] Another tradition is the use of horsetail hair, or grass-blade rope knots, for ten head counts.

[11] John Rae, *Statement of Some Principles on the Subject of Political Economy*, (Boston: Hilliard Gray and Co. 1834), 251-255

[12] James Peter and Thorpe Nick, *Ancient Inventions*, (New York: Ballantine Books, 1994),476

[13] As new digs present new evidence, we will redefine these scientific frontiers, to include coexistence and gene sharing of different species of humanoids. http://www.youtube.com/watch?v=hD1gFWMTUY8&feature=share

[14] J. J. O'Conner and E. F. Robertson, "The Arabic Numeral System."
[15] Another tradition is the use of horsetail hair, or grass-blade rope knots, for each ten head counts.
[16] David S. Landes, *The wealth and poverty of nations: Why Some are So Rich and Some are So Poor*, (New York: W.W. Norton & Company, 1998), 64-65

[17] Professor Ott uses the culture of organizations that could clash with organizational cultures (among companies), or with (this is author's addendum), the larger national culture (i.e. Vietnam area conflict between militarists and the American society antiwar cultural movement).

J. Steven Ott, *The Organizational Culture Perspectives*, (Pacific Grove, California: Brooks/Cole Publishing Company, 1989)

CHAPTER 4

SELECTED DEFINITIONS OF VALUE AND PRICE

One of the longest interesting economic arguments is about the value in entities, items, and things, produced and used by people. How we price each item has been the source of many written arguments and different school of thought in economics.

On Value

Ricardo and Marx are among a large number of economists who define the value of all products equal to the values that labor embodies in them. After Sir William Petty (1623-1687) lesser-known work on labor, John Lock (1632-1704) wrote of labor theory of value. He wrote, labor "puts the difference of value on everything."[1] Schumpeter wrote that Ricardo understood the time cost in production and did not explain it, but Marx included it in the labor-embodied value. He further credited Aristotle with the recognition of just value reached, by exchange in non-monopoly markets.[2] The actual practice was long established, in the Bazaars, and even earlier in tribal barter and exchanges in gatherings of central Persia dating close to village-cave formation period in human history. Schumpeter traces origin of the one-factor production function of Ricardo and Marx to Galiani, "fatica" and labor quality, and "talinti" counting for the different prices among labors. Hence, skill was also introduced, as a measure for price differentiation. So far, labor, time costs, and skill add to the value of a product. Galiani, 1588, explained the value-paradox of golden calf being of more value than a real natural calf, in use and scarcity. While the point is made, he meant utility by usefulness.[3] Turgot 1766, and Achille Nicolas Isnard 1781, further formulated the relation of value to price, before Adam Smith.[4] Alas, a clearer explanation of marginal utility, application of it to costs and distribution, and unification of the subjective notion in some use and utility and objective costs of production are reflected in the work of Jevon and Menger.

Jevon's definition alters the focus that cost of production determines supply, supply determines final degree of utility, and final degree of utility determines value. Economic value is determined in use, or in exchange. Stone-age societies used established use-values for each needed item, until the barter system created another force in establishing value. Once an item is produced, its owner can give it any value, yet unless one other person agrees with that value, the item is of no value in that exchange.

The marginal utility of each added parcel of a good consumed declines, " law of diminishing marginal utility" that all goods in the individual consumption basket have the marginal utility of the last unit of currency spent on them equally, "the law of equal marginal utility per currency unit". Thus, this is establishing an ordinal mechanism, to reflect choice by a negatively sloped demand curve.[5] Thus, regardless of the use-value and how much labor is embedded in an item, or the production costs involved, its exchange value may be much less, equal or greater than labor-embodied value or use-value. This can be a major source of disequilibrium and distribution problems of income.[6] In addition, in the longer run it can determine that certain items are not produced at all, or they are produced with additional tax-subsidy costs, or produced only seasonally. The short-term misinterpretation of scarcity-value system and market value system has let human society to life endangering abuse of two most abundant resources water and air.

Scarcity value system assuming only scarce resources have value, and market value system assigning a currency number according to the scarcity of resources from market exchanges. Both water and air abundant as they are, gained international recognition after pollution, toxic wastes, acid rain and deforestation and fish kills, nuclear accidents and nuclear clouds, as byproducts of an ever more expanding production systems of market economies focused global attentions. R. H. Coase and other economists have introduced negative and positive externalities in Pareto Optimum theory to account for failure of market mechanism to give value to otherwise valuable resources, and misapplication of scarcity value theorem. So then, the state through tax, fee, fine, and subsidy strategies compensates for market failures to account for the externalities, in assigning value exogenously determined outside market. This will induce more efficient and prudent use of societal resources by establishing representative values for the resources. Technologies in economic activities and as production variable also have a phantom nature (with externalities), which fail to assign them representative market values. Without this recognition, the inefficiencies cannot help but to encourage counterproductive implications.

The costs of production, reflecting costs of raw natural resources (lease, extraction, marketing, and transportation), labor, land (rent), management, interests on funds, and expected profits–given access to technology–determines supply. Theoretically, for maximum-profit equilibrium in competitive conditions to hold, expected marginal revenue product of inputs (as defined the expected marginal revenue of each added sale of produce time the marginal physical product of inputs) equates the market price of inputs. Thus, firms employ factors until the marginal costs and expected marginal benefit are equal.[7] The post-tax disposable income (which beside wages includes return or flow of cash from stock of capital, rent, and invested funds), and perception of utilities of produce in further production or for consumption determines demand. Supply and demand determines relative economic value, for a short period per each isolated exchange, or per mass for each institutional transaction and the contract-periods of time, when supply equates demand economic value equate to the relative market price. Relative market price can be much less, than the economic value because relative price can be equal to the cost of one input and lead to less efficient use of other inputs. This was hinted at by Richard Cantillon (1680?-1734) assay "On the Nature of Commerce In General," Cantillon wrote this, it was found two years after his death by Stanley Jovans (1881).[8]

"... The price or the intrinsic value of thing is the measure of the amount of land & of labor, which enters into its production, taking into account the quality or produce of the land & the quality of labor. But it often happens that several things that now have this intrinsic value do not sell in the market according to this value: that will depend upon the whims and fancies of men, & upon the amount they consume."

Thus, the lower value is causing relative underdevelopment of certain resources. That is production cannot continue in the longer run, if the relative market prices remain below costs of production. In fact, this is one of the Hayek's conditions, which causes capital to be consumed. However, the capital consumption can be applied to maintain production, with the same technology until we run out of that capital. Alternatively, Capital consumption can be applied to new technologies in a more profitable production venture, after a transitional process. For example, if production costs (supply-sided, and institutionally, and monopolistically set) did not reflect optimum taxes to maintain the infrastructure (roads, education, etc.) in a region, can this region still be nationally or internationally competitive in the end? Thus, it is paradoxical and false for some future economists to formulate a system explaining all economic life to the exclusion of human society. Yet another outrage is conjuring economic systems for the benefit of a limited class by a capital-only production function because robotic computer technologies can replace manual workers. Unless it is a computer-generated economic model, void of a human theory of value and dangerous nonsense, such model can evolve in some dictatorial outcast nation, in a state of fascist fratricide and hegemony-power politics and genocide, and it will be socio-politically unstable.

The universal set determining values can reflect subsets domination of economic (profit-motives), political (vote only motive), or social (theological motives) to the exclusion of others with higher degree of instability and inefficiency. These subsets can all be assigned subjective relative economic values or indices to avoid ignoring them. Here is the potential of a non-Marxist revolution, when a non-democratic political system or traditional social systems block progressive democratic changes that economic development policies often start. Nevertheless, an example in an advanced economy is as all of the production is down by the automation, then where would the unemployed society come up with the income to consume the produce. Unless we already decided to become another failed communist experience of the next century, we best take a long-term analytical look at the future we plan now. The rate of technological adaptations in a sector can increase rate of unemployment in the same sector for the short run. In the longer run, in a market economy, investment opportunities should increase the employment rate, by increasing the rate of job-creation in the new technology sector and related sectors. Absolute automation schemes would need absolute socialistic redistribution to survive. It will cut off the self-corrective mechanism of market forces. The ownership-rights become questionable and dynamic entrepreneurial interjection fall short and immigrate, first to more productive yet relatively freer markets, as other income generating endeavors vanish. Second, they relocate to more suitable and more productive regions. These points are further developed in the next chapter.

R. H. Coase and modern welfare economists have studied the co-existence of Pareto Optimality solutions and externalities (negative or positive).[9] The results are helpful to market sufficiency and sustainability balance-issues, because, the over manipulated and imperfect private market mechanism fail regularly.[10] There exists a need for state intervention through fiscal and monetary adjustments in macroeconomics. Gerhard Mensch Wrote,

> "The question is how this disequilibrium can be overcome, the answer is through the provision of new types of goods and services that better

supply what people desire"[11]

Another way is through (True costs) tax-subsidy-regulatory strategies to compensate for the externalities in order to induce more efficient use of societal resources by establishing more representative value for the resources ignored, overlooked, under-valued, or undetected by the market mechanisms (intentionally or not!), at the microeconomic level. Another point of interjection is encouragements of the mechanism of innovation, where the new technologies are created.

The involvement of states (democratic or otherwise) in the economic process is no reason for any dogmatic assurances of long-run equilibrium or permanent stabilities. Because socio-political forces have influences and affects, which are not all known, or readily manageable by the market forces. In addition, practically most prisoners' choices (Hobson choice games theories) may lead to none market equilibrium in the end, away from more stable optimum welfare equilibriums, and far away from sustainability solutions without fine tunings. These are acceptable in few isolated cases, but en mass, away from the market optimum solutions and societal stability path. So we are adding to the 1776 "Wealth of Nations" ideas of Adam Smith's "invisible hand of self-interest" and the market checks of competitors' self-interests. That is, if greed in pricing and misery in wage-setting by one individual is checked by others, coming into the market to take their places, with prices and wages adjusting closer to true costs of production of items, and wages that would sustain current workers and retain skilled workers and replacements.

That is possible only in a market that operates under perfect competition assumptions. We are adding the other surgical hand of regulations, and organization (monopsony, and Unions against monopolies). Where market imperfections, monopolistic imperfections (regulatory, technological, regional), or oligopolies exits. When market weakness, pollution, and longer term true costs are not given a chance to be part of the immediate market decision-makings. Therefore, they are excluded from the perfect markets' pricing system. While we need to avoid the debunked ideas, or non-market solutions that have some universal appeals, but they have proven to be counterproductive to markets, and destabilizing to the whole systems.

On Technology

Technology initially was the collected information about primitive tools, later expanded to the agricultural practitioners, and later, it includes the medical and industrial arts. Thus, technology is the societal pool of disembodied and embodied social and physical knowledge used in production of all technologies (ideas), goods, and services.[12]

Its origin go as far back as humanoids venturing in early migration passes from Africa to Persia to China, to Tibet and India, and eventually to Mediterranean costal, Europe, Russia, Japan , and south east Asia, and America taking with them the wood, stone tools and the skill to use them. That earlier migration routes predated the silk roads, it evolved as ice-cycles relented. The tribal-units predated the Mesopotamia cultures. They were earlier humanoid settlements as Asia separated from Africa by the plate tectonic separations, 2 million years ago, plus the emigrations waves from Africa. These tribes formed in the Central Persian Plateaus and cave-villages. They were among some thirteen or more technological advancing tribal units, dating as far back to 15,000 to 65,000 BC. They grow around the other less known twin rivers Karoon and Dez by Shush to the Persian Gulf to the south.[13] The tribes traveled beyond the Caspian Sea over time. They ventured to the frozen ice caps of the north (in Russia) and North West, and Tibet and to the East.

A plant and animal rich region, land locked and, landlocked mountain-meadows were safe from easy marauding, which allowed early developmental usage of dogs, donkeys, sheep and goats, and range hen and birds domestication, use of small grains, and grapes as wildly ubiquitous useful plant and animal species available to cave, and cave village dwellers. It is easy to understand that summer-winter feed flock movement strategy had to predate tribal en mass migrations, as present day Lure tribes continue the same practice in harsh conditions of central Persian plateau, which they survive regularly (twice a year) even in modern times. Moreover, of course the Political ventures of Mead and Elam tribes west to Syria and Mediterranean shows up in old and recent digs and led to the greater Persian Empire 650-530 BC.

Nevertheless, there were elemental political and theological social skills and controls evolved with urbanization of tribal units, which influenced economic tendencies and ideas that also defused to Mediterranean and European centers along with technologies. For Example early use of wool, cotton, and linen and upright single looms used in Persian rug weavings and use of linen and cotton in clothing shows up in Persian 12,000-20,000 BC to Syria and Africa to the west and south, and Tibet to India to China regions to the East. Use of handlooms with waving wheels in central Persia used in wool strings used in rug and other fabric formations, being found in clothes in desert dig past Tibet and in south east China. A more complex silk-multiple looming system comes back from China to Persia and goes to Egypt and then Europe. Ink from painting elements, two of, which are common plants endogenous in south-central to north of Iran is derived from skin of Persian Walnuts by soaking, ageing and sun drying in earlier times, but later by soaking and cooking the samples to produce ink. Further developments of oil based paint also added to the body of knowledge. The linen-paper pulping was noted and spread (by diffusion) in central China from second to seventh century AC, The "development of use and diffusion" of it in Persia started in Samarkand in 751 AD. It was reported in Bagdad by 793, in Egypt by 900, in Morocco by 1189, in Spain by 1150, in France 1189, Italy by 1276, and in Germany 1320.[14]

Imprinting as in pressing impressions came after a number of technologies were formulated. The chiseling of historical events in rocks or mountainsides already exited. The painting of cave wall and chiseling hunting events in mud cylinders, and stone was common. The weaving of colorful, historic, and beautiful impressions and designs in cloth or Persian rugs was present. Then mass production of material by pressing wooden engraved blocks on paper was reported in China by 6th century AD. Use of wine pressing, goldsmith, and engravers in Europe, combined with hand coping of Hesab books, and poetry in Persia and

Middle East had to predate the one very important technology of single book printing of paper books, then, the block multiple book printing in 1470 Europe materialized.

Technological change consists of all advancements in the societies' technology over time.[15] New principles applied, new methods used in production of old or new products. New management methods, new marketing techniques applied. For example, a corn seed developed by genetically selective pollination increases output per same amount of seeds and acres per set amount of cultivation and fertilization. This constitutes a technological change in the field of agronomy, but also it influences animal husbandry, dairy, poultry productions.

There are two definitions for technological change. The more general definition allows for the kinds of progress ranging, from the embodied technological changes (hardware), which primitive toolmakers, early artisans were engaged in, to the modern and scientifically methodical technological changes, which only takes place in modern, well-equipped research labs of big businesses. The disembodied technological changes (software) could be better infrastructures, organizational changes, or better basic education.[16] This could reduce the retraining time of the dislocated unemployed in for their new jobs that technological changes often can create. The following is a limited scope view what increase the wealth of a nation.[17]

> "The continuous upward shift in educational background has upgraded the skills and versatility of labor and contributed to the rise of national income."

Better health and nutrition of workers also contribute to productivity. This is, in short inputs, adds national wealth.

Inputs augmentation characters of technological change have implications for efficient allocation of resources in all economies. When new methods of production, more "mechanized" than the older methods produce. This reduces employment, "thus offering less employment than the average per unit of investment." The example uses Mexico 1971 when Multinational Cooperation share of sales are 25 percent, but their share of employment are 9.9 percent.[18] Particularly, when the embodied technological changes are formulated for highly skilled labor economies, to the disadvantages of the local population, constructive result will be elusive. The labor saving or capital-using technologies products are transferred, and yet they dominate production methods in developing nations. Then, they are transferred to highly populated, developing economies, which require more labor-using, appropriate technologies and or limited capital economies. Another aspect of appropriateness of technological changes has to do with how abundant or scarce raw material resources are in an economy. Assuming the market imperfections and other difficulties are minimal or stable in the economy, "if the market system is operating properly." New methods of production can be used for optimal resource use, "technological change will reduce and conserve the use of increasingly scarce raw materials."[19] So the appropriateness of technology change extends to optimum use of capital, labor ratio, and optimum use of available and scarce resources.

In Figure 5, however, it will bring much larger returns in machinery sectors at (k), on the budget line tangential to the new production-possibility frontier, at the point of production will reflect lower costs and better return in capital used in production of machinery, versus that used in food production. Therefore, less food is produced and more machines are put out by the economy.

Production possibilities locus showing different production methods and inputs given all resources available to an economy is illustrated. While the same ratio of k/L in machinery sector give use more machinery outputs, an explanation for that is that technological progress reflected in new production methods (a new production function for machinery utilizing better technologies along (Pmt).

Another supply expansion occurs when technologies are injected in the new

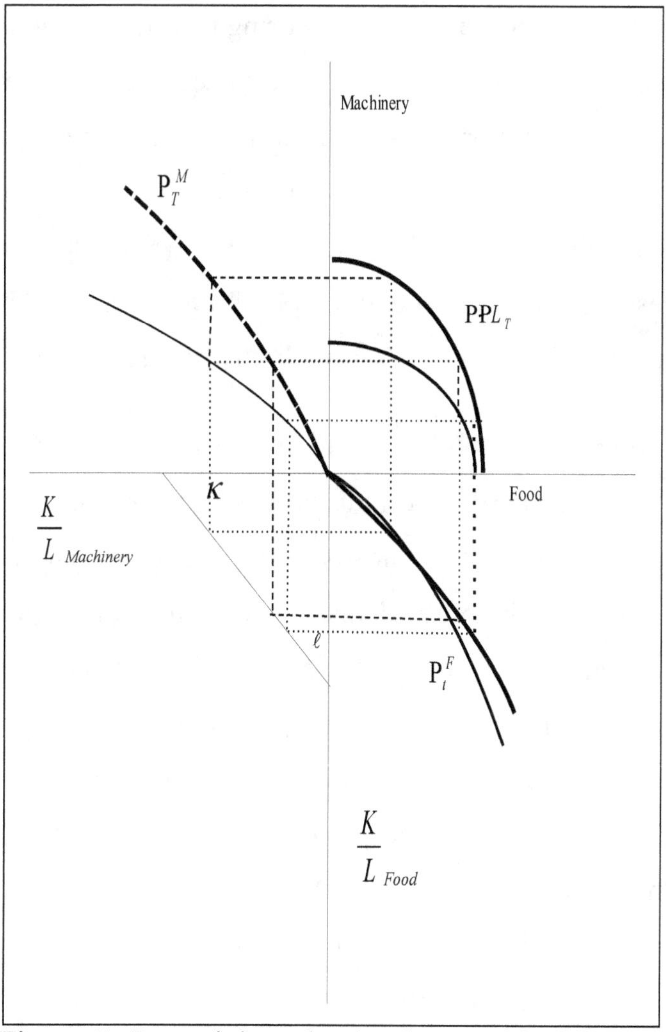

Figure 5. Potential production locus with different technologies.

production function producing food (Pft). The increased economic activities and production will expand production possibility curve outward favoring the industry, which uses technologies to produce more of machinery at lower resource time or costs. This is shown in the new outside potential production locus (PPL_t). The advancement in technological adoption and increased economic activity result in the new production possibility frontier. The injection of the same K/L will only bring minimal return in food production (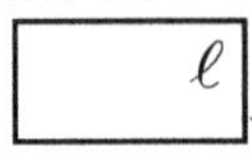).

The starting point usually is that agrarian economies have more workers, mostly unskilled, somewhat under educated than more advanced economies, which are often industrial economies. Yet, advanced economies tend to produce more of agricultural product beyond their local demands, using technologies and adopted-scientific methodologies in their production. Therefore, they sell off their over supplied agricultural output. Never the less their main revenue generating goods and services is the high costs item of machinery, service, or technological product, which are in demand, and they have higher sale value relative to their production costs.

A fundamental aspect of development is the process of shifting and timing such shifts from one method to another, if the institutional bases are there to start with.

Moreover, saving or funding for such shift in technological methodologies favoring different sets of capital, technology and labor methodologies of production to meet market demand generated out of their particular economies. In Figure 6, The locus of all hypothetically continuous production methods with different level of capital and labor combination reflect two different aspect of an economy, or two different countries one using more capital and technologically endued, and one using more labor intensive methods of production. When the statistical ratios and indices are measured they will confirm, which relays on capital more than the other sector or economies.

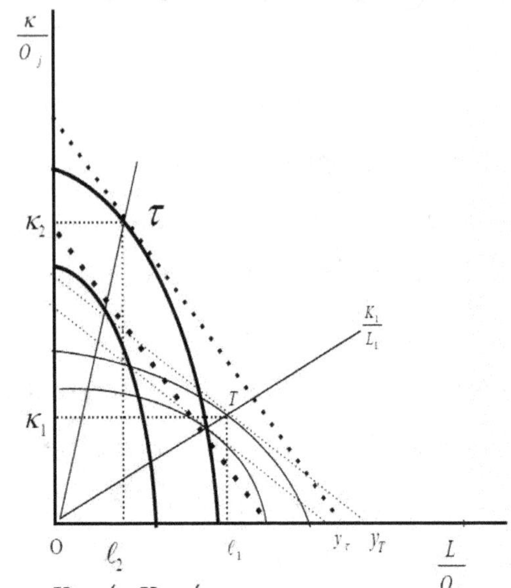

$$K_2/\ell_2 \rangle K_1/\ell_1 \therefore \alpha_\tau \rangle \beta_\tau \forall \tau, i.j \rangle 0$$

Figure 6. The locus of all hypothetically continuous production methods.

Figure 6, Potential Production locus (t, T), reflect different bundle of goods and services produced using labor (L), and capital (K) units more extensively for different bundles. That income at YT is greater than at Yt. That is, one can afford either production process or technologies. This further studied under classification of technological changes.

The U.S. Patent Office, to grant rights, uses the specific definition of technological changes.[20] A technological change index based on the number of patents is also used.[21] Nevertheless, given all that is excluded in its narrow definition, the value of such index may remain in question. It may reflect the growth of synthesis between the technological change and scientific methodology, where capital-intensive investments in technological changes are occurring. That is, to convey more scientifically and methodically technological changes are taking place.

Measurement of Technological Change and Problems

Initially, the use of productivity was used to measure output to input (labor hours, or capital value) ratios. One of the reasons for increases in this ratio is technological change.[22]

Table 6 shows an increases in non-farm business sectors (1977=100 percent), quarterly data, and seasonally adjusted (1950-1984).[23] Calculations from (Table 1) show the percentage increases of output are from 1.4 - 2.08 times higher than the percentage increase of hours of labor. In addition, the real hourly shares of labors have declined, and the labor hourly productivity has increased.

Nevertheless, the increase in labor hours was smaller in 1980-85, 1.2 per year versus 1.9 percent per annum of the 1970-1979. The real hourly compensations have kept to a relative decline. From the (0.84 percent) per year in

1970-1979, to (0.26 percent) per year increase of the 1980-1985, the share of labor hours productivity index percentages over the output percentage

Table 6 shows output, worker productivity percentages.

Table 6. Outputs, labor productivity percentages.

Years	Output	Hours	Output/ Hours All workers	Real Pay Per Hour
1950-1959	13.8	7.3	12.5	16.4
1960-1969	26.3	14.0	18.0	17.7
1970-1979	27.9	19.0	10.0	8.4
1980-1985	12.5	6.0	5.8	1.3

1- Output is gross domestic product originated in the sectors in the 1982 constant dollars.
2- Hours of all person working in each sectors.
3- Labor hours productivity index.
4- The hourly compensation divided by consumer price index.

increases have more than doubled, from 3.5 percent per annum in the 1970-1979, to 9.2 percent per annum in the (1980-1985).

When the same family unit on a given plots of land starts rotating crops and experiencing an increase in their crop yields for basic knowledge of what crop to use and, which of the three plots of land not to plant, it would have been difficult for those farmers not to see the line of causation over the years. When national farm outputs increases in short-term under unchanged conditions, except for new supply of mixed fertilizers, it is difficult not to admit the impact of the mixture of chemical fertilizers and the embodied knowledge in chemical formula of each potash, phosphate, and nitrate used. Whatever ways we want to explain production function, there is a line of causation between the increase of input fertilizers and increase in national farm output, if we measure the output in kilograms of produce in kind or current dollar value of each produce, or a real-value currency of output compared to a base year.

There are other factors, which would have an effect on production costs, for example currency value-fluctuations, to speculative jolts, monetization, or inflationary devaluations, etc. However, the primary increase in outputs is established. Now, the synthesis of science and technology have produced genetic engineering leading to designed plants and animals, for example, crops can be selected to use environmental nitrogen, or to be herbicide-resistant. The family on the same farm now invests in some machinery and can do all the work faster, so the family can go to college and obtain new skills, in order to obtain more output for less labor hours. On the labor side, about (65 percent) of population were engaged in agricultural activities in 1850, that dropped to (3 percent) of population staying in agricultural sectors.

On the supply side, the productivity of average farm worker was to supply food for three people in 1850. The productivity increased so average farm worker in an advance economy could supply 78 people in 1980. The food supplied by farm-worker index (food labor index) increased by 26 times.[24] Thus, the rate of growth of labor productivity index can be affected by a number of other variables, such as the use of machinery to substitute for human labor given the budget constraints or diffusion of knowledge or access to the best relevant techniques of production.

Other circumstances as positive economies of scale and improvement in health or nutrition of individual laborers could also affect this index. Thus, a new productivity index was needed to take into account more factors than labor productivity index. Even the aggregate output, after we note the use of oxen-pulled plows and tractors, from sharecropping to the use of modern agribusinesses and multi-nationals, the capital equipment of all ages will keep expanding. The expansion occurs due to genetically selective plant breeding, genetic engineering, by quantity or mix of fertilizers, and better financial managements, better communications among variables and market participants. With these expansions of due to technologies, there comes a time that every objective observer sees the lines of causation.

The agricultural produce and production possibility curve has expanded. The circular flow should show an increase in transfer of the increased sum from higher produce to more participants in the economy.

Total productivity index studies only the change in an estimation of output with respect to changes in labor and capital estimations. The capital-labor productivity index is calculated by dividing the percent change in quantity or value of output over the same value in a base year by labor and capital values calculated as a percentage change over the base year values, times their shares of output.

Total productivity index (TPI) is for TPI calculated as follows,

Given the Production Function, O = l x L + k x K,

$$\Rightarrow \frac{\mathrm{O}}{\ell \times L + k \times \mathrm{K}}$$

The O is for output, L and K are inputs of labor, and capital, l, and k are marginal products of the same inputs.[25]

This assumes the marginal products of inputs are

influenced only by technological change, and the ratios are independent of inputs quantities. This approach also will have difficulties if the distributions of shares of output are due to imperfect competitions, or other market imperfections, or socio-political factors by convention or tradition other than market valuations and technological changes influencing market valuations.

Aggregate Production Function, Technological Progress

The use of aggregate production function has led to the latest method of measuring technological change. There is little argument against a statistical relation linking an estimation of output, national or international, to estimations of capital and labors, yet, the transformation of a micro-economic relation of the same variables causes' considerable argument about the assumptions.

The pioneering micro-economic relation was developed by Charles Cobb (1928) and Paul Douglas.[26] The formulation was as follows,

Production Function,

$$Q = \rho \times K^{\beta} \times L^{\alpha}$$

Constant Return to Scale Rule,

$$\alpha + \beta = 1$$

The objections rose to constant return aspect of this function specially when larger economic variables are measured or technological aspects are studied at Macroeconomics level.

It was the work of J. Tinbergen (1942) and Stefan Valavanis-Vail (1955), which led to use of aggregate production function to measuring of technological change. J. Tinbergen used an exponential time trend method to estimate technological change from aggregate production.[27] Then, S. Valavanis-Vail used the productivity term of Cobb-Douglas to refer to an estimation of technological change.[28] Jacob Schmookler (1952) applied the use of factor shares method to the United States.[29] Later, John W. Kindrick applied the same methods.[30]

The findings among these studies for American economy all show a positive index for the rate of growth of total productivity. Stefan Valavanis-Vail showed a cumulative rate of growth of productivity of .75 percent per annum over the period 1869-1948. J. Tinbergen's estimate was 1.1 percent per year. Jacob Schmookler's number was 1.01 percent per year for the period 1869-1928. His analysis included agriculture. He calculated an increase of 36 percent for output per unit of input for the two periods of 1904-1913 and 1928-1938. John W. Kindrick's rate of growth of total productivity was 1.7 percent for the later period of 1899-1953. The later studies all are very close estimations of each other.[31]

Another important point to our thesis is the estimations about the later periods keep increasing over the earlier periods. It was assumed and later estimated that up to 90 percent of growth of output per head could not be linked to increase of capital per head in American economy, thus it could be related to some form of technological changes. Abramovitz focused the need for research,

> "Since we know little about causes of productivity increase, the indicated importance of this element may be taken as some measure of our ignorance about the causes of economic growth in the United States and some sort of indication of where we need to concentrate our attention."[32]

Solomomn Fabricant calculated 90 percent of the increase of output per capita was due to Technological progress.[33] He used a different method than the neoclassical model of Robert M. Solow (or neo-neoclassical methods so named by Joan Robinson), it is more general and divides output by weighted sum of inputs.

It also held implicitly that technological changes were neutral, and the production function was a linear mathematical relation. Thus, it was not different from Robert M. Solow's production model.[34] Robert M. Solow estimations applied to American data for the period1909-1949 showed the increase of gross output per person-hour doubled.[35] The increase of gross output per increases use of capital was 12.5 percent. The increase of gross output per technological changes was 87.5 percent. A. A. Walter later applied the Cobb-Douglas production function and exponential time trend of R. M. Solow's (1909-1949) data.[36] He found the production function was homogeneous of degree 1.26, and 1.37, and effect of technological change was 1, and 1.25 per annum.[37] Distinctions are made, between increases due to technological changes, versus increases due to added inputs.

Classification of Technological Changes Types

Technological changes are classified with respect what types of inputs they most utilized and what alternative input they save in the new production method they advance. The technological changes can be classified neutral, meaning equal effect on labor and capital inputs used in production. The same technological changes can be labor using, which by implication also means capital saving. These would be more useful in developing economies needing more employment strategies (job creationists' solutions). The technological progress can be classified as capital augmenting, capital using, and labor saving.

These types of technological advancements are useful in advanced and developing economies both, targeting higher income consumers and markets. The most revenue enhancements strategies for sustainable economic growth are in these fields. Moreover, large amounts of resources are wasted on deed-end technological advancement by developing economies. How these different types of technological changes are measured? Following the pioneering works on neutral technological progress, the logic was extended to study changes of relative factors of production due to changes of technologies.[38]

John R. Hicks in studying the issue of constancy of factors' shares over time, defined neutral adopted technologies, as those that change the inputs' marginal products (returns in competitive market conditions) equally, from the initial given ratios. John R. Hick's thesis points out the following conditions will take place. One, higher capital accumulation with respect to labor tends to reduce capital shares. Two, the subsequent higher wages of labors relative to price of capital goods will increase uses of capital-using technologies, which in turn reduce the labors' shares of outputs.[39] This is often rebutted that levels of living of labor in capital rich economy like United States have been increasing.[40]

Yet there is another fact, that the growth of employments in service sector can employ the dislocated, unemployed labors. Nevertheless, the dynamic real rate of disposable income growth must increase to prove these assertions. Unfortunately, it does not.

In Table1, we see that the relative real hourly compensation has declined. Is it due to Hicks second proposition? Alternatively, the service sector alone cannot generate enough jobs to employ the dislocated labors. If you remember in line with the fully computerized or robotic economy, the issue remains. Who then remains to purchase such outputs, beyond the satiated marginal utilities of the 5 percent or the highest-income individuals to keep a dynamic employment and production in such a nonfunctional unstable economic system?

Roy F. Harrod focus was long-term equilibrium growth. His neutral technological changes were defined as the changes that in a constant interest rate economy will hold the same ratio of capital to output.[41] Nevertheless, he also introduced the idea of other classifications for technological progress,

"...to define a neutral stream of inventions as one, which shall require the rate increase of capital equal to the rate of increase in income generated by it. If the stream of inventions requires capital to increase at a greater rate, then it is worker-saving or capital-requiring and conversely."

M. Brown and J. Popkin used different measurement to classify neutral and non-neutral technological changes, and returns to scales, reflected in output changes.[42] Given the elasticity of output with respect to labor and capital, the following formula determines the classifications of technological change as,

$$\frac{\alpha}{\alpha + \beta} \cong \theta$$

$\theta = 50$ Neutral;

$\theta \rangle 50$ Labor Saving;

$\theta \langle 50$ Labor Using

They found for 1890-1918, technological change was labor saving, (2= 0.66). For the period of 1919-1937, (2= 0.42). The labor using technological change biases declined for 1938-1958 period, since (2=0.49).

M. J. Beckmann and R. Sato came up with four different definition and calcifications.[43] These were product using, labor using, capital using, and factors saving technological changes, which can be adopted in production processes.

Classification of Criticism

The needs for these aspects of econometric modeling of technological changes have been realized. The objections to some aspects of the methodology have multiplied as well.[44] Alas, the extensive and modern use of econometrics has not been rolled out. The technological changes left unmeasured had been ignored, until the last end of last millennium. Despite the impression, and the facts about variables being rough estimations, objections will not stop the job yet to be done to completion, on the subject of measuring the impacts of ubiquitous technological changes.

In fact, the body of research and critics are focused on the core and center of activities, and they do not randomly spread away from it, as if it was obsolete. There are three main subjects of debates,

1. The measurements of inputs (especially capital)
2. The use of Cobb-Douglas production function
3. The aggregate production function issues

The criticisms are divided in different classification. They are either theoretical or empirical. The theoretical criticism aim at the assumptions related to the following areas,

A. The assumption of Cobb-Douglas production function

B. The assumptions of aggregate production function.

The empirical objections are either economical or statistical, and they reflect the difficulties in finding appropriate numbers representing actual economic variables and conditions.

Some of the objections to Cobb-Douglas production function are,

1. Neutrality of technological change.
2. Unitary elasticity of substitutions.
3. Constant return to scale.

Robert Solow's model is criticized because,

4. The assumption of disembodied technological change.
5. That all vintages of capital contribute the same share to technological change.
6. The factor shares are determined in a perfectly competitive market place.

In Solomon Fabricant's work the result seemed focused, while the methodology was different. In fact, further studies continue to support the Cobb-Douglas production function form, if not the distributive implications of the same. Thus, Charles Kennedy, and A. P. Thirwall remarked,

"It will be reassuring to those whose religious is Cobb-Douglas that no matter how technical change is specified the estimated production function invariably turns out to be close to Cobb-Douglas form .... None of the possible misspecifications of the Cobb-Douglas function considered so far have caused us to reverse drastically the conclusion of the pioneering studies that the major determinant of growth is the rate of technological progress (technological changes)."[45]

Some criticism is due to cloudy definitions.[46] The technological progress is argued to yield to the following,

1. The substitution of capital for labor
2. The increases of quantity and quality of inputs
3. The economies of scales
4. To learning by doing
5. Improvement of educational or organizational Infrastructure
6. Major resource shifts
7. Measurement errors

In fact, technological advancements are in the proactive manufactured processes. In the larger definition of technological changes, most of these issues are classified under the embodied and disembodied technological changes in dynamic production function.

On Capital

This economically significant word, capital has evolved with economic theory over time. It is difficult to imagine any economists that have not struggled with these most explained terms. Webster defines capital as,

"Stocks of accumulated goods, value of them, accumulated goods used in production of other goods, accumulated possessions to bring in income."[47]

Most of the elements considered as capital like land were not freely tradable entities until post enlightenments introduced the ideas to European institutions undergoing cultural liberalization with blood and revolts, to allow social experimentalism and market infrastructure forming. Solutions to technology progress "sheep herding" displaced "independent farming yeoman" and landowners, manor owners and legislators localized the displaced worker to parishes by law and on marginal help. Then they labeled them "migrant paupers, robbers, beggars, tenants, or agricultural day laborers." In addition, prescribed "whipping, branding, and, mutilations, and deportations" as readily as it could be arranged.[48]

Commercialization and free mobility of capital and labor was fought against, and it took Europe from thirteen to nineteenth century to allow market systems and market system-components like " Labor, land, and capital" to come to market.[49] Therefore, from the start the one component was not included human capital, or ideas and skills, the technological change. It is difficult to study technological changes without consideration to capital, because in capital goods, and human skills technology is embodied or disembodied in capital, or as human capital shows the mix of technological and market conflicts about it. Then the economic modification of the traditional usage will identify the modern definition of capital.

The retrospection on the word capital goes back to Greek usage of a practice long in use in Persia, India, China, and Egypt Urban and trade original systems. The Greek usage of the word-defined capital referred to the principal sum of money of money or quantity of goods (grain, wine) that was loaned. Like, the Greek for word head, (caput), was the Latin noun from the adjective word (capital), used to describe the amount of the loan, (capitalis pars debiti).[50] The practice was common among the practitioners and (Bazar) people, and caravan masters a much-closed band of adventurers and risk takers, even before risk taking was defined. However, this kind of risk taking was more targeted. The cave developers risking taking was higher. The cave people risk life to venture walking out of caves for food.

This kind of time-risk factor had a potential material gain added to the generic sailors, travelers, and caravan traveler's aspect of risk for adventure sake. In addition, its origin goes as far back as humanoids venturing in early migration passes from Africa to Persia and beyond. There were elemental socio-political and theological controls evolved with urbanization of tribal units, which influenced economic tendencies and ideas, which also defused to Mediterranean and European centers.

Other technologies needed to present. The use of paper in book printing, wool-rug weaving and linen, cotton with upright loom and handloom in cloth weaving technologies from Persia, book keeping, algebra and numerical accounting including zero from Persia, India, Mesopotamia, use of coins first for royal gifts and rewards, and later change to notes for payments in thirteenth century Europe. Therefore, the practice of loaning in kind a container of grain for two at next harvest was not unusual. The problems got complicated when the quantity borrowed increased in product-poor barter systems. On the demand side, in hardship one saw convenience in consumptive borrowing, but saw ethical and theological reasons and difficulties in more than equal repayment of capital plus interest for the time-use. On the supply side, in greed sometime lenders sought to get more than a reasonable interest. So negative type castings (stereotypical usurious money exchangers, merchants) had to be ignored, or countermanded by most honest productive people. They had to practice their crafts very honestly while facing high risks. The negative impact were immediate on merchants, as they need to borrow non-consumptive loans to pay for ship and sailors and costs of shipments back and forth to trade overseas, and for the caravan masters and merchants to trade over land, facing bandits, pirates, war parties and marauders.

Trade of spices, salt, paper, rug, and cloth, of silk, cotton, and linen, pottery, of wine and beer jugs, dishes, and jewelries, were common to anthropological dig-sites. From Africa to Persia and china, India to Pars, Shush, and Persian Gulf to Arab Peninsula to Syria and Greek and Rome on land, later by sea north to England, and south to costal Africa to Persian Gulf and India, to South East Asia and Japan humanity has been very mobile, very early. People found ways to improve their lives in astatic worth, cloth, medicine, tools, and method of production far beyond any previous dreams. Sometime, in small alteration in spearheads, or rock cutting tools, sometimes, in large technics of group hunts.

So cultural, theological, and traditional discouragements were the norms, but they had only tentative hold on mortality. Usury laws were supplemented with distaste and disdain for risk and reward in commercial ventures, or sale of land. These social barriers also were needed to be removed. Nevertheless, the harsh dictatorship, or imperialistic centrists governing of the East have been blamed for slow arrival of industrial revolution. That is not true, universally. Persian imperial dynasties of Akmanid were the most decentralized and local based system of governance of that world, the system was replaced by more self-centrist and militarist system with only generous borrowing from the experiences of Persian early Dynasties abroad. Where, they are now referenced, optimistically, as the source of Western democracy. The enlightenments had to overcome religious intolerance and traditional tendencies domestic to their region and time. The economic ideas and philosophies were in conflict as well.

Mercantilism notion of wealth was centered in accumulation of gold and silver, and self-centric opportunistic plundering rather than trade. It is a strategy used by England to bypass Holland commerce around 1775 to1870. As Adam Smith noted the British navigation acts impacted Dutch sea power. Alas, this caused problem for inevitable idea of "Free Trade." When the notion found its merits beneficial, the benefactors and the receivers of the notion were not so certain of the mutuality of benefits, considering the source.

The Physiocracy in person of M. Quesnay a physician in "tableau économique" introduced related wealth (away from the gold and silver version) to production (as in agricultural productivity) circulating hand to hand (with elements of laissez faire) like the flow of blood in human body.[51] However, they only looked at agricultural activities as reasonable commerce, trade and manufacturing industry were not acceptable economic activities. Those notions gave over to the enlightenments' forces. Moreover, intellectual debris of industrial revolution wiped them out. While manufactured concept of capital was seen initially related to the unsavory practices of usury on consumptive loans of barter economies. It morphed in the capital as principle sum loaned to merchants, which it gained more acceptance.[52] They were used in commerce or trade, which yielded a stream of revenue, income, rent; beside, it employed people and generated wages. These basic attributes of concepts of capital and interest kept them alive among the practitioners, public officials, and political economists and philosophers of the time, until other technologies evolved.

Capital was not initially an economic term. It was used in law and business. Roman jurists defined the principle of a loan as capital.[53] Economists up to seventeen century used terms like "Riches, wealth, treasures, stocks" as capital. Capital was defined one-way in the barter economies in biblical writings and before. The practitioners and merchant class of the same time defined it differently. Later, it was also defined, as any tool complementing human labor in production of goods with value exchangeable for goods in any market, not unlike some of the more modern definition. For example, Joan Robinson writes capital goods are "all the goods" at a given moment, they have purchasing power "value", they can be classified under physical specific groups, they are age specific (they have a useful life spans , and they are depreciable), they can be used by one or more people.[54] The rate of their output can be explained, as a function of the number of bodies operating the equipment. How did we get to this new definition?

On Capital Theories

Cantillon and Physiocrats defined capital theory, that is, identification of capital as part of an economic system.[55] The use of economic system appeared in Quesnay's work in the use of blood circulation in human anatomy to explain circular flow ideas, and Turgot's use of a term in physics to explain "equilibrium" in explaining economic issues. Quesnay's "avances" are the same as fixed and working Capital. He uses given advances and annual advances, as goods that can be consumed or produced, and they can be valued in money.[56] In Turgot, "riches mobiliaires" are the stock of goods and money saved. In addition, landowners are the only people with enough income to save, because all other classes get a subsisting income enough to meet their consumption.

Anne Robert Jaques Turgot, Baron de l'Aulne (1727-1781), in his work "Réfxion sur la Formation et la Distribution des Richesses" stated "Whoever acquires each year more goods than he finds it necessary to consume , can lay aside the excess and accumulated it. It is these accumulated goods (valeurs accumulrées) that are called capital."[57] He linked money to goods accumulated and wealth as a factor in production.[58] Moreover, he changed the notion of capital from money to other goods.

Richard Cantillon (1680?-, Murdered 1734) was an Irish banker from Paris. His systematic exposition "Sure la Nature du Commerce en General" predated Adam Smith's "Wealth of Nation." His description of farm activities set up many terms we take for granted in modern economics. He wrote that farmers take the products from their farms (earth, soil) "produit de la terre" and sell it in the market for market prices, then divide it three equal parts "les troise rentes", these were to cover their initial costs (workers contracts), land-lords share (land-rent contracts), and their own profits.

Thus, Cantillon introduced profit, and entrepreneurs in persons of farmers facing uncertainty of market prices, and of town merchants. The town merchants "marchands et entrepreneurs" received up to half of farms' outputs, one sixth from the farmers (1/4 * 2/3=1/6), and the land owners 1/3 (1/6+1/3=3/6=1/2).[59] All face the uncertain harvest and harvest prices.[60]

The Physiocrats capital theory determined that the landowners do investment on capital. Turgot listed different ways to employ the capital.[61] Thus, savings of the landowners were employed in the following fashion,

A. Purchase of land
B. Investment in agricultural, manufacturing, and commerce
C. Lending for annual interest

Physiocrats ideas about interest were incomplete. They noted it was a portion of output going for use of capital for a period.

Adam Smith a contemporary and acquaintance modified Quesnay and Turgot definitions of capital. Adam Smith identified fixed capital, the kind of capital, which generate revenue of profit without "circulating or changing masters." [62] He classified some accumulated goods for consumption, and other accumulated goods, those, which yield a flow of income. The former, is bought for resale for a profit, thus it is a circulating capital good. The latter, is bought for the (income) flow of its revenue. It will generate revenue periodically, less the cost of its upkeep. He stated that societal arrangements reflected those of the individual making it up.

Adam Smith divided individual and societal possessions for immediate consumptive goods and longer-term concerns. Especially if individuals have small amount of these positions to maintain themselves for a short period, like a few month to a year. In the longer-term periods, beyond the point of immediate self-satisfactory consumption, the concerns turned to generating revenue. The revenue generation occurred by two types of capital. One, capital is as means of acquisition of revenue (interest). Two, capital is as means of further production. The fixed capital does not change hand, or change form during the production process. So fixed capital does not go from one producer to another as inventory to be altered into consumable goods. Machinery, factories, business buildings, modified and improved land. The societal learnt skills and "useful skill" were listed as example of fixed capital. The circular capital is the kind of capital, which changes hand and form from one producer to another.[63] That all fixed capitals originate from circular capital, and maintained and repaired using circular capital. Examples of circular capitals are money and inventories of incomplete goods (part of cloth, furniture, made in one workshop), or completed products in the hands of merchants to be sold in (as wholesalers' or retailers' inventories). A woven and painted cloth sold to a Taylor.

Say in "Vide Epitome des principles fondamentaux de l'economie politique" stated capital was an accumulation of values, and "richesse" were a sum of values, "la somme des valeurs," In addition, value was what a thing was worth, so determined by market choices.

Among other English classic economists, Ricardo linked capital with labor. David Ricardo defined capital as,

"...that part of the wealth of nation a country, which is employed in production and consists of food, clothing, tools, raw materials, machinery, etc. necessary to give effect to labour."

Malthus defined it as,

"...that portion of the stock of a country kept or employed with a view to profit in the production and distribution of wealth."

Senior defined it as "an article of wealth, the result of human exertion," employed in the same manner. John Stuart Mill defined capital in his detailed way.[64] He defines capital as "stock, previously accumulated, of the produce of former labours." He explained the way capital contributes to production process,

"the shelter, protection, tools, and materials, which the work requires, and feed and otherwise maintain the labourers during the process. These are the services which present labours requires ...from the produce of past, labours."

Other important developments came thereafter. Herman defined land as capital but unlike Adam Smith, he defined all durable goods in personal use as capital.[65] Karl Knies (1821-1898) a German historian defined capital as the existing good applied to the need of future, or to "The satisfaction of the demand in the future."

Here are number of ideas, which were refined or adopted after modification later, but they added to the way definitions and attributions of capital grow over time. Some were dropped, while portion of the idea moved on. The notions of existing goods as capital under goes more changes. While the definitions of capital identified it as an entity used in production.[66] Knies defined "consumption, acquisition, or production goods" as capital goods. Leon Walras divided all goods into durable goods or capital (i.e. Land, persons, and mobile-durable), and fuels, raw materials, and food as (French "revenue") or income. Landry added ideas, and services due ownership of durable goods.

Künast a lawyer, declared value of the certain goods as capital, "the value of production power residing in material goods," but not the concrete objects themselves. Time in production period and the link between capital income, and interest were reintroduced by Böhm-Bawerk.

He expounded Adam Smith idea of social capital to define "notional" capital to study the interest rate theory. He also introduced production period, to define the life of capital used in the round about production.[67] However, he defined it as the time between "the first time application of productive powers and the completion of the product," which says nothing about the useful life of original "productive power" capital goods. Another difficulty is that in aggregation, it does not explain the duration of the useful life of capital goods in use. Entropy of individual entities of capital (notional or social) is problematic. Certain of his assumption cause more difficulties. His assumption that more (complex) round about methods of production (with more technologies), will take much longer to produce, than a less round about method of production. These ignore new facts, that technological changes are timesaving, input saving, as well as resource saving. However, proper representational governance requires regulation to modify the wealth accumulation unabated on one side, and displacement and human obsolesce on the other side. civil societies can remedy these very dangerous volatility and disability conditions readily. Only the most backward of underdeveloped, uneducated societies would fall in such an obvious technologically induced dualistic trap, often for ideological obstinacies and over biased imbecilities. Unfortunately, humanity sees far too much of these conditions.

Styles of Governance and Political Teconomic Progress

The importance of legal institutions in inducements about ownership, capital use, and protection of private rights of ownership and conduct of business activities also play an important part in the process of technological progress, and capital formation. Austrian economists (L. V. Misses, and F.V. Hayak) paid much attention to the system-implication of such institutions and further progress, which aided progress.

In light of Soviet Union (now Russia) and Eastern Europeans' economic systems and institutional changes in 1980s, the work of L. V. Misses, and F.V. Hayak attracted renewed interests. The following were some fundamentals about legal rights and returns on capital, which also have current implications for use of capital,

1. Ownership and use rights were absolute.
2. The relative market price of capital, return, or interest reflects the scarcity of capital.
3. Risk of losses of different capital made their returns different.
4. Interest on funds are the minimum, bellow that the return of other capital cannot go, in order to remain an investment opportunity.

The importance of such infrastructure and the impact of technological-changes have been over looked, or miss-applied. Thus, slowing construction to correct the repeated dangerous past experiences. United State depression and WWII experience found two solutions after the historical globalizations of early misapplications of "laissez faire" of Adam Smith. So the Hayak solution out of Hayak and Keynes roof top paradoxical solutions to the only alternative of Marxism let to the Keynes-ism, since the Hayak solutions had been assumed tried and failed in the " laissez faire" era of pre-depression. F. D. Roosevelt and others tried Keynes, which was pulled to the Statists' extreme in the post-depression and WWII experiences of United States. It is not surprising that the less informed students of economic, and political economics now mistake swing to Hayak solution as repudiation of Keynes, when they mean repudiation of Statists' extremism, and the Stalinism's branch of Marx, which has made a comeback in some regulatory and policy circles. In one hand, with the aid of old fusion political centralism, in another hand, by inducement and encouragements of financial capitalism in cooperate centralism and distributive misallocations of both political power and funds, they have tested other dark dead ends of political economic miss-models. The following graph in Figure 7 shows political economic systems and market dependencies. It is an over view of some infrastructure links.

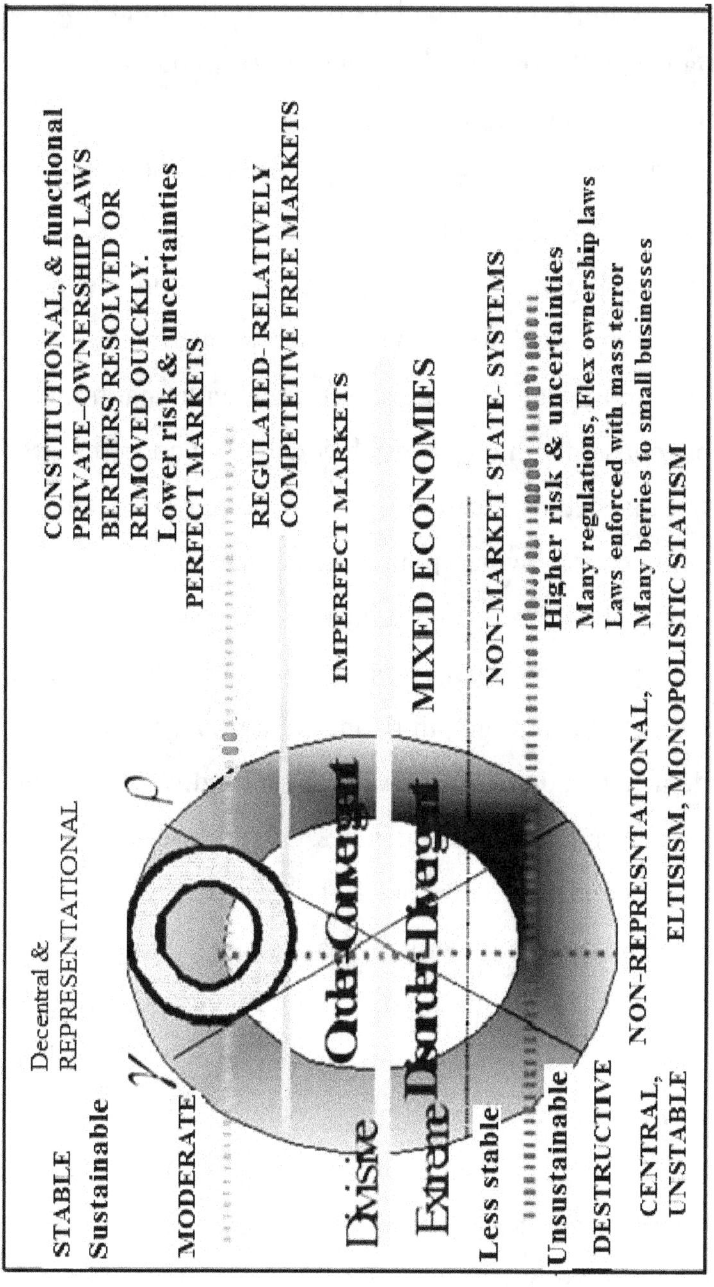

Figure 7. Dr. B.Fakhraie's Political-Teconmics system analysis for innovation.

The impact of regulatory risk to free capital flow, or human capital alone can influence most if not all international investors.

That is not the reputation of ever more ubiquitous mixed economies, taxes, and fees on one side, jobs, and reasonable higher real wages (especially reasonable lower executive pay packages) on the other. Governments will still misapply "laissez fair" again, even with unanimous global consent, which will with equally sad consequences. Only enhanced by technology of "mass and immediate" communications will expound the potency of the past failures. Therefore, "buyers be aware" gets a global refurbishing in political economics, macro-economic and international economic, in finance and trade, again! All academics can do is to forewarn the alerted, well read, and educated proactive constituencies.

Argentina, South East Asia, Mexico 1990-2002 ought to be yet other alerts to "Laissez fair" Monetarism from guarded scholarly branches of Monetarism, which are alluded to later. Governments globally spend political and financial capital on inappropriate technological transfers. Which have no infrastructural-foundations in their political system or regulatory systems? Some of the most recent examples are reflected in the totality of what is explained as Arab spring.[68] The 2008-2010 Islamic countries closely allied with the west and United States, initiated a series of political economic alterations, which will reverberated globally, as much as the 1980s Russian system alteration had affected the global realignments. A small individual business owners' reaction to extreme diversions from economic equilibrium at his expense reverberates in Tunisia set off a chain reaction of predated events that had implication for governments of Tunisia, Egypt, Libya, and Yemen, and all other states, which are in transitions or will follow.[69]

They readily adopt regulation neutralizing what they spend inordinate amount of national capital to obtain and operate, in a rigid political system, which will expunge itself of newness of others, thoughts, technological knowhow, and commercial actions. Moreover, most comically, are the political leaderships, whom will load innovation metamorphism readily, and wage war on its elemental adoptions mercilessly. One-step forward for profit maximization, and two steps back for optimization and sustainability. Figure 7 non-market state-systems are illuminated by thee examples from Tunisia, Egypt, Libya, and Yemenis, and others to come.

The longevity and sustainability of the governmental leadership is not a matter of historicism, the propagandists' militarism, or media-led triumphalism, they will remain a matter of importance for future academic research. The special contribution of technological progress will play a prominent factor in these futuristic advancements phenomena.

Earlier American Economists on Capital and Interest

The intellectual boiling pot of Western Europe from 1300-1700 century had certain names in common. The some notable American names also appear on the constitution of United States. Benjamin Franklin was closely associated with Adam Smith, Quesnay, and Turgot. However, the economic experiences of United States were in its embryonic phase. The head starts in less exogenous conflicts, unlimited land (from the economically uninformed inhabitants <and under armed indigenous population>, that included all nations of American Indians). The extremely motivated populations, without direct controls, and constraints of Governments took advantage of all resources. Uses of other human labors, without appropriate economic or market constrained as slave labor was a prize worthy to fight a civil war over it. Access to international supply of current knowledge in terms of embodied capital with immigrants other than slaves. While some immigrants were employed, they were treated as quasi-slave workers (Chinese immigrants working for the west-east railroad-tracks). Despite some setbacks for the

Irish, Chinese, Japanese, Latin, and Middle Eastern immigrants, the immigrants were highly motivated and grateful. They were unconstraint with dictatorship (physical and litigious) brutalities beyond the water, so they helped to unleash an economic powerhouse. That leapfrogged United State economy ahead of the European industrious advancements.

That is not to say bad ideas did not or do not travel over the water, alas, the constitutional rights and markers tend to overcome office feudalists over the long run, and elections are institutionalized periodical (sometime) peaceful revolutions. Therefore, independence revolution, or north and south war, and emancipation revolution were not bloodless, and labor-management problems took place. They increasing take place in most honest elections. So honest democratic elections remain a lot more amicable, and less destructive, never the less, they remain as technological advancements.

Early American economists Simmon Newcomb, John Rae, John Bates Clark, and Irvin Fisher theoretical innovations modified and added uniquely to the capital and interest theory. The special contribution of technological progress played a prominent factor in these unique American phenomena. America spent less time (less than 200 years) relative to England or Europe, starting at about the same level of progress as Europe to obtain the economic and industrial leadership of modern time. The longevity and sustainability of the economic leadership is not a matter of historicism, the propagandists' militarism, or media-led triumphalism, they will remain a matter of importance for future academic research.

Simmon Newcomb (1835-1909) a mathematician formulated an equation of exchange in monetary theory, later useful to I. Fisher's work. He also expounded the ideas of Cantillon and Quesnay's circular flow as "societary circulation" demonstrating the flow of money and goods, and from opposite direction the flow of services.[70] He also reintroduced the ideas of, "flow" and "funds" as income and capital.

John Rae (1796-1872), was a Scottish economist, which resided in Canada. He wrote in "The Sociological Theory of Capital" under headings of personal finance, about Roman Empire fall and decay. When the mass indulgence and present self-consumption squander, uses up all of the wealth and future of the empire. He is the lesser-known economist by public, with extremely important writings and effects on important economists. Böhm-Bawerk, Irvin Fisher, wrote of his influence on their writings. In fact, Irvin Fisher credited John Rae for (in his 1834 book) for relating events and interest rate. A body of work, that is still in full fruitions, in scholarly studies of current notables like J. Hirshleifer and others.

John Rae work on capital goods "instrument" stated the common factors among the capital goods,

1. They are byproduct of labor.
2. They have a "capacity" to produce "events," which satisfy human wants.
3. They are "exhausted."

He further wrote of formation, selection, and prioritization among different capital goods. J. Rae applied three criteria to prioritize capital goods,

1. By higher yield, or return.
2. By lower costs
3. By the shorter time, between formation and exhaustion

The first and second criteria are also in Fisher Model, if Marshal's net return is used. There are some issues with the last criteria. If the longer time-use of a capital good and increased demand increases the net return of capital good over time relative to the shorter time-use instrument. Perhaps an example can point out the error better. That is, a steal, an iron, and a wooden plow can last for a long time, in the order they are listed. Their usefulness also reflects the same order. Therefore, the revenue-life associated with the steal plow will naturally far exceed the revenue-life of a wooden plow stick, thus the contradiction. In studying computers technologies, the obsolescence period grows shorter and values in prices drop. The focus of the work was on causes of national wealth. The four causes were,

A. Natural resources
B. The desire to accumulate
C. Wage rate hold constant as in " existing circumstances."
D. The inventive faculty

He measured capital goods by the workers accumulation in capital goods. He also identified amount of workers that each capital good would replace, but holding wage constant. First, the objection was raised that "to compute the capacity of goods," the concern should be with wages and not "mental and physical exertions" of workers.[71] Only the first part of this makes sense. Since the replacement of workers by capital goods will make the supply of workers increase, therefore, Wages fluctuate, that in the short run wages mainly decline. This also affects the rate of capital goods formation. In the longer run, the demise of demand will halt the innovation process.

Synchronous Adjustment of Capital

There is more of an onionskins-quality to comprehension of this concept. John Bates Clark (1847-1938) contributed to capital theory. From Turgot to Adam Smith and Böhm-Bawerk, capital was an advance or loan, which was partly used for subsistence of the producers, and it was partly applied (as capital goods) to production. Turgot specified how the revenue from production is spent. He stated the revenue from business should be enough, to pay for interest of capital, a profit for the care, labor, talents, and risk.[72] Moreover, the revenue must be enough so the process can continue,

> "Replace the annual wear and tear of his advances,--that he is obliged to convert from the very first into effects, which are susceptible of change, and they are exposed to every kind of accident."

John Bates Clark divided the concept of capital into an abstract whole, and concrete parts.[73] The abstract-whole capital was called the "true capital," which is a "fund of value" or "productive wealth" that remains durable. The concrete-parts capitals are the material capital goods, which make up to the whole of "true" capital fund, or the capital stock. This concrete-part of capital is destroyed or consumed. A process called synchronization between production and consumption maintained the Permanent capital fund.[74] Therefore, for each tree used up for wood fire, one tree is planted, for future use. His theory of capital was called "mythology of capital" by Böhm-Bawrek., and it was void of time dimension. Thus, it could not yield a dynamic theory, but led the field to the general area. When the revenue from material goods is applied to repair and maintenance, life of capital is extended.

Therefore, it was not bounded by "production period" the way Böhm-Bawerk viewed it. In addition, the useful life of capital after formation and before exhaustion (John Rae's production period) is extended. Especially, its life is extended, when technological advancements, improvements, or modification delay obsolescence, too.

The concept of synchronous adjustments, in innovational capital formation theory is relevant. It is a recent discovery. Therefore, important solutions are beneficial to all systems, currently facing increasing unemployment of resources regarding innovational capital formation issues, and speedy obsolescence, while maintaining, or increase capital fund to increase national wealth. This is viable (sustainable), if an adequate redistributive mechanism of wages is functional. That is necessary to maintain the higher velocity of money, and ensure adequate aggregate demands in the economic system.

Notes

[1] H. W. Spiegel, *The Growth of Economic Thought*, (North Carolina: Duke University Press, 1983), 122, 155, 164

[2] Joseph A. Schumpeter, *History of Economic Analysis*, (New York: Oxford University Press, 1954), 61, 598

[3] Ibid., 300-302

[4] M. Blaug, *Economic Theory in Retrospect*, 3rd ed., (London: Cambridge University Press, 1978), 637

[5] P. A. Samuelson, *Economics*, 11ed. (New York: MacGrow-Hill Inc. 1980), 408-412

[6] J. William Baumol, *Economic Theory and Operational Analysis*, 4th ed., (New Jersey: Prentice-Hall, Inc., 1977), Chapter 21

[7] P.A. Samuelson, *Economics*, 11ed. (New York: MacGrow-Hill Inc. 1980), 499-519

[8] Arthur Eli Monroe, Early Economic Thought, (Cambridge Mass.: Harvard University Press, 1924)

[9] Author, "Economic Indices", (Paper and class presentation based on I. Fisher work and modern welfare economics in Prof. Lawrence Nabors class, Microeconomic 622, University of Utah, Spring 1979)

[10] E. K. Hunt, and J. G. Schwartz, *A Critique of Economic Theory*, (Maryland: Penguin Books, Inc. 1972), 162

[11] G. Mensch, *Stalemate in Technology: innovation overcome the Depression*, (Massachusetts: Ballinger

Publishing Company, 1975), 2

[12] Edwin Mansfield and others, Technological Transfer, Productivity, and Economic Policy, (New York: W. W. Norton & Company, Inc., 1982), 1

[13] River dez, flows north south by the city of Desfil, (dez-pol), and Karron flows north southwest by the city of Shushtar, both cities are major urban centers in the providence of Khoseztan, Iran. There are caves defensibly located over the rivers that show proof of ancient activities, predating Achaminds, or the dynastic phase of ancient Persia.

[14] Abbott Payson Usher , *A History of Mechanical Inventions*, (Boston: Beacon Press, 1959, Harvard 1929), 239

[15] Edwin Mansfield and others, *Technological Transfer, Productivity, and Economic Policy*, (New York: W. W. Norton & Company, Inc., 1982), 1

[16] Richard C. Lipsey and Peter O. Steiner, *Economics*, 5th ed., (New York: Harper & Row, Publisher, 1978), 800-801

[17] Edward F. Denison, *Trends in American Economic Growth*, 1929-1982,(Washington, D.C.: The Brookings Institution, 1985) 15

[18] James p. Gander, *Technological Change and Raw Materials*,(Utah: Bureau of Economic and Business Research, U. O. U., 1977), 94

[19] Ibid,

[20] Nathan Rosenberg, *Technology and American Economic*

Growth,(New York: M. E. Sharp, Inc., 1972), 7

[21] Edwin Mansfield, *Technological Change*, (new York: W. W. Norton and Company,1971), 36

[22] Ibid, 23

[23] Author from data in the following sources calculated the table: Department of labor, Bureau of labor Statistics. U. S. President, *Economic Report of the President*, (Washington D.C.: U.S. Government Printing Office, 1988), 300

[24] Wayne D. Rasmussen, "The Mechanization of Agricultural", *Scientific American*, Vol. 247, No. 3 (September 1982), 76-90

[25] Edwin Mansfield, *Technological Change*, (New York: W. W. Norton and Company, Inc., 1971), 29

[26] Charles W. Cobb, and Paul H. Douglas, "A Theory of Production," *American Economic Review*, March 1929

[27] J. Tinbergen, "Zur Theorie der Langfristigen Wirtschaftsentwicklung", Weltwirschaftlicha Archiv, May 1942

[28] S. Valavanis-Vail, "An Econometric Model of Growth, U.S.A., 1969-1953," *American Economic Association Paper,* May 1955

[29] J. Schmooker, "The Changing Efficiency of the American Economy 1869-1938," *Review of Economics and Statistics*, August 1952.

[30] J. W. Kendrick, "Productivity Trends: Capital and Labour," *Review of Economics and Statistics*, August 1956

[31] Charles Kennedy and A. P. Thirlwall," Surveys In Applied Economics: Technological Progress," *The Economic Journal,* (March 1972),17

[32] M. Abramovitz, "Resources and Output Trends in the U.S. Since 1870," *American Economic Review, Paper and Proceeding,* XLVI, (May 1956),5-23

[33] Solomon Fabricant, "Economic Progress and Economic Change, "*34th Annual Report of the National Bureau of Economic research,* New York, 1954

[34] Robert M. Solow, "Technological Change and The Aggregate Production Function," *Review of Economics And Statistics,* August 1957

[35] Ibid

[36] A. A. Walters, "A Note on Economies of Scales," *Review of Economics and Statistics*, November 1963

[37] Charles Kennedy and A.P. Thirlwall, "Surveys in Applied Economics: Technological Progress," *The Economics Journal*, (Match 1972), 27

[38] C. E. Ferguson, *The Neoclassical Theory of Production and Distribution*, (New York: Cambridge University Press, 1975), 216

[39] John R. Hicks, *The Theory of Wage*, (London: Macmillan, 1932)

[40] Charles Kennedy and A.P. Thirlwall, "Surveys in Applied Economics: Technological Progress," *The Economics Journal*, (Match 1972), 20

[41] Roy F. Harrod, Toward a Dynamic Economics, (London: Macmillan, 1956) 26-27

[42] M. Brown and J. Popkin, "A Measure of Technological Changes and returns To Scale," *Review of Economics and Statistics*, November 1962

[43] M. J. Bechmann and J. Sato, "Aggregate Production Functions and Types of Technological Progress," *American Economic Review*, March 1962

[44] Joan Robinson, *Contributions to Modern Economics*, (San Francisco: Academic Press. 1976) 97-98

[45] Kennedy, Charles and Thirlwall, A.P., "*Surveys in Applied Economics: Technological Progress*," *The Economics Journal*, (Match 1972), 19

[46] Ibid, 22, 27-28

[47] Webster's Ninth Collegiate Dictionary (Massachusetts: Merriam-Webster Inc., 1985)

[48] There are parallels to study, in western neo-fascism, slavery, colonialism, or Hitlerism. Alternatively, what inappropriate transferred technologies can cause in the Developing economies?

[49] Robert L. Heilbroner, *The worldly Philosophers*, (New York: Special Edition Time Inc., 1962), 23-24

[50] Eugen Von Böhn_Bawerk, *Capital and Interest: Positive Theory if Capital*, Vol. II, Trans. G.D. Hunke and H. F. Sennholz, (Illinois: Libertarian Press, 1959), 16

[51] Robert L. Heilbroner, *The worldly Philosophers*, Special

ed. (New York: Time Inc., 1962), 42

[52] Eugen Von Böhn_Bawerk, *Capital and Interest: Positive Theory if Capital*, Vol. II, Trans.

[53] Joseph A. Schumpeter, *History of Economic Analysis*, (New York: Ox ford University Press, 1954), 322

[54] Joan Robinson, *Contributions to Modern Economics*, (San Francisco: Academic Press, 1978), 1979), 79

[55] H. W. Spiegel, *The Growth of Human Thought*, (North Carolinas: Duke University Press, 1883), 197

[56] Ibid, 195

[57] Eugen Von Böhn_Bawerk, *Capital and Interest: Positive Theory if Capital,* Vol. II, Trans. G.D. Hunke & H. F. Sennholz, (Illinois: Libertarian Press, 1959), 19

[58] J. A. Schumpeter, *History of Economic Analysis*, (New York: Oxford University Press, 1954), 323

[59] Note the Physiocrats mistaken assumption about who benefit the most from agriculture, the landowners, or merchants in "marchands et entrepreneurs."

[60] Joseph A. Schumpeter, *History of Economic Analysis*, (New York: Oxford University Press, 1954), 217, 221-222

[61] Anne Robert Jacques Turgot, *Reflection the Formation and distribution of Riches*, (new York: The Macmillan Company, 1922), 81

[62] Adam Smith, *An Inquiry into The Nature and Cause of Wealth of Nations*, Edited by E. Cannon, (Chicago:

University of Chicago Press), 1st ed. 1776, 1976), 296

[63] Ibid, 299, 305

[64] John Stuart Mill, *Principles of political Economy: with some of their applications to social philosophy*, (London: John W. Parker, West Strand, 1848, reprinted Augustus M. kelly publishers, 1987), 54

[65] SSTaatswirthschaftliche Untersuchhngen, chs. III and V

[66] Eugen Von Böhn_Bawerk, *Capital and Interest: Positive Theory if Capital*, Vol. II, Trans. G.D. Hunke and H. F. Sennholz, (Illinois: Libertarian Press, 1959), 24

[67] Ibid, 464

[68] Bob Simon, *How a slap sparked Tunisia's revolution*, CBS News, February 20, 2011 7:58 PM, http://www.cbsnews.com/2102-18560_162-20033404.html, "Bob Simon reports from Tunisia, where protests against the repressive government not only toppled its autocratic ruler, but sparked the uprising in Egypt that forced President Hosni Mubarak to resign."

[69] Yasmine Ryan, *Tunisian revolution yet to solve inequality*, Al Jazeera, April 11 2011, http://www.aljazeera.com/indepth/features/2011/03/2011331172249350413.html, "Hassine Dimassi, an economics professor, wants fairer distribution of wealth in new Tunisia."

[70] Henry William Spiegle, *The Growth of Economic Thought*, (North Carolina: Duke University Press, 1983), 616-617

[71] Eugen Von Böhn_Bawerk, *Capital and Interest: Positive Theory if Capital*, Vol. I, Trans. G.D. Hunke and H. F. Sennholz, (Illinois: Libertarian Press, 1959), 211

[72] Anne Robert Jacques Turgot, *Reflection the Formation and distribution of Riches*, (new York: The Macmillan Company, 1922), 83

[73] Eugen Von Böhn_Bawerk, *Capital and Interest: Positive Theory if Capital*, Vol. I, Trans. G.D. Hunke & H. F. Sennholz, (Illinois: Libertarian Press, 1959), 618

[74] Ibid, 620

CHAPTER 5

SELECTED DEFINITIONS OF CAPITAL

We know that institutional adjustments and liberalizations of these institutions had took place gradually over time in order to yield economic progress, even before the industrial innovation programs could take place. The retrospective on concept of interest also takes back to the old world. The importance of these issues plays in the importance of the part they played in technological progress that evolved in the past, or will bloom into the future.

Interest, Capital, and Income

The difficulties with notion of interest were complicated by theological ideas about it. However, the modification of the opinions, were also introduced early on as remedies and solution for business activities. St. Thomas Aquinas mentioned the selling of wine cannot be different from the use of wine, and no one should be charged twice for the same good, money may not be paid as price and then as interest. He identified an exception, in cases, which money was used by the borrowers as pledge or guarantee, and then the premium was just. St. Antonine stated the difference between coins for exchange or transaction can be sterile -- in Aristotelian terms-- but money capital obtained for business was different.[1]

The practitioners choose to do differently. The Eastern practitioners used older traditions like (Havaleh) a Persian word and practice for village to village, multi-regional, and multi-national transfer of funds or goods in trade via verbal promises, or reminders and notes, predating silk road and caravan trades. In addition, after the application of Aristotelian's logic to interest, the Islamic solution was sharing in profit instead of taking time-money-rent implied by the idea of interest. A version of that we noticed, was being practiced in European agriculture as explained by Turgot. Amidst political and theological conflicts Netherlands emerged as a relatively freer state, the canon doctrine was contradicted. Interest, in the forms of compensation for loss, and risk, and in place of profit (more like a time-rent idea), were commonly practiced.[2] In fact, Claudius Salmasius in his three books, starting with his first work, "De Usuries" in (1638), classified and defined interest in line with the market applications and needs for it.[3] He classified interest "jus naturale," therefore, "jus divine" in the canonist traditional polemic dating to St. Thomas Aquinas.

The Physiocratic ideas about interest were

incomplete, but more complex than past ideas. They noted it was a portion of output going for use of capital, and to entrepreneurs. Cantillon and Turgot stated interest was the price paid for use of capital, in such a way that allows for the price of the finished product to be greater than the sum of all parts that made it, thus a surplus. Output price, thus a surplus for the entrepreneurs, exited.[4] While they held each portion is equal, the market conditions and dynamic changed these proportions. The interest on the money lent tended to increase, as prices of land dropped. Because demand for land would increase, and lenders themselves would rather buy the land than loan out the money.[5] Thus, the interest would go up, until the money lenders would rather loan out rather than buy land. That contradicted their initial idea of equal proportions, and explained the supply and demand condition for loan-money. The ideas were not expounded any further.

Turgot linked interest on loan amount to rent in the following example, a certain amount of capital fund had to yield a certain amount of interest, because the same amount of capital fund could buy land, which yields a rent equal to the amount of interest. In fact, Turgot stated it must be higher to account for the risk of insolvency of the borrowers. That is for a land with price of 100,000.0 units, and rent of 10,000.0 units, interest cannot be lesser than 10 percent. So he wrote about the divisions of alternative returns, of the same invested sum. That the return from land is less than the interest on loans, which would be even less than return from production involving labor.[6] As problematic this may be, he did not explain the changes in the rate of interest, which by discounting affect the price of land using the equation above,

$$\frac{i}{p} \cong r$$

$$i \times p \cong r \Rightarrow \frac{r}{i} \cong p$$

So holding rent constant changes in interest from 10 percent to 5 percent, changes the price of land from 100,000 to 200,000 units. Alternatively, an increase in the interest to 20 percent will reduce the price of the same land being rented, to 50,000 units. A value and goods problem that was explained later, when the time dimension was added.

After, the physiocrats, classical economists expounded on the nature of net revenue, until Alfred Marshal.

The larger question of multi-market causation of interest, capital value calculation, and income in time continuum were not developed or uniquely linked and formulated until Irvin Fisher work. In the present valuations of production market, the supply and demand for and of the input mixes of free and mobile workers (with skills), most recently advanced machines, funds, and technologies determine net revenues. In the financial market the supply and demand for money, international free flow of capital, and an ever-increasing number of risks to freedom and mobility of labor, capital, technologies, and funds are reflected in the rate of interest, which will affect the supply (availability) of fund in the production market. Technology in the second field also eases the flow, and assists with the institutional skills, which even advance economies periodically tend to misplace, while facing an increasing supply of better competitors.

The present versus future time line, all economic agents make a decision to save or spent their current income for either current consumption or an expectation of better future consumption, equivocal to a higher future income. By doing so we make decisions linking multiple markets and over time, and in perfect markets, act as the invisible corrective hands, then out of individual self-interest "beyond immediate self-interest" we assist the overall economy. Moreover, sometime out of these complex economic decisions, even with partial equilibrium, if scio-political democratically corrective institutions are also active, a system may function in a corrective manner over time.

In fact, until Irving Fisher identified "stock of wealth" with capital, which generates income, the notion of capital had been defined too generally. John Rae defined instruments as capital, and all tools and machinery as instruments.[7] All instruments need to have three characteristic in common,

A. They are formed by human labor, and other instruments
B. They help to supply the human wants
C. They are exhaustible
4. There is a time period before formation and exhaustion. There are causes determining an amount of instruments a society is willing to form,
5. The quality and quantity of accumulation
6. The propensity to accumulate, "the effective desire of accumulation"
7. The rate of wages
8. The progress of the inventive faculty

It will take some amount of labor to make any instrument; the same amount of labor can be currently applied to satisfy wants. Therefore, if one is willing to sacrifice the amount of current want for greater future want, certain instrument will be formed.[8] Otherwise, it will not. If one relays on short-term "self-gratification" and its invisible hand enough, one will not see satisfaction of greater future wants. He defined the effective desire of accumulation as,

> "The determination to sacrifice a certain amount of present goods, to obtain another greater amount of goods, at some future period ..."

So longer-term view over the short-term self-interest, intellectual power instead of intellectual weakness, societal stabilities versus instabilities are enlisted to assist in the desire to accumulate.

Irving Fisher identified "stock of wealth" with capital, which generates income. In the production process, a capital tool produces physical entities as goods that may or may not have values in financial term to be determined in the market place. Therefore, a physical capital makes goods that have financial value or a stream of income values, which determines the value of capital. The financial value determined from the sale of physical goods produced by capital periodically then is "income value," which in turn sets the "capital value."[9] If we use the Turgot land of $100,000, and let say it produces crops with value of $10,000, and in a market, that interest is 10 percent. It is the $10,000 value as annual income (y), with 10 percent discounted interest (i), which determines the $100.0000 discounted value of land as value of the "discounted value of income." Moreover, not the physical land as physical capital by itself.

$$\frac{y}{i} \cong dv \qquad \Rightarrow \qquad \frac{\$10{,}000}{0.10} \cong \$100{,}000$$

I. Fisher defines capital as its value as a source of income. In addition, it is calculated by discounting or capitalizing the expected income. Ownership of capital entities total or partial as in shares is reflecting in the entitlement to the income stream of the capital. The rate of interest is defined as a premium above the principle sum, which is given up presently for it to be back in hand after a period like a year or so later.

Böhm-Bawerk introduced present versus future wants, as the base of theory of impatience and current preference theory, the multiple-links were not introduced.[10] Unlike Irving Fisher, he did not cover the complex links and balance among the consumers, savers, investors, and producers, which often are the economic agents. The very connection of financial capital (fund) as a source of income generation as in interests, and the converted capital applied as a tool in production process, or net revenue generation as another kind of income generation.

Thus, the deferent want-satisfaction valuation in different period (present and future), allows for saving (accumulation) out of present income and decision about lower consumption in present period for a chance for future want-satisfaction (future-consumption).[11] The distinction between the same level of consumption, or less current consumption for the expectation of more future consumption involves the use of present savings in production process of consumption goods, skill (technologies), and other services. The dynamic of this process with risk causes,

9. Increase in future consumptive goods, skills, and services
10. Increase in future income stream
11. Link present savings to interest and income and capital
12. Link of capital value from income stream to capital goods

The rate of interest is defined as a premium percentage paid for use of good or money now versus their use in a future.[12] Thus, in "money market" price of holding money "price of money" is determined and it is equal to interest rate. There is a premium for spending money on current certain consumption or risky future consumption, involves renting out the use of cash for certain amount in percentage and of the same fund, as price of money. Therefore, capital value is the capitalized value of future stream of income generated out of application of capital good, with labor and methods in a production process over time. The stream of income is generated by sales of produce yielded by the production process above. Therefore, capital formation relays on the different consumptive utilities and the saving out of income streams in different periods, and the attitudes about saving.

Attitudes On Saving

After current income is taxed, and if the disposable income is high, enough to pay for the inflated prices of consumer goods and services, if anything is left, that is defined as saving. Therefore, the high real disposable income only meets the necessary condition for saving. However, it does not meet the sufficient condition for saving. Individuals' attitudes determine the sufficient condition for saving. The negative or positive attitudes about saving are based on sets of characteristics, which are learnt behaviors.

Variety of causes can induce pro-saving or anti-saving characteristics. Perennial conditions of natural plenty, where food grows year round may discourage saving of perishable goods. Because, the same environmental elements that encourages growth of food also induces growth of bacterial and pests. Here are also a set of technologies beneficial to this life style. Multiple crops, all seasons continues planting of crops, crop rotations, animal domestications and husbandry can be some of multitudes of initial and essential skills accumulated over time in warmer climates. Harsh climate, periodically snow-covered regions may encourage selectivity of skills, which benefitted the survival of habitual savers. Storage of foods and grains, in containers or above the grounds, in stands and structures for storage of hay and cut grasses are some examples. Then, there are special regions, but few are available globally.

Nevertheless, regional locations like in central southwest Iran, where cold harsh climate and warmer climate are close, for a few days walks, hike or animal travels. Rich natural crops like wild grapes, Persian Walnuts, Pistachio, grass and small grains are common in mountain meadows, or cooler climates. Moreover, wild sheep, goats, lions, wild horse, and donkeys were common to the warmer flat lands. Exposure to lava, gas fires, natural forest fires were also common experiences. The cold are cold enough to look for shelter in the caves and built tribal cave-enclosures for early village centers. The water sources are in short distances from meadows and surface of grounds to induce channeling and well digging (Qanat, or locally pronounced Qhanat), it before seasonal water is drained, or lost down the hills. In addition, the presence of earlier larger and smaller humanoids (100,000 - 75000 BC) encouraged natural selection, and skill accumulations.

Cultural or theological teaching and practices regarding working, saving, and diligence, and honest toils can cultivate related attitudes. However, the Greek thinkers did not look in commerce for honesty, greed and profit were not too far from each other, and love of justice and laws of God or man did not favor accumulations of Treasure, which was defined to include profits, coins, lands, herds, etc. Some of these pronouncements did prevail in religious thought and most recent times. St Paul statement about "love of money is the root of all evil" is an idiom. However, the care and concerns for family, the welfare of kin, tribe, and society relented some opposition to savings. The accumulation of knowledge, and other non-self-indulgences, and non-hedonistic practices did further encourage some saving practices.[13] The importance of saving attitudes is in its deterministic role in choices between present versus future spending of individuals. It is important in availability of funds and the desire to purchase capital goods.

The non-savers have the propensity to spend most or all of their real disposable income as soon as possible, assuming it is more than their real consumption. Their non-saving attitudes shape their economic decisions, too. They tend to have a shorter time planning periods in mind. They may not plan longer terms, or fail to have any financial plans to direct or aim their efforts, at least, at their life-stage level. This can leave their decisions subject to less self-control, or assertion of the less self-control. That is, they are emotional and impetuous buyers. They are habitual spenders. They tend to be more self-centered. They may not have and thus less concerned about surviving children and family, and futures. They are slavishly dependent on current fashion.[14] At a social level, such economic agents (individuals) could be in states or nations with sociopolitical instability, and irregular circumstances of law and order, too. They tend not be dominated by highly educated mature people but younger populations, and their social benevolence would be all encompassing.[15] In view of such a list, it would be difficult to see such individuals as capital accumulators. They have capital because they have inherited capital, or they are captains of industry.[16]

It is fortunate, that most people under go changes in different stages of their lives as free agents. That is, they can change to higher disposable real incomes, and attain higher degree of specific educations, under some specific conditions and types of governments. Therefore, the alteration of the above non-saving attitudes' list would not be too difficult to change under all circumstances for all people. In a certain portion of economic cycle, as in troughs, it may be beneficial to have such a population or encourage such behaviors as well.

The savors have a propensity to like better future incomes, even if they have to spend some of their present real disposable income for or on a suitable plan and the mechanism to obtain that higher real disposable income.

The savers also have certain attitudes, which tend to direct their spending and economic activities. Savers have better or studied foresight. They tend to be future minded. They are willing to exchange and withstand some current hardship if they can conjure something better for their future. Therefore, they will be more mindful of how they invest their saved disposable income. They tend to be family or social mined. They are willing to benefit their environment and surroundings out of their higher real disposable income. They do tend to have priority lists. They are capable of short and long-term planning and strategic designs for themselves, their families, and their communities.

They have detail financial plans to direct their short and long-term efforts, at least, in some life stages of their lives. They have will and self-control to abstain from spending their present real disposable income, net of basic consumptive needs in order to save. They will need to have the characteristic to save and invest.

That is, they need to directly, or indirectly purchase capital for its income steams over time, to increase their potential real future disposable income, enough to justify all these actions and risks. They will be habitually thrifty. It is not without good reason that highly successful business people are extreme practitioners of such frugality. They will have positive expectations for long and prosperous lives. They can act independently from dictate of fashion and salesmanship.[17] They are highly educated and trained members of stable – law and order – states and nations, with mutual affections.[18] The importance of appropriate governance is repeated for good reasons.

There are profiteering and industrious forces, which have found ways around regulation to defraud savers. The difference between good and bad government and regulations are in the supports and practically, to encourage proper saving and reducing crimes against savers. Fraudulent overcharges, fees, tool taxations, usury and mortgage frauds by banks and institutions, unusual and flex legalisms, and multitudes of other criminality that also evolve in and out of government. These are some of elemental aspects of commerce inductive to long-term business activities, beside profit–self motives. While being a saver can create the financial positioning for investing, it will not, by and of itself makes entrepreneurs out of all savers.

Entrepreneurs are the economic agents between

savers and capital formation and the potential for higher real disposable income. In an inadequate state, with a government short of appropriate financial institutions, entrepreneurs will often apply their own savings to risky ventures in order to obtain capital formations and the higher income streams. This is not about money and currency.

It is the set of appropriate technologies assisting an abstract process, which can easily be under mined, or negatively impacted, and derailed. Most financial institutions also do not ready engage in risky-unknown ventures, which are often the harvest aims of the entrepreneurs' field of dreams.

Proper managers have to be skilled savers and investors. They are often not innovators. Skilled workers lucky enough to have positive net disposable real incomes may or may not be good savers and investors. However, all economic agents living in modern money economy, which hope to educate their families, and have modest retirements need appropriate-personal financial-management plans for saving and investing to succeed.

All economic agents, in such a money economy, are capital owners. Weather, we are concerned with individual skills, training, and education in human capital or the machinery and structures, which are employed as tools and instruments in creating income streams.

Modern economies are here because we have harnessed the best initial aspects of the concept of capital employed in the current state of industrialization, and advanced beyond that into information and service industries.

The fact is, each generation defined capital, harnessed its benefits and suffers its initial and subsequent costs and lost. Some dutifully, some out of self-interest aid in its formation, innovation, and evolutions.

Sometime, humanity resisted its mobility, but it remains mobile, they resisted its diffusion and social impacts, yet it has defused, they resisted its innovation, yet it is re-invented. Whether it is done knowingly or not, capital and the technological-changes encompassing it are all around us. They will continue to influence all aspects of human life as they grow and decay, entropy and atrophy, and evolve in cycles and recycles again.

The political dogma will sway at its will and ways. The subsequent generations of economies stumble into all of the consequences, and create new hypothesis and leave their marks. That is why functional honest democracies have a better chance of success.

The New Definition of Capital and Related Assumptions

Definition of capital as we have read has evolved like most usefully manufactured entities, and it may do so again. There are a few observations and numbers of assumption, which would benefit the taxonomy of capital,

1. Capital is a stock, which is measurable in money, or any currency or any means of transactions other than money.
2. Capital stock combines with natural or raw resources and workers time and skill in a production process (a methodology of production) and organization (given the state of technologies available) to make a produce, which can be goods, services, or skills (methodologies) to be used in current consumption or for future consumption, in a further production process.
3. Capital stock when is activated in a production process generates a flow of future incomes, a stream of revenue, over a period. There by an estimation of its value can be measured as the present value discounted from its true or estimated revenue, estimated useful life, market interest rate, net of initial costs and estimation for periodic entropy, currently miscalculated as capital consumption costs.
4. Capital stock is not often used up entirely in the process of production, even for some time periods. Exceptions are made for long-term ware, capital consumption, entropy, and time-varied market determined obsolescence. Of course, items like misses, bullet, and tools that are used once.
5. Other production inputs can be transformed into and act as capital stocks. Some of the

work force I as human capital), land, natural resources, raw resources can be transformed by use of capital stock.

6. The more transformed and complex a stock of capital becomes the more end use specific it becomes. Also the more transformed a stock of capital becomes the less free to all other uses as capital stock and functions it will be. This make it even more important to set aside fund from income flow and present consumption for future regenerations, technological progress and technological obsolescence, saving, and future consumption.
7. Funds used as capital stock also need to be treated as capital stocks. That is, only part of their income flow can be used for current consumption. The rest of related income flow from the funds needs to be saved for capital(stock) fund regenerations, opportunities related to technological innovation (or financial market innovations), and for future consumption.

In view of these assumptions, the following definition will identify more entities as capital stock, which are often used as capital stock, but are not defined as such.

Capital stock are goods, services, educated and retrained skilled workers, technologically innovated methodologies, partially processed natural or raw resources, improved lands. These are used in a production organization with other inputs like , natural resources, skilled workers, and other forms of capital (i.e. tools, computers, and machinery) to produce other goods, services, or methodologies, in order to be used in current consumption, repairs, depreciation and replacements, more production, and future consumption. The generated flow-income or revenue will be partially consumed, and be partially saved. The saving will be held in fund-investment forms, replacement parts, new production tools, or newly innovated equipment, useful inventories, and by-products of technological innovations from research and developments. The aggregated value estimation of social (national) capital or pure capital is an estimation of the sum of present value of capital. It is calculate from the estimation of generated future income, estimations of life of service and market interest rate.

Econometrics estimation of social capital (Domar) has been developed to estimate better values for capital. This will be studied in detail as teconometrics. The pure capital fund will allow periodical withdrawals to replace older material capital (instruments), or constructions and production of newer more innovated new capital in new machineries and instruments, methodologies. This definition of capital and the lists of propositions and assumptions, and the list many forms of capital related to it allow for dynamic, complex, and modern economic usage of the world capital.

Definition of Capital Forms

The better understanding of capital and its relation to technological changes, which reformulates it constantly, requires a better definition of capital forms. Mansfield stated the links between capital and technology and technological change as follows,

"Technology is the society's pool of knowledge and art ... Technological change is the advance of technology, such advancement often taking the form new methods of producing existing products, and new techniques of organization, marketing, and management. Technological change results in a change in production function."[19]

The following classification of capital forms is to better identify its many forms.

A. Human capital, is the abilities that exceed innate natural limits each person has in life void of education and training of any kind. The basic survival and life of Homo Erectus could serve as an example, close to basic work, but not totally void of complex skills. The innate survival and stone tool-techniques were learnt, stored, and passed on, from learning by doing or mimicking, at some point of human development. Early tools, use of stone, bones, fire, cave shelter and cave-and built structure villages, use of seeds, use of plant materials and seasonality and timing of it, all signify how early human capital existed and become internalized with human work.

B. In modern time, human capital is embedded in the education and skill of inhabitants. The substantial financial investment that flows to educations signifies the importance and influence of human capital embedded in members of society, which are trained and retrained through the educational experiences of each culture. Off course, there are the higher incomes. Higher wages and level of living correlated to higher education levels.

C. The level of human knowledge is not consumed after use, it is a stock, when it is appropriately utilized, it can produce and generate a flow of future uses and thus income streams, unless, the obsolescence in industries cause obsolescence of skills. Alternatively, the changes in an economy can demand a new level of skill, a more specialized version of human capital, entrepreneurship, and financial and regulatory accommodations, and economic condition inductive to entrepreneurs' profit and activities.

D. Technological progress in storage of knowledge tools, stored knowledge (applicable now, or in the future), the passage of earlier skills by allegory and fire chats to post computer chips methodologies via super speed of audio visual multi-media communication signify the importance of storage and inter-generational transfer of these types of capital stocks. Fire or pests could destroy paper. The modern digital storage and instantaneous global access to it are significant accomplishments.

E. Stored (on the shelf) knowledge, is the accumulations of trials (success or failure) of different methodologies of production of goods, service, and skills over time. While specific set of knowledge could become obsolete, some aspects of it can become part of some synthesized new process or methodology. Therefore, contribute to generation of new flow of income streams in a new way. In fact, use of Patton, trademarks, copyrights, and registrations are institutional tools to complement the relatively free market to insure financial survival of innovators, and to protect such flow of income essential to the inducements of capital-generating activities. Beside methodologies of combining resources for production, there are important subdivisions that have been accumulated. These are the organizations and efficiencies involved in the production itself, and the organization, which firms are shaped as, and essential governmental organizations, which modify where market mechanism fails.

F. Tools, machinery, instruments from flint stones, fire, and hunting and gathering to agro-industrial multinational corporations and electrical robotic manufacturing, human lives have evolved around tools, machinery, and instruments. These types of capital stocks are most commonly identified as capital.

G. Unfinished produce, partially finished goods, are also capital stocks. In Neolithic times bones of fish and hunted games could be altered and used as needle or cutting edges. In modern times, economic integration and globalizations have yielded automobiles, Flat screen television, computers, and cell phones, which are partially, build in different countries. Parts of a computer or a car could be made in one country (circuit chips for television or a computer in Malaysia), and tires of a car in Mexico, its engine in Japan, interiors in Iran and its final assembly in USA, or other countries.

H. Financial capital or funds as set aside for capital stock creation or purchase. This form of capital is loaned for purchase of other instruments for flow of income equal to the principle plus a sum as interest for the risk and use of the initial sum over a period. This is modified according to customs or tradition and religious practices in some areas. Interest may be restricted to a portion of profit only.[20]

I. Skills and technologies involved in the metamorphic evolution (transformation) in forms, Which capital stocks take over time must be better understood. Marx wrote the production and circulation of commodities led to capital.[21] Thus, C-M-C, goods is transformed to money, and then back to goods, or M-C-M', (M'>M, by the amount of surplus value). That is , money is transformed into commodities and later commodities are changed to higher amount of money equal to surplus value, and capital <stock> is defined here as both commodities and money. Therefore, this process is defined as transformation of capital <stock> to money, and re-transformation of money back in capital <stock> as metamorphisms of capital.[22] The importance of capital stock metamorphisms should become very clear. Economic condition change enough over time, inventions and innovations and changes make most static initial forms of capital stocks obsolete. Thus the accumulated flow of income generated from the initial forms of capital stocks less the present consumption (or saving), less capital consumption, less replacement costs, held in investment over time can aid to smooth capital stock metamorphisms for human societies. Many important economists have ignored that nominal savings and depreciation allotments can be offset by changes in inflationary prices of the newly innovated forms of capital stocks. The saved funds are often assumed as accumulation of wealth, and riches, however they are mostly over run by the costs of innovation and unaccounted for inflationary costs of the process. The capital stocks cannot accumulated in a sustained rate, or even grow at a constant rate. Thus the funds are spend on less capital stocks, which would lead to less income flow, and diminishing saving will follow a decay path, instead of a growth path. Thus, the infamous capitalists' deflationary cycle, one of, which M. Keynes worked on. The class divisions among landowners, workers, and later the artisans and state workers have been adopted throughout the history of economic thoughts, almost blindly. An example in modern times is the assumptions, which states workers consume only (all of their income) and capitalist invest only, a preposterous modified version of Turgot's landowners and peasants divisions. Of course, worker kept on subsistence real income or in the very early parts of their life-phases can have all their nominal income eaten up by current consumption. It is important to note aside from the corporate criminal activities, computer fraud and flash crimes, and miss-managements of funds, a great source of capital formation funds are the reinvestment of labor pension funds. However, labor-manager conflicts have demand curtailments and counter-beneficial results as well. In all of its forms capital stock is committed to a production goal, and once committed to a production it cannot be applied to any other production or present consumption. Thus in parts or in whole an instrument a machine as function of the capital stock becomes more specific-use focused, it become less of use to other production functions. Nevertheless, some types of capital stocks can be sold for their present value related to their future flow of their income plus a salvage value. However, money-capital stock (funds) when used in present consumption stops all future flow of income and future consumption that was attached to its original form. Therefore, two aspects of this proposition garnish special care. One, those alternatives, which require this amount of fund, must be prioritized with an opportunity costs and returns of each option, after the expenditure in mind, versus market rates of return. Two, due to personal financial innovations and revolutions in financial and investment instruments (stocks, bonds, futures, options on futures) have been creatively designed in markets to aid transformation and re-transformation of capital stocks.

J. Time, a smaller part of the time space continuum, is the limited span of time each person gets, it is the time each capital stock has before it become obsolete or useless due to laws of entropy. This form of capital is potentially the most valued from of capital stock. The potential value also decays at a varied rate, pending on what use of time is made. Thus, the quality use of time can benefit future business activities. Therefore, the distinction between neutral passage (forced or voluntarily) of time, or time well planned and utilized make it possible to gauge time utilization, or opportunity costs associated with time. Thus, can a stream of future income be associated to time spend in completion of capital instrument, learning a skill? The answer is affirmative. Thus, capital stock is formed, or used up, with a time components.

The last few volumes of works in production and technological injection, and capital formation and economic systems are expansively explain the complexities of economic system that advanced economies need to sustainable remain in productive and distributive capacity, functionality, and system stabilities. Occasionally, certain class, feudalist of the middle ages Europe, Cooperates'

Chief executive officers of modern cooperation, government functionaries of totalitarian, dictatorial, even socialists and democratic system can bend and twist the rules and conducts of economics systems into wealth concentration mechanism by over dishonesty, often without transparency. Alternatively, if transparency exists in none democratic systems, then the system relays on brutality and militaristic means, and by police force.

The difficulties arises as economic cyclical system development and progress, even with technological injection can ran into the governmental counter cyclical developments, civil unrest and even revolutionary deconstructive phases. that is why the final chapters' details specify case studies in such subject matters.

Notes

[1] Joseph A. Schumpeter, *History of Economic Analysis*, (New York: Oxford University Press, 1954), 105

[2] Eugen Von Böhn_Bawerk, *Capital and Interest: Positive Theory if Capital*, Vol. II, Trans. G.D. Hunke and H. F. Sennholz, (Illinois: Libertarian Press, 1959), 22-26

[3] Ibid

[4] Anne Robert Jacques Turgot, *Reflection the Formation and distribution of Riches*, (New York: The Macmillan Company, 1922), 83

[5] Ibid, 84

[6] Ibid, 82,84

[7] John Rae, "*Statement of some New Principles on the Subject of Political Economy, Exposing the Fallacies of the system of Free Trade, and some other Doctrines maintained in the Wealth of Nation,*" (First print 1834, New York: August M. Kelly, Bookseller, 1964), 91-94

[8] Ibid, 118-119

[9] Irving Fisher, *The Theory f Interest : AS Determined by Impatience to Spend Income and Opportunity to Invest It,* (New York, The Macmillan Company, 1930), 55

[10] Eugen Von Böhn_Bawerk, *Capital and Interest: Positive Theory if Capital*, Vol. II, Trans. G.D. Hunke & H. F. Sennholz, (Illinois: Libertarian Press, 1959), 283

[11] Mises, Ludwig Von, *Human Action: A Treatise on*

Economics, 3rd. Rev. ed. (Chicago: Contemporary Books, Inc., 1949, 1963), 283-288

[12] Irving Fisher, *The Theory f Interest : AS Determined by Impatience to Spend Income and Opportunity to Invest It,* (New York, The Macmillan Company, 1930), 12-15

[13] John Rae, *Statement of some New Principles on the Subject of Political Economy, Exposing the Fallacies of the system of Free Trade, and some other Doctrines maintained in the Wealth of Nation,* (First print 1834, New York: August M. Kelly, Bookseller, 1964), 26-129.

[14] Irving Fisher, *The Theory f Interest : AS Determined by Impatience to Spend Income and Opportunity to Invest It*, (New York, The Macmillan Company, 1930), 81-85

[15] John Rae, *Statement of some New Principles on the Subject of Political Economy, Exposing the Fallacies of the system of Free Trade, and some other Doctrines maintained in the Wealth of Nation,* (First print 1834, New York: August M. Kelly, Bookseller, 1964), 119-124

[16] Ibid, 125

[17] Irving Fisher, *The Theory f Interest : AS Determined by Impatience to Spend Income and Opportunity to Invest It*, (New York, The Macmillan Company, 1930), 81-85

[18] John Rae, *Statement of some New Principles on the Subject of Political Economy, Exposing the Fallacies of the system of Free Trade, and some other Doctrines maintained in the Wealth of Nation,* (First print 1834, New York: August M. Kelly, Bookseller, 1964), 119-124

[19] Edwin Mansfield, Microeconomic: Theory and

Application, 2nd ed., (New York: W. W. Norton & Company Inc. 1975), 465

[20] (Islamic: Ghazerol "Hassaneh")
[21] K. Marx, *Capital: a critique of political economy*, Vol.1 ed., F Engels, Trans. S. Moore & E. Aveling (new York: International Publishing, 1977), 110

[22] Ibid, 146-155

CHAPTER 6

SELECTED DEFINITIONS OF ACCUMULATION

It is clear that saving and accumulations over time are important in economic system, which favors dynamic sustainability. They generate capital formation over time, which employs more workers and transfers income to them for more consumption in each period.

On Accumulation

The differences between Quesnay and Turgot about capital accumulation have also survived time. Quesnay unlike Turgot considered saving the same as misery and the cause of poverty. Turgot and Smith works on saving and investment formulated the classic orthodoxy until Keynes macroeconomic work and the work of a lesser-known economist John Rae.

Turgot while mentioned misery and hoarding, defined business saving or retained business income in terms of money, which will be transferred into capital (capital stock). Thus saving would not be leakage out of the system and did not cause unemployment, In that kind of a close system the transformation from money into capital was assumed immediate and continuous.

The same ideas are followed by the logic of Adam Smith, in "Wealth of a Nation." Accumulation of capital would lead to division of labor, which will in turn improve and ease the work conditions; therefore, it would add to employment and more capital accumulation.[1] Adam Smith wrote,

> "The quantity of industry, therefore, not only increases in every country with increase of stock <accumulated capital stocks>, which employs it, but, in consequence of that increase, the same quantity of that industry <due to the newly added innovational capital stocks> produces a much greater quantity of work <higher level of employment>."

Granted certain elements add newer perspective to Adam Smith work. There is a time lag, where the rate of job-displacements may be greater than the rate of job-absorptions and job-creation. Adam Smith also did not note that, it is part of the newer addition to Smith's system.

The most serious of economic misjudgments, the most dangerous of economic misreads, the dumbest possible economic mistake ever, and this mild rebuke or denouncements, is confusing wealth, treasures, bullions, nominal money with the economic wealth of a nation or an state, which sustains employment and economic productivity of all willing and active economic agents within it. It is astonishing the number of otherwise educated members of different societies and even some so-called republic democracies, which fall back to this shrill voice of economically self-destructive radicalism. The amount of national budget spent on this endeavors are enormous, under different and ever so newly invented flags (patriotism and wars, anti-drug or terrorism, war on poverty or hunger, class wars are just a few example, anything but creating or sustaining jobs, and the national real disposable income per capita).

The hoarding in its classic terms involved putting away, coinage, bullions, jewelry, and non-perishable commodities, which increased the market prices by reducing the supply of coins and produce. Under the economic limitations (lack of free flow of workers and capital) of the time, it was very much possible to do so; however, in modern economic systems this may be more difficult phenomenon –not impossible in unstable, sociopolitical, and economic conditions– to create. The rate of production of debased (not based on gold, or gold certificates) paper currency can easily be adjusted for the health or psychology of the market, if the economy can avoid major self-destructive (mentioned mistakes), and trust shattering experiences to the minimum. Alternatively, a degree of universal trust in governments can be maintained to remedy corruptions as they are divulged. This makes sluggish response of some governments and their agencies to their stock market abuses, the declines of protective rights and shares of the smaller stockholders and workers in the profit margins, and the astronomical rise of managerial pays out of the same profit margins even more puzzling. Because they add to the rate of decay in the trust and reduce real disposable income per capital.[2] The ownership designs of the private market, credit system are constructed on those pillars and foundations.

Therefore, saving in most institutions are reinvested in the economy, directly by the corporate teams, or indirectly by other financial institutions representing individuals, workers, and all economic agents as investments in the dynamic process of capital formations. In fact, individual savings, (or all the booties, treasures, and caches, and confiscated loots) will not be singularly enough to obtain productive and complex organizations of production, factories, and machineries, and instruments, skills, diversity of production required in the integrated global market place. The accumulation of saving from combined sources with integrated skills of educated workers from different countries must converge creatively and often freely to synthesize any number of complex machineries, public goods of the information age, some of the infrastructure of modern international trade and finance, and most of research and developments of modern economies.

Accumulation, Production, Employment, and Invention

Fundamental propositions of the early concerning capital theories tend to survive over time, because of their relevance to societal changes. John Stuart Mill's following propositions are among these fundamentals concerning capital stock.

1. Industry is limited by capital <stock>
2. Capital <stock> is the result of saving
3. Capital <stock> is kept through generations, by reproduction, not preservation
4. Demand for commodities is not demand for labor

The third fundamental allows for the rebuilding of machines and instruments, which lets innovational in production and use of new machines in to the system, or allows for the technological changes needed to develop new capital stocks. The first and the last of these fundamentals are ongoing concerns of economists. Wicksell explained the issue in the following statement, ".... That demand for commodities is not demand for labor –unless it results in accumulation of capital." Adam Smith's explanation was, "The general industry of a society never can exceed what the capital of society can employ."

Hayek pointed out that modern subjective theory of value by linking the increased value of consumer goods to value of pure inputs, is not proof of a direct and unbreakable link between demand for products and demand for all inputs, and elasticity of input substitution is not the same given value in all case.[3] Clearly, accumulation and labor division were identified important in forming new industries, which also expanded work.

In trade cycle and long term dynamics, in welfare theory formulation of economic systems, or in any equilibrium propositions among economic, societal, and political implications, there is a need for some acceptable equitable balance among the mix of inputs and the distributions among them. Therefore, demand for commodities cannot be demand for only labor or capital in other than the most isolated of cases. That is, the demand for present and future goods and services, and technologies, are the derived-demand for an efficient and diversified mix of all available inputs, with Pareto Optimum, equity, and societal and political balance in mind.

It should be noted the supplies of land and labor are different from the supply of capital. The supplies of land are relatively fixed. The rent of land reflects the quality of the marginal lands added to the supply (Ricardo). Technologies can add to usefulness and value of these more marginal lands, and effect supply that way. Labor supplies are more given by the rate of population growth of available workers. Technologies can influence supply and pay here as well. Institutional interventions (technologies) like unions and, immigration laws, and freedom of mobility combined with skill (level of training, and education) can also modify supplies and wages. Therefore, it will be logically inconsistence, to claim a pro-growth policy, while cultivating hostile anti-immigration policies, and budget shut off on the educational advancement. Technological progress can also determine the mixes of inputs and affect their charges. The supplies of technologies are influenced by individuals' inventiveness, and instructional interventions from educational and governmental institutions, as well.

John Rae objection to the classical economists is their attempt to equate saving of individuals and nations to accumulation of capital, void of innovations or state help or direction.[4] Off course, this is another step –be it an incomplete one– toward the recognition and importance of technological progress in any sustainable economic growth. Yielding to increased production, and increase in the rate of formation of new and improved capital stocks, given a complementary and optimum adjustments in the real disposable income per capita of the population is taking place. This also involves national intervention in creation and "augmentation of capital," which also involves complementation of "invention."[5] That is, different from simple additions of older (on the shelf) technologies, which are accumulations or duplications of existing forms of capital stocks? Individuals easily and profitably can accomplish this. Legal and institutional technologies about franchising are known under franchising laws in most Western and Eastern economies, some further modifications can perhaps improve the reach of these technologies. The unlimited and injudicious additions to supply of existing capital stock reduces profit margins, but additions in the forms of newly invented capital stocks, thus of rarer but acceptable capital stock supplies would yield a match higher profit margins. The secondary impact of demand for the innovated capital stocks also uplift the employment in skill and training markets for workers, thus improve real disposable income, therefore, creating a multiple chances for accumulation.

John Rae misses the importance, impact, and roles individuals have in the incremental inventions creation. They create inventions during and at the front lines of productions, and in organization of production. Adam Smith, John Rae, The classical economists, the Austrian economists did not recognize the essential agencies of individuals in invention, nor the entrepreneurs or their profit in innovational progress and sustainable growth. John Rae also did not reflect on the negative impact of the state interventions, or replacement of the privet market mechanisms. The Austrian economists developed some ideas later.

The dysfunctional impacts of states, with intrusion of control versus contractual relationships leave significant mark in all market exchanges.[6] The relaxation of private ownership rights, regulatory confiscation of living quarters, cash and bank accounts, intervention in legitimate earning of a living, the draining and exhaustion of set-aside funds (savings) by excessive taxation, or other market interventions, in-appropriate or under representation of large portion of the economy facing fraud and abuse are some example of serious governance problems.[7] Furthermore, the irregular enforcement of those contractual agreements or financial regulations, enforcement of such regulation on major financial institutions also influences the motivation and behaviors of market participants.

The Rate of Capital Formation

The new capital stocks and duplication of old capital stocks, in a dynamic economy, can be produced at different rate of growth.[8] These varied rates of growth of capital stocks can serve as one of the main inputs, which can enhance and sustain economic growth over time.[9] However, the return to of all capital forms, the net income flow over time or capital value divided by the initial investment can prioritize all capital-stock forms in the market place. Some of these returns can be much higher than the market interest rates in modern economies. That is, the rates, which supply and demand for money meet in short or long run is a bare minimum, most facial money managers would want to be earning more than that rate, in normal non-recessionary and competitive economies.

Economies riddled by non-competitive markets or political and exchange risks will be burdened by higher capital return requirements to attract investors. Thus the would be capitalists, if you are still delusional who is a capitalist look in the mirror, they need to meet many challenges and risks and be forward looking in their prospectus, at all times, whether they are in the market or not. Such delusions are fortified by states picking up banners of superpowers and other nonsensical aversion of logic and engage in technologically enhanced destruction of all forms of capital stocks, beyond the consensual defensive need and stopping of genocidal maniacs. Such wars only lead to bankruptcy of treasuries, and eventually their owns and destructions of a lot of capital stocks in the process, which humanity can ill effort as its population explode exponentially.

Every time we globally raise a finger to destroy or defraud, we are harming ourselves and scare off more would be capitalists, ourselves. The technologies of market integration, globalization, and instantaneous communications have progressed along this lines all beyond the undoing phase, so we need all to learn how to live with the consequences of open and exposed society syndromes. Alas, the would be capitalists, all of us, need to study the rate of return of the capital stocks, rent on capital stocks, the internal rate of return of investment projects, also the rate of changes in related prices, and the interest rate on loan or funds needed in the market. When all the dusts settle and the sand falls motionless in its golden waves, the individuals build up the globe.

In a dynamic economy, any numbers of variables affect these rates, and combined with expectation they can make these rate change differently from one another. In a dynamic economy, even simple issues like project duration and rate of obsolescence due to technological innovation can add to the risks-list and make it more logical to set a much higher rate of return of capital stock, much more than the market interest rates to attract investors. Another highly significant variable, which is under studied is the human capital skill embedded in workers-immigrants. All of these risks heavily affect them, as well. This is a list of risks, which affect decisions. Some of these risks are as follows,

1. Market risks
2. Business cycle risks
3. Currency exchange risks
4. Fundamental or more permanent taste change risks
5. Regulation change risks
6. Political change risks
7. Climatic or natural disaster risks
8. War and regional conflict risks

A person's decision or a group's decision (individually, or in partnership and corporations) to purchase should be after considerable calculations about expected revenue (expected flow of income over time) from such capital stocks less other costs of investment.

John M. Keynes included assets purchased at stock market, and "fixed capital, working capital or liquid capital."[10] Keynes definition of aggregate investment as equal to net investment is "the net addition to all kinds of capital equipment."[11] Besides calculating the rate of return of capital stocks, these rates of returns need to be compared with the market interest rate, government bonds, or other relatively safer liquid assets.

Investors can expect much higher rate of return(r), when opportunity costs and risk costs are greater than the interest rate (i). Since, the expected revenue (ER) includes the costs of operation (OC), plus a premium for risk (RP), deducted from the estimation of future revenues (FR).[12] Thus, assets costs (AC) are calculated using the following formula,

$$AC \approx \frac{FR_n - (OC + RP)}{(1+R)^n}$$

IFF RP $\underline{=}$ 0 , n = 1, 2, 3 …

This is compared with the present value of invested funds equal to the market value of capital stock purchased at the its market price.

$$PV \approx \frac{R_n}{(1+i)^n}$$

Then if

$$AC \geq PV$$

That is a buy signal.

However, when (RP>0), conditions become more complex.

$$\frac{AC}{PV} \geq \vartheta$$

Or,

$$\frac{r}{i} \geq \theta$$

Then the constants are: $RP > 0\ ,\ \vartheta, \theta > 1$

In presence of higher risk, the purchaser of capital stocks or investor still need to determine at that point of difference between r and i, they like to make their capital purchases.[13]

Proportionally, the rate of return of risky ventures and longer-term projects ought to be higher than the rate of returns for safer, shorter-term projects, or safer government bonds with guarantee of return of principles. When priority lists of such projects are presented to the economic agents, who have limited their present consumption for higher future rewards, consumption, utility preference curves present a new set of options to the economic agents, regardless of their location or backgrounds. A new set of choices are presented, an innovational set of choices influences the capital purchase decision making.

Planning, actions, evaluation, control (shut-off, turn on) are parts of the dynamic production process module, which will adopt technologies to modern modular production decision process. This is to control extreme negative externalities associated with technological advancement in an inappropriate fashion.

Figure 8 shows a dynamic production-action process model, with four distinct elements.

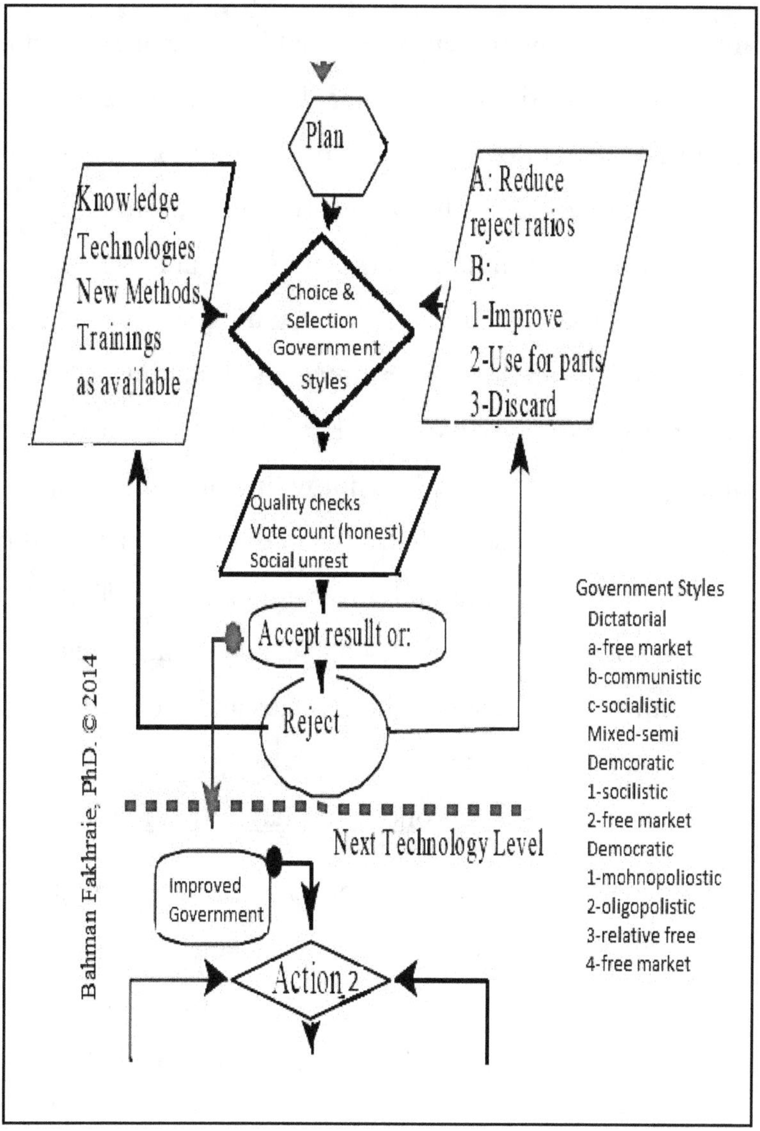

Figure 8. Government technologies and dynamic modular production process model.

In case, of positive initial result further advancement, to the next level of operation will continue. This is worker-manager teams' dynamic process of quality control action modules. In government styles that induce honest voting systems of functioning democracy will temperate the historical methodology of periodical interruptions of violence, revolts, revolutions of most inappropriately controlling and failing government styles and systems.

Naturally, we understand that all system insist that their versions are the only rational and functional possible alternative that should exists. However, while allowing for many exceptions, if they are not willing to test that in a free and democratic fashion their hypothetical styles, they self-define their conditions and governmental style. This also does not mean automatic discourse, and social unrest. Nevertheless, it increases the chances and probabilities for unsustainable conditions.

Non-Synchronous Capital Formation

The estimated value of physical capital, capital stocks in aggregate, given the average life of capital goods can be estimated. That is, a portion of capital stocks can be newer, and a portion older than the average, but a value estimate can represent capital stocks. When the rate of capital stocks duplication, and the rate of new capital stocks formation, and the rate of capital stock replacement combined fall short of the rate of capital stocks obsolescence and rate of capital stock entropy, then the rate of growth in production of outputs will suffer. When this rate difference goes into the negative, a rate of decay of production can be noted. In a globally integrated and competitive market, such a non-synchronous and mal-adjustment will lead to market share losses and diminishing and vanishing profit margins. While initially a microeconomic situation, it will lead to unemployment and under-employment of resources. Of course, the macroeconomic variable, and international trade and finance issues can easily initiate and reverberate back to multiple non-synchronous capital formation difficulties and imbalances in the economy.

Modern cooperation dominated production processes are dealing a newer phenomenon. The speedy obsolescence of their main products, an example is in computer and electronics. In addition, the consumers' willingness to skip generations of innovational products for newer or different products, an example here is in communication industries.

The personal-electronic computer industry was content with a six-month product cycles. The difficulty is the financial problems any institution would have in major changes in capital stock requires every six month, if all of the overhead was to be abolished and remade anew, in such a short product cycle, and production period. In 1980-1990 solutions, some out of Japans' re-invention process, which allowed for post war reconstructions with newer technologies with capital stocks and the application of quality control with statistical methods applied since 1930s in United States industries.[14] These were updated in 1970s and 1980s, when they system was introduced to Japan by Dr. W. Edward Deming to all aspects of production processes, they applied to all processes.

Quality Control and Relative Market Competition

In a relatively competitive market, final quality of products and improvement due to quality control of the processes are technologically advancements, which add valuable to the final sales, thus they are valuable to the economy. The quality control evolved to a combination of methodologies beyond profound knowledge and total quality control and 14 points of Dr. Deming to include the Japanese concept of Kaizen "Ki-Zen" meaning gradual and continual (dynamic) improvements and change.[15] However, general and unorganized information like those of the 14-points, or a conceptual knowledge that "we need continual progress" would hardly be sufficient, in scientifically methodological technological-advancement. There is other more advancement, which have evolved around management-technologies to benefit different aspects of manufacturing and production process.

Combinations of problem solving strategies, benchmarking approaches, may get to the planning stage of a production process.

The forces of market competition, multitudes of product differentiations, consumer alerts and proactive interventions, and health and safety regulatory monitoring are among the more positive enforcements at work to upgrade product qualities, and counterbalance the profit only self-control mechanism. The negative forces, of litigious nature of consumer societies combined with short-term profiteering motivations, limitations and strict political immigration-controls of skilled or motivated workers, capital mobility restrictions can exponentially explode costs and cause bankruptcies.

The new production methodologies are formulated in the following fashion,

1. Some assembly lines are maintained as overhead
2. Land and some capital stocks infrastructures are
    a. maintained
3. Part of assemblies are shifted to competitive
    a. workers outside the factory, however,
    b. quality and costs both go into bid-selections
    c. decisions
4. Worker-manager teams work much closer inside the factory.

   They follow four steps system,

   A. Plan,

   B. Act,

   C. Check (measure),

      a- adjust,

      b- improve and go to next step, or

      c- reject and send to first step for parts or sell or discard,

   D- Act Quality control, team units'

      a. productivity are quantified and compared

      b. as part of the process and at all levels, the

      c. boardrooms to factory floors, not just at the end of process in one big way, but all along the process by each unit.
5. Rejected items are not pass on to the next level,
    a. unless they meet closer post improvement
    b. scrutiny. They can be reused for parts
6. Rejection ratios are examined for ways to
    a. reduce them
7. Parts and inventories are computer linked
    a. narrowly to final demands
8. The lists of demanded items firms can produce
    a. are prioritized from the highest values per
    b. currency investment needed to get them to
    c. market to lower values per dollar investment

   d. needed
9. Task flex and adjustable robotic assembly lines
   a. complements demand signals, existing
   b. infrastructures, worker-manager teams,
   c. and continual training. They are taxed for
   d. retraining funds, and accord costs to the economy.

The new process much quicker with a lot less costs absorbs the innovation due to technological progress, where it benefits the operations the most. The worker-manger teams learning are the sources of most technological progress injections in the process. It is important to understand no rejected parts are forwarded to the next workstation or action decision module. An assembly line will have more than one action modules along the same line. At each point, where one can measure a change or an addition, an action module will be formed for it as unit. Data collection and statistical methods are used at these points as well.

The embodied technological progress in augmented capitals stocks yields to adjustments in the hard and soft ware of robotic and assembly lines, or partial upgrades and replacements in the same.

The disembodied technological progress associated with the same changes is passed on as retraining to the core employees, or training to newly hired, who start from the bottom and earn their ways up. The formulation combined with the statistical graphing, and

Data taking along each step of production process, combined with clear and comprehensibly defined-quality samples taken regularly quantify and improve the achievement-targets.

$$\frac{B_{jt} - W_{jt}}{\delta\sigma_{jt}} \approx QC;\ for \delta \cong 6,5,4$$

These data are also used to aid retaining process of manager-worker teams considerably.[16] Using Best choice for upper limits and worst choice for the lower limits from acceptable mean and variance of the targeted items, reflecting the quality criteria consumers or users of the item would closely identify. Another set of methodologies like Stochastic Process Control of production (Figure9), and total quality control (TQC), are used to identify, measure, and tests quality and processes for errors and adjustments along each step of production process. The machineries have had to bend to the realities of modern market place, shortened product life cycles, and continual upgrades of production technologies.

These are measured for specific time, and variance of the same item for the same time. Figure 9 shows the application of stochastic quality control process (SQCP) of the dynamic production.

For, 4, 5, 6 multiplicands, can establish three quality control zones, along the production line of the same item, starting when parts are bid for and purchased from sub-contractors, to inputs picked up, to workers hiring, to assembly lines production modules. The quality control indices when shoot into error zones, swing wildly into error zones, or bellow mean bar they show the need for quality improvements.

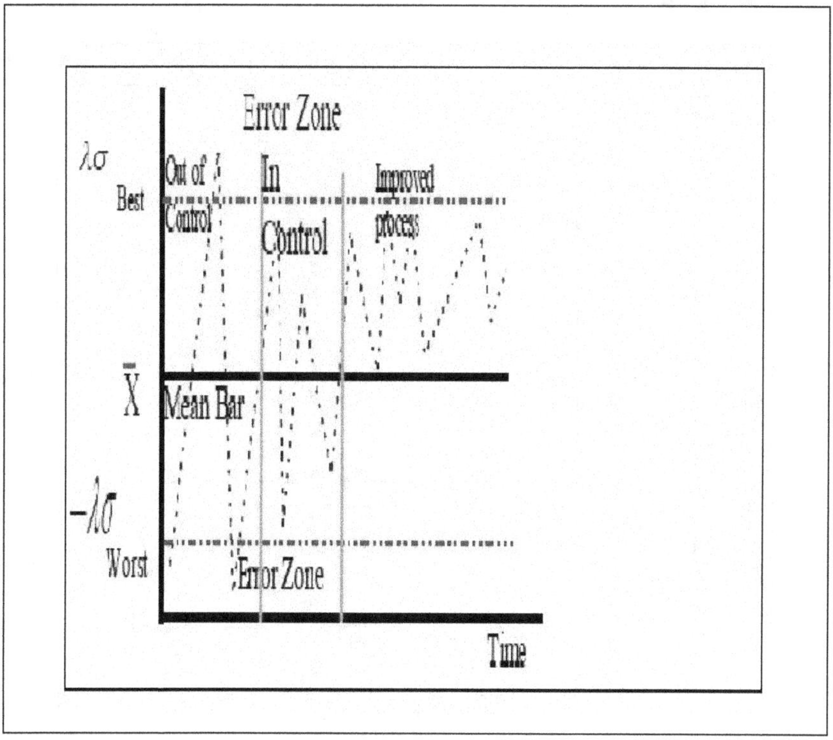

Figure 9. Application of stochastic quality control process (SQCP) to production.

All parties are asked about all elements, which what contribute to the best quality produced item, and with that data the preferred multiplicand is 6, or ∀3 around mean, or in the (+3), the positive-variance control-zone. Five and four represent second and third best choices, on way to 6. Figure 10 shows Dynamic Stochastic Process Quality Control. DSPQ is the innovative technological advancement introduced in this work that adds to sustainable improving averages.

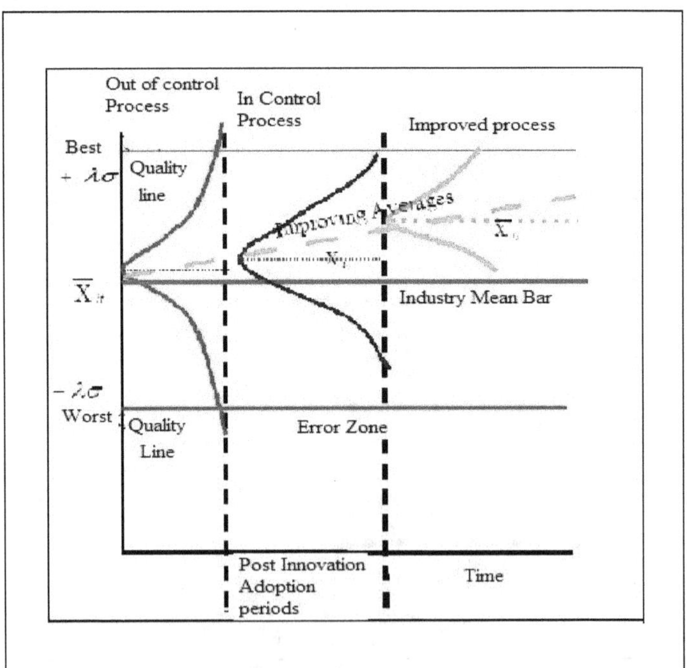

Figure 10. Dynamic Stochastic Process Quality Control.

Moreover, 6 is the closest to the control zone and upper limits of acceptance. Higher Costs are related to narrower zones and the quality control process and are factored in the choice decisions. This process will need to repeat for new elements, and shocks, which may occur periodically.

Knowledge is utilized to duplicate success, and identify and repair failures. Repairing failures are not blame lists, or firing lists, but an educational menu for retraining, for all of the teams. The negative connotations label on the Total Quality Control procedures will taint all results. Negative emotional energies are monitored, as waste and not as managerial tools.[17] In addition, excuses for not trying or studying new ideas are studied as part of the negative block-lists against gradual improvements. Since the process will require to be repeated, rather than one time trial experiment, it will requires all due attention.

The priority listing of products by their expected returns per each dollar invested to produce them allows for good choices, knowing that higher quality results in higher prices. The estimation about net revenues and future higher profit of target products justify the investments. These costs have to include positive and negative externalists and sustainability condition in their decisions matrix as well.

Therefore, the simple maximization of profit

formulations has long evolved to more complex-studies. The following formulas give you the statistical initial steps.

$$A \approx \sum \frac{X_i}{n}$$

$$s^2 \approx \frac{\Sigma (X_i - \overline{X})^2}{n - 1}$$

$$\sigma = \sqrt{\frac{\Sigma (X_i - \overline{X})^2}{n - 1}}$$

The Industry Mean Bar could be reference marker in the initial stages of establishing a new process or a new business, estimated from similar processes ($\overline{X}_{it}$). The best and worst quality lines are also calculated as comparative markers. The dynamic conditions from each stage of development and the innovational process create new set of data specific to the process. From the data we can calculate the new and improved mean ($\overline{X}_{t_n}$) and standard deviation and squared root of the Standard deviation (sigma σ) for each subgroups. When the mean and variance fall within the Industry Mean Bar and the Best Quality line and consistently stays in the same range the improved process has been reached for a period. The duration is flexible, and subject to other innovational changes and processes taking place, which will leave behind any slaking industries. Therefore, at each period the means and variances will improve as innovational injections are adopted, and they are internalized in the production process.

Figure 10, shows the Dynamic Stochastic Process Quality Control, developed in this study. The innovative operators find the right mix and after competitive adjustments start working on the operators, marginal operators and processes will star shutting down.

The competitors may also become fewer as some do not adjust fast enough to survive the changes and their consumers move on to competitor. Schumpeter studied this as the creative destruction built in the capitalism processes. This will occurs in any processes in a dynamic setting, especially with some access to innovations. When the process is new and operating out of control, there can be a lot of operators, that explain the marginal operators spending too much on innovation and doing better than the Best Quality Line error zone, and some operators go for saving and no innovational adaptations and operating bellow the Worst Quality Line error zone.

Few operators will reach the optimum mix of innovation and minimum costs of efficiency and quality control in the improved-zone. Figure 10 shows the dynamic production processes adjust and updates continually. Technological advancements are gradually injected as part of the dynamic processes.

Wide Angle versus Zooming Methods

Scanning, discovery, problem defining phases of any process requires general techniques, these we study as (shot-gunning, bird-shooting, strategies), wide-angle method. In early stages of production process, a larger 8 in (8Φ) allows for such an approach. Study of common methods of the more successful practices, along known statistical markers is titled "Bench Marking." After identification of problem-areas in need of improvements, the improvements along known methodologies with further training and new software and hard ware takes shape. This requires narrowing the 8 of (8Φ), or rifling techniques to focus resources toward specific solutions, or creations and adaptations of appropriate technological advancements.

That is the zooming method. The λ (lamda), becomes and smaller multiplicand of (8Φ), until the natural limitation and new bottle necks are reached and remain unalterable.

The dynamic production process will soon resume new dynamic adjustments, as technological innovations become possible. Then for, $0 \geq \lambda \leq 1$, σ is calculated.

Accumulation, Aggregation, Innovation and Capital formation

The main point about accumulation has been its role in increasing capital stocks, we saw here, that is also, where technological changes are injected in production. Therefore, the accumulation of capital stocks, duplicated, replaced, or newly invented capital stocks increases the productions. The increased in productions increases future consumption goods, services, and skills, therefore, increases employment. While the classical economists thought the increased employment only comes at the set subsistence wages, we know that the injection of skills and increased employment should also increase the real wages.[18] Thus real income increases to maintain the appropriate level of demand for increased productions, unless market imperfections, regulatory naiveté, mishaps, and unfortunate fiscal policies severely hamper the economy.

The classical economists assumed wages constant at subsistence levels.[19] Quesnay thought saving is causing under consumption in present time; therefore, frugality causes poverty. However, Turgot's work and Smith's writings on saving and investment were the classical orthodoxy, until Keynes studies.

Turgot while mentioned misery and hoarding, defined business saving or retained portion of business income in money or currency, which will be transferred into real capital stock. Adam Smith defined saving not to be leakage out of the system, and did not cause unemployment, because the transformation from money saving to real capital stock to employment and production were assumed immediate. Individuals, saving and its transformation to capital stocks are duplicated in national level in aggregation.[20] That will result in national actions of saving-investments, and capital formation.

John Rae recognized the need for invention, and importance of national resources in capital formation.[21] John Rae as identified the legislative actions, which benefit the creation of new capital,

A Progress of science
B Progress of art
C Discovery of new arts <and Science>
D Improvements in the existing art <and science>

The new capital creation need to exceed past rate of capital creation by individuals, for economic and population growth rates. States have to bring the needed elements of higher complexities together, assists in division of labor and retaining, and fund such notions, which market cannot vision any market advantage in (no immediate profit), in order for such new capitals to come to fruition. The factory maintains some assembly lines and lands infrastructures, some parts of assemblies have been shifted to contractors outside the factory on competitive bases.

In invention-generation skips the use of cell phones instead the heavily infrastructure investment in the landline base phones systems in most developing nations. This is a new way of saving the massive front-end infrastructure funds required to for lines-posts and land, which the older system's needs. Every update requires further reinvesting in digging up old systems and replacing them with new cable and equipment.

Notes

[1] Adam Smith, *An Inquiry into the Nature and Causes of Wealth of Nations,* Edited by E. Cannon, Chicago: University of Chicago Press, 1st ed. 1776, 1976), 292

[2] These pillars were tested in 1990-2008, swaps, mortgage securitization, and risk bundling. Thus the worst economic downturn since the 1929 depression.
Bahman Fakhraie, *CURRENT ANALYSIS OF CASCADING ECONOMIC DECLINES,* 2011

[3] Friedrich A. Hayek, *The pure theory of capital*, (Chicago: University of Chicago Press, 1941), 442- 439

[4] John Rae, *Statement of some New Principles on the Subject of Political Economy, Exposing the Fallacies of the system of Free Trade, and some other Doctrines maintained in the ,Wealth of Nation,* (First print 1834, New York: August M. Kelly, Bookseller, 1964), 14-15

[5] Ibid, 264

[6] Ludwig Von Mises, *Human Action: A Treatise on Economics,* 3rd. Rev. ed. (Chicago: Contemporary Books, Inc., 1949, 1963), 195

[7] Ibid, 682,855

[8] Bohm-Bawerk in developing his theory of interest made a distinction among "original" factors (land and labor) and the produced factor (capital).

[9] K. Blaug, *Economic Theory in Retrospective*, 525

[10] John M. Keynes, *The General theory of Employment, Interest and Money*, (London Royal Economic Society). Keynes definition is different from the gross investment definition currently in use.

[11] Ibid, 74-76

[12] Keynes is in agreement with Irvin Fisher's methods used (1930) in the" theory of interest," where instead of marginal efficiency of capital, the rate of return over costs is used.

[13] Ibid, 135-140

[14] Walter Shewhart's book, Economic *Control of Quality of Manufactured Product*, (Van Nostrand, 1931). He was a statistician at the Western Electric (Hawthorne plant). His book is the foundation of modern statistical process control (SPC) and provides the basis for the philosophy of total quality management or continuous process improvement for improving processes according to Sis Sytsma, in "Quality and Statistical process Control," Ferris State University, on line.

[15] Online at: http://www.kaizen-institute.com

[16] There is a W. Edward Deming web sites, there also is an institute in his name. Library of Congress of United States (after filing request page) allows more extensive search of his work. Alas, the volumes of research have evolved passed that marker as the only source.

[17] This part of curriculum fails inclusion efforts in hedge fund MBA educations, stripe and sales managerial characters, and modern finance and business ethic courses, and even some economic courses.

[18] Recently on more than one occasion, I recall the conversation I had with the late great professor Milton Freedman at USU that real wage cola of 3.2 percent was required to keep up with the natural real rate of growth, which included population growth, but it did not account for the perverted executive-pay exaggeration in those estimations. That combined with the no tax fiscal policy model are academically failed and dangerously instable economic models.

[19] Monetarists and modern mixed-encomiasts operate under economic conditions, which require balanced increases in real aggregate wages. However, not the distorted indices, which excessive executive pays distorts.

[20] Smith, Adam, An Inquiry into the Nature and Causes of Wealth of Nations, Edited by E. Cannon, Chicago: University of Chicago Press, 1st ed. 1776, 1976), 292

[21] John Rae,, *Statement of some New Principles on the Subject of Political Economy, Exposing the Fallacies of the system of Free Trade, and some other Doctrines maintained in the Wealth of Nation*, (First print 1834, New York: August M. Kelly, Bookseller, 1964), 15

CHAPTER 7

TECHNOLOGICAL ADVANCMENTS, DEMAND

Technological advancements are the progress of sets of knowledge and skills used in new production or productions of new capital (human and non-human), new goods and services.

Progress of technology is not just the result of individualistic curiosity of inventors or scientists in an intellectual vacuum. The economic variables are among a host of stimuli, which now guide institutional interest in technological advancements.

In one of the oldest form of the language, Dari, Dezfuli, Farsi, the word "KARDON" explains the same terminology. It means individual who is knowledgeable of the work skill. In Sanskrit, "TAKASATI" mean fashioner, or fashioning. Latin uses "TEXERE" that means weavers. Greek most recent of definitions explain it, "TEKTON," which means builder, and carpenter, and the word "TECHNIKOS, or TECHNE" that means art and skillfulness. Finally "TECNOLOGIA" that is the didactic and systemic treatment of an art, and logy, implies the erudition study of the same subject.[1] The epistemological study of the word implies that it has been with human cultures for a very long time, and conceptually it had been very useful.

Governments are interested in the increased productivity and economic growth, thus the partial impact of technological advancements on potential increase in the level of living. Private firms like the potential profit attached to the same inputs' costs producing more output, leading to more sale, and possibly more profit, or the reduction in cost, which less inputs (with more productivity) producing the same output will yield. Therefore, potential markets influence resource allocation and investment in new and appropriate technology generations from applied and basic research. Before an invention can be used and lead to economic growth satisfy national needs, or be supplied to advertised-induced consumer demands, it must undergo its metamorphosis.

The new idea must be perceived as a marketable good or service, be applicable to a production process, or become a new machine with other old and new parts. The process is a very expensive one. Often, old capital must be discarded before full depreciation has taken effect, while a risky new way is tested for feasibility and profitability. Thus, the need for increased saving and investments or upwardly adjusted investments should be clear. In addition, the need for a functional financial market (credit market) is essential to allow economic agents (entrepreneurs) to do the needed conversions of capitals' many forms. Moreover, the economy, which can risk much of the resources, must already be financially a sound and functioning economy.

The Derived Demand for Technological Advancements

The derived demand for techno-advanced goods and services is the sum of segmental demand for goods and services with embodied and disembodied technology by consumers and other producers. In addition, the derived demand for technological progress in the production process, then of capital in use and innovation, by entrepreneurs and producers. Then the demand for inventiveness leads to the demand for inventions, research, and scientific activities.[2] That is, theoretically inducements (through market mechanism) induce the entrepreneurs, innovators, and inventors to innovate.[3]

The one segment of the economy determines the ultimate success or failure of technology in goods and services. The most dominant purchasing power (70-90 percent) of gross national product is consumption in a market economy. Producers are the other economic agents most utilizing technological embodied and disembodied goods and services used in production of other goods and services. They are not the delusional-whole of the consumption sector, but a part of it.

Despite the importance of technological advancements (embodied and disembodied in human and non-human capital) that exists in development of the history of human economic growth, they are not fully understood. This is never the main economic reason behind the demand for them.

Reduced Price and Techno-Progress

Consumer and producers both respond positively when they can use any new product as a substitute for higher-priced commodity, service, and input, or if they get a perceived large enough
improvement subject to their financial constraints.

Consumer Demand

Consumer utility function guides the consumer demand; therefore, it also guides the most dominant purchasing power of the economy. Thus, consumers buy the kind of goods and services, which would be within their sets of budgetary constraint. The byproducts of process of technological advancements (invention, innovation, and capital in use) must meet the same criteria.

That is, the new good or service must be priced low subject to the consumer budget to allow attainment of a higher indifference curve, or produce a low-price substitute to what makes up the consumption basket. Alternatively, they produce such a novelty item, which would modify the taste of the consumer. Moreover, it must be within consumers' income constraints, it must be within the budget.

Techno-advanced Price Reductions of Commodities

The most recent and vivid example of modern consumer durable product of technological advancement of many combined scientific fields is the personal computer. A many-roomed big multiple mess of wires and bulbs, costing many times the annual revenue of the world's biggest institutions and nations were called computers in the 1970s. Most households and students had no access to it. Comparatively, now in the 1990s, a nicely packed mix of computer chips and a few short cables, a desktop personal computer is available, priced less than the average monthly salaries of an employed advanced-economy worker. Clearly, for the consumers who prefer such an item, the technological innovation embodied and disembodied in the personal computer has made it possible in two decades to have something they could not have before. They still are able to buy other items in their consumption basket. There are still high-priced computer systems in the world, but the choices and the alternatives have increased at the end of this technological advancements process.

Another vivid example is the price-impact of inventions, innovations, and capital in use related to agriculture. In the history of early colonial America (the eighteenth century), the same imported technology was used in agro-production, which was mostly for familial consumption.[4] In the Europe of the eighteenth century and in present rural India, like most rural agrarian life of developing nations, it takes of 50 percent of income to obtain food.[5] By contrast, 10-20 percent of average income of an employed worker in an advanced economy is allocated to food.

Techno-advanced Price Reductions of Substitutes

There are often a large number of commodities in most consumers' baskets, which are substituted for others, as seasonal price-changes occur. When prices of close substitute are reduced due to technological advances, consumer demand for such commodities can increase. The present consumer demand for home central heating and air condition systems has increased consumer demand for gas versus wood, coal, or petroleum products.

In fact, demand for a commodity (cable, for example) will change directly (increase or decrease), if a technological advancement changes the price of a substitute commodity (a VCR, for example). The cross elasticity of relative demand for a television would be positive with respect to the relative technological advance and price change of the VCR, video cassette recordings.[6] With technologically advanced product, there are cases, which replacements take place. At some point, obsolesce of certain products are realized. Cell phone technologies have made them smaller and more indispensable than landline phone services. Students and mobile business people have totally made the shift cells or other technological devices (flat-screen computers).

Techno-Advanced Price Reductions of Complements

Technological progress also affects consumer demand of complements. These goods are commodities used in relative fixed percentages of each other. The demand for television sets will increase if innovation changes reduce the electricity. The demand for VCR changes, if the price of the videocassette changes. The cross elasticity of relative demand for VCR quantities would be negative with respect to the relative techno-advance price changes of the video cassette.

Techno-advancements and Consumer Taste

In earlier history of most advanced economies, in most developing nations, may not meet sufficient demand to sustain their development and use, unless consumer taste does change much of byproducts of technological progress.

A large set of exogenous variables (sociological: education, culture, politics, theology) to economics may affect the endogenous variable demand, via consumer taste to halt or expedite technological progress. This is one reason to explain the faster rate of technological change in the utilitarian colonial America, versus British custom or class tailored demand for consumer items.[7] The existence of the phenomenon shifts much of the earlier focus of inducement for innovation adoptions from producers' isolation and suppliers' bases, to a demand and supply base inducement clamoring for progressive changes.[8]

The initial geographic dispersion of familial, rural America with accumulated land and livestock imposed certain needs for transportation and information. The general store, Montgomery Ward and Sears and Roebuck ordering catalogues, likeness of Ford's Model T to horse buggies all preceded modern advertisement and auto industries.[9] The importance of consumer taste has led to multi-billion dollar producer-supported advertisement industry. The purpose of the public relation advertisement industry is to modify taste and preference of consumers, thus consumer demand for goods and services. Many sets of psychological and communication innovations are so financed to modify consumer demand.

It is important that when a culture has taken an adoptive and utilitarian position in her tastes and preferences toward an innovation, such an innovational progress has taken effect. In way of explanation, an adoptive culture may have reduced the risk factors facing entrepreneurs on their way of supplying novel ideas, technological advancements, or new products. It stands to reason, not to further risk presenting new ideas, if every new idea has a 50 percent chance of getting the inventor jailed, killed, or bankrupt.

Here is another reason nondemocratic or even poorly managed police state democracies cannot keep up with technological advancement mechanism of modern times. The organizational cultures do not retain the skill and flexibilities to resolve inner conflicts dynamically.[10] However, if the novel idea gives you the same odds for financial rewards beyond your dreams, versus some manageable financial losses, you will risk more. This also explains the relative economic growth of more democratic economies, which have matured resolving organizational difficulties in time.

Techno-advancements and Consumer Income

One of the most important byproducts of technological progress and availability of cheaper goods and services is the relative increase in income to consume and invest more. The choice made will directly affect the future income and level of living. Take the example of the reduced cost of food in an advanced economy. Workers spend 20 percent of their disposable income on food, a large sum of individual resources remains for shelter, entertainment, and improvements in such a consumption basket. Perhaps about 80-90 percent consumption expenditure of the disposable income, leaving 10 percent for education of the households as an investment or saving for future consumption and investments. Firms or the governments in most economies cover health care often, because it plays such a big role in the competitive productivity edge most advanced economies are seeking.

Education, basic and retraining, is also gaining recognition due to its role in productivity increases in the internationally competitive markets. If there is such a large allocation of available income for consumptive goods and services (entertainment) over investment in education (10-80 percent), one should also see a re-allocation of resources and national focus.[11] However, consumers are also supplying work input to the production process, which is becoming more responsive to an innovation-using evermore-competitive international market. The producers would only pay high income to the workers who are constantly increasing their self-embodied human capital by education and retraining. Perhaps it is an easy skip from this logical need for skilled worker to the paradoxical argument that robotization will replace the need for workers. While this is no longer a technological impossibility, and aside from the political Neo-Con (new cons) and neo-fascists' backlash, this supply sides' dream-logic is confronted with the basic need for workers' income. That is, the workers' real income that generates the sustained aggregate demand to buy the products. Who will buy the high-priced innovational junk?

There have been multiple attempts to blame fiscal stagnations on technology, while real disposable income and workers' wages have been held tightly flat or grown much less than the 3.5 percent of their natural rates. In addition, job creation has been fought against or abundant except by slick political verbiage. All workers employed in all segments of the economy, with sufficient incomes can afford to purchase the supplied products, pay sufficient taxes for the optimum services demanded in such an economy. Alas, mindless market mechanisms have been known to do significant damages before, market or governmental breaks, regulations, and modifications have been added. When and where the rates of technological changes increase enough, the potential for such deviations and externalities become more profound and important.

The technology products like other commodities can be either normal or interior goods. Since the dynamic aspect is the issue, the innovation byproducts should initially be a normal good, and later, an inferior good.[12] That is, the demand for such a commodity should increase with increases in income, then fall. Therefore, the income elasticity for number sold with respect to real disposable personal income over time should be positive for new products, but negative when they become obsolete or other novel and useful commodities replace them.

For the most part, 1940-1970 has been an important innovational period for passenger cars, initially uncomfortable, now a balance of electrical, combustion and other multi-systems of technological advancements. In the following table, the income elasticity of real disposable personal income and number of passenger cars are studied. Table 7 reflects the positive attitude of consumers about the technology embodied and disembodied automobile.

Table 7. Income elasticity of consumers for cars.

Year	1940-50	1950-60	1960-70
Elasticity	3.95	.004	1.52

Note: Real 1972-dollar disposable personal income and numbers of passenger cars sold are used in these calculations.
Source: Historical Statistic of the U.S., 1967, Statistical Abstract of the U.S., 1967, Economic Report of the President, 1984.

In application of the same economic measurements to a number of agricultural products is even more interesting. From the decline in usage of use of mules and horses, to more pronounced rise and fall in usage of combines, corn-pickers, and tractors show in agriculture production and in the economy.

Table 8 shows income elasticity for agricultural products for approximately three decades.

Table 8. Income elasticity for innovational products.

Year	IE: DI & Tractors	IE: DI & Combines	IE: DI & Corn Pickers	IE: DI & Mules, Horses
1940 -45	1.3	2.5	1	-0.4
1945 -50	6	12	23	-4.7
1950 -55	1.6	2	3	-2.5
1955 -60	0.5	0.4	1	-1
1960 -65	0.08	-0.5	-0.5	N/A

Note: Real 1972-dollar disposable personal income and numbers of farm animals are machinery are sued in these calculations.
Source: Agricultural Statistics, 1967, Economic Report of the President, 1984.

The income elasticity of consumers for this number of agro-products show a positive index and it peaks for complementary new products. There is negative ebb in index for the substitute or obsolete product.

The more real disposable personal income of American agriculture base families increased the more they spend on new more machinery that is productive and less on traditional modus operandi on farms. Later, since the percentages of people on the farm also declined for larger-scale operations, urbanization, and international suppliers, the indices also changes for some innovational machinery over time.

Producer Demand

Producers will be motivated to take risks, borrow, and invest in the uncertain outcomes of technological advancements ,if they perceive some profit potential from the above mentioned vast consumer market demand for innovational and novel products. The profit formula, Profit equals revenues less costs. The producer to increased revenue must find customers or other producers to sell more output to them. Better products, and innovational methods to produce these or older conventional commodities, to produce better and cheaper, can help. However, for the reduction in costs, the producers must have cheaper and more productive input or a cheaper alternative to his present input or a better combination of input to produce more, which means better production techniques to reduce costs. In the above table farm producers, among others, comprise different market demands for novel products used in production of other output.

Increases in economic activities in different businesses are assumed to induce more concentration of innovational work. The increases in international demand for electronic imports from Japan have followed by an increase in Japanese patents in electronics.[13] Changes in family size, urban-rural mixes, economic growth, are among the variables, which may influence profitability-risk potential of technological progress.[14] Some other changes in population growth and the age compositions per capita income growth, change in related innovations also can affect demand for innovational works.

Producer Demand and Techno-advanced And Price Reductions

Producers, entrepreneurs facing the same profit formula and risk prospects tend to choose least-costs appropriate production techniques. Since they are kin to market price mechanisms, they would upgrade their production method with respect to relative prices. Thus, American homebuilders would use more wood relative to the British or Middle East builders, which use more brick or masonry.[15] Naturally, more invention may target least-resource cost appropriate techniques to guide their innovational talents.

Institutional Demands-Induced Techno-progress

Governments during wartime, universities, and corporations now regularly finance research and development. It is true that in times of war, military needs induce many such demand-pull inventions.[16] While the institutions may have a general wish and wish lists for certain technological advancements, they do not have little direct control on the creation of inventions. Their means of directing inventions are as follows.

1. Freedom to research, finance the researcher or a team of researchers.
2. Collect relevant information for the team, reduce risk and increase reward and incentive.
3. In the case of governments, allowing for stable but responsive systems of governing allowing innovative changes to take place.
4. Also, be present in case of negative externalities of technological progress and market mechanism failure.

Some of these factors are in use already. Government regulations are applied in patent systems and copyrights are used to protect the inventors and other creativity. Anti-trust laws are used to reduce monopoly market blocking.

Some military and quasi-military institutions are

financed for their inventive productivity and the diffusions of products. DOD (military) and NASA (Space Research) are a few famed examples. Government support of civilian technological progress also exists, whether it is in guaranteed buy of products or in winning of contracts. An example would be the financing of some avionic innovations of post-WWII by the United States and other Western economies.

Governments can be internal to the economic process. Central banks by interest rates and exchange rates can create cyclical trends, which will induce selective technological transfers. Trade regulations can also play a far more pivotal role in the import of appropriate technologies and enhancement of market mechanisms to induce such flow, research area yet unexplored.

Notes

[1] www.merriam-webester.com

[2] Charles Kennedy and A. P. Thirlwall, "Surveys in Applied Economics: Technological Progress," *The Economic Journal*, March 1972, 12

[3] Colin G. Thirtle and V. W. Ruttan, *The Role of Demand and Supply in the Generation of Diffusion of Technological Change*, (Switzerland, 1987), 8

[4] Nathan Rosenberg, *Technology and American Economic Growth*, (New York: M. E. Sharpe, Inc., 1972), 3, 43-44, 48

[5] Theodore W. Schultz, *In*vesting *in People: The Economics of Population Quality*, (Berkley: University of California Press 1982), 4.

[6] George J. Stigler, *The Theory of Price*, 3rd Edition. New York: The Macmillan Company, 1966, 31-34.

[7] The acceptance of standardized machine-made but quality products in America allowed for customer versus producer based inducement for technological progress and mechanization. (Rosenberg: 1972. 43-44)

[8] J. A. Schumpeter, *Business Cycles*, Vol. 1, (New York: McGraw Hill Book Company, Inc., 1939), 73.

[9] Nathan Rosenberg, *Technology and American Economic Growth*, (New York: M. E. Sharpe, Inc., 1972), 48.

[10] J. Steven Ott, *The Organizational Culture Perspectives*, (Pacific Grove, California: Brooks/Cole Publishing Company, 1989), 2, 12.

[11] Such a misallocation of resources and national focus is not hard to find. Refer to the author's work "Hollowing Headless Nations on Taxation and Education," and many excellent publications about the American high-priced athletic ventures (multi-million dollar executive contracts, with averages 8 to 20 million dollars, plus benefits and other pay bonus packages). Next to the massive under-funding of program related to education, and job retraining or creations (av. salary range of $20-$40 thousands).

[12] The percentage change in quantity sold is taken relative to the percentage change real disposable personal income. The more standard definition of normal and inferior goods and income elasticity is available in economic literature. (Stigler: 1966. 33-34)

[13] Jacob Schmookler, *Invention and Economic Growth,* (Massachusetts: Harvard University Press, 1966)

[14] Nathan Rosenberg, *Technology and American Economic Growth*, (New York: M. E. Sharpe, Inc., 1972), 40.

[15] Jacob Schmookler, *Invention and Economic Growth,* (Massachusetts: Harvard University Press, 1966), 55.

[16] The Manhattan Project yielded one of the most complex inventions of human history: access to atomic energy. Its good and bad potential are still ongoing. The invention of synthetic rubber instead of South East Asian natural rubber is another example. Ibid, 42.

CHAPTER 8

TECHNOLOGICAL ADVANCMENTS, SUPPLY

Technological advancements are the progress of sets of knowledge and skills and all of the inputs used in new dynamic production methodologies locally, nationally, or globally. The supply of progress of set of knowledge and skills used in new production, or productions of new capital (human and non-human), and new goods and services.

The Supply of Technological Progress

The supplies of technological advancements are identified as two initial types. One is the set of knowledge, which is subdivided into, basic and applied scientific knowledge and inventions. Two, is the set of skills and qualitative improvements added to the basic inventions, in order to apply them in the process of production. Innovational changes and improvements in forms of new capital (human and non-human capital, i.e., new machines and tools) are of the latter kind. Thus, the more general definition of technological advancements is used.[1] That is, the progress of set of knowledge and skills used in new production or productions of new capital (human and non-human), new goods and services. The genetics in new hybrid grain or pest-resistant seeds, new marketing, managerial skills, financial development or another electronic time saver would meet the definition of technological progress.[2] The post-Schumpeterian focus of economists on the post-innovational phase may have clouded some political judgments, may have led to resource misallocation away from other phases of technological progress.

For an invention to end up in the form of a final novel product (new goods or services) or a new production process, it must go through the qualitative process of innovations and capital in use phases.[3] Thus, if the patent-holder innovators are unable to use it in production, other agents must be induced to do so. That is, innovators and scientists must first supply the new idea, in form of innovation. Then innovators and entrepreneurs would take that invention or a new combination of older inventions, and apply them (as new capital in use) to supply a new product or a new production process to produce an old product.

Inventive Process and Supply and Techno-Advancements

The contribution of inventive process to supply of technological progress is explained in view of two factors. One is the synthesis of practitioners' methods, with the scientific methodology. Two, is the discovery of inventiveness process.

Internal logic of scientific discovery reflects motives for understanding. While practitioners' motives for technological change was for use in production.[4] Historically, practitioners would discover their skills without knowing the scientific logic of them. It has been noted that extensive innovational changes can take place without any new inventions, often based on new combinations of old inventions. Nevertheless, the synthesis of technology and scientific methods have speeded the rate of technological change. Moreover, the complexity of new discoveries, mostly concentrated in the research of applied science, where financial resources can be spent on teams of researchers focused on certain problems.[5] When the expected benefit and probability of enough profit-induced resource allocation to the targeted problem, where the rate of relevant technological advancements tend to increase.[6] In fact, over the last two decades, the federal government and industries spent more than universities on research and development programs.

Next, the inventive process is presented, which can explain the emergence of a new ideas and the development of ideas to inventions, innovations, and capital in use as a process of supplying technological progress.

Emergence of Novel Ideas

The subject of much fascination, novel ideas have been studied by anthropologists, historians, and sociologists before applied scientists, economists, and econometricians. Therefore, introduction of teconometrics is not such a giant step in this study. Yet, it is a giant leap for economics, but the time for it has arrived.

The Transcendentalist Approach

Novel ideas attain a mythical, mystical, and inspirational attributes. Only special persons, agents of creations conjure new ideas with uncommon intuitive acts of genius.[7] For most of human history, practical ideas were guarded from public.

Theologically they were kept inside temples. Professionally fathers passed them on to their sons. Theologically, they were revealed only to high-ranking religious peoples. Secularly, essential truths would pass to aspirants as inspired people of rare natural gifts, and rarely outside paternal circles. The process of supplying ideas would become implausible. Especially in a competitive industrial production, setting new ideas revive dead-commerce repeatedly.

The approach failed to explain the cumulative additions to collected human knowledge and critical reason over the historical long run.[8] Insightful acts are not as rare, or person-specific, as presented. Specific problem pre-conditioning may increase the possibility of such acts of insight.

The Mechanistic Approach

The definition of mechanistic method formulates the process of creation of inventive ideas is as an accumulation of small parts over a long time. Finally, in stepwise fashion all small parts are formed together in such a way to form the new idea as complete whole, in a much larger functional whole.[9] The stress of needs and formation of some known elements in a setting like a factory would help make the process to happen.[10] Given advancement in knowledge and social relation and the cumulative synthesis, make the whole of an inventive idea to be accumulated. This approach has been accredited for one, the cumulative synthesis of many smaller parts, two, for presenting it as a long process.[11] Nevertheless, they do not present the detail of the process, underrating the role of inventors and they give it a deterministic certainty.

The Cumulative Synthesis

This approach is the middle of the two extreme processes. The cumulative synthesis process subsumes the previous processes, but minimizes their negatives. It is divided into two segments.

A. One is the creation of individual insightful acts, which they may not be an inventive idea.

B. Two, is the cumulative synthesis process, this is a combination of more insightful acts with many other ideas and parts toward forming a whole, having a more probable chance of being a strategic invention.

This would be the most likely process of creating inventive ideas, because, the multi-associative synthesis of ideas are concentrating and converging in this process.

The insightful acts and organizational formation can occur in the first process, like clouds. Some clouds produce rains, and some do not. Selectivity, filtering, rejection, revaluation, and recombining can formulate a more productive invention after the second process.

The Gestalt Theory

The Germanic Gestalt pattern used to explain a formed completed whole, whose parts belong together. A recognized pattern, which is the organized-whole, a complete product, is made up of the distinct segmented parts. In addition, it is new. These are more complicated than bright ideas. Moreover, they have a quality to them in that organized-whole, which is different when juxtaposing them with their parts randomly.[12] Inventions, as whole-organized forms (Gestalten) are a massive synthesis of smaller whole-entities (products) insightful acts that are syntheses of other acts of insights.[13] Thus, by setting the initial proximal stimuli combined "in space and time" they would form a certain kind of predictable perceptual organization, that is, an act of insight.[14] Then a social process for invention exit, which does not depend on mystical impossibilities nor systematic determinism and can account for historical progression in mechanical technologies.

There are four sequential phases in the initial process of emergence of novel ideas or emergence of insightful acts.

1. One, unfulfilled wants, needs, demands, or an incomplete pattern would initially present the problem.[15] The need will focus individuals' concentration.
2. Two, combination and collection of initial relevant information to satisfy the need and fulfill the demand. The practitioners very early used fumbling, trial and error at this stage which pure chance playing a big role.[16] Later, the scientific method and organized experimentation with a more probability for successes were to lead to relevant acts of insight. Nevertheless, not all conditions and information may be available for all possible people. In addition, people may be subject to a number of forces, which make them unsuccessful?
3. Three, the relevant insightful acts presents a solution. But the solution is found by Chance so an exact timing of such activity is not possible nor there is an assurance that it would take place every time in a deterministic or mechanical fashion.

4. Four, this phase is for critical study, revisions, thus mastery of new ideas. Then the new idea is a 'technique of thought or action."[17] It becomes more important if it useful with the rest of experiences and cultural accumulations of the group.

The accumulation of such events could then lead to inventions and the process of cumulative synthesis. This can be a great start, but as an explanation either it falls short of the real life, or the importance of inventions have attracted much more resources and focus for economic reasons, either way, the regularity of applications and existence of inventions and innovation in modern economies requires further study.

<u>The Accumulation of Ideas and Cumulative Synthesis</u>

Accumulation of ideas and improvements in communication cross-cultural and over time increased the rate of cumulative progress of ideas. The process of organizing the related ideas to a relative whole, which constitutes an invention, is called the cumulative synthesis process. However, the dynamic cumulative synthesis presented in this study is even more likely to yield innovation.[18] The cumulative synthesis process is a collection of the four steps in emergence of novel ideas, combined with a large number of old and new inventions, ideas, experiences into a massive synthesis process.

This process explains how the scientific need for pure understanding and discovery of the supply-push argument is combined with the institutional and economic need of the demand-pull argument in fruition of a strategic invention.[19] That is, the scientists' need for discovery can play a role in the desire to complete the incomplete pattern in the process. Moreover, it explains how the institutional funding and economic needs become relevant to the setting up of research teams and are internalized to the social process of inventions. Practitioners, inventors, innovators, and scientists use the massive synthesis process alike.[20]

The four steps of cumulative synthesis are,

1. The perception of incomplete pattern phase, this could be the result of innovators' need To use, or the scientific need to understand, or it is the institutional area of focus. While individualized means of measurable inventions have been on the decline, individuals (even in team research) play the unique role to the process.
2. Setting up the stage, the recent requirement for research is more complex. The individual researchers have large sums of human capital invested in them over the years. They are self-financed or state or federal capital invested in them. Then the institutional-infrastructure for the research to take place, the needed equipment is also parts of non-human capital for the setting-up stage.[21] Thus, financial needs of researchers and the institutions become internalized in the social process of cumulative synthesis, and societal allocation of resources become deterministic, when international

competition is involved. Nevertheless, all of the preliminaries should be cleared, and all the data and information should point in the direction of invention. In case of a major invention, all relevant inventions would be already available. Industrial research laboratories and agricultural experiments stations are two American examples, which have utilized these facts. The establishment of experimental laboratories was a clear recognition of benefit from the applied process.[22] Alas, regardless of Henry Ford's background as a bicycle repairperson and availability of information on horse buggies. Still, it was Henry Ford and none other who invented, innovated, and utilized resources in a unique way to make the Model T car.

3. The act of insight phase, as part of cumulative synthesis, it implies a special at of insight combining other inventions and many acts of insights. Thus, a more complex process requires some knowledge of previous inventions. A more complex learning process of previous knowledge is suggested. Henry Ford could understand and fix a bicycle. Bicycle repair induced no one else to invent the Model T.

4. The critical revision and mastery phase is also a part of cumulative synthesis. Failures serve a historically important service and are internalized by A. P. Usher to the process on creating novel things. There may be inventions or scientific works already discovered but not used or applied. Because the fourth phase of cumulative synthesis has not applied to them. It could be after other inventions and future critical revisions, which full mastery other inventions, are found. The wheels, wagons, and rails were in coal industry, but they waited for steam engine before steam locomotives materialized.

The modifications needed here are reflective of changes in modern economies to allow for financing of the activities, which are both costly and financially risky, before they ultimately become marketable entities.

The Dynamic Cumulative Invention Synthesis Process

They dynamic cumulative synthesis process would repeat the four steps, while the set of novel ideas and inventions are increasing over time. A. P. Usher introduced the first and second phase as parts of the second cycle. The historical relevance of having few strategic inventions for any socially important achievements was known.[23] For example, the personal computer invention took place after relevant electronic inventions, use of digital numbers, and audio-visual communications were already invented, before the earlier personal computers were available. Further inventions have added to the expanding base of personal computer knowledge. Besides the continuity of the process, the inter-disciplinary and intra-disciplinary discoveries have further increased the rate of technological progress.[24] The firms recognized the potential benefit of the process. They internalized the process and allocated funds to finance it, as a part of research and development systems. The following table represents the categories of research and development funding.

There is a need for governments' allocation role to

finance research. Table 9 shows the diminishing federal funding of research and development. In fact, the next table will show the value different advanced economies have given the invention process in their economies by allocation of non-defense research and development funds to advancement of knowledge.

Some arguments favor anti-immigration laws and delusions of constitutional laws to enhance growth, among a canned list of misfortunes as they occur unabated, or induced to occur. That would do little but shut off the capital mobility to the American economy, while baby--boomers portion of population will explode and wage earners and real wages have been manipulated to be kept low.

There are social benefits not accounted for in the private firms' returns or in the researchers' returns.

Table 9 shows total research and development funding and categories (in Millions of 1982 dollars).

Table 9. Total R and D funding and categories (Millions of 1982 $).

Categories	1970	1975	1980	1985
Total R&D	62407	59883	73237	96999
Fed. as source %	57.1	51.7	47.2	47.9
% of GNP	2.6	**2.2**	2.3	2.7
Basic/totalR&D%	13.7	13.7	13.5	12.9
Fed. as source %	70.2	69.2	70.2	65.7
Applied/totalR&D%	21.9	22.0	22.2	22.6
Fed. as source %	60.2	57.4	55.5	53.1
Devlpmnt/R&D%	64.4	64.1	64.3	64.5
Fed. as source %	55.4	48.5	42.6	45.0

Note: Total R&D includes basic, applied, and development funds.
Source: U.S. Bureau of the Census, *Statistical Abstract of the United States*, Washington, D. C.: 1989. 577.

When the minimum wages are raised 10 cents for the working poor, you hear political voices everywhere about the implosion of the economy, about inflation. You will not hear any political voices or sound laws to remedy against looting capital markets by the executives' wage-packages at more than 40 times, 100 times, 200 times, or even 500 times the national average income of the wage earners.

The sound policy would deal with the knowledge

advancement needs and fill the R and D 50 percent gap, so the U.S. can compete on an equal level. Eventually, that advancement in knowledge would lead to some innovational entities in the very competitive international market. Since 1976, improvements have been made but the following table should alert the comparative need for resources in advancement of knowledge.

Table 10, shows percentage of non-defense R&D funds going to advancement of knowledge in some advanced economies, 1976.

Table 10. Percentage of Non-defense R&D Funds for the Advancement of Knowledge.

Type	United States	United Kingdom	France	West Germany	Japan
Non-defense R&D to Advance Knowledge	8	37	37	58	56

Note: This is calculated from Mansfield's defense share percentages less 100. The data excludes U.S. general university funds. Dates cover 1974-75 Japan, 1976 U.K., 1976-1977 U.S.

Source: Mansfield, E., and others, Technological *Transfer, Productivity, and Economic Policy*, New York: W. W. Norton & Co., Inc., 1982. 193.

Science Indicators, 1978. Washington, D.C.: National Science Foundation, 1979.

Experimental spirit makes inventors or academic mavericks, which are important and unique to the invention process, as entrepreneurs play an important role. They alone, or as a team, are those with the inventive-insightful acts. That is, their endowed human capital would specifically make them unique and valuable. The costs of the human capital, higher education, and training, books, educational and trade periodicals have increased above all others. However, all other costs of maintaining a family also have increased as reflected in the growth of disposable income, GNP, or inflation, CPI. Moreover, the relative value of teachers, professors, researchers have declined with respect to others. The cultural perception is important.

Table 11 shows the growth rates in government spending (in1971 U.S. $), and scientists-Years, and gross national product GNP (in 1984 U.S. $) in different sample countries.

Table 11. Growth rates in gov. (71 U.S. $), and scientists-Years, GNP (84 U.S. $).

Countries	Gov. Av. Spend. `54-74	Scientific Man Years `54-74	GNP `75-85
Brazil	32	32	1.27
Columbia	2.5	11	1.58
India	5	2	2.52
Indonesia	62	115	1.25
Korea	11	4	8.23
Mexico	11	14	1.31
Malaysia	10	22	4.71
Pakistan	3.2	4.2	4.06
Sri Lanka	2	5.6	3.76
Taiwan	6	0.6	4.27
Thailand	15	13	4.27
Turkey	15	41	1.37

Note: Population estimated from the U.S. Abstract, and other sources.[25]

That is, a definite allocation of private national resources, which has taken place contrary to the best interests of the whole, as noted in this study. In fact, that is why education has become such a fundamental point of technological competition push for the future. However, no longer a private, small-funded venture can really turn around the national economy of any nation.[26] At least, they cannot affect it enough to meet, compete, and lead international class-multinationals or the giant-industrial market. The developing nations have also increased resources to these endeavors. A large list of developing nations, which have allocated increasing amounts of financial resources and scientific person-hours have sustained growth in their economies. The internal and external barriers are far greater in smaller developing economies. The real per capital growth rate per year of expenditures on agricultural research during 1959-74 in the Islamic Republic of Iran was 28 percent. The scientist person-year per capital per annum growth rate was 4.4 percent.[27] These have been duplicated in many different nations as the importance and science in the process of inventive and innovative synthesis further discovered.

The extended explanation of dynamic invention cumulative synthesis process was to restate,

1. One, it is organized, and to some degree more

continual than first thought.

2. Two, in the case of institutional and mechanical inventions, which are patentable, and the creative and scientific works that are issued copy right, the invention base set (basic knowledge and creative works) is increasing. Therefore, their potential use will be increasing, too.
3. Three, make explicit the unique value of the inventors, researchers, experimenters, and scientists with the creative human capital to this process of dynamic creative (inventive) cumulative synthesis.
4. Four, governmental protection of their ownerships, their property rights, and agricultural productivity will have a positive effect on the future productivity in this area.
5. Five, the intellectual property ownership rights of the individual are opposite to those of some politically and financially powerful interests, or some institutions and governments.

Since, the inventors' roles are valuable to the whole of human societies. Specifically, there is a law targeted by the institutional interests (PACs, political action committees), which aims to pass the right of ownership of intellectual property rights (i.e., copyrights, etc.) from the creators to the institutions where they are working as part of labor salary contracts and in addition to their works performed for hire.

This is an intellectual enslavement act, and it should be discarded, next to the unfortunate communal agro-productivity experiments of our starving international neighbors. This is a direct attack on inventive-productivity motivation. The motivation, which is known to the institutions. The Economic Report of the President (1990, 112-113) stated, "Thomas Edison, after unsuccessfully trying to sell his first invention (an automatic vote counter), vowed that he would work only on ideas for things that people would buy." International protection of intellectual property rights was such an issue on the administration agenda.[28]

Whenever, institutionalism, statists, corporatists have replaced so egregiously self-interest and individualism of the suppliers we are set up for another disaster, like the communal production in agro farming. In addition, important economic incentive is removed from a production process.

There has been a decided shift away from rights of ownership to institutional control. That we will find to be an intellectual dead end for dynamic societies depending on individual invention energies as much as any advanced economy must depend on such inventions and multitudes of creative solutions of different kinds.

Distortion of worth and values in favor of short term profiteering, is a field of folly well cultivated by monopolies, oligarchies, plutocrats. It will substantially add to the forces, which overwhelm assumptive competitive market forces, and add to the market failures, disproportionate instable wealth concentration, and in decay of wealth of nations. All great nations have had to correct that economic misdirection, some repeatedly with bloody discontent. Brain drain gained much publicity and recognition in the second half of last millennium; apparently, we are still confused about the mega impact it has on the process of innovational advancement.

Innovation Process and Techno-progress

The process is a special class of dynamic cumulative synthesis process, which is not in J. A. Schumpeter's theory of innovation.[29] In this study with a new dynamic cumulative innovational synthesis (DCIS), different from the dynamic invention cumulative synthesis process, the speed and direction of innovation also are influenced. Given there is no guarantee, an increased probability of breakthroughs exist. The statement of V.W. Ruttan (1960, 604) may clear some issues,

> "The focus of conscious effort to affect the speed or direction of innovation centers around the second and fourth steps in the process as outlined by Usher–in setting the stage and in critical revision. By consciously bringing together the elements of solution–by creating the appropriate research environment–the stage can be set in such a manner that fewer elements are left to chance."

In addition, the planning phase of what is in J. A. Schumpeter's theory of innovation.[30] Economic agents study the old and new inventions, innovations, insightful acts, and different sets of economic feasibility sets in order to establish the potentials for a new production function.[31]

These notes new and old innovations were made possible when some new inventions were supplies. Alternatively, old inventions were mixed anew, or an old innovation can now be used in a new way. This is to combine Usher's developments and Schumpeter theory of innovation, in order to make an explicit link between invention and innovation.

$$\Omega \equiv f(\mu, \Omega', t)$$

$$\mu = f(\frac{\mu}{t}); iff \Rightarrow f \geq 0$$

$$But, \Omega' = f(\frac{\Omega'}{\mu}, \frac{\Omega'}{\mu'}, \frac{\Omega'}{t}); iff, f \geq 0$$

Identities show innovation, Ω is new inventions. μ is a mix of new and old inventions with old innovations (Ω ‘) to yield an innovation over time. So planning for new factories and new equipment, new innovative firms and old innovation-generating firms and entrepreneurial spirits in risk-taking (other than financial risk-taking, unless new ventures are self-financed) or experimental spirit are also essential for the innovational process. Alas, the formulation fails phenomenon of new ideas like the computer microchips evolutions into industry-computerization of business, governments, and educations, without any significant a priori road maps.

The design and building of a new factories and rebuilding of older ones, exist the chance for the adoption cost-reducing innovations, available inventions. There two cases, which may require more explanation, the issue of duplication of factories and replacement of old parts of a factory may not include innovation.

The duplication of factories involved innovation, if it occurs at the early part of diffusion and adoption phase of innovation, if it is in a new market, region, and country. Moreover, it occurs always by the use of newer, more innovational production techniques, new innovational factory reorganization, or innovational marketing strategy, to affect supply curve of the same factory. There is little to be gained from the innovation residual there, if it is a duplication of a product at the end of its product cycle in the same area, saturated by other suppliers.[32]

The replacement of old parts, with the same identical parts, made at the same way and same costs would certainly constitute no innovation. However, new parts made of better material, which would last longer (i.e., use of steel for iron) made much cheaper would entail innovation, inventions. Table 12, shows the number of patents issued and copyrights registered, which often measure the effect of creative and inventive efforts. Nevertheless, patents on new inventions are used as an innovations index.

New legal entities representing the entrepreneurs do engage in innovative ventures. The legal entities are sole ownership, S-corporations, C-corporations, or trusts, which conduct all

Table 12. Annual growth rate of Patents issued by categories, and Copyrights Registered.

Periods	Total Patents	Foreign Corp.	U.S. Corp.	Individuals	U.S Gov	Registered Copyrights
60-65	6.6	14.7	6.7	4.6	4.7	4.1
65-70	0.4	10.4	-0.14	-3.2	2.6	1.5
70-75	2.6	9.8	-1.2	5.6	1.8	5.4
75-80	-2.8	-0.1	-2.9	-4.5	-9.4	3.1
80-85	3.3	9.0	1.3	-0.06	2.0	3.2
85-87	7.9	12.3	3.9	9.3	-4.5	3.9

Note: Column 3 includes patents to foreign governments. Data includes patents for designs, botanical plants, reissues. Source, U. S. Bureau of the Census, *Statistical Abstract of the United States*, Washington, D.C.: 1974, 1985, 1989.

business activities. Alas, they would normally engage in innovative actions if they plan to set up new factories, build new equipment, or design new organizational relations and marketing strategies. The innovative older firms have maintained an inner innovational team.[33] They systematically engage in economic competition, through innovational process. The distinction is drawn between, competitive capitalism and "trustified" <institutionalized> capitalism, when size of the firms are in question, in

Schumpeter. There is a good chance that the "giant" firms (i.e., monopolists, multi-nationals) could engage in non-economic means (legal, etc.) to stop entry or shut out innovative smaller firms to certain markets. While they will have to compete with other big firms their own size by more innovation and by economic means. At least, they might, due to fear of retaliation. The U.S.A. anti-trust laws are frequently cited in such cases.[34] Others, big or small, will naturally die out if they do not adjust by innovation to the new economy conditions.

The Entrepreneurship

The economic agent entrepreneurs discover new economic possibilities where none existed before, they perform economic insightful acts in the dynamic cumulative innovational synthesis process. The Classical economists did, not recognize J. B. Say's role of entrepreneurs. For classical economists, profit was the capitalist's share only. It emerged after the marginalists' revolution again. In addition, the neo-classical economists noted entrepreneurs' role and profit in the 1980s, but it disappeared from the theoretical work.[35] The theoretical works of J. A. Schumpeter, and F. Knight reintroduced the subject to economics again.[36] The entrepreneurs with the injection of innovation and production methodologies will change the consumer satisfaction obtained in demand terms, and the yield derived from supply terms, from resources, mutatis mutandis in any given period.[37] They behave in a manner specifically different from other economic agents, because they will break through the traditional modus operandi, the conventional ways of thinking, the status qui. They are involved in all innovational economic activities.

The entrepreneurs' skills make them uniquely aware of the relative economic possibilities around them, either for a short period or they may choose to keep informed of such relative economic conditions, laws, and social phenomenon relative to their economic activities, such as people as specialists in each such field would learn to do. The entrepreneurs' decision set resembles his awareness of the economic and non-economic conditions around him. There are shortened or cheat-sheet versions of entrepreneurial characteristics, as capital < financial> market arbitragers, which miss defines both agents of capital formation process.

However, we will see the processes involving the transformation of choice ideas to applicable technologies, and successful production processes and economic ventures are far too complex for individuals unaided and non-synchronized to conduct with balance the economic purposes of national or integrated global economy.

The 1920s and 1930s deflationary implosions, in the West, 1980s military-costs implosion in the East, repeated financial meltdowns on cyclical bases are not assuring testimonials of our academic understandings.

Notes

[1] Charles Kennedy and A. P. Thirlwall, "Surveys in Applied Economics: Technological Progress," *The Economic Journal*, March 1972, 12.

[2] Edwin Mansfield, *Technological Change*, (New York: W. W. Norton & Co., 1971), 9.

[3] Vernon W. Ruttan, "Usher and Schumpeter on Invention, Innovation, and Technological Change," *Quarterly Journal of Economics*, vol. 73, 1960, 596-606.

[4] Edwin Mansfield, *Technological Change*, (New York: W. W. Norton & Co., Inc. 1971), 10.

[5] Ibid, 11.

[6] Ibid, 17.

[7] Ralph Waldo Emerson (1803-1882), as leader of New England Transcendentalism, explained "transcendental forms" were identified by Emmanuel Kant (1724-1804) as an important class of ideas which come by intuitive thoughts rather than experience, "New England Transcendentalism," by Michael Moran, The Encyclopedia of Philosophy, 1967

[8] Abbot Payson Usher, *A History of Mechanical Inventions*, revised ed.,(London: Oxford University Press, 1954), 60

[9] Chicago sociologists W. F. Ogburn and S. C. Gilfillan are credited for the mechanistic process. Usher, Abbot Payson, A History of Mechanical Inventions, revised ed., (London: Oxford University Press, 1954), 61

[10] S. C. Gilfillan wrote that the invention would take place because of need and the process or individual may not be necessary. Ruttan, V. W. "Usher and Schumpeter on Invention, Innovation, and Technological Change," *Quarterly Journal of Economics*. 1960, 601

[11] Abbot Payson Usher, *A History of Mechanical Inventions*, revised edition, (London: Oxford University Press, 1954), 61

[12] The founders of the Gestalt theory were three German psychologists: Max Wertheimer, Wolfgang Köhler, and Kurt Koffka. "Gestalt Theory," by T. R. Miles, *The Encyclopedia of Philosophy*, 1967 edition

[13] The social process would yield us a close circle when initially there would be incomplete circles (i.e., David Kaz: proximity, closed forms). Kafka stated laws of maximum simplicity, regularity, and symmetry would help the stimuli to yield a good psychological organization (Gestalten). "Gestalt Theory," by T. R. Miles,*The Encyclopedia of Philosophy*, 1967 edition.

[14] Köhler experiments show a chimpanzee using a tool placed close to food to retrieve the food while no previous experience existed. Kafka identified the act given the setting of the stage as an act of insight. Arthur Koestler draws a parallel: Archimedes already had the problem in his head before his bath. Thus, the combined mental fields became one and the solution was not invented, but found. Usher, Abbot Payson, *A History of Mechanical Inventions*, revised edition, London: Oxford University Press, 1954. 61-64.

[15] Primal needs for food is a very basic demand, which Gestalt psychologists noted. In the history of human development, the set of needs have evolved to more

complex issues.

[16] Ibid, 65

[17] Abbot Payson Usher, *A History of Mechanical Inventions*, revised ed.,(London: Oxford University Press, 1954), 65

[18] While V. W. Ruttan (1960, 1987) identified the second and fourth steps needed in innovation, the distinctions between the process (the emergence of a novel thing or cumulative synthesis) were not made. The same was also true about E. Mansfield's (1971) presentation. A. P. Usher (1954) found the cumulative synthesis as the source of any inventive creations. Ruttan, V. W., "Usher and Schumpeter on Invention, Innovation, and Technological Change," *Quarterly Journal of Economics*, 1960, 604.
Colin G. Thirtle and V. W. Ruttan, *The Role of Demand and Supply in the Generation and Diffusion of Technological Change,* (Switzerland: Harwood Academic Publishers, 1987), 5.
Edwin Mansfield, *Technological Change,* (New York: W. W. Norton & Co., Inc., 1971), 48

[19] Colin G. Thirtle and V. W. Ruttan, *The Role of Demand and Supply in the Generation and Diffusion of Technological Change,* (Switzerland: Harwood Academic Publishers, 1987), 9

[20] It is noted in 1900, 80 percent of the U.S. patented inventions were issued to individuals. BY 1957, the individuals' shares were 40 percent of patents issued. Edwin Mansfield, *Technological Change,* (New York: W. W. Norton & Co., Inc., 1971), 65

[21] Ibid.

[22] Thomas Edison is credited for the first research lab (1876) in the United States. Some others credit Eastman Kodak (1893), B.F. Goodrich (1895), and General Electric (1900) applied the industrial laboratory idea as a new process for inventions.
Mansfield,1971, 40-41

[23] Like the portion of savings, which is invested in new capital to generate more income, new savings, and investments, and newer capital, a dynamic cumulative synthesis looks at the role of added inventions in generating more relevant-inventions.

[24] Frank Lynn's study introduced the average time interval of incubation period form (1885-1919), 30 years and (1920-1944), 16 years to (1945-1964), 9 years. The rate of innovational process implies were the same or the commercial development for the same data were 7, 8, and 5 years. Edwin Mansfield, *Technological Change,* (New York: W. W. Norton & Co., Inc., 1971), 76-77

[25] Other sources for this table are,
Schultz, Theodore W. *Investing in People,* Berkeley: University of California Press, 1981. 50-51
Boyce, J. K., and Evenson, R. E., *Agricultural Research and Extension Programs\,* New York: Agricultural Development Council, 1975. Appendix II
U. S. Bureau of the Census, *Statistical Abstract of the United State,* Washington, D.C.: 1989. 822.

[26] Part of Japan's push to generate basic research has been to quadruple their engineers and scientists from the current graduation rates of 2, 9 for every 100,000. This passes the British 10, 7 and meets the graduation rate of nine scientists and twelve engineers per 100,000 Americans. Valery, 1989, 7

[27] Source for population data was the International Financial Statistics, 1983. Currency was constant 1971 U.S. dollars.
Theodore W. Schultz, *Investing in People,* (Berkeley: University of California Press, 1981), 50-51
J. K. Boyce and R. E. Evenson, *Agricultural Research and Extension Programs,* (New York: Agricultural Development Council, 1975), Appendix II

[28] Ibid. 114

[29] Abbot Payson Usher, *A History of Mechanical Inventions*, revised ed., (London: Oxford University Press, 1954), 68-69

[30] J. A. Schumpeter, *Business Cycles: A Theoretical, Historical, and Statistical Analysis of the Capitalist Process,* Vol. I., (New York: McGraw Hill Book Company, Inc., 1939), 87-97

[31] Carolyn Shaw Solo, "Innovation in the Capitalist Process: A Critique of the Schumpeterian Theory," *Quarterly Journal of Economics*, 1951, 422.

[32] Two examples are the retailers' multitudes of stores, used as temporary occupation, European artisans' businesses, where age and tradition dictate business formation.
J.A. Schumpeter, *Business Cycles: A Theoretical, Historical, and Statistical Analysis of the Capitalist Process*, Vol. I, (New York: McGraw Hill Book Co., Inc., 1939), 87-97

[33] It is stated: "It is, therefore, not the new firms which innovate and the old firms which react, but all the competing firms which innovation, some succeeding,

others failing." Carolyn Shaw Solo, "Innovation in the Capitalist Process: A Critique of the Schumpeterian Theory," *Quarterly Journal of Economics,* 1951, 425

[34] Ibid, 96.

[35] One can claim that financial alchemy subsumed it, for executive pay and other institutional financial criminal mischief.

[36] M. I. Kirzner, *Discovery and the Capitalist Process*, (Chicago: The University of Chicago Press, 1985), 1-14

[37] Peter F. Drucker, *Innovation and Entrepreneurship, (* New York: Harper & Row Publishers, 1985), 33

CHAPTER 9

TECHNOMINCS OF PRODUCT DEVELOPMENT

Traditional approach defines a product from an on-the-shelf technology in an existing factory. This and other writings extensively challenge the uniqueness of this notion on-the-shelf technology. Therefore, in this chapter a two-product model is used to show how technological change evolves to accomplish the transferences from technologies associated with product (a) to different technologies in producing new product (b).

Dynamic Planning and Product Development Utilizing New Technologies

The dynamic and sustainable development of new-products, utilizing new and appropriate technologies is developed by a transformative application of product life cycle planning, and budgeting yield.[1]

In this model sales of at least two products (a, b) are used as an example of two level of technologies reflected in methodologies producing (a, b) over time. The phases of are divided into different stages to make the process a manageable series of events.[2] There are certain variables and characteristics to look for in each phase,

1. Phase 1, initial development of product phase, The sales of product increases at different rate, initially at increasing rate enough to encourage the added costs of research and development, advertising, and high labor and overhead expenses.
2. Phase 2, growing of new product sales and production, While the sales will be much more than in the initial phase, the point of inflection in this phase goes from increasing of sales at increasing rate to increasing sales at decreasing rate. The capital market can be approached to finance production expansion. The research and development focuses on production technologies issues. However, the funding becomes available to study product differentiation and new product development. If that is impossible at this stage, it will become essential in the next phase. The process generates Jobs.
3. Phase 3, Product maturing phase, Some shops or small businesses stay in this phase, they also pass it on as inheritance, unless or until they completely shut down the operation. In larger operation, this becomes the takeoff-phase of a new firm. They present it for public shares and apply the generated access cash flow to launch product differentiations and new lines of products as they expand. The phase start when the sales revenues are growing but at the decreasing rate. Still the sales are higher than before, but the second mathematical differentiation start being negative. The employment rank increased, and salaries and skill improve as well.
4. Phase 4, shut off or expansion decision phase, This moment comes to all operations. For managerial team or owners of firm the profitability of operation the need to cut losses, or make a graceful exit are ongoing concerns, but the sales of product start decreasing after zero growth for a time, and they start to decrease at increasing rate. The options in new

markets or technological changes are few or unsuitable for conditions faced by the operation related to product (a). Nevertheless, the hope and options related technologies and product (b) are either expanding or also declining. Therefore, the sum of net revenues generated are increasing or changing directions. If there is the net revenue from either operation take a negative turn, the shut off plans need to be implemented. Alternatively, the mops up operations after the shut-off phase are orderly closing down and termination.

5. Phase 5, the follow up phase, in revisiting phase 1, a successful product (b) will require the same actions but perhaps with most new technologies, retooling and retraining for new skills. Larger institutions do create such flow of inventions and activities, and they can raise the needed cash flow from the capital market to enact their plans. The research and development internal to the businesses usually yields such great returns.

The net earning potential line can also represent profit from the two endeavors (a, b), however, the operational and related expenses can differ in different firms. There are some very peculiar notions about implications of excessive wage packages. It is assumed, they are good to be kept low at the lower ends, and limitless at the top end. Both notions are inappropriate, the former, for starving the economy, and the later, for looting capital markets and the shareholders.

Earnings, Net Revenues, Profits, and Capital Formation

Operations without earnings are terminated.

Alternatively, production methodologies, applied technologies are shelved. Even with earnings, it must be sufficient net earnings to cover operational expenses,

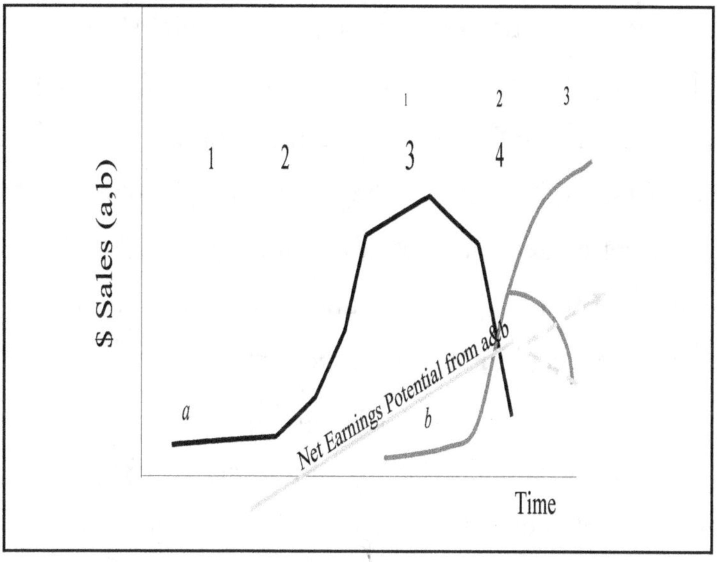

wages, and rents, purchases of overheads, and machinery to justify prolonging the operation, until the sales pick up.

Figure 11shows dynamic-sustainable products development, using technologies (a, and b).

Figure 11. Dynamic-sustainable products development, using technologies (a, and b).

At some point, the sales and earnings increase the cash flow sufficiently to have funds left over the operational expenses and taxes, which is often profit.

In most small business, this is often put in expanding

the operation by purchase of more equipment or capital stocks. In larger operation, higher earnings, often is passed on to shareholders as capital gain or equity yields. The existence of earning and the degree of risk stock holders assign to each stock determines the prices earnings ratio, 7, 17, and 27, which the stockholders are willing to hold on to a stock. The earning divided among the number of stocks determines the initial value of the stocks. At this phase, often large-set-aside funds out of earnings goes for research and development, new products, and new markets, and purchase of new capital stocks, embodying the new technologies, or replacing older technologies.

The earning can also be looted for wage packages, and unreasonable benefits of executives. It is reasonable to argue for the following formula for limited number of executives. However, larger obscene sums are now common in millions and billions of dollars.

Formula,

{[Yi] x $ 42,600 (AV U.S. INCOMES) x 0.80 = Base Value)}

Base Value x [1 ± r];

{r = Rate of growth [r <= 20 percent],

or decay [r<= 0.80 percent] of cooperate earnings};

i = 1...n; Y = 10... 100

Table 13 shows a wage matrix that links the wages to

average national income, and performance indices.

Table 13. Wage matrix.

Base wages + %1.20 + %0.80	Low	High
	$ 613,440.00	$ 749,760.00
	$ 3,067,200.00	$ 4,430,400.00

For example,

(10 x $42,600 x 0.80 = $ 340,800 base value) plus bonus

$ 340,800 base value x {1.20 or 0.80} = {$408,960.00 or $272,640.00}

(100 x $42,600 x 0.80) => $3,408,000.00 x {1.20, 0.80} = {$4,089,600.00 or $2,726,400}

The executive retirement fund portion as the 401-k of workers' retirement can be matched with stocks, for holding for at least up five years after leaving the firm. Any options are needed to be purchased in free markets like any investors' purchases. Any stock purchases have to be done in the market, at market prices. Any loans need to be available in the market place to everyone shareholders, workers and executives alike. The profits go to shareholders or in smaller firms to owners. Executives are workers no less and no more than any workers in the firms. Of course, executive and workers would benefit the same as shareholders if they are holding shares, purchased at the market place, without discounts, without any hidden behind closed door of the board room mechanism or policies, otherwise not available to other shareholders. To do otherwise, to over pay, to introduce elitism, and other market imperfections, and dishonest accountings are to harm the system not a new management skill, or innovative management model.

The much larger numbers are reflective of deterioration of democracy and market imperfections now long established. They go back to Nixon-ism effect in political ethics, dependencies of the same political structures on business funds for campaign advertisements for legal favors. An example is the abolishment of 1933 Glass-Steagall Act (GSA) without protective-clauses for regular customers and voters.[3] The depression era law was designed around the insightful concerns Senator Carter Glass, after real life experiences of two publicly held companies and a commercial bank loan and security department turn a $15 Million dollar bank loan into a $25 million dollar common stock, and $30 million dollars bond. Then, bankruptcy of the $ 70 million-dollar company brought the fraud on taxpayers out of the back rooms into the media. The GSA made it illegal for banks to engage in sale of common stocks for the entities they loaned. This also did not allow the accounting firms to consult the same entity they audited. The act established legal firewalls between activities, which aid greed-induce criminal activities. It is now a common daily media affair to see the result of recent modifications of the same law in the 10 to 20 infamous legal cases of mega corporations, despite the apologists' blinders, and the <pretzel> politicians. When the banking, investing, and auditing interest groups approached the representatives to suspend the GSA, they had a captured audience. Most of mechanisms put in place to protect the public economic welfare have failed in a major ways.[4] They got another one of those 1990s fast passages. Realizations of current magnitude of risk to financial and capital markets, and the universality of conflicts of interests, The GSA should have been extended (not suspended) to cover all loans, securities, and financial institutions, and fire walls for all insurance, auditing, and consulting not just banks. Campaign funding reform acts are other golden sources of analysis of gradual deterioration of ethics and morals of politics and commerce, and sustainable damages to any democracy.

Most fast cast law patches in the recent past have been anemic, superficial, and further eroding to capital formation and capital market. Until, this issues are met fast responses, cosmetic publicity stunts, are delaying proper repairs to market trusts. Specially alarming, is the silence of those (in political leadership positions), who scream about minor increases of dimes and nickels in minimum wages for working poor, and growing hordes of the un-insured workers, the legacy costs of blue color retiree. Nevertheless, they are dismissal of these obscene multibillion dollar executives wage packages and their retirement severance agreements (the severance agreements), which are looting and divesting the capital formation markets, and shareholders' equities, and workers retirements and future wealth of a nation. All the while, the same executives, and their paid political operatives scream legacy costs, about the contracted funds of the lowest paid middle class wage earners, professors, teachers, police, and firefighters.

The importance of net revenue to technological advancement is related to the size of net earning left after such activities. The impact on demand is also important, when shareholders' income and worker retirements-induced higher demands' funds are raided to add to miss concentration of wealth. The economy will recess to lower level of activities.

Concentration of wealth as a political end has always been harmful to American economy and global economy, along the anti-property laws, and market imperfection laws, they are all chronically deflationary. They reduce and limit formation and circulation of wealth creation, exchange theory of wages, appropriate circular flow of nations' economies.

Notes

[1] Lloyd L. Byers, *Concepts of Strategic Management: Planning and Implementation*, (New York, Harper & Row Publishers, 1984), 194

[2] R.S. Savich and L.A. Thomson, "Resource Allocation within The Product life Cycles," *MSU Business Topic* (Fall, 1978), 38

[3] The following internet exogenous source depends on the web hosting it:
http://www.google.com/search?q=cache:wdFhB-bLugcC:gsbwww.uchicago.edu/fac/raghuram.rajan/research/randy1.pdf+glass-steagall+act&hl=en&ie=UTF-8

[4] Internet sources are subject to frequent modifications at their source.
Gordon M., "Watchdog System Failed Enron ," *AP Business Writer*, Mon Oct 7, 1:58 AM ET
Senate report:
http://www.senate.gov/gov_affairs/100702watchdogsreport.pdf

CHAPTER 10

TECHNOLOGIES, INFRASTRUCTURES AND WELFARE THEORY

Global economy is defined around the larger national and international businesses, mistakenly or by design, it will include the larger formal and informal smaller entities, individuals (on, wheel, donkey, bicycle, motor bikes, trucks, boats, etc.) in variety of locations and shops. It includes small farmer, and their distribution means. They all benefit of exiting and up-graded infrastructures technology investments that accommodates them supplying the market with more of their products.

The infrastructures technological advancements can be a new higher speed digital connection in advanced global markets connections. They can be cell phones in the hand older villagers and farmers linking them to updated information, prices and market needs in timely fashion. The overall implications for supply and demand sides' adjustment will be that consumers and producers surpluses can expand. Thus, the infrastructures technological advancements will increase the real disposable income and level of living of active and alert members of the economy.

Production function

Production formulation is as follows,[1]

$$y = Ae^{a}c^{\beta}l^{\alpha}k^{\vartheta}e^{u}$$

$$\ln y = lnA + alne \quad + \beta lnc \quad + \propto lnl \quad + \vartheta lnk \quad + ulne$$

$$\ln y = \cancel{lnA}\,0 + a\cancel{lne}{=}1$$

$$+ \beta lnc + \propto lnl \quad + \vartheta lnk \quad + u\cancel{lne}\,1$$

$$\ln y = a + \beta lnc + \propto lnl + \vartheta lnk + u$$

Such that,[2] RTSt=f (a, v1, v2, v3, v4)

The following equations are the log linear econometrics of production functions and proof equations.[3]

$$y = Ae^{a}c^{\beta}l^{\alpha}k^{\vartheta}e^{u}$$

$$\ln y = lnA + alne \quad + \beta lnc \quad + \propto lnl \quad + \vartheta lnk \quad + ulne$$

$$\ln y = \cancel{lnA}\,0 + a\cancel{lne}{=}1$$

$$+ \beta lnc + \propto lnl \quad + \vartheta lnk \quad + u\cancel{lne}\,1$$

$$\ln y = a + \beta lnc + \propto lnl + \vartheta lnk + u$$

Such that: RTSt=f (a, v1, v2, v3, v4)

And RTSn=f (a, v1, v2, v3, v4)

Proof: RTSn>RTSt

The data have passed correlation fitness tests, F-type, and R-square tests. Their R-square regression fitness tests are significantly high.

The Optimization

The optimization issue is maximizing profit subject to the cost of variables and production.

Here the firm production function is

$q = f(v1, \ldots vn)$.

Moreover, vi is the quantity of its ith input used in production, it is positive.

The profit is given by,

$\vartheta = p \times q - c1v1 - \ldots - cn\, vn \qquad \text{and } vi > 0$

Profit maximization conditions for producer of a single product are,

$M\vartheta / Mvi = 0$

That is,

$c = c' + e'$

$q = q' + k'$

$M\vartheta / M(q' + k')i = 0$

And

$$p.\ M(q' + k')i / Mvi = (c' + e')i$$

Technological injection as knowledge included in the process is shown by (k), and the prices, wages of inputs and variables are augmented by the externality (e).[4]

Therefore, the price multiplied by the added unit equals the determined cost of each variable, including the externalities. This denotes a premium added to the value of each variable for technology, and the premium added to the cost for externalities associated with new technologies. The second order of Sheppard Lemma condition requires that the rate of technological substitution be the inverse of variables (inputs) prices.

The Lagrange Formulation and Sheppard Lemmas

Q = f (vi) for vi > 0

And

L= f (vi)-(y-(c.vi)) = 0

Minimization condition,

First order condition,

$$\frac{\partial L}{\partial t} = 0$$

Second order condition,

$$\frac{\partial L^2}{\partial t} \geq 0$$

Maximization condition,

First order condition,

$$\frac{\partial L}{\partial t} = 0$$

Second order condition,

$$\frac{\partial L^2}{\partial t} \leq 0$$

$$fvi\ fvn > (fvi\ vn)^2$$

Thus,

$$\forall\ Vi > 0 \quad (i = 1.\ 2.\ 3 \ldots .n)$$

Maximum Minimum Dual Formulations

This is a non-linear formulation for profit maximization as primal production, and cost minimization as dual condition.

Function q = f(vi) for (i = 1,2,3,…n)

and for all vi > 0

Max

$\vartheta = \ \leq ri$

Min

$C = q-(c-vi) \geq ri$

Technological Infrastructures and Economic Surpluses

Benefits of technological infrastructures are studied as economic Surpluses in this study. The new research uses teconometrics comprehension of technological advancement in modular production-function under production theory. There are new graphic models to study the influence of technological injections in welfare theory of economics. Specifically, the measurement of additional benefits from consumer and producer surpluses for an economy that advance toward the new economic development model presented in this study and a few volumes associated with the same author.

The optimizations of resources have been to use best methodology that is best available technology to procure the maximum products, therefore most profit of the products. While minimizing the waste, pollution, and cots of variables in the production of goods and services, use technologically advanced methodology available to assist in the process with the optimality conditions in mind.

The use of duality condition also known as dual conditioning, or maximization of profit from our production given our variables, subject to cost of those variables, is the primal condition. Moreover, minimization of costs subject expenses associated with the methodology, technology of variables, pollution, externalities are the dual problem associated with the same process.

Technological advancement as it is injected in methodology of production is very expensive, therefore, it is necessary to understand the benefit of such injection. The study of consumer and producer surpluses tailored to technological injection will aid in this field of inquiry.

Cost Benefit of Technology and Supply Expansions

The addition of new roads to a village is a new technological infrastructure, which brings stream of new benefits to an area over time. A conversion dirt road to larger payment road, which expand trade and traffic and increases commerce as the result, access to health care and urban medical benefit can also further expand the benefits. At least, the increase in the traffic is measureable.

A secondary railroad bridge with two or more lines can multiple the volumes of transferred products into and out of a region substantially. It will contribute to the economic activities as well. it will garnish multiplier effect, increased money velocity, with added jobs and increased commerce.

The benefit increase is the shaded area under the demand curve and marginal costs. It is not considered as an increase in welfare of the village, unless the real income partly or in aggregate increases, without harming the real income of other people in the village.

Figure 12 shows the added benefits from utilizing new infrastructure. Ever, in the initial developmental stages, when the supply expands and more supplies are available for the given the same level of demand function for that population.

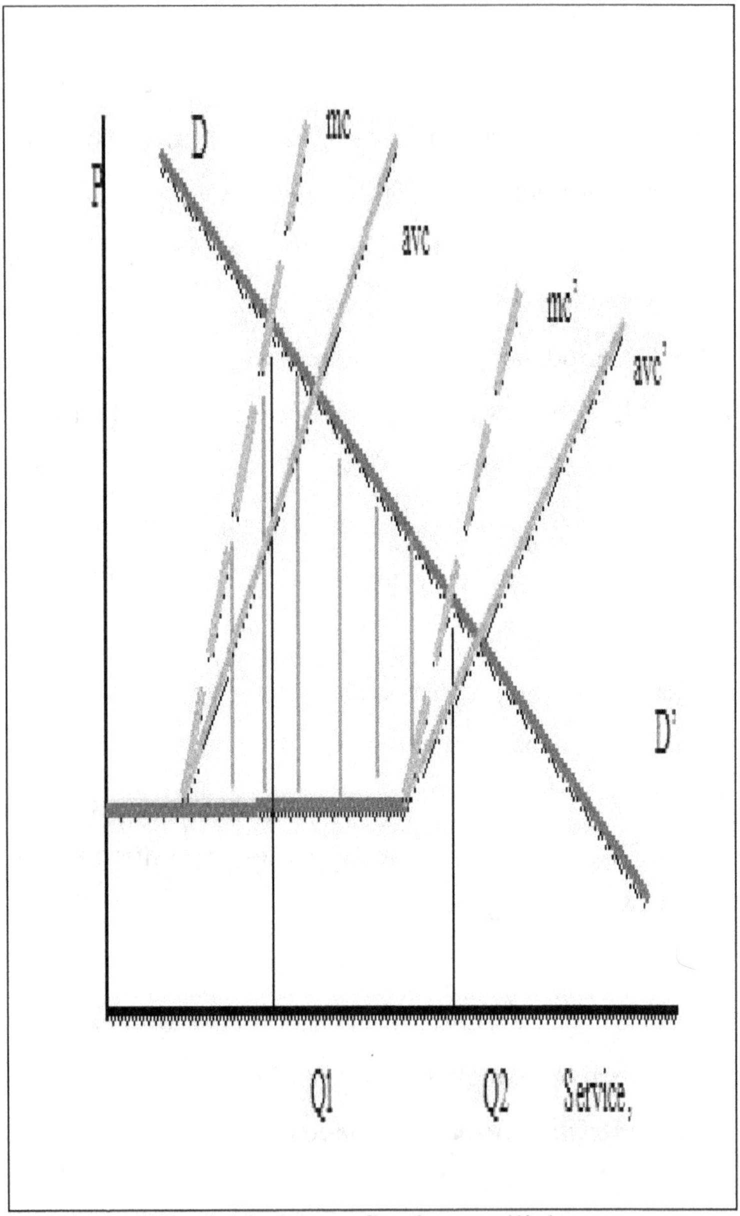

Figure 12. Added Benefits from utilizing new infrastructure.

Producer Surplus

Total cost of all variables used in production of quantity Q, are the values under the curve identified by OSDQ.

The curve is supply curve, which is the marginal cost curve of production function. In case of perfect competition condition, the profit can go the zero, while rent or producer surplus is greater than zero.[5] In this graph, Producers' surplus is shown by SCD. This goes to the suppliers of the firms' productive variables.

Figure 13 shows producer's surplus or rent.

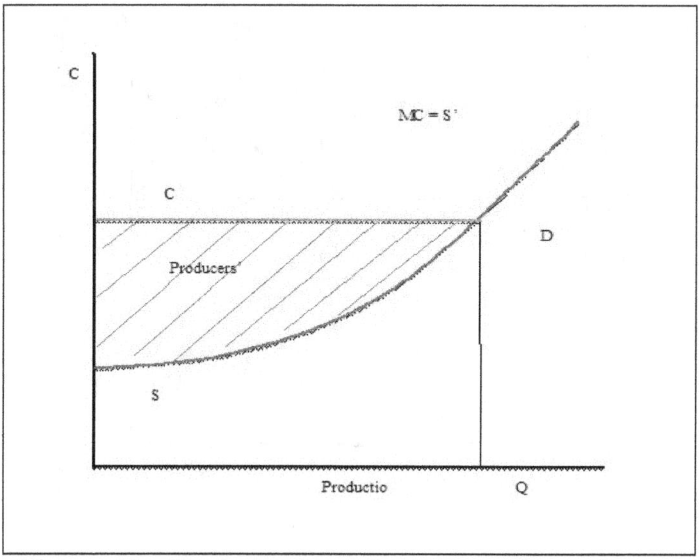

Figure 13. Producers' surplus, or rent in perfect competition.

Figure 14 shows the increase in the producers' surplus after the injection of technologies has shifted the supply curve outward. The area designated as D1D2S', shows the difference, and the increase in the producer's surplus, after a technological change has shifted the supply curve. The price remains the same by assumption.

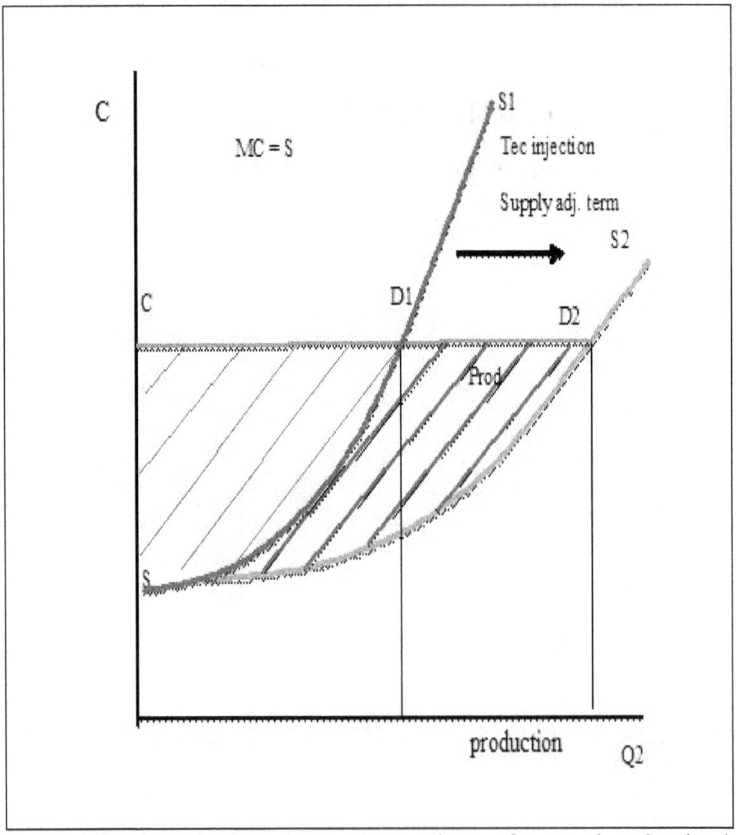

Figure 14. Producers' surplus, after technological injection, and supply curve shift.

The alterations of certain conditions influence the ceteri paribus and the market conditions, therefore, the arithmetic of benefit calculation in the economy. When a technological injection expands the supply curve outward, the consumer can afford to buy more of the same good or service at the lower price. The consumer surplus increases by amount of the present larger surplus less the previous amount of nominal surplus.

Figure 15 shows the effect of such technological injection. In addition, S1S2P' is this producer surplus under the demand curve.

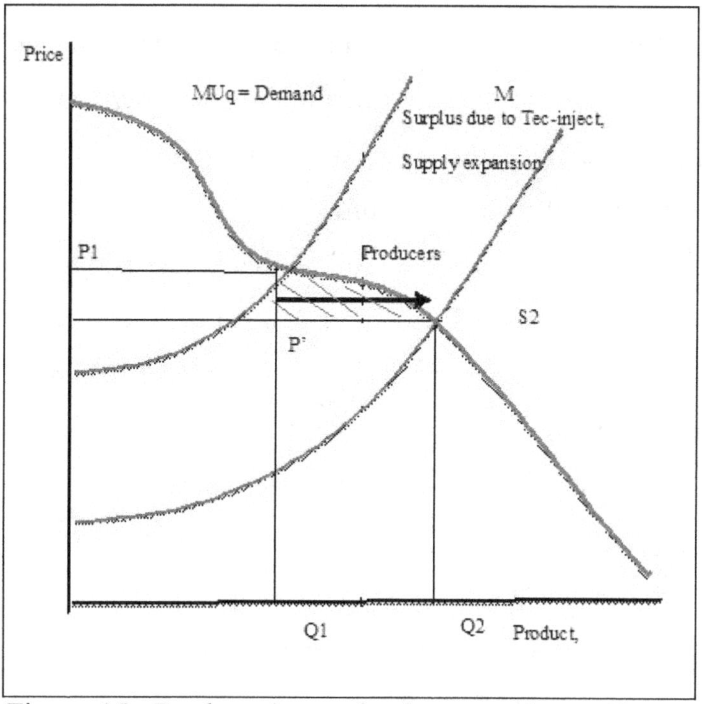

Figure 15. Producer's surplus increase due to Tec-injects and supply expansion.

Consumer Surplus

Consumers and producers that come into the market place gain an additional degree of satisfaction per each additional unit they buy or sell, until the value of the additional unit drops to null. That is the last unit traded. The accumulation of these added benefits are titled consumer and producer surpluses, which is measured.

When marginal utility of each item consumed equals, the marginal cost of the production of each unit, goods and services prices, consumer purchases the most possible basket of goods and services, subject to his or her budgetary constraints.[6] What the consumer purchase has a nominal price and shadow value to the consumer above the market price that is the nominal worth of individual consumer surplus for each purchase.

That odd item, a golf club at the garage sale sold for $10, while the buyer thinks it was $80 at the sport outlets, just last week. Therefore, the consumer buys it feeling it was a good buy.

The rare painting of dead western artist of "bovine roping," sold at $50 at the church rummage sale, consumer buys it, because it looks good. The buyers googled it (look it up on the internet), and then ran it down to the local dealer, he was told $50,000 or more at a real auction! The arbitrages $40 for the golf club, and $50,000 less expenses, are the consumers' surpluses. The consumer obviously cannot measure the astatic of the painting, but he or she can measure consumer surplus nominal index. The former example is not sufficient to increase the real income; however, in the latter example the real income will be much higher after the sale. Therefore, the welfare of at least the seller will have increased substantially.

All those people seen at garage sales are there under the dictate of consumer surplus economic model, even if they did not know it. They seek the largest arbitrages, they can find, if they understood they are there to increase their consumers' surpluses.

In figure 16, total utility of q versus how much the consumer pays for it, constitute consumer surplus. Total revenue spend on the q is shown by OPD'Q. The demand curve is constructed under certain assumptions. Perfect competition and ceteris paribus as we have studied it are complex assumptive construct to uphold.

Figure 16 shows consumer surplus from utilizing each additional product q. Consumer surplus is shown by DD'P.

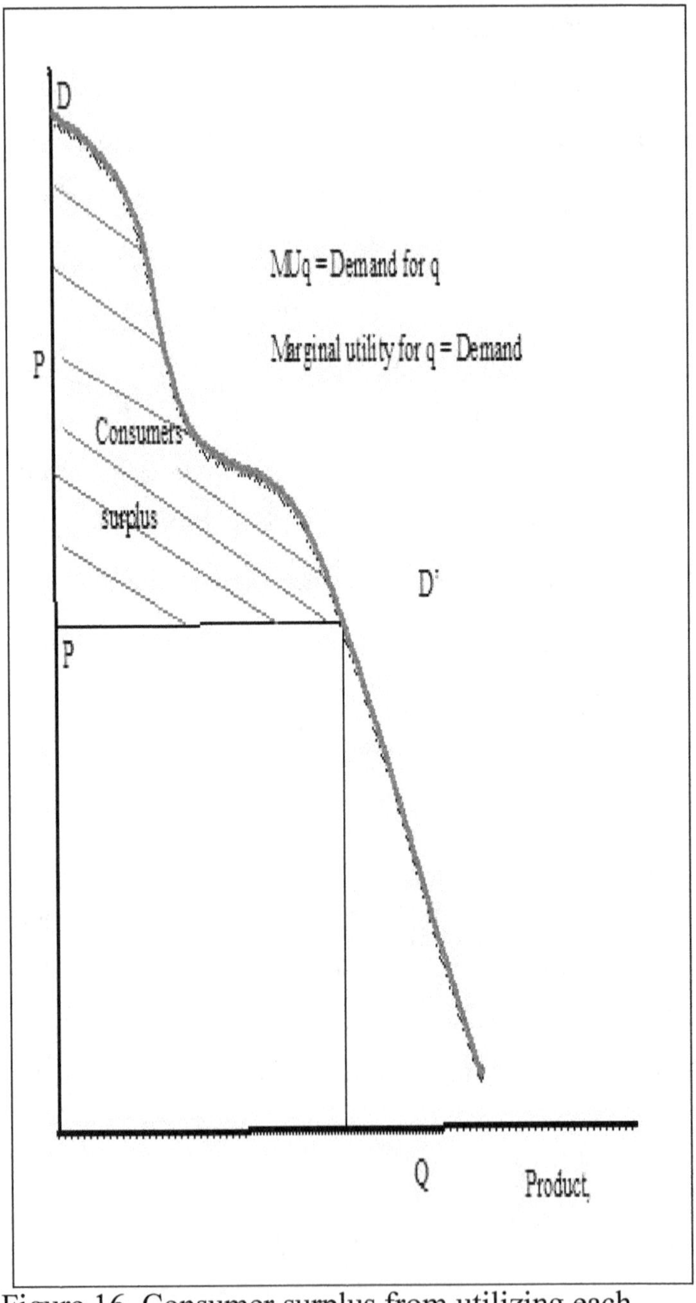

Figure 16, Consumer surplus from utilizing each additional product q.

It does help to understand what they are. These assumptions are perfect knowledge of market participants, population size, tastes, prices of all other goods and services, given incomes, nominal or real, thus distribution issues. The changes can alter elasticity and shapes of demand and supply curve, thus the benefit estimations.[7] While we use equalities rather than equations, there is a need for cautious analytical comprehensions.

The demand curve is downward sloping; therefore, it is not a case of Geffin good. The money income is assumed constant. In this specific case, a reduction in price of his consumption good increases the benefit to that consumer. It has the same effect as rise in the real income, thus it is an increase in the consumer welfare.

Figure 17 shows the shorter-term effect of technologic injection and the related price adjustment. The consumer surplus increase is shown by PDD'P'. Figure 18 shows the effect of technological injection, which has expanded the demand outward.

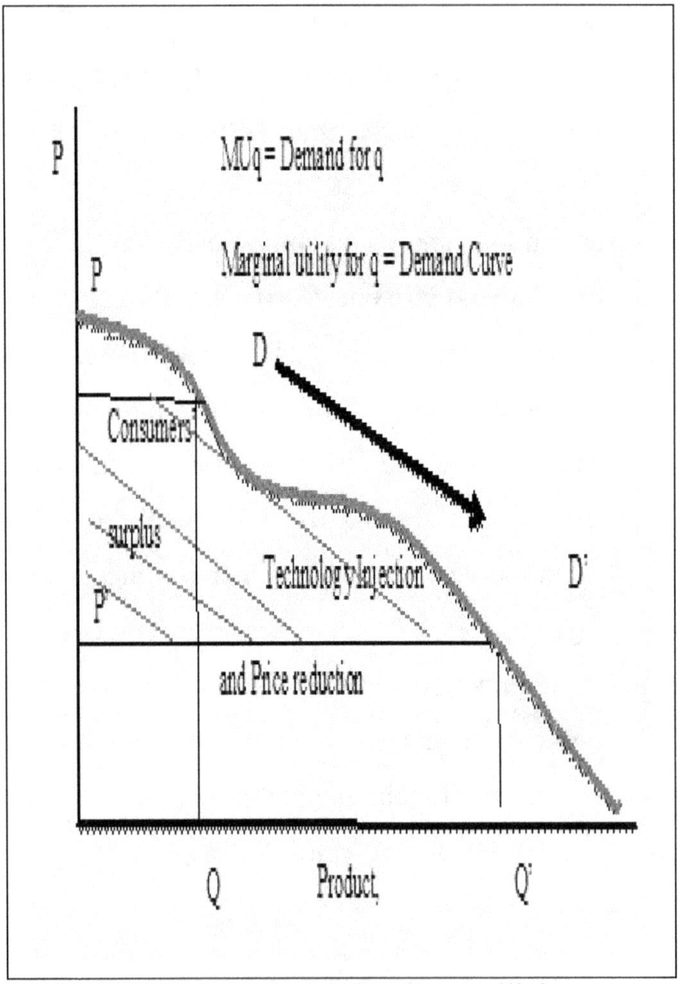

Figure 17. Consumer surplus from utilizing each additional product q.

Figure 18 shows Consumers' surplus increase due to Tec-injects and demand shift.

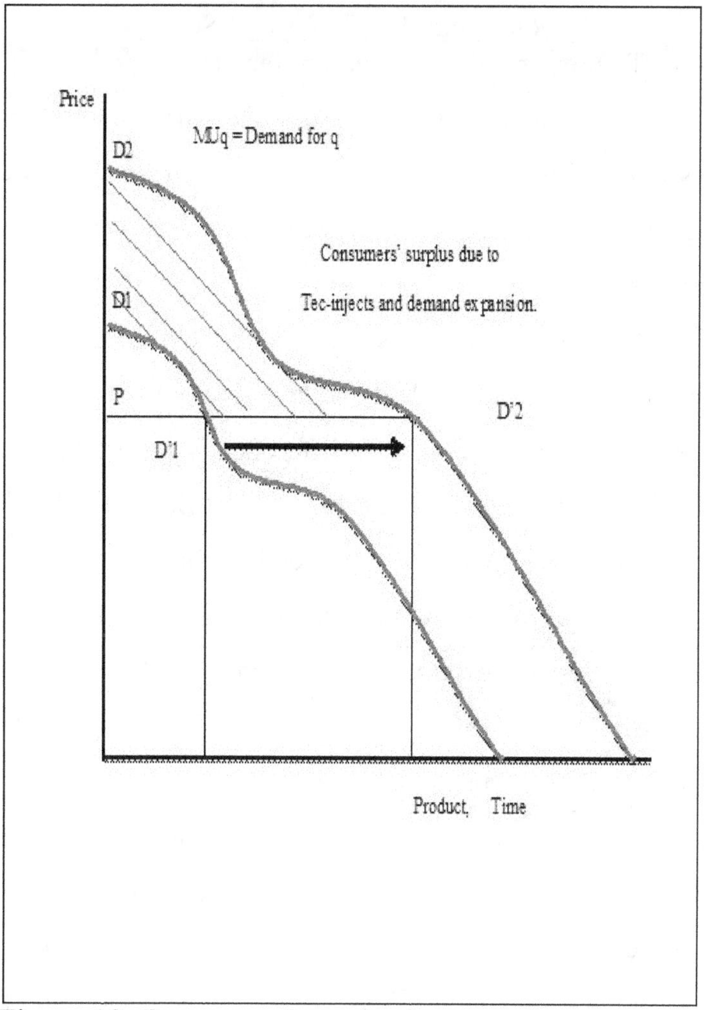

Figure 18. Consumers' surplus increase due to Tec- injects and demand shift.

Figure 18 shows the effect of technological injection, which has expanded the demand outward, prices, and nominal income staying the same ceteris paribus, D1D2D'2D'1 shows the consumer surplus increases due to the technological injection.

Technology Injections and Surpluses

The technical advancement leads to expansion of curves, the downward sloping demand curve, and the positively sloping supply curve. In order to measure the consumer and producer's surpluses, the price is assumed constant.

Figure 19, Surpluses increase due to Technological injection, which expands demand and supply curve outward. Consumer surplus difference is shown as SS'1D'2. The producer surplus is identified by S1D'2D'.

The implication of increases in appropriate technological injections benefits both the consumers and the producers proportionally. Therefore, in figure 19 the industrial benefit from technological injections are felt and motivate both parties to encourage the increase of technological injections, and advancement of the knowledge in the economic activities. This proof of science contribution to industries, which still the anti-science crowds, the political biased few, and motivated luddites have difficulties with its overt implication.

The proof traveled well from Persian Empire, Chinese's expansive history, from Asia, Middle East, and Africa to southern and northern Eurasia to Americas. It is somewhat difficult, even overtly moronic to intellectually push arguments similar to defending a square wheel argument in the face of the evidence, faith does not does not make one closed minded, or logically incapable of studying the evidences.

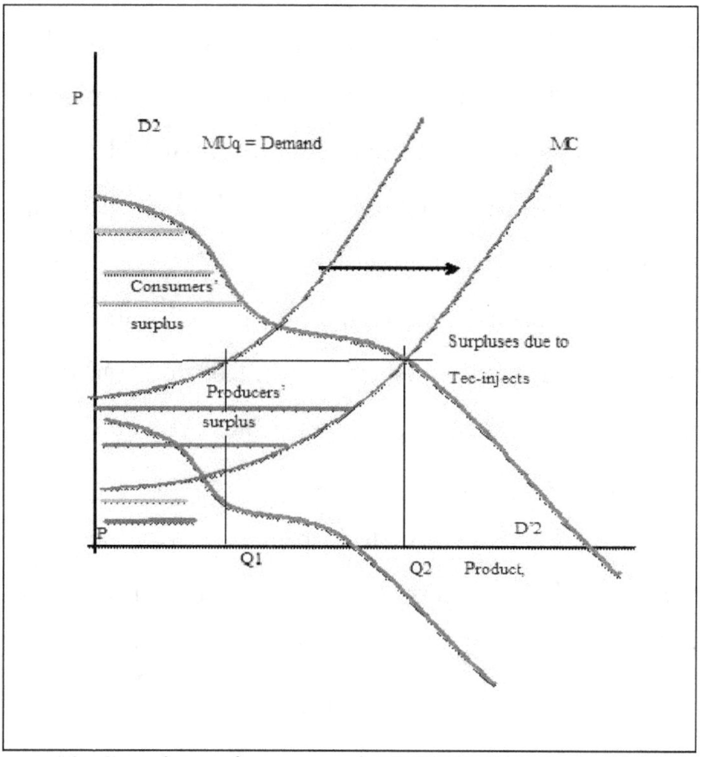

Figure 19, Surpluses increase due to Tec-injects causing supply and demand shifts.

The Distribution Theory Implication in Teconomics

The policy implication of limited resource allocation, requires distribution of limited variables as inputs to production of commodities goods and services (including technologies), and distribution of goods and services among various the consumers, and the maintenance of economic functionality on a slight growth path determines the sustainability of a productive and developing economy.

Optimization in Microeconomic and welfare theory of economics means the operational maximization of resource or produce uses in satisfaction of consumer utility function.[8] That is, in Pareto optimality formulation we will find marginal utility ratios of goods and services equals their prices, and costs ratios.[9]

The producers' profit function is set for maximization subject to the variable cost of wages, salaries, and rents. The marginal product ratios of variables are equal to the ratio of wages, rents, and wages of variables.

In recent political history, redistribution theory, exchange and value theory, socialism, red baiting and other issues have been utilized to cloud and confuse the proper discussions and implementation of distribution theory. Since it is a necessity economic tool for any functional market economic theory. This has been done for the following reasons. One reason is it maintains a broken political economic model to keep taxes lower than functionally possible in a macro economy of market oscillations of a market economy. Two is, a dishonest placement of an institutionally fixed arrangement to set pay packages higher in cooperate executive markets. Three, a most perverse new political tool to break social, governmental, and cooperation contracts after, in order to deny workers their portion of pay-packages in their retirements. This is yet another criminally insane idea to underpay variables bellow their equilibrium wages.[10] It is an unhelpful backward move to the Marxian maxim, which called this method of under subsistence pay in microeconomic capital production market as a brutal method. John Bates Clark concluded his economic theory of distribution from marginal productivity theory of distribution.[11] Clark could have not had these levels of abuses and machinations in mind. The negative externalities implied are too large to be ignored.

In modern economies, when we here about free market, the assumptive foundations are about perfect competition in the free market economies. However, when it comes to redistribution in modern economies, the vandalized discussions only parrot the assumptive foundations, but they are monopolistic or institutionally are twisted to enrich the very few. They falsify the indices to look like everyone is properly employed, productive, and benefiting from proper distributions of wealth. However, the decaying disposable real income of the population presents the ultimate facts.

In that light, the growing deficits are theft of public wealth to enrich the few, a perverse wealth concentration models that has brought many market economies ruination. The socialization of risks and costs, and the privatization and wealth-concentration of beneficial profits are not perfect market solutions. That is not only a road to serfdom, but also a high way to predation. A perfect example is 1920s, and 1930s United State pre-depression economic machinations, and the refined but dishonest verbiages about the gliders and bling of triumphalism predating the prolonged disastrous results. It is astonishing how political organizational culture has also ventured off the democratic path, which parallel perfect completion when voters and not the moneyed-interests are represented.

Small deviations from perfect competition at micro level yields to improper distribution in market place. In aggregation and at macro level, especially in the age of mega corporations and multinationals, there are distributional misadventures, which would yield to unsustainability conditions, stated with comfortable degree of certainty.[12] Author studies the macroeconomics case, and the injection of corrective measures is a technological injection.[13] In the market economies, which are consumer demand driven economies, there are profound influence in form of prolonged negative oscillations of the economy.[14]

For example, the use of real disposable income over time will show if economic welfare has increased, decayed, or remained flat. In same time, the surpluses and the positive externalities have taken place. The impacts are the underperformance, and unemployment due to such insufficient and improper distribution of national wealth.

Income and Substitution Effects of technologies

The study of sustainable development refocuses new resources at serious global issues. Water use, energy source and use impact on global warnings, health and food (feed) shortages, or miss allocations, global population explosions in post regional wars, are not new problems. However, the recognition of the magnitudes and speed of collective impacts of mainly consumer oriented technologies and production processes on minimum sustainable bio-diversity is so pronounced and immediate that ignoring it will have consequences. Not in alarmists' way, that the life had changed behind hope in a nihilistic polemics, but some species have already paid for this with their permanent vanishing acts.

Therefore, doing nothing, and not even studying the matter is a foolish notion. Abusing resources in madness of crowd mass hysteria, wasteful world war revisionism, militarism beyond defense, government-size waste and fraud, and destructive movements leading the financial impulsions common to readerships of the last millennium are not road maps. Perpetuating famine, diseases like AID, Malaria, and other viral infections, hegemonic bents, and violent political movements are not glory ideas. Humanity cannot easily survive intact the impacts of these manufactured-self-destructive cycles. Such silly delusions and other miss-interpretations of modernity need more contemplation in true democracies, free intellectual environment, sound international laws, and international courts, which will need to be reintroduction globally, in place of industrialists' group agreements to violate humanitarians' established principles.

If current level of production was being manufactured with early 1900 technologies, the level of death from pollution would even astonish the mindless apologists of the worst kinds of capitalism, as it did in the coal mines of United Kingdom, or industrial smog of North East United States and England in early stages of industrial expansions. Nevertheless, technological changes have evolved in the same two nations and others gradually, to less polluting and toxic production processes and better level of living. Figure 20 explains this phenomenon. The X bundle of goods and services reflect the older technologies requiring increasing usage of carbon base fossil fuels, more polluting than alternative processes.

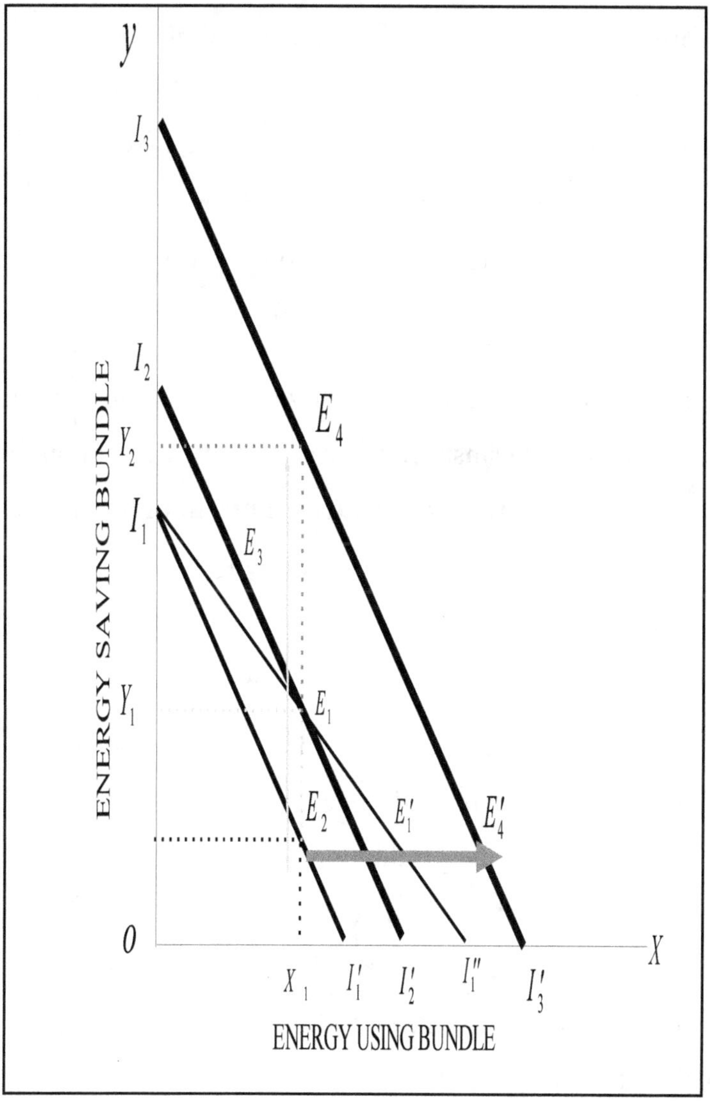

Figure 20. Income and substitution effects on technological change.

The multiple-infrastructural supports, substantial transformation of resources and human capital across the globe, with substantial number of new technologies in the form of institutional arrangements, new laws, private property protections, industries fortify otherwise illusionary sustainable development out of economic growth.

The Y bundle of goods and services are more appropriate and less polluting technologies, conversion to natural gas in manufacturing and transportations sectors of the economy, smaller liquid gas cooking or water-pumps in more villages and rural-settings, better automobile engines (H-cell or dual fuel), and cleaner factories in larger urban cities. Initially along budget line I1 I"2 , at E'1 true price of bundle X will rise showing health and environmental costs, but also as we run out of the fuel. This will lower the consumers' income and it will rearrange the production and redeployment of resources at a different production possibility frontier, shown by income (budget) line I1 I'1 at E2, this shows a major reduction in consumption of X. Consumers will soon recognize benefit of reduction in purchasing X in larger amount of Y they can consume instead, this will increase their real income over time, therefore their welfare will increase, as well. The substitution of Y, for more costly X at E1 is called the substitution effect. This yet again reflect different technologies and resource allocation the positive externalities or consumers' benefits are measured by I1 E1 I'2 and their negative externalities from the change will be equal to I"1 E1 I'2, the loss related to increasing price of X. In a sustainable development model, a large injection of real (disposable) income, more education, and retraining will entice another shifts to using more of Y bundle. At the new budget line I3 I'3, at E4 the consumers will be at a higher welfare level. However, in a developing economy this may prove to be more of a complex proposition than it is proposed on our campuses or political halls, if it even is discussed anymore. Therefore, in most cases, we adopt technologies to arrive at E'4 for sustainable economic developments. Nevertheless, we really need to plan to be at E4 wasting much less of diminishing resources. This results in some very peculiar non-market notions as well. One is that cheaper or subsidized fossil fuel is just beneficial to sustainable advancements of economies. Ignoring efficiencies that market price will generate, or negative externalities, which a true price can modify. If a free car was given to every human on earth will that strictly, benefit humanity. If every village had a coal factory, will the globe survive this benefit? These are example of fallacy of composition, which their negative externalities are not too hard to grasp, but it will not always survive the stronger notions of private gains, and ignorance.

The temporary discourses from the Pareto optimal allocations and economic welfare equilibriums alone can be difficult to overcome. Gather all Nash-disequilibrium you wish, you would not add them up to a Pareto Optimum Equilibrium Stable system. The ample application of Keynes and monetarism was fought past the 1929 business cycle. The conservatism of Hover-ism was circumvented with the World War Two expenditures and reallocation of purchasing powers. The second proposition is totally ignored, or fought as redistribution of income. Often the very people who were helped by it in their mixed economic strategies called it a socialist notion.

It is not without cause that it is hypothesized here, that perfectly free market economies are chronically deflationary, because they tend not to be perfect nor always free, nor legal and political institutions understand the damage they can do to structure as they accumulate rules or centralize power eroding the same systems. It is matter of life and facts that most developing economies do not have the socio-political infrastructure commonly taken for granted in the advanced economies. In addition, moving from one phase to another creates great taxing of fragile systems, and requires not only newer appropriate technologies, but also means to adopt and improve dealing with bottlenecks, as they are formed in the process. These are facts reflected in the major injection of income, as budget line shows. It also reflects the need for food, medicine, the minimum infrastructure required, before any sustainable strategies for economic growth or development can be successfully formulated.

We have accumulated a long list of unfortunate private and governmental attempts to transpose development models, mostly along a projected line towards E'4 in less developing economies. Even gradual and segmental movements toward adaptations of appropriate technologies and the improved production processes will prove more beneficial in the end, when and where such adjustments can be made.

All productions and Pareto optimal allocations of economic activities of supplies and demands fall within the set societal utility of production and consumption frontier.[15] Naturally, all productions possible with all technologies will fall within this set. Social welfare indifference curves reflect choices and satisfaction possible such that there are sets of points, which are preferred and do benefit the global well-beings, and meet minimum required limits for the survival of bio-diversity versus other sets of points. However, we cannot represent this as unique solution points, because we are studying societal norms, individual Pareto Optimal points of satisfaction fall on or within the bounded sets of numbers in the graph, in a way that they are not worst off without benefits, or excluded without sound legal cause or reason, to do otherwise is often to cause harm. It is at E4, which more of appropriate technological advancements and sustainable progress, and higher and improved satisfaction exists using more of Y bundles of goods and services. These are produced using better appropriate technologies, with optimum employment and real income to justify and meet such prices. Either movement from E2 will be a considered an improvement. At E4 we have a higher indifference curve and possibility for sustainable progress in globally active economies.

Figure 21 shows a comparative of the societal utility of productions and consumption (S = D) frontiers, sum of all Pareto possible solutions society chooses from bundles x and y combination possible.

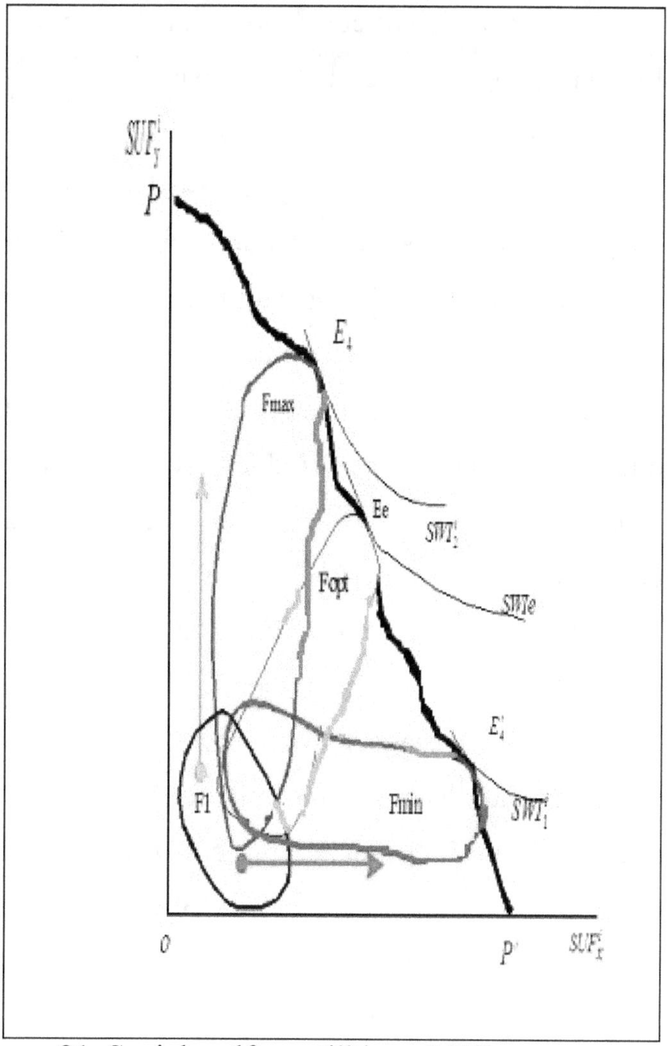

Figure 21, Social welfare utilities of different technological solutions over time.

The duplication of consumptive units has very resource limiting future, globally. The population expansions require innovative scholarships to find the sustainable development comfort zones. The bounded set E4, include more of Pareto Optimum locus of individuals' satisfactions at different levels within the set, with generally more market imperfections and more true costs (externalities linked prices), than at the bounded set (Fopt: optimal). The bounded set {Fi}does not narrow but either stays the same longer, or expand over time, reflecting the intertemporal investment in appropriate technologies and increasing consumer Pareto Optimum and preferred satisfactions in the future by diversifications of resources and prolonging the usage of diminishing resources. This in the set (Fopt), also show initially effect of limited corrective actions in the market place, but reality reflecting market true conditions and narrowing of the set start as pressure on limited resources shows. The narrowing bounded set at E'4 reflects even more of the market imperfections and imperfection of democracies, which stifle rights to vote or opinions and diminishing resources. The general understanding assumes that it is very difficult to set conditions or systems to satisfy humanity in totality, however, satisfying the most 80 percent at (Fopt)-Ee, and 60 percent at (Fmax)and E4, and finally 40 percent at

(Fmin)-E'4 with harming the least seems to be the best condition we can assume at this time. More free competitive markets, and free trades, and free nobilities of capital and workers, a rational currency exchange mechanism will do a lot to minimize harm, where rational beings may exchange their differences rather than engage in conflicts. Each failure, knowingly or otherwise, waste resources, replaces functional systems and reduce trusts in any further attempts to correct fundamental short comings present there or transferred there. Alas, the horrendously poor circumstances and Dickensian inhuman conditions around Asia, Africa, South America, and elsewhere (granted, beside developing economies, positive examples as South Africa exists), these invites the need for ideas to improve level of living globally.

Simply going back to military models of last millenniums will prove to be the most destructive and mutually resource wasting of all options. Even employing the most constructive of the militarists' solution, the Marshal plan, with the old technologies, without thought provoking selections among appropriate modern technologies can be very limiting.

The benefit of non-military appropriate technological advancements will become clear, when they make possible a production possibility frontier reflecting the new transformed economy, which allow for adaptations without triggering the fallacy of composition. The current models duplicating advanced economies' discarded-technologies will trigger the fallacy of composition.

The concept of all nations doing the same thing, producing the same products for jobs or profits is counter intuitive, and conflicts with comparative advantage argument of international trade policy, and fallacy of composition.[16] There are actual hopeful signs. When skipping certain technologies a generation for more efficient ones, like the wired phones for new digital-cell phones, or use of propane instead of wood or coal or oil fuels are adopted readily in a larger segment of the global households not knowing the extend of technologies in an actual advanced economies' households. However, the other wonderful modern technology of communication may yet have other surprises for us. For a long time, the world looked at the implosions of Soviet system, not understanding how communication made comparatives realities so unbearable. That did not materialize after spending three trillion dollars and many fiendish minds in clandestine operations. It came as, the customers of the system turned on their television sets, and the contrasts came around the globe over the satellite antennas in front of people. The world suddenly could vote by their eyes, legs, and opinions. We will revisit this phenomenon again in business cycles, capital concentration, income and wage package economic distortions, and human capital mobility globally, until we can grasp its true significance.[17] A current development around social networking and electronic gadgetries is titled "The Arab Spring," there is a temporary grasp for democratic devolution. Yet, there is the idiom, "hope springs eternal."

A realistic study of global economic conditions leave very few choices away from constructive and cooperative endeavors, however non-passive it gets, toward minimization of conflicts for better cooperation for improved economic employment of resources, human and non-human capital, and shared functioning economies on shrinking productive soils. At times, when humanity is not on one of the many destructive side roads, we are optimistically closer to the path of allowing international trade and finance to expand market economies. Moreover, this will allow for a democratization methodology that encourages democratic supplementations of governments, which can nudge different populations toward economic growth and development.

Notes

[1] Bahman Fakhraie, *Technological Injection, Dynamic New Capital Measurements, and Production Theory in Economics*, (Utah: PhD Dissertation, University of Utah Economics Dept., 2010), https://order.proquest.com/OA_HTML/pqdtibeCCtpItmDspRte.jsp

[2] All variable meet this condition that is, they are greater than zero.

[3] Henderson and Quandt, *Microeconomic Theory; A Mathematical Approach,* 2nd ed., (New York: McGraw-Hill, 1972), 191-199, 280

[4] William J. Baumol, Economic Theory and Operational Analysis, 4th ed., (New Jersey: Prentice-Hall, 1977),573

[5] William J. Baumol, Economic Theory and Operational Analysis, 4th ed., (New Jersey: Prentice-Hall, 1977),595 [or ibid 595]

[6] This is when an under payment bellow subsistence level, will have a magnified impact on demand and supply, thus on the aggregates of the national and global economy. The ceteris paribus conditions do not apply.

[7] Edward Joshua Mishan, *Cost-Benefit Analysis*, 4th Ed. London: Unwin Hyman, 1988, 55.

[8] Jules Dupuit, uses monetary units to measure consumer 'surplus as the area under the demand curve and the paid price line.
J. Dupuit, "On the Measurement of Utility of Public works," (1844)

K. J. Arrow and T. Scitovsky, eds., *Reading in Welfare Economics*, *American Economic Association*, Vol. XIII, Homewood Illinois: Richard D. Irwin, Inc., 1969

[9] Vilfredo Pareto, analytical work in constraint maximization to obtain maximum utility of each consumer, without harming another in Pareto optimality.

[10] Kerr ed., *Das Kapita*l, Vol. I, Chapter VI, 189-192.

[11] John Bates Clark, *The Distribution of Wealth*, New York: The Macmillan Company, 1899, 7-8
"the different classes of men <people> who combine their forces in industry have no grievances against each other… <under the perfect competition the distribution> gives every agent of production the amount of wealth which that agent create."

[12] Ibid, 1-2.

[13] Bahman Fakhraie, *Technological Injection, Dynamic New Capital Measurements, and Production Theory in Economics*, (Utah: PhD Dissertation, University of Utah Economics Dept., 2010), https://order.proquest.com/OA_HTML/pqdtibeCCtpItmDspRte.jsp

[14] John Bates Clark, *The Distribution of Wealth: A Theory of Wages, Interest, and Profits*, (New York: The Macmillan Company, 1899), 9.

[15] Hirshleifer Jack, "*Price Theory and Applications*", (New Jersey, Prentice-Hall, Inc. 1976),438-443

[16] Professor Samuelsson beggar-my-neighbor policy example is also relevant.

Paul A. Samuelson, *Economics*, (San Francisco, McGraw-Hill Book Company, 1979), 663

CHAPTER 11

MACROEOCONOMICS OF TECHNOLIGICAL CHANGE

While the basic inputs for production have been known as workers, capital, and natural resources, the skills involved have changed over time. Theoretically, the dynamics involved have been studied under different sub-headings. Growth theory, macro-economy, and development theory have evolved some time apart from each other, and mostly by use of static analysis of the classical economists (Mill, Marshall). The earlier part of this century, the post-war-era economists were finding solutions for the major changes of the consumers' demand as they and their families take a war-era saver or hoarder characteristic, which seems to be hard to change after the war, even in modern times.

The Keynes focuses on unemployment, and the F.D. Roosevelt New Deal was expunging the negative feelings of fear and poverty out of desperate populations. These were some of the well-known concerns. Another line of theoretical evolution from Austria was concern with capital, interest rates, and system analysis, which had a longer outlook to it. Eugen Von Bohm-Bawerk, Ludwig Von Mises, and the American Irving Fisher covered their concerns with interest and capital, Mises, F. A. Hayak, Joseph A. Schumpeter, and Evsey D. Domar were concern with the systems, and the misunderstanding and miscalculations of capital by the system. This last concern gathers force and importance; they are studied in chapter 1, and chapter 2. The human and non-human capital also reflects societal pool of technologies embodied in all capital forms, and disembodied skills about use of capital and yet other sets of technological tools. These tools can be a new mix of monetary and fiscal policies, or other governmental and societal skills, as I have introduced them to coordinated and encourage the adoption of new technologies in political freed, quasi-market economies (formerly communist nations). All nations are evolving and expanding dynamically, as progressive and constructive uses of such complex mixes impacts the many nations forming the developing human society.

Emerging democracies often look wishfully on the finished products of the developed nations, and their present advanced economies, hoping to copy readymade systems. Nevertheless, this often proved a self-defeating first step. We often forget it took European nations from the fifteenth to the twentieth century to get at their present developed mixed economies. Even with a good many readymade technologies transferred, it took the United States good part of two hundred years to obtain the present status quo. Japan is one of the modern miracles of transferred, copied, imitated, and self-made post-war technologies have had twenty-five years of capital and technological transfusions. Japan is a homogenous society, with a strong and stable mixture of familiar and command system societal characteristics, very hard to find anywhere else, except maybe for the Germanic culture. Yet, Japanese population and their age compositions have modified the older economic growth model. However, most nations and states have more diverse and heterogeneous mixed populations, thus more complex problems to resolve.

The Real Flow of National Products

The historical perspective in physiocrats and classical economists as noted in chapter one point to the micro-foundations of macro-economic, in the economic division of output. Nationally, such divisions and distributions are primal to all economies. The divided portions of real national output constitute the share of production factors from real national production of all goods and services.

Therefore, beyond a threshold subsistence level of current consumption, a portion of individuals' share of output may be put aside for future consumption. In that portion saved of real output, national accumulations and savings, investments, capital formations, new capital formations, and technological progress, thus economic growth and potential development, find their fuel. Thus, a portion of national output will go to workers, to lender, to owners of land, resources and capital good, and all other service providers involved in the national output production process.

The National Production Process Flow Model

The modern mixed economies are far more complex than the classical economists envisioned them. That number of economic agents, agencies, and institutions involved are far more than what even believed possible, or survivable from the Malthusian model point of view. Nevertheless, an important part of technological progress has been the evolution of governmental and private agents and institutions engaging in national production process, and with the expansion of goods and services produced and consumed nationally. So increasingly more advanced flow charts have been produced to show such economic activities.[1]

The Theoretical Origins of the Model

Since Physiocrats used the blood flow in the human body to explain the exchange mechanism and functioning of the relatively free-market systems, the flow charts of various complexities have been applied to simplify and explain economic exchanges.

The more complex Department of Commerce models explain in detail about the flow of goods and services in the economy. This model is used to show the complexities of advanced modern mixed economies. It shows the flow of goods and services from private and public institutions to consumers from the markets of institutionally-set prices and taxes (fees, etc.), and consumers paying out of their disposable income obtained from performance of their services for wages, salaries, earned interests, dividends (and capital gains), and government transfers (entitlement).

The Kaleckian flow showed a distributive aspect of circular flow. The Kaleckian's flow model elucidates the shares of output going to workers and capitalists, and in favor of the capitalists, as the traditional economic theories still mistakenly generalized. The capital owners (capitalists) were in position of saving, because their share of output (production surplus) were much larger than the iron law of wages (institutionally) pegged the workers' shares of output Therefore, the capitalists were the only ones able to save and invest. Moreover, a major source of class division was taken for granted.

Why do we need a new way to explain the flow of

goods and services made by the national production process? The problem, which is the historical division between workers and owners of capital, has been addressed. The evolution of ideas to development of technologies was explained. Moreover, the need for maximum involvement of all production agents in the process, for optimum level of technological progress was pointed out. Besides, the evolution of capital ownership, and residual capital ownership in corporate shares, in modern mixed economies (capitalist systems) have run far ahead of all academic, political, and international arguments, the isms, and older production relationships. Then, among the last remaining macro-economic problems to explain are how to minimize the instabilities, which dynamism of technological changes create, after the waves of new technological injections in most economies with other (business) cyclical. Therefore, an important number of institutional innovations have taken place. The technological progresses accumulated have created a critical need for the new circular model.

The Schumpeterian Circular Flow

The Schumpeterian circular flow without the presence of change-agents is represented as the aggregate equilibrium of all economic activities.[2] It is defined here as the static equilibrium state. The model historically fits most agrarian economies. The consumptive motives dominate economic behavior. The only capital good is land. Heredity determines the ownership of land institutionally. Workers are paid by their productivity and by the Iron Law of Wages. They are not paid much more than subsistence levels. Therefore, they consume all their income. Thus, no savings or accumulation takes place. Such an economy will find it difficult to initiate major expansion out of its present circular flow without agents of change, major innovational expansion in their present institutions, or external economic forces.

The level of wages at subsistence, lack of institutional accommodations of savings, institutional blocks against ownership have far more impacts on the continuity of status quo, the static equilibrium circular flow will continue unabated. The consumption motivation as defined by Schumpeter or Paul Sweezy has an impact, too. Without the essential financial institutions and sufficient interest rates, consumption is postponed, at least, by the capitalists (landowners). For example, capital consumption here has been ignored. It is equal to soil erosion or damaged waterways on the farmland, which would require landowners saving for repairs or improvements of such capital assets.

The agents of change, unlike consumers or producers,

are missing as an integral part of most other economic theories. The entrepreneurs are identified by J. A. Schumpeter to initiate the needed changed in the economy, which would remain in an equilibrium state with circular flow. The entrepreneurs are not confused with inventors, but are identical to innovators. Like all other economic agents, they interchange their task as consumers, producers, managers, inventors, and innovators. Nevertheless, their ultimate capacity to see and act on any potentially higher profitable situation makes them unique contributors to economic progress. In addition, without them, theoretically at later stages of perfect competition, all firms would operate at shut-off points, no major surplus, no savings, and no accumulation, no technological progress. Moreover, if that were the case for all economic activities for the whole system, then no economic growth and development would be possible.

Critique of the Schumpeterian Model

There are few objections to the assumptions and definitions of J. A. Schumpeter. Which have to be modified before the proper appreciation and contributions of his work to this study are noted.

J. A. Schumpeter identified change as economic growth, which is not quite the same.[3] Even the change in many internal economic variables may or may not cause economic growth, let alone sustainable economic growth or development. Change for change's sake may alter relations and balances enough to stress the balance identified by the set intersection of socio-political and economic forces. It could build up conflictive energy among the population to block constructive changes due to economic growth. Another important argument that is historically inescapable if not a truism is the idea of postponement of consumption, which forms savings and capital formation, innovation, and technological progress out of past accumulation. Schumpeter himself rolled out the arguments. Perhaps some logic exists about the past accumulations being fixed in the present circular flow, when the method of production and the processes are in effect. However, the present condition is built upon the past accumulative efforts initiated by the consumers first, then by the other accumulated skills in the specialists' classes involved. Then, the fixed capital in the method of production also is accumulated.

The redefinition of J. B. Clark's automatic synchronization as was noted excluded the dynamic effects of capital consumption over time. Because J. B. Clark's capital fund and Schumpeter's cost-return versus profit-loss adjustment mechanism do not identify the agencies or fund the process of technological advancement, nor do they counteract against the negatives of capital consumption.

Modification of the following factors affects the Schumpeterian circular flow model. One is the removal of the institutional blocking of capital goods (workers') ownership. The replacement of the Iron Law of wages by more modern free agency of workers, and the monopsony-monopoly nature of labor-union versus management team-wage settings, have created a higher real disposable income to allow workers' accumulation to take place. Two is the evolution of financial institutions to accommodate accumulation and formation of capital. Three is institutionalization of technological progress. Four is the recognition, evolution, and accumulation of entrepreneurship as a new and internal economic agency.

Static Equilibrium and the Dynamics of Technological Change

The circular flow in the Schumpeterian model has a tendency toward static equilibrium, both before and after innovational shocks has been absorbed by it.[4] The static equilibrium he defined as the "static" idea of J. B. Clark. The circular flow, static equilibrium meets the conditions of optimum allocations of resources due to price adjustment formations, allowed in the relatively free market. The dynamic changes to the system have the following characteristics. One is they are internal shocks to the economic systems, not to the exclusions of other economic systems (international trade and competitions). However, excluding external aspects to the economic systems, like the natural disasters.[5] Two is they are innovational shocks affecting economic variables (capital, population, and consumers' tastes). Three, they take place over longer time spans. Four is, after dynamic changes have taken place, the new circular flow and economic relationships would tend to settle at the new equilibrium.

However, the new equilibrium level will be at a different equilibrium from any previous levels. The new and improved static equilibrium will not imply all relative factor prices are held constant, even in real terms. Because certain factors will experience increases or decreases in market value, as new production methods meets the oscillations of the demand and supply for them, ex post to technological progression.

The same tendencies toward static economic equilibrium also appear in the free market economic systems. It seems to be the tendency toward a set of equilibrium arrangements formed out of the internal constructive-competitive forces even after a major shift or shock to a lesser-developed or smaller economic system has occurred. That adds the basic attributes of free markets to find marginal worth (wage, rent, interest, profit) relative to marginal contributions, even in some of the value-confused systems like in the non-market economics (with state-capitalism or communism), or like the capitalist top-management salary and benefit systems. There is also reluctance to move away from any stable or relatively stable system at any equilibrium, because it is a known system relative to the unknown of the new and possibly unstable system. The reward in favor of change is a higher level of living for individuals (also a higher social welfare frontier attainment), but the change also will have a high-risk probability that it will remain unstable for an uncertain length of time for a lower social welfare frontier attainment.

There is an experiment, which may visually help with these points. Crystal salt, soy seeds, and sand are poured into three equally sized balloons. Periodically, the crystal salt balloon has to be adjusted to hold more salt. The salts are reshaped, organized, and well ordered into a perfect half-globe, and additional room is made for more. The soy seed balloon takes far less adjustment and holds more soy seeds. Sand balloons would hold even more. There is also a risk that beyond a given point, all balloons burst. More recent theoretical works (chaos theorem), studied systems' responses to changes in the initial conditions and found some systems do respond less rationally to a given set of initial stimulations, enough that futuristic projections would often be in error. Mind you, economics is partially praxeology based on human behavior. Moreover, human behavior, taste, and preference changes over time and in response to the changes, which economic growth and development would cause over time.

So dynamically, we can depend on change including changes in both human behavior and all future economic systems and models based on those conditions. In addition, certain well-behaved models become chaotic beyond a threshold level. Moreover, the last point, technological systems in operation can have a different break-up limitation, at a higher threshold level than their human operations. The result proves too costly to the human elements. The newer fighter jets proved this most drastically.

It is no less drastic when a society (the human element) with different internal stability threshold levels (i.e., homogeneous versus heterogeneous societal system) with democratic verses less democratic political systems face transferred technologies specifically (in forms of socio-political reforms, new economic units, new markets, new factories, etc.) in any or all of their economic growth and development models.

Why would society take on such bad odds and risk all

for the changes to come? Because, it is possible that some societies like the first cave societies know the improvements of any or most of their conditions depend on taking the risks to change. Furthermore, those changes, those modifications and modernizations, will improve the lives of many in the cave, the group, the society.

In modern times, economists theorize that hopefully others' situation if not improved in the groups; at least, they are not worsening by these changes! In the cave people days, no such luxuries were afforded; the ultimate risks were present in most case. If these new ways mean new technologies, in new capital, in new methods and new way of life, so be it. If the odds are known or estimated, and as the majority of the society perceive these risks, or see the result of appropriate technology-adoptions on the societies around them, rate of diffusion of the technologies will increase. Then, modern societies are not taking such great chances when they adopt new and improved technologies, prudently.

Nevertheless, the majorities are led by socio-political manipulations, ignorant of the negatives, or oversold on militarists' technologies beyond defensive capabilities. Thus, the prolonged struggles then political difficulties multiply, and economy suffers.

The forces for equilibrium are partly out of socio-political needs for less confrontation and partly out of more comfortable economic arrangements among the group for the sake of continuity and longevity of beneficial (marginal rewards) of relatively free trades. It is not clear or certain that all changes, developments, or system shifts are always stable. Often, at some uncertain point, a point of political combustion causes longer-term instabilities. Even after seemingly minor regional economic changes, socio-political alterations needed such developments to become sustainable. The more homogenous, more democratic cultures have better patience capacity than less democratic and more heterogynous cultures. Thus, logically decentralization, democratization, and free trade combined with alertness for the adjustment of combustive mall distribution of income among such developing or developed hopeful would benefit longer-term stability causes.

In fact, the intent of saving is future consumption. Moreover, future consumption would depend on present investments. It is by investment that growth is possible, which makes development probable. In addition, the dynamic process involves change, metamorphic evolutionary equilibrium states bigger, better, or just different from the previous states of equilibrium.

However, along the way, either continuously by

means of democratic election changes or periodically in less-politically developed system by means of governmental interventions, legislative adjusters, monetary or fiscal political, tax-subsidy adjusters, the over-all system stabilities at each level of equilibrium along the way must be maintained. These are hardly the true classic laissez-faire, hidden-hands economic policies. At least, we are talking about a relatively mixed economy with especially alert and flexible, and more stable government.

Aggregate Demand Slide

The postponement of consumption in aggregate determines the magnitude of current savings. Nevertheless, the aggregate demand is dependent on the income, thus wages of individuals in the economy.

These determinants are the level of past savings and the rate of their conversion to proper ratio of capital goods to produce and meet the present levels of consumptive and productive goods and services.

The Monetary Relationships

Wages among the production agents ought to reflect productivity and the organizational worth and values allocated to each members or agents of production, in advanced industrial economies. Alas, historically, they are often set out of the competitive but constructive conflicts of the workers' trade unions and managements or firms' representatives sometimes with the assistance of the federal (governmental) mediators. Traditionally, they also reflect culture, discriminations and negative power plays, or habits.

The wage rigidity in current prices does not grant high real wages. Thus, it is overlooked as the new complementary source of saving and capital formation. Prices (CPI) could easily increase at a higher rate than the rate increase in current wages, enough to ensure stable and declining real income levels. The accumulated rate of taxation at federal, state, local, sales, or value-added taxation would further deteriorate the real disposable income of consumers enough to leave no positive margin to save. In addition, inappropriate wage setting among the workers according to the institutional arrangements (among the board teams) about the divisions between management and workers could easily harm the productivity bases appropriate division of output among the worker-consumers, enough to affect income, savings, and sales, thus profit.

Some helpful non-scientific hints can help. One, the wage gap should not start larger than two to one in early stages of development, and 3-5 to one in more prosperous stages of development. The ratio gap limits counteract against initial negative and uncomfortable reactions against the new changes and the socio-political constraints technology progress entails in systems. Two, the highest-paid wages must be less in number (often one per group or organization) and not exceed two to five times the averages of the lowest paid workers. Because high-multiple executive salaries would take fund out of profit, capital reformation, new capital investments, and the production process, just as high wages of all workers would do. Three, the average of the lowest paid workers out to be above a comfortable level of poverty given the sum of prices for the basket of goods and services required for such a modest living.

Keep in mind that education, health, and general well-being of workers and their family members are closely correlated to their productivity, and the higher real wages. Preoccupation of workers in their fields of their non-specializations only wastes time from their most effective use. Thus orderly care, prolonged sickness due to improper or no medical services, time in queue for other goods and services, are all time out of the best uses for workers time. In addition, they are more frequently predominate uses of time in most of the developing nations. In fact, if any aspect of the work involved governmental regulatory services, waste can be measured in months rather than days, instead of hours. The control in private organizations will reflect productivity, where wages are equal to margin productivity of workers. Thus, laws ought not apply or limit the revenue of individuals from all entrepreneurial sources, while they enact gap-limited ratios for individual enterprises. For example, they use legal and legitimate multiple investments for other sources of income. That, should initially and often be rewarded because it helps the motivated, skillful workers to also be investors, factory shareholders (capitalism), and multi-productive sources of national wealth. Remember the development, modification, and application of new technologies often is initiated and is helped at the many worker levels. Thus, the difficult part will be the creative taxation to fill the gap between the needs of the unskilled, orderly, and youths for health care, education, retraining, job-creation, and investment targeting, which normal private entrepreneurial skills do not cover and basic worker pay cannot pay for.

When all else fails, even advanced economies are left with no choice other than to get back to the real basic of wage settings, equal to the ratio of the marginal product of inputs. The relatively suitable, functional, and democratic political systems would give the national, those uniquely untenable flexible political realists, whom will take the spiked punch away from their best constituencies' party. In other words, none of the following, the democracies, and the mixed relatively frees market economies, and mostly dynamical human behaviors are about perfections or perfectionism. They mainly are about second best, third-best sets solutions and systems, which allow for human errors and multiple failings, learning and relearning, readjustments and retraining. Thus, allowing for controlled experimentalism and scientific discoveries, not relativism (the social kind), but relative chances of error. In fact, when science passes through intellectual barriers to absolute relative to human factors, it is the human agents who tend to lose the most, often en masse, until new limits are learned. Two examples are as follows. One is the sub-atomic technologies, nuclear energy conversion, and a more complex mixed system of electronic, hydraulic, metallurgy, embodied, and disembodied technologies. Two is in super-sonic jet plains and their human operators with humans' physiological limits. Alas, we are more concerned about such a mix of technologies with less-trained and more heterogeneous human societies around the globe.

Real Disposable Income, Consumption, Long Term

In addendum to the static Keynesian functional relation of current real consumption with the real disposable income, the consumptive behavior of individual in long-term tends to differ relative to their productivity, their accumulated skills, savings, and knowledge. Thus, their disposable income will differ.

The permanent income hypothesis and the life-cycle hypothesis were developed to give a more dynamic monetary explanation. At the time, Dr. Milton Freedman was concern with the dynamic issue. He confronted and advised about the essentials assumptive corrections, thus the economic growth took place. Unfortunately, during the last three decades, the data shows that real disposable income, and real wages have stayed the same or declined, which support the FRDI model, leading to stagnation or stagflation conundrums experienced during the 1970-80 business cycles. There are no guarantees about future reoccurrences of the same problems, given we use the same assumptive bases. Therefore, this reaffirms the paradox in the monetary neoclassical model.[6] Alas, growing real disposable income GRDI, developed here, will further explain consumers' long-term behaviors, adding an explanation void of money a non-money illusions, between workers and the so-called capitalists. The differences are learned skilled and accumulation of human capital possible with a higher level of real disposable income. The two models below will relate these modern works with our analysis.

Flat Real Disposable Income Model

The modification in the former models is minimal. At the initial working age, workers-consumers receive their share of national output in terms of given real disposable income level, which stays with him or her, the rest of their working lives. This FRDI tends to be the same as or more than his real consumption, which stays flat until the worker's retirement age. Then, the level drops to a 50-60 percent of the former level because of social security's pension-level payments. Often, these workers know their dilemma but are under constraint, be it financial, familial (for example, teen mothers), or lack of education. So they cannot even ask for proper state assistance, if available, to educate, improve their employment skills. The more social, political, and economic constraints there are on the population, the larger the working class relative to the rest of the population. These paradoxical stagnant economic conditions are common in poor regions of advanced economies, or in developing nations. These create stagnant economic conditions, which the economy cannot outgrow by perfectly competitive market forces.

Growing Real Disposable Income Model

At the working age, the growing real disposable income, GRDI starts to increase periodically as the workers, in expectation of future higher rewards, increases their skills, while the consumers' real basic consumption can remain the same or slightly increase until retirement age. The increases in GRDI are saved methodically. They are also invested for retirements, health, and education, durable goods. Beyond a higher GRDI sealing, some workers take more direct, entrepreneurial control. Therefore, the worker would be very involved with the capital. The worker will own capital passively, by investing (purchase of mutual funds or shares of a corporation), in the form of stocks, bonds, or by their pension. More directly, the workers will save and buy capital or starts a new, innovative business. They are also indirectly saving their postponed consumption in banks and other institutions like money market mutual funds, so they are capitalists defined in two ways. One is as owners, two, is as lenders. However, the degree of ownership control is another matter, because managers or executive management teams may very well have altered older definitions of ownership or lender controls of the capital in capitalism in multinational corporations. Other modifications can take place, for example, new laws by a pro-active legislative branch or a judicial dysfunction can affect ownership control, shareholders' rights, etc.

At retirement age, often these workers would leave

closer to 70-80 percent of their real consumption. The higher retirement real consumption would be financed by social security, pensions, and returns on investments.

The GRDI model explains more logically the two hundred years evolution of the United States economy and the post-industrial revolutionary dynamics of the twenty-five year development success experienced by the Japanese, or any new developmental experiments, because, it explains the combined impact of knowledge and technological progress due to consumers' decisions. It also raises the probability of systems' success. If the systems depend on maximum numbers of the population finding solutions, then being relatively free to carry them out for optimum rewards. The probability of a systems' success decreases, if the socio-political and economic barriers cut the number of the participants to fewer, less-motivated groups, if real wages are kept low, if the fees and taxes disproportionally increase on the working classes. Granted, specialization plays a very important part in this success, but workers, as well as trained specialists, theorists, and practitioners all together can make a lot more contributions in cultivating growth environments.

The Changed Class Divisions in the Free Market (by Saving)

While all of early development of market economies

the Kaleckian model and other harsher interpretations of capitalism held more consistencies that are logical. However, the post-WWII United States relatively free market approach and various socio-political forces enforced another dimension on traditional economics. The wartime needs or all kinds of workers (all minorities, blacks, women, etc.) combined with wartime scarcities of consumptive goods forced the postponement of soldier and civilian consumption. In the post-war capital market, much less distinction was made among class division than capital holdings.

Residual Postponement of Workers' Consumption (Saving)

The accumulation (of savings) of soldiers and civilians took the form of learned work skills of minorities employed in domestic war industries (another use of the savings) and funds saved and held as currencies or precious metals. Those combined with other socio-political movement created social freedom, and later, political freedom (like the non-violence movement of Gandhi for freedom from the United Kingdom's colonization of India. In addition, Martin Luther King's civil right movements in the United States, which created hopeful and conducive conditions to allow the employment of minorities in the post-WWII civilian production. In addition, pro-black and brown socio-political and civil right and reconciliation movements of Mandela that took place in South Africa. These allowed for more participation and savings. Especially as the economic growth yielded higher real disposable income in excess of depression levels and war, modified consumer demands (real consumption expenditures).

Residual Postponement of Capitalist's Consumption (Saving)

Either the capitalists (owners of post-depression capital, if any) had their accumulation in the form of more convertible capital, or they received government credit extensions. That allowed for their involvement in the wartime production and thus more major accumulation of capitalists' savings. Then, essentially, they created the post-war corporate demands for additional workers to utilize the forced savings in the form of new consumer-capital goods so they could produce and meet the post-WWII consumer demands.

Aggregate Supply Side

The postponement of consumption of all economic agents will become capital in one form or another. The entrepreneurs, managers, investors discount the present value of income streams of capital goods and services, thus establishing priorities among their decisions. The microeconomic foundations play important defining parts, in calculating revenues over costs. But also the interest rates determined by supply and demand for money in the financial markets. However, the impact of these decisions made in the present is about the kind of new capital formations, employed in future production operations. Indeed, the increase in decay rate, increase in charges of revenue relative to costs could signal shut-off in certain operations and terminate plans for any multiplicative investment in that line of production. Financial markets also determine the need for change in the future operations.

Interest, Credit, Market Innovations, and Capital Formation

The real interest rates tend to increase as innovation uses of capital goods requires capital funds to be applied in the process of production and production and purchase of new capital goods. After the transformation of capital funds to capital goods, the supply of money drops, the real interest rate rises. That signals the need for more risk-taking and entrepreneurial contributions and new capital formation, with a higher rate of returns above the market rate, until high enough real interest rates will cause a down turn in business activities. Because savers, lenders, and fund-holders reduce their risk and keep liquid or the capital form of choice will be the capital funds, as the estimated rate of return from new ventures will be equal or fall below the higher real interest rates. The supply of money will increase, while the demand for money remains the same or subsequently drops. Then, the real interest rate drops. Thus, the inducement of lower costs of risk taking would sustain the process. If innovational forms of new capital are available, entrepreneurs will overcome the psychological fear of the business downturn and apply the technologies in new combinations and productions processes.

Schumpeterian Credit Expansion and New Capital

J. A. Schumpeter had a microeconomic definition of credit affecting entrepreneurship.[7] In the static equilibrium, the interest rate was assumed zero, entrepreneurs did not have any savings or funds to apply to new capital in production.[8] They either used credit or convinced others to allow the use of their funds, their postponed consumption. The credit, if granted, gives the entrepreneur the needed purchasing power in order to formulate the new technological combination applied in the production and starting new firms.

The principles of the loans (amount of the credit), plus interest on it, were paid out of the operational revenue or entrepreneurial profit. At this stage, past accumulations are complemented by newly created purchasing power.[9] It is true, the financial institutions and entrepreneurs can create innovational changes, new firms, and improve the probabilities of economic growth and development. But the distinction between the accumulation, postponement of consumption, or thrift out of income (GRDI) embodied in human and other forms of capital is overlooked, because the innovation microeconomic arrangement of credit-purchasing power between the financial institutions and entrepreneurs ignores two fundamental kinds of capital. One is the human capital endowed in or accumulated by the entrepreneurs as education and skills. Two is the accumulation of capital in the dynamic synthetic process, which even on the shelf-technologies would have as embodied and disembodied technologies. Thus, the entrepreneurial credit will allow new purchasing power to obtain the essential agencies of innovative capital (human and non-human), workers, processed goods, location, to be assembled together in a "new combination," resulting in the application of innovative capital in production and establishment of new firms.

The initial and future wages and payments would create more purchasing power, create new markets, and enhance the level of living for more people associated with the new venture. If successful (profitable), then the multiplicative investments in the innovative venture would increase. Moreover, the micro-economic oddity will bloom into a macroeconomic wonder. The market success of the innovative ventures increases lending of credit to expand operations. This kind of credit is the operational credit, with reduced risk, therefore, increasing national real production growth. The sustainable economic growth then makes the growing of real disposable income possible. Hence, the probability of economic development is increased.

In modern business, investors-entrepreneurs need business plans, credit histories, previous success, and collateral to secure entrepreneurial credit. Nevertheless, entrepreneurs are not immediately trusted with even small business loans. Therefore, trust is very important component of economic success.

In fact, it is the experience of regional poverty in the developing economies and the inner cities of advanced economies, which have recently gained uncomfortable recognitions. That is, the geographical, institutional, and socio-political barriers can block access to the credit market for smaller, newer entrepreneurs.

This explains the positive impact of micro-business loans by the non-governmental organizations in the same areas. Moreover, their success in economic growth and development, even in villages of the developing nations reinforces their impacts. In addition, the last kind of credit, the high consumption-credit, much like the government-deficit spending on non-appropriate investments, can cause demand-pull inflation, monetary constraints, higher interest, and contractions. If the consumption-credit is too low, it can cause under-consumption, supply glut, under-employment of resources and workers.

In a zero-real interest rate period, which is more probable zero-nominal rate of interest, the access to credit should assist formation of new innovative capital and the new combinations of new capital in the production process. Therefore, they are assisting in economic growth. It should also be clear that monetary policy or international interventions affecting the level of real interest rates would, thereafter, influence credit expansions or contractions, and persuade or dissuade lenders and investors to continue or discontinue with the transformations of capital-funds to new capital goods. This will depend on the balance of real rate of return at real interest rate fluctuations from positive to zero.

Changed Class Divisions (Investment)

The same socio-political environment of freedom and unbiased (principle-based) democratic representation rather than purchase-limited participatory democracies and nondemocracies cultivate conditions for investment of the accumulated savings. Thus, the socio-political flexibilities added to relative freedom in the marketplace induce rather than ensure the chance of reward over risk after participation.

Linkage of Savings, Investment, Technology, and Capital

Historically, the gradual savings and capital accumulations preceded all economic activities. In the post-Keynesian and -WWII periods, the injection of income in excess of consumption presented a more managed, but faster, macro-economic effects of savings-investment affect the economy, out of the down side of oscillation. Given at least theoretically, that all infrastructures, services, and required institutions are in place, and they are efficiently and competitively functional.

In such a state of golden bliss, the mechanism of invention and innovation would in response to market forces of supply and demand, also affect the economy.

The projection of economic activities in response to market signals would, through research and development introduces successful technologies, new capital, and new products. More importantly, new jobs and higher government and busies revenues.

Capital Formation, Capital Consumption

The only successful experiments for periodical episodes show the micro-economy of neoclassical development has led rather than followed top to bottom macro-economic policies, which has benefitted the whole economy.[10] However, in the same experimental economic models, imperfections have decidedly imploded the system in massive unemployment and income distribution insufficiencies.

Therefore, it seems logical to ask what has made capital formation more sustainable there and less possible in this other places? In addition, what are the more probable conditions, which would induce such a renovation process? Historical in the 1909 to 1919, to 1929, the overt wealth concentration strategies and subsistence wages (iron law of wages) have not yielded sustainability. In all other cases, the most controlled systems or state-controlled, to less rigid systems monopolistic regimes of state industrial policies within the market economies, to even less control strategically managed institutional version in the relatively free markets, the successes have improved or sustained the profitable systems for shorter periods.

A tentative statement could be made that under the right micro-economic systems, in a less rigid and less volatile socio-political system, with a balanced functional distributive system, the national production processes have better long-term chance of successful growth (at a more sustainable process) than with all other arrangements.

Note

[1] This may also be the cause of underestimations by neoclassical monetarists, and Keynesians for adequate policy responses and remedies lately.

[2] Paul M. Sweezy, "*The Present as History: Essays and Reviews on Capitalism and Socialism*," *Monthly Review Press*, 1953 (New York), 278, 60

[3] He modified the J. Clark argument of "automatic synchronization" by equating adjustment of costs and returns by oscillations in profit and loss. But the main divergence from the evidentiary history is states as "the introduction of new methods of production (by innovation and technological progress) requires on the whole no previous accumulation of goods." Unless an imaginary state of instantaneous circular flow with ubiquitous equilibrium is meant, which he did not mean, the argument becomes too strong.

[4] J. A. Schumpeter, *The Theory of Economic Development: An Inquiry Into Profits, Capital, Credit, Interest, and the Business Cycle*, Trans. Redvers Opie., (London: Oxford University Press, 1961), 60, 64, 70-74

[5] The costs can be absolute in terms of human life or relative in terms of societal instabilities. Whether that leads to chaos, revolution, or a change of government is only party dependant on the political system and the social makeup. Nevertheless, it may be too strong of an argument to deduce that social liberal democratization is a socio-political cure-all and it will not lead to absolute costs. In fact, in a society (a political movement) so misled may be uninformed about the cause, but revolt and revolute with the economic and absolute costs, before getting to all the

perceived or imagined political and economic benefits of the relatively free markets in both spheres.

[6] Other problems arise when the chronic issues lead to wealth concentrations and older models, rather than the targeted wealth creation models and circulatory enhancements, as define in Dr. Fakhraie studies,, and books.

[7] Ibid, 100

[8] While credit supply is different from money supply, but the latter affects the process as well.

[9] J. A. Schumpeter, *The Theory of Economic Development: An Inquiry Into Profits, Capital, Credit, Interest, and the Business Cycle*, Trans. Redvers Opie., (London: Oxford University Press, 1961), 70-74.

[10] Bahman Fakhraie, *Technological injection, dynamic new capital measurements, and Production Theory in Economics*, (Michigan: ProQuest LLC, 2010) and, https://order.proquest.com/OA_HTML/pqdtibeCCtpItmDspRte.jsp

CHAPTER 12

SELECTED DEFINITIONS OF TECHECONOMICS

Economic tools have differentiated enough to be of skillful utilities in different conditions. In macroeconomics, countercyclical interventions have long been of intense interest to governmental and private commercial interests for obvious reasons. Stability and sustainability are among those reasons.

On Business Cycles and Capital Formation
Counter-cyclical Interventions

Masterful utilization of monetary and fiscal policies in relatively free markets formulates the counter cyclical strategies of functioning economies.[1]

Given there is sufficient real disposable income to encourage postponements of current consumption, monetary policy would play an important role as a counter-cyclical tool. However, creation of credit in order to create new combinations of resources to formulate and form new capital by innovator-entrepreneurs, and appropriate laws by lawmakers are ultimately important contributions of institutionally powerful central banks. This aspect of monetary policy was part of the Schumpeterian definition of credit, after the needs for appropriate technological progress were introduced to the economic growth and development. It is a natural extension of the centrists' intervention-stabilizing policies because, in a Schumpeterian circular flow, all sources of funding innovational ventures are assumed occupied in competitive activities. In addition, entrepreneurs are not capital owners; therefore, they do not risk their own capital. Thus, the central banks have to ensure other capital owners of the private sector to invest in entrepreneurial ventures or they have to fund such ventures. Given the remoteness of access of some smaller entrepreneurs to larger institutions, either non-government organizations or government institutions have to fill the void of the missing lending-agencies. It is important to realize that a majority of new ventures would fail. Then, either the front-end training can reduce the risk, or risk-insurances has to be established, in order to stop major money-drain from the new capital creation activities. The money-drain would cause the interest rates to increase above any normal levels, as interest rises due to technological progress. In each case, the central bank can supply enough funds to moderate the trends and counter-speculative oscillations. This could take place without fueling inflation, as long as the supply of goods and services would increase in the market for the excess demand.

The fiscal policies of governments can apply to infrastructure, front-end training of new entrepreneurs, and the retraining of the unemployed, technology-displaced workers. The tax-subsidy strategies also can target regional under-utilization of resources by redirecting the entrepreneurial resources. Institutional development of appropriate human capital, research, and development, establishment of universities, agrarian and manufacturing research stations and outputs, educational financial aid and research grants can enhance the economic growth and development process.

Individual educational choices and lifetime learning have become universal enhancement in national human capital. While the personal investment choices are made for purely private income enhancements, the benefit are sufficiently national in scope to justify education-saving tax shelters from taxes to allow to private financing of educations, risks to the lenders, the variations introduces differential degrees of risk needed to make distinctions between entrepreneurial and consumption loans. This will restore the recognition by financial and governmental institutions of the missing entrepreneurial agencies. This study has repeatedly mentioned economic paradigms that have been ignored. Other policies can ease the establishment of non-bank financial institutions (for business micro-loans) at more remote regional geographies to assist smaller entrepreneurs.

The main aspects of good fiscal policies still will be to stabilize the economic fluctuations, which may wipe out most businesses, starting with the new and vulnerable firms. Still, among the appropriate fiscal policies are maintaining proper tax rates to keep the income-ladder incentive effective in the economy, which is one of those rare American experiences that for a long time supplied the America economy with the capital (human and other kinds), and willing multi-national emigrant and entrepreneurs. That is, all newcomers and poorer segment of the population would fully understand their hard work, investment in education, and applications of their marketable skills will take them up the ladder to an income proportional to the level of their acquired skills. That the policy will reaffirm, their savings-investment strategies have a decided plan, path, and clear forecasts.

Fiscal policies can also monitor and counteract when needed against unusual international economic trends. When unusually, high amounts of currencies are dumped, or are drained in the domestic financial markets, these cause higher instabilities, and risk premiums. They can overwhelm monetary policy and keep interest rates counter high for new capital formation.

A different degree of alertness is also required from other regulatory, educational, research centers, and institutions against competitions, when entities, military, or governments plan and carry out with exactness.

Economic Growth, Schumpeterian, Kaldorian Theories

The Jevonian policy implications extended the static equilibrium of perfect competition. Later, the ubiquitous universal implications of it were assumed to apply to the economy as a whole.[2] While theoretically, it still has a revolutionary contribution to microeconomic analysis of firm operations and laissez-faire. Nevertheless, the macro-economic policy implication of the equilibrium static and laissez-faire, reasonable at microeconomic level, have had some pernicious effects at macro-economic level, which leads to major cyclical and aggregate variable swings of output and employment. The recognition of possible divergence effect of exchange value and purchasing power of consumers (distribution-effects, or the redistribution question), and the improbability of universal multiple-equilibriums did not encourages government policy makers of classical creeds to act.

The arguments against the notion of universal equilibrium state were detailed in Chapter One. Whether we take imperfect competition, oligopoly, monopoly or the divergence of relatively free market exchange values due to purchasing power deterioration, the aggregate number identifies extreme cases of dysfunctional market inadequacies, disequilibrium. The disequilibrium conditions (extreme unemployment, factor valuations, or wealth concentrations) are either due to endogenous economic situations (imperfect competition), or they are due to exogenous (institutions, governmental intervention). Often, in both cases, at the macro-level of the problematic conditions are too large for any changes at the micro-level alone to resolve surgically. Especially, the intersections of the socio-political state sets exerts time limits (the next election), which requires the immediacy of macro-economic interventions in democratic economies. Moreover, all major macro-economic problems (mass unemployment, etc.) become socio-political problems, before or at election time.

Infrastructure Technologies and Economic Growth

The policy makers also took the laissez-faire with Adam Smith interpretations of the "hidden hands," and avoided proper interventions on monetary or fiscal ends until the cyclical impacts of the 1920s and the contraction-unemployment of the 1930s yielded a realization of complexities, far beyond the capabilities of the Jevonian economic and static micro-model capabilities. It was time for improved infrastructural technologies and more resources to help the invisible hands.

The laissez-faire's French original economic model is more explicitly telling an interpretation of it. In fact, French rural agrarian farmers-producers in the economy of that time faced state-agents (legitimate and otherwise) at each village, and between villages and towns. Therefore, fees or multiple-taxes, payout, bridge tools, (mustache taxes, and bribes) were repeatedly levied at each market-entrances or bridges.

In sum, all regional or central government agents had confiscatory impacts on production revenues. Moreover, the ruling class or government used up the levied fees (revenues) in the up-keep of armies. Rarely infrastructures or public capitals were the serious aim of any governmental agencies. When nation-state or the central governments became more powerful that the regional centers of powers (Magi, priest, feudal, khan, gendarmes, magistrate, etc.), then the state taxes subsume the extortionists' fees, road robberies.

The balanced mixtures of the property rights with exponential explosions in the producers' revenues and in the state tax revenues have yielded good results, until in recent history.[3] Nevertheless, like all good things in life, there is a limit (of optimum taxation and ubiquitous fees) beyond which even laissez-faire will become counter-productive, dysfunctional, unsustainable, and finally instable.

The proper uses of tax-revenue from appropriate products have helped commerce. They have even improved it. From the earlier times, the wall of China reduced risks of attack on the farmers and urban areas. The upkeep and guarding of the Silk Road helped commerce, as more supplies of spices and silk and products were traded.

In ancient times of Elamite and Achaemenian cultivation of multinational scholars, the Achaemenian multinational empire-governance, to Aztec road building of South America, such global and marginal contributions existed with human groups outperforming others in their own-time periods.[4] Since, the middle ages, the contributions of church, then state, then the democratic evolution of nation-states have constantly added to explicit responsibilities of the states.

Therefore, the states are increasingly less about war, genocide, victimization of others, and more about the defense (of self or the victimized), and infrastructure advancements, accommodations of commerce and trades and stability. Accordingly, as they help create the appropriate conduct of business, reduce thefts, fraud, and crimes, they help to improve commerce. No doubt, beyond a certain optimum level, the taxes they collected contributed more to present capital consumption, less to infrastructure, stability, future investment, and new capital formation. That is why deceptive ideologues and least educated researchers hoot "mixed economy" as a euphemistic metaphor for anti-American communism, in the post-1950s United States of America.

The inexperience academics have advanced recent research in this field, deeming all governmental investments devolutionary in all micro and macro cases! It is defined as such by the least informed and most outdated of political ideologies.[5] It is the greater ratio of government versus private applications that matters the most in dynamic down cycles and low unemployment periods. The reverse antithetical can be presented in peak cycles, low unemployment periods, where real disposable incomes have not had a 30 years rate of decay data representing them.

Any application of economic tools required in modern economics, sociology, and political knowledge unhinges the intellectually infirmed. In addition, the related tax financing of national projects, which may have more political than economic logic make them incendiary.

Thus, a widening gap will develop, away from the initial economic reasons.

Neither Fisherian income and investment criteria, nor the very limited Keynesians' multipliers can be blamed so acerbically and totally for the non-market selectivity of economic tools miss-applied.

The New Flow Model

The reality of modern mixed economies made the new flow model self-evident, ex post facto to the counter-cyclical policies of Western economics in post-Depression and -WWII England and the United States. The innovations in corporate financing made the ownership of corporate shares legal. The constitutional laws made that ownership and private property ownership a universal fact. Equal protections under clause of the law modified legal risks of shareholders' ownership. The majority of populations start owning cooperate-shares, other risks like market risk, oscillations-risks, and fraud were still the same.

The economic growth of post-war (WWII) adjusted American real disposable incomes above consumption level, without major international manufacturing competition from other economies. The export of capital goods also further improved employment and income. So the savings of the workers could accumulate at an increasing rate, combined with the capitalists' savings and the massive injections of new technological and applied innovations from the universities, agriculture land-grant colleges, agricultural research stations, and private corporate research and development programs, they formed the accumulation and production, which was the longest post-war sustainable growth and development period possible. In modern time, the triumph of follies, institutional miserliness has replaced and compounded individual tendencies of 1930s.

The intersection of the socio-political sets of an evolving but stable democracy and the relatively free market flex system took endogenous business cycle shocks (inflations, etc.) and exogenous shocks (the Cold War, Korea, Vietnam), but it learned, adjusted, and corrected mistakes, getting back to its economic growth path.

However, in 2009-2010 the Stalled Depression, the timid Keynesianism, and temporary quantitative monetarism did not penetrate the expectation barriers, in sufficient or sustainable manner, in order to pull the economy out of the defensive primal squats globally. If that was not enough of bad manufactured conundrums, political right forgot their patriotic duties as representative oppositions, and they gave to their demonstrated bigotries, xenophobic policies, and untimely abstractionisms. Thus, the second follow up infrastructure technological injections and rebuilding, job creation, and the actual stimulus fiscal injection did not take place.

All the worshipers at the pillar of dogmatic deficit control found their voice in opposition to the reelection of opposite party. They wanted to ignore that their policy fiascoes of 1990s, their anti-emigration acts of 1996, the disbanding of the (1933) Glass-Steagall Act, the covert and overt cooperate policy and deregulatory interventionism, the middleclass taxes and fees versus high income transferences cascaded in multiple failures.[6] Economic events culminated into 2008-2011 stalled-economies growth out of the down turn, and retrograded into some "double-dips." Other global situations European financial arrangements were also influencing the economy. These were disclosed, and they were discussed openly in 1995, 1998, and 2000s. Yet, the global economies walked into them eye opened shut.

This study is the accumulation of traditional post Keynes analysis, it dynamic cumulative synthesis of the Schumpeterian Growth and Development model, the Domar growth theory and new measurement of Capital. Capital consumption and replacement funds are included in reevaluation of new adjusted capital to study new capital formation. The speedy technological –obsolescence can be amortized and included in capital formation funds.[7] The conglomerations of scientific discoveries present will yield technological capital formation, and assist with the dynamic forces of sustainable economic growth model.

Notes

[1] Irving Fisher, *The Theory of Interest: As Determined by Impatience to Spend Income and Opportunity to Invest It,* (New York: The Macmillan Company, 1930), 341.

[2] M. Dobb, *Theories of Value and Distribution Since Adam Smith: Ideology and Economic Theory*, (London: Cambridge University Press, 1973), 211

[3] Bell City CA. USA, http://abcnews.go.com/US/bell-city-fires-manager-paid-president-obamas-salary/story?id=11236299 ;Tunisia, 2011, http://www.cbsnews.com/stories/2011/02/20/60minutes/main20033404.shtml; http://articles.cnn.com/2011-01-16/world/tunisia.fruit.seller.bouazizi_1_tunisian-history-street-vendor-police-officer?_s=PM:WORLD
Egypt, 2011, http://topics.nytimes.com/top/news/international/countriesandterritories/egypt/index.html
Libya, 2011 http://www.guardian.co.uk/world/2011/sep/16/libyan-women-our-revolution-too
USSR, 1988 http://www.huffingtonpost.com/bennett-ramberg-phd/the-soviet-occupation-of_b_369105.html http://iis-db.stanford.edu/pubs/22468/No_108_Stoner-Weiss_domestic_and_international_influences_on_collapse_of_USSR.pdf

[4] Achmaaenids, sometime written Achamnid are pronounced in Farsi, "Hakhamanesh", and as a dynasty, "Hakhamaneshian."

[5] One wonders, if business schools advancing such assertions, have returned federal funds, or government

funds to the treasury lately!

[6] No corrective remedies followed all of those statements of "mistakes were made." There were huge advertisements "spin" budgets, campaign contributions, but no attempts to cultivate any academic studies to follow up. They did not like academics, or researchers asking hard questions! The last two decades, must have been the decades of ignoring foretold events. Read about the long demise and the chronology of the 1933 Glass-Steagall Act, its demise in the 1990s at the following link, sthttp://www.pbs.org/wgbh/pages/frontline/shows/wallstreet/weill/demise.html

[7] Bahman Fakhraie, "Technological Injection, Dynamic New Capital Measurements, and Production Theory in Economics," (Utah: PhD Dissertation, University of Utah Economics Dept., 2010)

CHAPTER 13

TRADE, TECHNOLOGIES, AND SURPLUSES

Technology changes and international trade surplus from international trade and finance often supply the sources for increasing level of living, and the increase in the real income. The complexities of the process do get murky. It is noteworthy that without technological advancements and production possibility growth, even trade will not benefit or increase the benefit to the economy sufficiently.[1] The exchange line shift from T1 to T2, and as noted in region A, the economy falls back to the lower public indifference curve.[2] While with technological advancements in both economies we move to region C, beneficial to both trading economies, at the given exchange-trade line T1 resources and higher population are employed better in the end. The level of living also improves. X1 and X2 show trade surpluses in both countries 1 and 2 in Figure 22. Investment in new technologies shows the two period shifts from one technological production locus to another by giving up

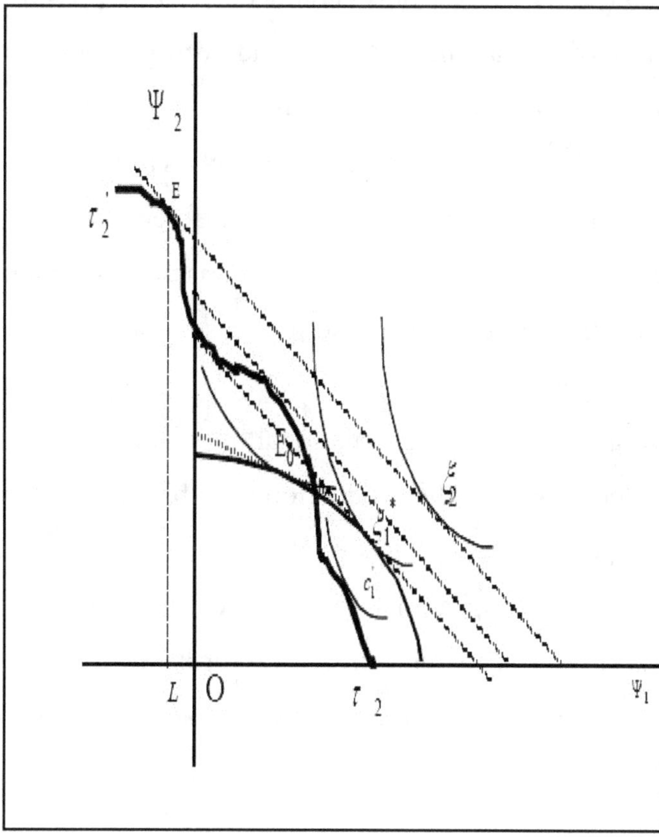

Figure 22. Investment in technologies, temporal modular production.

current consumption and falling back to a lower preference at the current period, and investing it in new technologies. Trade after investment in new technologies, shows the two period shifts from one technological production locus to another by giving up current consumption and falling back to a lower preference at the current period, and investing it in new technologies.

The consumer surplus is reduced at c1, in present period, in order that the save fund and borrowed funds purchase new technologies, and improve the consumption level at a future period at level E2, which is a substantial jump in consumer surplus level. The difference, not consumed from the budget line at c1 consumption level, pays installments for the loan to purchase new technological capital.

Figure 23 shows, international trade after investment in new technologies, the production possibilities frontiers, locus of possible production levels are assumed to retain its normal concave appearance in time, but initially reflect the irregular nature of methods available for investments. Figure 23 and 24 shows the improvement of the economy after the technological transfer.

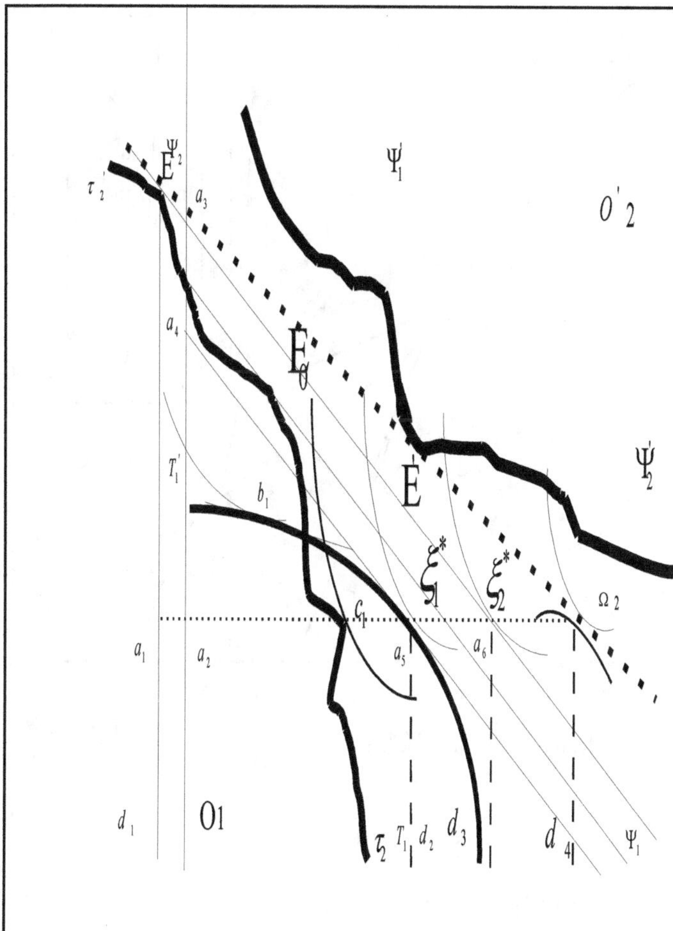

Figure 23. International trade after investment in new technologies.

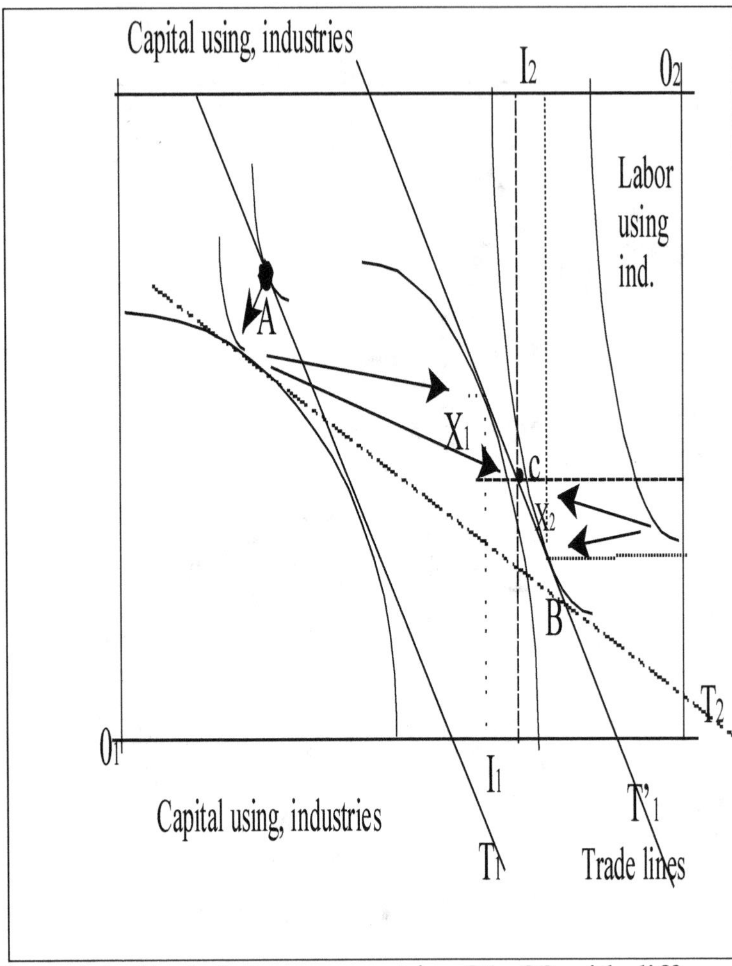

Figure 24. Trade between countries O1, O2 with different technologies.

The exchanges after the technology transfer and new production adjustments will improve the economic conditions in both cases.

That is a real income increase, following the growth in their gross domestic products over time can yield to welfare-improvement, which benefits both economies after the transfers of technologies and international trade and finance. Many assumptive accommodations have to take place as well, for optimal conditions to occur in both economies.

Global Trade and Real Growth Rates

The united nation data for real growth of gross domestic products of groups of nations are studied for their rate of growth or decay over time (1970-2010). The technological portfolio of each group of nations can be studied for their comparative contributions to the growth rates of GDP in those countries.

The graphic presentation shows that developing economies with technologies as the major exporter of manufacture goods, Organization of the Islamic conference counties, (OIC), and High-Income developing economies visit the decay zone, less frequently. They stay in the 2 to 6 percent growth rate zone for longer times. Figure 25 shows the average annual growth rate of GDP in $82 for the (OIC), the organization of Islamic conference nations.

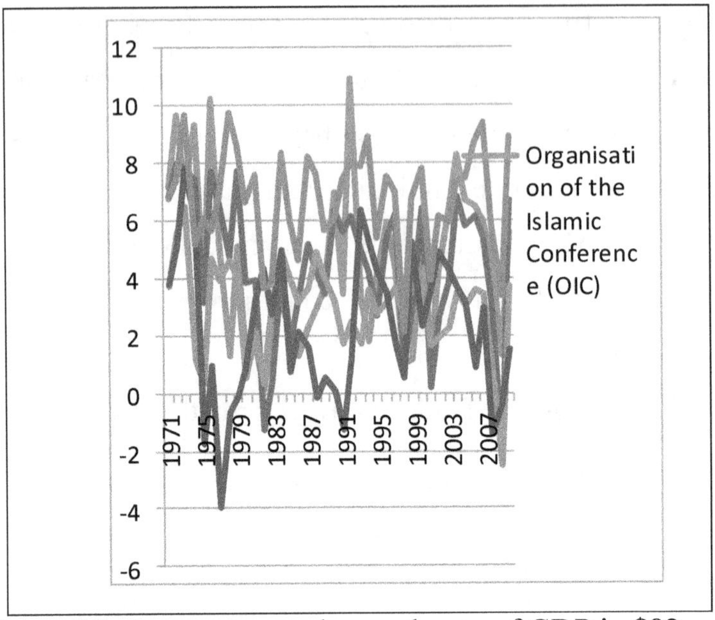

Figure 25, Average annual growth rate of GDP in $82. "UNCTAD, UNCTAD stat"

However, major exporter of manufactured goods, (2008-2009) and major petroleum exporters, developing economies 1975-79, 1991, 2008-2009, do have outliner swings into the negative rates. Thus, the technological advancement of the former groups can guide independent studies for appropriate technological conditions, which would garner contributive result to the essential strategies for future growth models.

Globally, in trade groups of economies, certain economies can complement the technologies of their exporting strategies to modify the violent swings of their economies. That may prove more stabilizing to the price of energy, or essential commodities, therefore stabilizing socio- economic and political conditions in the future. The multifactorial influences can complement economic growth models. The sustainability of those models can help with the development of these economies.

Set Theory Calculation for Trade Surplus

The complex concept of mathematical optimization was introduced with three lemmas. These are the necessary condition, sufficient condition, and the newly proposed Sustainability condition.[3] Lemma 1, is it necessary? Lemma 2, is it sufficient? Lemma 3, is it sustainable? Since the advancement of the second best theorem, in complex optimization formulation in welfare economic theory, this is the first prominent study that advances the economic science toward economic sustainability condition.

The application of advanced set theory cloud calculation is not simple picking and choosing out of chaos, but the accumulation built on of logical foundation in different fields of study.

The transfers of technologies by most developing countries are often to extract valuable resources, or assist with important national needs. In most cases, it is an important task to prioritize for best choices possible. Therefore, it is equally significant to these countries to have best and second best union of potentially viable subsets to filter their decision choices through.

Figure 25, general topical subsets present the fields, which all three condition has to be met. The technological choices have to be subjected to these fields. The area of focus will be economic, social, political, environmental, and global variables sets. Figure 26 shows the union of subsets, which present conditions for sustainability. These secondary sets of conditions allow for choices between maximization or optimization and sustainability.

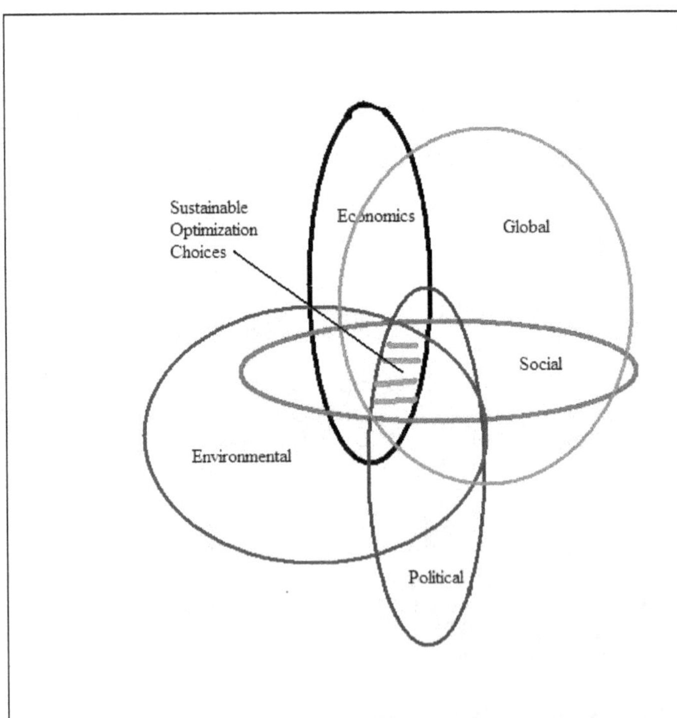

Figure 26. Union of topical subsets for sustainability.

It is not accidental that there are unsustainable possibilities, versus sustainable maximum profit making possibilities. There are examples, which elucidate the issues further; however, it has been important to establish the scientific reality as it exists, and as it is attained. Future examples will help.

The Multivariable Model of Sustainability

Economic decisions are not isolated events at bets of time. They are often more complex in more difficult times. The set theory, empirical analysis of production theory and trade surplus sustainability among universal sets of economic, environmental, political, and global trade factors are studied in the following example. The following conditions are used to demonstrate what decision makers have to deal with on dynamic bases.

In this model, four different hypothetical conditions are portrait,

1. Economic conditions
2. Environmental conditions
3. Trade conditions
4. Political conditions

The economic conditions refer to economies, which are functioning under perfect completion market, or under different degrees of imperfect completion. In the case of global trade, free trade versus balanced free trade, or constricted finance and trade play significant part in functionality of the markets. That is a wide field of operation. Those include mixed and socialist economies, and monopolistic Stalinist newbies. Political economy also will point out the risk level associated with the conditions of governing.

Environmental conditions refer to general operational situation, which have proven to cause lethality and toxicities, which require course of action. Three mile Island, Chernobyl, and the Japanese post tsunami nuclear disasters are on top of any lists.

Figure 27 studies the union of subsets and conditions for sustainability

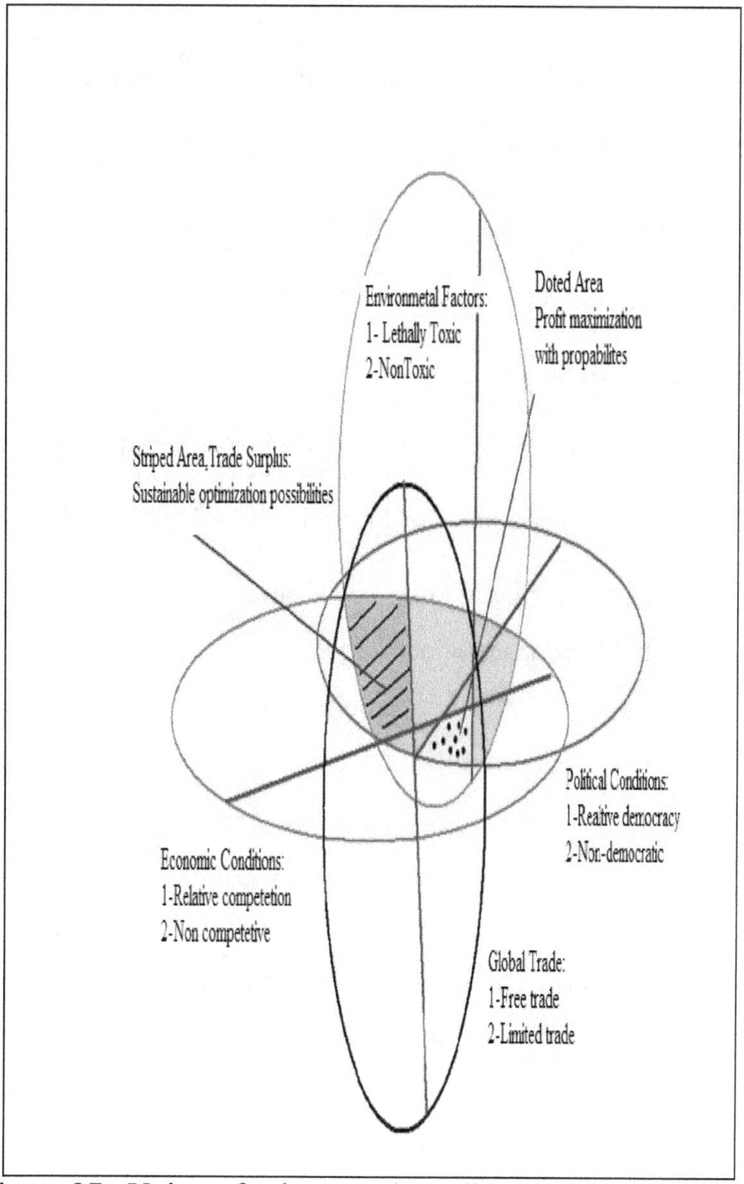

Figure 27. Union of subsets and conditions for sustainability.

The dangerous and volatile level of carcinogens and toxin in well waters related to non-sleeved fracking technology for natural gas is relevant. . Longer lists would include Prince William's oil tanker disaster, the British Petroleum Mexican Golf disaster. Presence of led and mercury toxicity in fish and water due to coal industry.

The Quality of Decisions Choices

The quantification and observation of three conditional lemmas produces at least two types of sustainability possibilities. You thought after all that mathematical conditioning, the stay at equilibrium, or optimum condition ought to be for good. Unfortunately, the duration of stay in the paradise, is conditional on the severity and continuation of all the sinning, otherwise, static assumptive conditions are always changing. The concepts of maximization-minimization, primal and duality conditions models can be useful in such complex situations to assists in finding solutions.

Two examples can demonstrate the difference quiet aptly. One country uses outdoor atomic testing, under national security and wartime hysteria forgoes democratic vetting, normal scientific questioning, and public involvement. Three or four decades of silence killing of their citizen, they discoveries establish a confrontational public, private, and government trisected conflict. The conflict establishes guidelines and forced regulatory mandates, which controls toxic waste and industrial mushrooming in that field. Consequentially, another country forgoes all aspect of representative or democratic government for speedy development and advancement without control. The asserted scientific methodologies are not enough incentives to allow for the discoveries of defects in nuclear factory, and core meltdown, and toxic clouds ensue. Large portions of the countries natural assets are toxically inaccessible to human encroachments and any developmental activities for 10,000 years.[4] The former, is an optimization possibilities solution, the latter is a profit maximization-possibility solution, neither are dominant long-term sustainable solutions. The qualities of decision-choices leave distinguishable causal footprints, among the set of conditions for sustainable optimizations, or shorter-term profit maximization.

Multivariable Game Decision Indices

Multivariable Bayesian (n-variables game theory) decision Indices of binomial technology choices shows an example of decision-making. There are five subsets of the universal sets available to study.[5] Prior probabilities, and observed data, are combined with the educated interpretational probabilities to formulate functional numbers. Given the field of studies in international trade and development theories, we understand that numeral representation in varied in different areas. There are some calculated some estimated assigned probabilities numbers to each subset, where certain items production, or aggregate production can be studies and assigned.[6] In this example, a more complex n-elements game theory situation is presented in different sub-set theory.[7] Five universal subsets are examined for constructive area of cooperation, with binomial choices, which the worst of at least two best possible options are selected. Bayesian probability estimation formula is as follows,

$$\text{Given, BPE} = \sum E\ (P\ Vi)\ ,$$

$$\text{then BPE aij} = E\ (P\ Vi)\ U\ E\ (P\ Vj),\ \text{ and }\ 0 < aij < 1.$$

The Bayesian formulation is,

$$BDIqi = EPVi * 1/ (\sum EPVi)$$

$$BDIqi = \{EPVi\ x\ [1/ (\sum EPVi)]\},\ 0 < EPVi < 1$$

Table 14 presents multivariable Bayesian decision indices (MBDI) of the binomial-technology choices. Table 15 presents the BDI for subsets of alternative technology choices, and the quantitative enumeration that assists the decision makers.

Table 14, Multivariable Bayesian decision Indices of binomial technology choices.

General Description	Binomial Tech a, b	Probability of Maximization	Probability of Optimization	Probability of Sustainability
Production A	less-energy	60	20	80
B	Max output	50	25	75
Environment A	Non-toxic	40	35	75
Condition B	Toxic-lethal	35	-20	65
Economic A	RFreemrkts	40	45	85
Condition B	Restricted	35	40	75
Intl. Trade A	RFreeTrade	40	45	85
Condition B	Restricted	20	25	45
Political A	Democracy	40	35	75
Condition B	Restricted	35	-10	25

Notes. RFreeMrkt, is subset of choices made in relatively free market, where assumptive aspects of perfect competition are practiced. RFeeTrade, is subset of choices in relatively free trade zones, reciprocity and comparative advantages are practiced as much as possible. Restricted, implies regulatory and imposed legal and market interference. Max output uses the most energy in production technologies.

Table 15 shows BDI for alternative technological choices.

Table 15. BDI for subsets of alternative technology choices.

Choices	Tec As	Tec mix, 50/50	Tec Bs
BDIqa	4/5= **80%**	3.4/5= 68%	2.9/5= 58 %
BDIqb	3.95/5= **79 %**	3.35/5= 67 %	2.85/5= 57 %

Note. In the 50/50 two highest BDIs are selected as Tec As choices, and two Tec Bs choices are added. In this example, economic and relatively international trade yields the highest indices.

Therefore, using the estimations regarding the probabilities of sustainability a BDI matrix is constructed to assist in the decision makers, production processes using technological method A or B, yield the best BDI numbers if all other subsets of Tec As are chosen at 80 and 79 percent. The subsets of Tec Bs yield the lowest numbers at 58 and 57 percent. In addition, the most usual choices of middle-income developing nations, which is a selection of possible alternatives, and not necessarily the best Tec As choices are reflected in the 50/50 alternative. In this example, Tec mix yields 68, and 67 percent. This will still put the choice BDI index above the worst case of all Tec Bs subset alternatives.

In addition, given the assumptive and very constrictive choices presented by the real condition of developing economies, that A12, and most likely A 22 are the choices they are presented. However, Table 15 shows many alternative combinations among max, and opt choices, which can recalculated and present new BDIs. Therefore, Table 16 is only one sample of likely decision choices.

Notes

[1]. Viner Jacob, *Studies In the Theory of International trade*, (New York: Harper & Brothers, Publishers, 1937) pp. 521-522

[2]. Richard E. Caves and R.W. Jones, *World Trade and Payments, An Introduction*, 2nd ed., (Boston, Little, Brown and Company, 1977)

[3] Bahman Fakhraie, *Technological injection , dynamic new capital measurements, and Production Theory in Economics*, (Michigan: ProQuest LLC, 2010)

[4] Japans nuclear disaster, http://www.guardian.co.uk/business/2011/dec/27/fukushima-nuclear-disaster-firm-bailout ; http://www.nytimes.com/2011/12/27/world/asia/report-condemns-japans-response-to-nuclear-accident.html ; http://www.guardian.co.uk/business/2011/dec/27/fukushima-nuclear-disaster-firm-bailout ; Three Mile Island nuclear disaster, http://www.nrc.gov/reading-rm/doc-collections/fact-sheets/3mile-isle.html ; Chernobyl: http://www.unscear.org/unscear/en/chernobyl.html ; http://www.nrc.gov/reading-rm/doc-collections/fact-sheets/chernobyl-bg.html.

[5] John Von Neumann and Oskar Morgenstern, Theory of Games and Economic Behavior, 2nd ed., Princeton , N.J.: Princeton university press, 1974

[6] William J Baumol, *Economic Theory and Operational Analysis,* 4th ed., New Jersey: Prentice-Hall, 1977, 452

[7] Aris Spanos, *Probability Theory and Statistical inference: Econometric Modeling with Observational Data*, United Kingdom: Cambridge university press, 1999, 569-570

CHAPTER 14

ECONOMETRIC STUDY OF DATA

The Econometrics of new capital measures and technological variables are presented in this chapter. In the following tables, some of the measurements are classified and presented together to study the impacts of the new measurement used for technology and capital in economic production. Thus, "Teconomics" explains these combined and amalgamated new training practices as a new addendum to science of econometrics, and social behaviorist economics.

Important research show that further studies of all relevant factors of production have technological components for their potential impacts on production process.[1] Those with optimum correlations advance to extensive testing as follows.[2] Other related work continues.

The initial test run includes available viable data for an overall period, in this case, 1963 to 2004. Then for two subsequent decades, other tests are done, for the period of 1963-73, and the period of 1973-83. The comparative evaluation will aid our understanding of the performance of our data and new variables. The iterations occur before the econometrics' tests applications.

These are the log-determined multiple-regressions results for technological modified and requested new parameters, and traditional and adjusted capital. They have passed T-test and Chi square test, Correlation test, F-test, and R-Square tests. At 95 percent confidence level they are within the sample markers, the variables are independent from each other, and they are non-zero.

The data undergo DW iterations, and second run results (if required) take place. Alas, the results are constructively positive. Moreover, they back the hypothesis as stated in the original and present abstract. This set of variables represents the traditional estimation of capital stocks and the adjusted capital measures. In addition, set of data representing each capital stock, and adjusted capital stock are subject to the econometric analysis. Both sets will include a new variable, the educational parameter.

The Long Run Econometrics Study of New Technological Parameters

Table 16 shows the newly re-estimated capital stock and related parameters for the 1963-2004 periods.

The econometrics displayed here are the data after the second run Durban Watson adjustments.

Table 16. Comparative analysis of multiple regression parameters.

a	0.28938	%	a'	0.13625	%
V1	0.00126	.01	V1	(0.0255)	(2)
V2	0.12334	12	V2	0.2681	23
V3	0.89979	87	V3	.89578	78
u	0.30948	-	U+	0.030743	-
RTSt	1.02340	-	RTSn	1.14021	-

Note: The control tag name for data is t2ndrun/dstdfc32710.
The control tag name for data is CSs+2ndrun/dstdfc32710.
Data is for 1963-04 traditional and adj. & new tech., parameters.

Further analysis and evaluations of data again assist us in the understanding of these new parameters and their significance in our work. These are the log-determined multiple-regressions results for technological, modified, and requested new parameters.[3]

Even to the none-initiated to econometrics, the significance of the finding resonates. The simple comparison of RTSn and RTSt reinforces the proof of the theses-statement, as indicated in abstract copy enclosed with the body of the research.

The following equations are the log linear econometrics of production functions and proof equations.[4]

$$y = Ae^{a}c^{\beta}l^{\alpha}k^{\vartheta}e^{u}$$

The natural log of the exponential production relation above is given as follows:

Lny = lnA + alne + βlnc + αlnl + ϑlnk + ulne

Such that:

$$\ln y =$$

$$\sout{lnA}\,0 + a\sout{lne}=1 + \beta lnc + \propto lnl \quad + \vartheta lnk \quad + u\sout{lne}1$$

$$\ln y = a + \beta lnc + \propto lnl + \vartheta lnk + u$$

Such that: RTSt=f (a, v1, v2, v3, v4)

And RTSn=f (a, v1, v2, v3, v4)

Proof: RTSn>RTSt

The data have passed correlation fitness tests, F-type, and R-square tests. Their R-square regression fitness tests are significantly high.

The variables explain over 90 percent of changes in the dependent variable. The Durban Watson iterations take place with their statistic.[5] Alas, the results are affirmative. Moreover, they back the hypothesis as we suspected all along.

These sets of variables represent the traditional estimation of capital stocks, the newer adjusted capital stocks, and the newly add educational parameter. The addition of education as technology variable is not that difficult to establish. The importance of it in dynamic adaptation, training, and skill development associated with technologies had been assumed endogenous to the process.

However, funding appropriately has been relegated to the realm of political whims. Subsequently, tax and subsidization issues of technological fields have been allowed a dangerous pass. That has inflected a double whack at the demand side. In no-unionization and in no-taxation polices fashioned by the of the same industries and political dependence of democracy on them, the social costs associated with the structural unemployment associated with these industry have been financed by housing and other industries unabated for the last three decades.

Even the new students of econometrics can comprehend the significance of the finding of the study. By comparing the parameters and variables over time, we will see trends that can help our understanding of the improvements.

The simple comparison of RTSn and RTSt reinforces the proof of the hypothesis statement. That is, RTSn>RTSt.

Longer Run Econometrics of Traditional Capital and New Parameters

Econometric analysis of data set (CT2nd run/dstdfc32710 (1963-04)) is detailed in Table 17. The multiple regression analysis of data presents the elasticity of parameters. The three independent variables include the new parameter for educational funding. They are calculated for traditional, adjusted capital, and presented the right hand side of the data column.

Tables 17, show the more extensive data for 1964 to 2004. Table 17, 18, 19, and 20, show more econometric analysis for the same data set (CT2nd run/dstdfc32710 (1963-04)), they study the longer run time 1963 to 2004.

Table 17. Regression tests results for (1964-2004).

SUMMARY OUTPUT				actu(Ps)	%(P/RTS)
		a	1.33561	0.28938769	
Regression Statistics		v1	1.00127	0.00126918	0.001
Multiple R	0.952923	v2	1.13013	0.12233484	0.12
R Square	0.908063	v3	2.4591	0.89979695	0.879
Adjusted R Squar	0.900805	u	1.03143	0.03094819	
Standard Error	0.030948	RTS=	4.59051	1.02340097	
Observations	42				

ANOVA

	df	*SS*	*MS*	*F*	*ignificance F*
Regression	3	0.35948	0.11983	125.109	9.6994E-20
Residual	38	0.0364	0.00096		
Total	41	0.39588			

Regression for data Set [CT2; 32710 (1963-04)]

Table 18.

Regression coefficents for 1964-2004 data.

	Coefficients	*Standard Error*	*t Stat*	*P-value*	*Lower 95%*	*Upper 95%*	*Lower 95.0%*	*Upper 95.0%*
Intercept	0.2893877	0.307632379	0.94069	0.3528	-0.33338149	0.912157	-0.33338149	0.912156882
ct	0.0012692	0.00459224	0.27638	0.78376	-0.00802732	0.010566	-0.00802732	0.010565686
h	0.1223348	0.271857624	0.45	0.65527	-0.42801214	0.672682	-0.42801214	0.672681822
edmils	0.8997969	0.065684704	13.6987	2.8E-16	0.76682522	1.032769	0.76682522	1.032768679

T-test for data Set [CT2; 32710 (1963-04)]

Table 19. Chi square test result for (1964-2004).

RESIDUAL OUTPUT

Observation	Predicted y$	Residuals	
1	1.501320825	-0.018027188	4.903676
2	1.446246508	0.079034221	5.188161
3	1.543310326	-0.029101239	4.758695
4	1.536450143	0.001939913	4.811114
5	1.603543844	-0.04862514	4.559329
6	1.601354596	-0.026677648	4.587576
7	1.571304548	-0.022525515	4.679972
8	1.624527463	-0.036082251	4.512352
9	1.615709976	-0.027587121	4.545669
10	1.639128115	-0.067831957	4.440087
11	1.636424552	-0.030692282	4.484674
12	1.601219346	0.0257396	4.640383
13	1.627847437	0.025668704	4.564826
14	1.700958139	-0.064180787	4.279874
15	1.673814419	-0.021313085	4.393188
16	1.64510073	0.036993172	4.528546
17	1.665718012	0.026914716	4.462873
18	1.668315615	0.051446313	4.480498
19	1.711396992	0.010368777	4.327927
20	1.692177157	0.015638385	4.382236
21	1.687003143	0.060207202	4.440197
22	1.697284307	-0.012450176	4.341008
23	1.708899962	0.023629163	4.347496
24	1.732084753	0.032832014	4.298822
25	1.742896408	-0.002097508	4.237429
26	1.736223028	-0.002257027	4.253565
27	1.739936285	0.00446055	4.2512
28	1.757538205	0.007374153	4.211582
29	1.767983512	0.002943377	4.182313
30	1.764357445	-0.000956877	4.187002
31	1.752786729	-0.006973775	4.208631
32	1.764729945	0.00743459	4.194509
33	1.747849996	0.024186009	4.251698
34	1.784854922	0.003824019	4.143688
35	1.779727155	0.000155419	4.151947
36	1.779495258	0.015458424	4.167791
37	1.806962752	-0.000579508	4.088634
38	1.811995792	-0.007507219	4.070348
39	1.819833356	-0.003669028	4.056624
40	1.828446886	-0.006308729	4.034857
41	1.815666405	-0.013519242	4.056092
42	1.814846961	-0.00728542	4.064163
X^2 pass			183.7713

Table 20.

DW test results for 1964-2004 data

Model Summary

Model	R	R Square	Adjusted R Square	Std. Error of the Estimate	Change Statistics					Durbin-Watson
					R Square Change	F Change	df1	df2	Sig. F Change	
1	.951[a]	.904	.896	3.157E-02	.904	119.299	3	38	.000	1.671

a. Predictors: (Constant), V2,V3,V4

b.Dependent Variable: V1

c.Data Set [CT 2nd run/dstdfc32710(1993-04)]

The Table 19 Chi square test shows with 95 percent confidence the variables are independent of each other. X^2c > X^2t => H0, hypothesis H0, (Vi are independent of each other) is accepted. Hypothesis H1 (Vi are not independent) is rejected.[6] This holds for (i= 1, 2, 3). Table 20 shows the Durban Watson autocorrelation test for the data.

Long Run Econometrics Analysis for Data Set

Table 21 shows the econometrics analysis associated with data [CS+2ndrun/dstdfc32710 (1963-04)]. In addition, Table 22 shows the Chi square test result for the same data. Table 23 shows the Durban Watson test.

Table 21. Regression tests results for (1964-2004).

SUMMARY OUTPUT					
			a	0.136254	
Regression Statistics			v1	-0.0255	
Multiple R	0.953561		v2	0.268131	
R Square	0.909279		v3	0.897585	
Adjusted R S	0.902117		u	0.030743	
Standard Err	0.030743		RTS=	1.140215	
Observations	42				
ANOVA					
	df	*SS*	*MS*	*F*	*Significance F*
Regression	3	0.359965	0.119988	126.9561	7.53526E-20
Residual	38	0.0359144	0.000945		
Total	41	0.3958794			
	Regression analysis of data set CS+2 (1963-2004).				

Table 22. Chi square test for data set (1964-2004)

RESIDUAL OUTPUT			
Observation	*Predicted y$*	*Residuals*	
1	1.501320825	-0.018027188	4.903676
2	1.446246508	0.079034221	5.188161
3	1.543310326	-0.029101239	4.758695
4	1.536450143	0.001939913	4.811114
5	1.603543844	-0.04862514	4.559329
6	1.601354596	-0.026677648	4.587576
7	1.571304548	-0.022525515	4.679972
8	1.624527463	-0.036082251	4.512352
9	1.615709976	-0.027587121	4.545669
10	1.639128115	-0.067831957	4.440087
11	1.636424552	-0.030692282	4.484674
12	1.601219346	0.0257396	4.640383
13	1.627847437	0.025668704	4.564826
14	1.700958139	-0.064180787	4.279874
15	1.673814419	-0.021313085	4.393188
16	1.64510073	0.036993172	4.528546
17	1.665718012	0.026914716	4.462873
18	1.668315615	0.051446313	4.480498
19	1.711396992	0.010368777	4.327927
20	1.692177157	0.015638385	4.382236
21	1.687003143	0.060207202	4.440197
22	1.697284307	-0.012450176	4.341008
23	1.708899962	0.023629163	4.347496
24	1.732084753	0.032832014	4.298822
25	1.742896408	-0.002097508	4.237429
26	1.736223028	-0.002257027	4.253565
27	1.739936285	0.00446055	4.2512
28	1.757538205	0.007374153	4.211582
29	1.767983512	0.002943377	4.182313
30	1.764357445	-0.000956877	4.187002
31	1.752786729	-0.006973775	4.208631
32	1.764729945	0.00743459	4.194509
33	1.747849996	0.024186009	4.251698
34	1.784854922	0.003824019	4.143688
35	1.779727155	0.000155419	4.151947
36	1.779495258	0.015458424	4.167791
37	1.806962752	-0.000579508	4.088634
38	1.811995792	-0.007507219	4.070348
39	1.819833356	-0.003669028	4.056624
40	1.828446886	-0.006308729	4.034857
41	1.815666405	-0.013519242	4.056092
42	1.814846961	-0.00728542	4.064163
X^2 pass			183.7713

Table 23.

DW result after the second test run (1964-2004)

Model Summary

Model	R	R Square	Adjusted R Square	Std. Error of the Estimate	Change Statistics					Durbin-Watson
					R Square Change	F Change	df1	df2	Sig. F Change	
1	.951[a]	.905	.897	3.145E-02	.905	120.311	3	38	.000	1.709

a. Predictors: (Constant), V2,V3,V4,

b.Dependent Variable:V1

c.Durban Watson test for CS+2nd run/dstdfc32710

Table 22 shows a Chi square test with 95 percent confidence that all variables are independent of each other. X^2c > X^t => H0, that is the hypothesis H0 (Vi are independent of each other) is accepted, for (i= 1, 2, 3). Table 23 shows the Durban Watson autocorrelation test result for the data.

Comparative Graphic Proof

In Table 24, there is the comparative study of the technological parameter of traditional and adjusted capitals. The adjusted capital parameters show a distinct econometric improvement over the selected time span. The indicators as summation of technological parameters with adjusted capital exceed the indicators calculated using traditional capital for the same period. Since the calculations include the new technological parameters, this will be further proof that these are important variables to monitor and maintain for sustainable economic advancements. Figure 27 shows the new parameters, including traditional capital and adjusted capital over the extended periods. This will serve as the proof of our thesis in a longer period. The adjustments have improved the slope and the results are significantly positive for this period and the data.

Table 24. Technological parameters for two data set.

		1963-04	1963-04
		ct	cs+
a		0.28938 8	0.13625 4
v1		0.00126 9	-0.0255
v2		0.12233 5	0.26813 1
v3		0.89979 7	0.89758 5
RTSt,	RTScs +	1.02340 1	1.14021 5

Figure 27 shows the proof of technological injections over time.

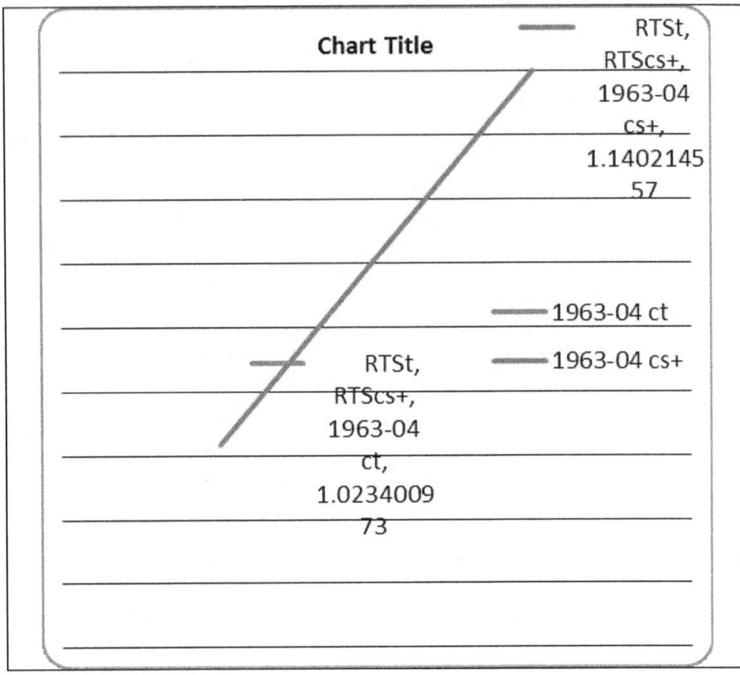

Figure 27. Comparative graph of data set from [dstdfnc32710.xl] .

The graph is sloping upward. The policy implication is remaining solid. That is, investing a dollar in investment choices returning 80 cents remains preferred to the set of the economic stimulus project, which returns 2 cents, or 20 cents. In a balance approach, one could balance out by investing more in the first set of investment with the higher retune, if it is necessary to invest in the second two sets, for lower returns. That is, return from technologies associated with adjusted capital stocks will be more positive.

Teconomics of Infrastructures

Modern Problems and Solutions

Application of Game Theory has found new students in applied econometrics and some social sciences are catching up to us. That is the way of science.

The applications of the methodology were productive in the early 1980s-1990s for the Western economic data and political economy, in related analysis of technological change and economic growth theory and social welfare economics.

First, a historical presentation of the rate of growth of some key data shows us the importance of our new parameter. The gap between the promises of investment in innovative advancements and the real rate of growth of invested-funds in these key representative variables is remarkable. Then, the real untold global unemployment disaster is also phenomenal.

The dynamic view of the United States economic variables in most of the last millennium prepared us for the difficulties of this millennium already starting on very shaky grounds. We heard loudly about the millennium projects, investments in innovational programs, higher education. Like West Coast ocean fog, with a little sun light and logic, the mist dissipates.

The calculations of variables are to show the importance of their relations. The econometrics data analyses focus on their importance in this research. These variables play an important part and affect the technological parameters under study in this research. The moderation in cycles and the pattern of these growth rates over an extended time, combined with the age-composition of the population affects workers immigration laws and demand side of the economy for years.

It is also true that economic cycles are repetitious facts. Since 1930s and 1940s, the violence of the large oscillations had been tamed. Until the recent two decades, when unguardedly, certain depression era laws were nullified, then risky innovational investment instruments (as deregulated securitizations) were introduced, which destabilized mortgage and bond markets globally. Once again, this proves not all changes are innovational changes that are good. The trends of externalities need to be studied very carefully, for their positive or negative inclinations. These are more reasons for more research and advancement of knowledge to study the follies. These areas should have received better treatment by researchers.

Figures 29 show a graphic presentation of the realities between what a nation wants to do, and what they actually do about rate of growth of technological advancements of knowledge by private and public means. From 1970s, to end of the 1990s, we see that rate growth in funding has been negative by both the private and governmental institution. These under funding had been taking place in face of increasing global competition. Figure 28 shows the growth rates for real GDP, (real gross domestic product, rG), the growth rate of population in the United States (rg_ResPop), the real growth rate of educational funding (Red), and the rate of the growth of real disposable income per capita (rdpipercapta).

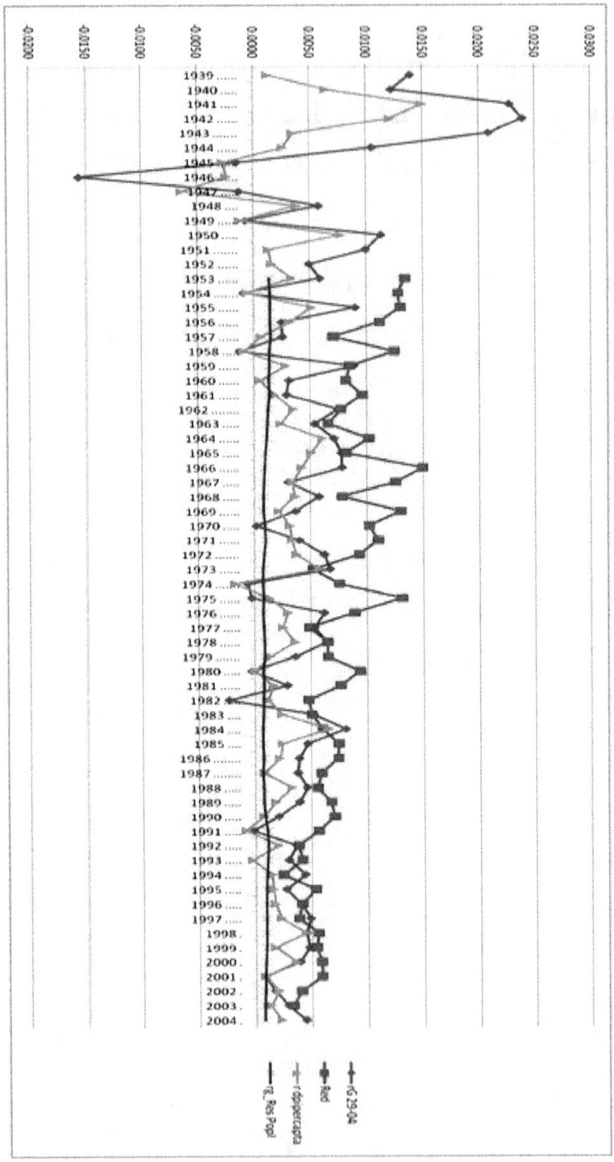

Figure28. USA dynamic growth rates in key data.

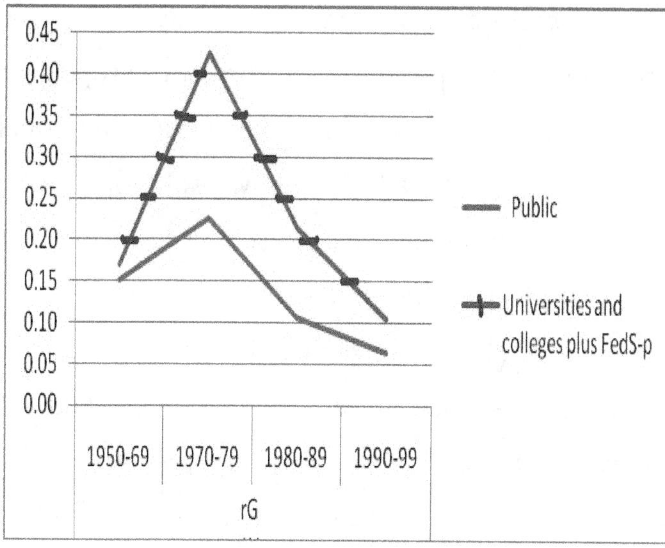

Figure 29. Growth rates of public invested funds

It is important to realize that the growth rate for resident population in the United States has declined. The reduction in growth rate of educational funding (Red) predates economic downturns.

A Global Catastrophe, Unemployment

In this shorter study, we look at the empirical data of Western economies and unemployment indices related to minorities and less represented elements of these economies, and study the correlation of their incidences of general social unrest in the same economies relative to each other.

The conclusion is not too difficult to ascertain, when the graphs are studied. What is more important is what each culture has designed to remedy the difficulties these complexities present. The very old European colonial strategies of blaming the underdog and policies in lieu of genocidal eradications, war-solutions, and exporting the problems have consequences that are more dangerous, while mere militarisms will not remedy. Those golden old strategies of beg thy neighbor, loot thy other neighbors, and burn thy neighbor books and knowledge sources, are as self-destructive now as they were then. Given the state of knowledge, let us all do better. We are all able to do better now. The following is a list of some negatives to avoid,

1. Fake assimilation to cheat the unknowing foreigners (immigrants) only delays and compounds the negative results.
2. Resource stripping them at home and cheating them out of employment at home and abroad will have definite economic consequential complications. One of which is no adequate demand in a competitive condition facing other products-differentiated supply economies. This is also true with racism, sexism, ageism, etc.
3. Undoing other democracies will guarantee you nondemocratic hostile alternatives. You will not like to deal with them, and they will not like to deal with

you, without paying for negative externality with much higher margins by all.

4. Torturing and border transgressions do not look good when dictators do them, they will not look good when democracies bamboozle themselves into doing them, using drones, gimmicks, and hand puppets.
5. Cheap tricks, multimedia theatricals are poor and consequential substitutes for the hard work of analytical diplomacy. Even, if the United Nation's words, gestures, or other institutions' actions supply the guarded-veils of indecencies. Communicational diplomacies are main necessary and sufficient tools for sustainable international policy, trade, and finance.
6. Deconstruction of viable infrastructure in public health, public education, immigration, incarcerations, and judiciaries for miserly saving will cost monstrous social costs, negative externalities, and add to unsustainable conditions in bad governances.

Militarisms have an inescapable self-terminating economic progression to them. They are dependent on functionality of the whole economy. They also have self-perpetuating monopolistic tendencies internally.

They are scientifically called recursive game theory models. Their finality is determined comes economically, they are self-terminating. Either you have an exit plan at the start, or a hurried one carries you out with your head handed to you at the exit, with the blood of innocence on your reputation for decades. Two of the most important examples came in Afghanistan, one happened to a colonial empire, the other to a super power. There may be pothers.

Therefore, doing the right thing is not a new Political Correctness, or a bit of wisdom handed to you in a Chayi khaneh, or café bistro, or psychobabbles in Western Infomercials.[78] It has the power and logic of mathematical theories behind it. The most harmed are the war initiators in modern times.[9] The finality of consequences are not at first overwhelming or outstanding. Creeping, crippling unemployment comes dynamically over time. Manageably deceptive at first, mission creeps and military industrial political complex (MIPC) will dominate the economy activates. Their impacts become clausal toward the end. They create their own niche, their own socioeconomics, and nihilistic politics. Democracies and want to be democracies will ignore those models at their own peril.

Dynamically, it causes blighted towns, cities, states, and countries.

The damages, the instabilities, become significantly larger, where imperfections thwart or dull the full forces of market and political signals. We have seen the harm it is inevitable. There, we will be seen again, the interferences with democracy and free market signals will harm progress. Policy makers if slow to respond will be nonresponsive to oncoming economic calamity as well. Often, the overconfident governments will not know what conglomerations of misfortunes will befall them.

Table 25 shows the estimation about the percentages of adult and youth minorities unemployed in some advance economies. It is very significant to comprehend that such statistic are difficult to obtain. Yet, they play such an important part in understanding of stability and sustainability of economic conditions in most economies. Reducing fees and streamlining appropriate regulations, increasing employment naturally adds to the stability and hopefully more rational discourses. No entity has the time or resources to pay attention or remedy to the perceived irrational discourses of all sides.

Figure 30 shows us, sometime it is wiser to pay attention and choose good policy. There are significant correlation and regression pointing at serious social problems in this area. The studies that link emigration and minority youth increased incarcerations by the dominant cultures are not isolated issues. Demagogic inflammatory rhetoric is harmfully destabilizing.

Table 26 is a Bayesian decision matrix. It points out a number of policy and regulatory moves and policy studies, which will reduce negative externalities associated with maligned neglects. The Bayesian decision matrix index of over 50 percent will require government intervention, investments, and job creation, etc.

Table 25. The percentages of unemployed minorities in advanced economies.

Country	Unemployed adults Foreign native		Unemployed youth Foreign native		Totals
France	30	17	17	7	71
Sweden	23	9	16	6	54
Spain					44
UK	14	11	10	6	41
Germany	12	7	13	7	39
Canada	-	-	-	-	30
USA	-	-	-	-	29
Australia	-	-	-	-	28
Japan	-	-	-	-	27
Netherland	-	-	-	-	19

Notes. From the President report 2004. Unemployment percentages of: adult (foreign, native), youth (foreign, native).

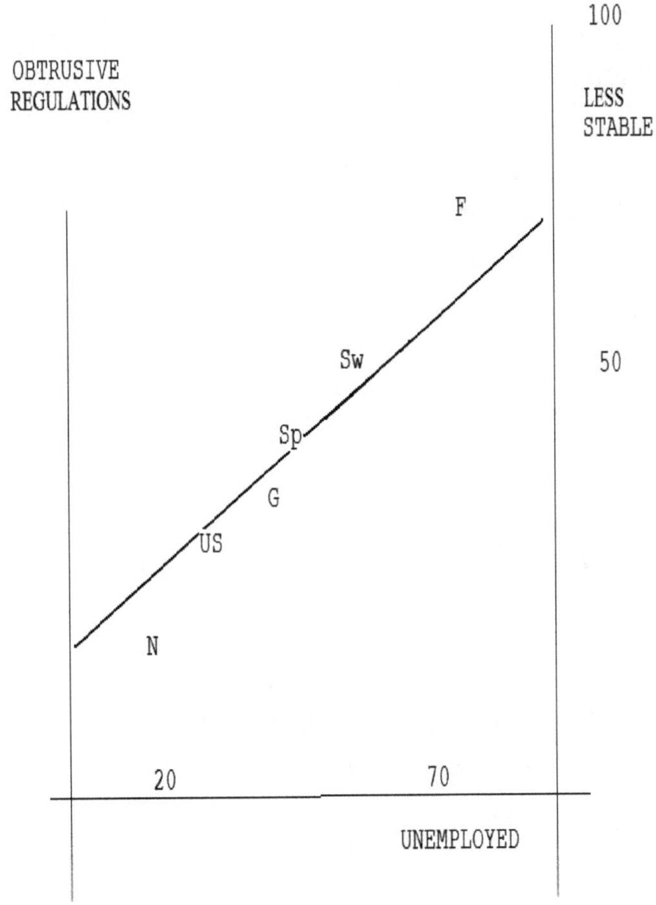

Figure 30. Policy matrixes for constructive trends.

Table 26. Using Bayesian decision matrix indices.

<table>
<tr><th></th><th>low
unemployment
Gov-assists+
Job-retraining</th><th>high
unemployment
Gov-assists?-
No job-
retraining</th><th>Less barrier to
Free & fair trade
Allowing mobility
of workers and
CAPITAL</th></tr>
<tr><td>Lower fees
and
abstractive
none
inclusive
laws,
Inclusive</td><td>< 20%</td><td>50-70%</td><td rowspan="2">BDMI >50%
Requires
Intervention
Gov. policies to reduce
it.
****
BDMI<50
Requires private
Ngo assists
To further stabilize.
****
Job creation
Fees-performance
Realignments,
Law reviews,
Non-alienation
Reviews,
Modernizations,
Ed.& job access</td></tr>
<tr><td>High fees
And
exclusive
Punitive
Regulations
Exclusive</td><td>20-50%</td><td>70-100%</td></tr>
<tr><td>Dangerous
politics;
Bigoted-
xenophobic
/exclusionary
racer bating
victimizing
policies</td><td>More
Stable
Less costs
Sustainable</td><td>Less
Stable
More costs
Unsustainable</td><td>Policy modification
required
Anti-racism
Anti-xenophobic
Exclusionary-anti
education

Bahman Fakhraie,
08;©®</td></tr>
</table>

Technological advancements are synonymous with development and growth. However, as we have studied it, with the externalities associated with it, it requires capital components, human, financial, educational, and stocks of capitals, in order to achieve sustainability of growth. That is, what will endure into sustainable development and maintenances of level of living most modern societies aspire to achieve.

The certainty and durability of such achievements are very dependent on high degrees of cooperation among all human cultures. Hence, free trade and free market associations are theoretical vanguards in modern human history for progress, as less self-implosive methodologies of acquiring improved-economic states.

Humanity also requires an accommodating political state to reason our path out of innate natural and genetic tendencies toward conflicts, to allow ourselves to obtain better lives.

Since enlightenment and discovery of scientific methodology, there are degrees of optimistic certitudes, at least among the intellectuals and academics, such sustainable states of cooperative coexistence through free commerce are possible for all humanity, despite the stubborn unhappy tendency amongst all of us to regress. Are we willing to take the positive steps to achieve such

Proof and Summary of the Pure Model

The thesis states the impacts of different measurements of capital stocks on embodied and disembodied technological variables on productivity and economic growth of national social products are tested. The role of a new capital stock measure introduced in the writing of Friedrich August Von Hayek, John Maynard Keynes, and further developed by Evsey D. Domar and ignored by most modern economist are examined. Therefore, we focus on the demand and supply side of technological embodied in capital both human skill and produced goods and services and the economy. Therefore, the thesis was to calculate adjusted capital and traditional capital measure, adopt reflective technological variables, and study their impact on production under the three-lemma conditions. This study has met those scholarly requirements exceedingly well. The econometrics analysis and graphic representation show the positive impact of those variables in the economy. The positively sloped graphic shows that dynamically, the adjusted capital measure combined with the newly added parameter reflect a constructive and increasing impact in the production over time.

In the derived demand for technological advancement, all-important elements that have encapsulated a growing focus and expanding financial forces to seek technological progress were studied.

In the supply-side analysis, the growing knowledge in human history has found its way into the production process globally. In this study, a theoretical expedition has woven the human history in scientific discoveries into the production process. The existence of good ideas in no way directly produces a bright and useful saleable product. The journey is the academic discovery and the story. How a scientist, a researcher brings these elemental disconnected abstracts to a holistically functional concept is still very important, it is very financially beneficial to the society and it should remain beneficial to the individual researchers, writers, scientist, and discoverers despite the evidence.

The most advanced aspects of theoretical economics have been delegated to the social welfare theories. The significance of these bodies of theoretical advancement studies the potentiality of good and bad side effects of the technological machineries. These externalities can easily misappropriate and destroy resources and human living conditions. They can do it technologically, exceeding faster than any living or existing defense mechanisms could repair their immediate damages, or longer term consequences. In this study, a theoretical moderation path accommodates freer trade, more resource utilizations, and more employment to enhance growth and employment of resources, while avoiding wasteful methodologies that only accommodates extreme ends.

The global options are limited. They are not always all we desire. They are redistributed unjustly, or without egalitarian ethics. This study of microeconomic analysis of technological advancement and contributions to the economy are encouraging. Therefore, with the open market mechanism, democracies (or relative democracies), and some added-infrastructures, the level of lives will improve in growing circles of humanity than present situations allow in large regions of Africa, Asia (including Eurasia), and South America. Nevertheless, it is comically insincere, for advanced mixed economies to become austere budget balancing capitalists as political opportunists. They are all beneficiaries of Keynesian redistributions' theories (with sustainable supply and demand sides' equilibrium and balancing mechanism). They become self-prescribed Adam Smith capitalists' economists on behalf of trans-global mega-monopolists.

Even Adam Smith would not recognize them. They become strict neoclassical monetarist economists on protecting their profits; however, they become flaming liberals and Stalinists' socialist in sharing their monopoly risks and operational deficits. The same myopic television tubes, which folds to totalitarians, dictators, militarists, and at least one global super power, are looking inside out at them, too.

The pretzel-convolutions occur, when the issue of North–South or sustainable development and economic growth for the South comes to discussion. Unfortunately, the current degree of human miseries and ubiquity of global communications are such that we will share the humanities' fortune and misfortunes alike, wherever we are, and regardless of any moral ambiguities, or theological complexities, and cultural or linguistic differences. Either, we are fueling the flames that burn us all, or we resolve our differences and agree to grow the trees and crops of heaven together to feed us all. Humanity can chose foolishly, glove up and go to fighting corners, misapply the instrument tools and technological of unifications, inclusivity, and competitive advantages to divisive ends, and waste inordinate amount of dwindling resources to ill ends.

Alternatively, humanity can chose wisely, in order

to reset its global trade-attitudes and superpower superiority-inferiority delusions, and come out to trade globally, but trade to include rather than exclude, to construct, and not to destruct. The value of a Great World War II President is that at the end of war, he became more protective of peace. His advice could have saved President Johnson a second term, A save in pulling out of the Vietnam war fiasco. President Dwight D. Eisenhower' speech has been a thorn under the inflated seats of many men and women of extravagant pomposities, beyond their own economic means, hellbenders on national economic self-destruction.[10]

"To all the peoples of the world, I once more give expression to America's prayerful and continuing inspiration,

We pray that peoples of all faiths, all races, all nations, may have their great human needs satisfied; that those now denied opportunity shall come to enjoy it to the full; that all who yearn for freedom may experience its spiritual blessings; that those who have freedom will understand, also, its heavy responsibilities; that all who are insensitive to the needs of others will learn charity; that the scourges of poverty, disease and ignorance will be made to disappear from the earth, and that, in the goodness of time, all peoples will come to live together in a peace guaranteed by the binding force of mutual respect and love."

The concept of national wealth building has expanded to include a global concept of wealth building, with thoughtful selection of appropriate technologies to accommodate sustainable strategies, along the integration strategies to improve human conditions globally. The adjusted capital and new technological parameters allow strategically to complement creative-destruction works, by dynamic creative-construction strategies to avoid the implications of economic failures, and to respond correctively for sustainable developments needs presently and in the future.

The following chapters study the implication of antithetical examples to the pure model.

Notes

[1] Author proposed new research to continue these studies and do more iteration, Grant.gov. Private funds and interests can contact the author, Dr. Bahman Fakhraie for more information, and the research packages at, dr.bahf.econ@ gmail.com.

[2] Michael D. Intriligator, *Econometric Models, Techniques, and Applications* (New Jersey: Prentice Hall, 1978), 288-292

[3] J. Johnson, *Econometric Methods*, 2nd ed., (New York: McGraw-Hill, 1972), 293

[4] Henderson and Quandt, *Microeconomic Theory; A Mathematical Approach,* 2nd ed., (New York: McGraw-Hill, 1972), 191-199, 280

[5] R.S. Pindyck and D.L. Rubinfeld, *Econometrics Models and Economics,* 2nd ed., (New York: McGraw-Hills, 1981), 157-164

[6] Data set used is (Ct2ndrun1963-2004 data se).

[7] Ghahveh khaneh, Chayi Khaneh, Coffee shops are common Eastern and Middle Eastern establishment. They are like electronic shops, pubs, and bars in the western countries. People congregate (smoke) drink tea or coffee, and trade or exchange information.

[8] Infomercials are a combination of television commercials mixed with tightly formulated trite information relative to the same commercials.

[9] President Richard M. Nixon termination of Vietnam War is one successful example, that the war dynamic was stopped, before its destroy the United States economy. Nevertheless, it had costs, and consequences.

[10] President Dwight D. Eisenhower's Farewell Address (1961)

CHAPTER 15

POLITICAL MONOPOLISTIC CAPITALISM AND WEALTH CONCENTRATION ARRANGEMENTS

It will be difficult to discuss futuristic visions, which does not involve the plight of educators, students, and recent graduates, middle class, working (includes women heads of households) poor, and the poor children and elderly Americans. The international economic implications of these misalignments have been lived. However, the effects are now pronounced and noticeable, morally by different religions, and ethically by different philosophies.

The demagogic history of the issues should not scare the reader away from an important discovery, that wealth creation element of free market, by job-creation and appropriate level of incomes in the relative free market mechanisms have been derailed by greed and self-indulgences.[1] They have been perverted away from the ethically accepted rules of capitalism in creation of decent jobs, livable salaries, sustainable functionalities system that feeds them, too.

Despite the fact, that well enumerated

inconsequential intellectuals are spinning mightily to present different middle class Americans' majorities as the new welfare-queens of the moment, and create another victim subclass to demagogue on the 24/7 fake news-channels, beside the immigrants and the brown, elderly, students, and women minorities.

There are malfunctioned wealth concentration arrangements realigning the wealth creation mechanisms in the once functional capitalists' economies. Since, this has been morphing over the last three decades the accumulated harm exceed the abilities of most small businesses to counter vial the currents.

The political monopolistic industrial organizations have mastered a self-destructive game, before they fully understand that they are its most likely victims, since they will have the most at risk. Therefore, they will have to finance most reparatory reworks. Therefore, cash-hoardings, minimum cooperate level tax avoidance are the wrong self-indulgences.

They know they are fulfilling a counter-productive duty to deflect and transpose the structurally widening real income gap in earnings and wealth concentration, and the breakdown of wealth creation in United States economy.

<u>Political Monopolistic Capitalism & Wealth Concentration Schema</u>

In fact, the unethical cacophony of monopolistic capitalism enslaved these once true representatives of this great exceptional American democratic republic so bad they readily overlooked, cooperate welfare queens, which are manipulating the social benefits and welfare system of the very poor to their underpaid-workers.

In face of historic profit, stock values, and CEO pay and bonus-checks, shamelessly, while they boldly under pay their taxes to refund the depleting reparatory systems. Those are the only reparatory systems available globally.

Modern Plights of U-graduates and U-students

In particular, It is important to understand the plight of modern university students, and recent graduate victims of the do-nothing political economic and great depression epoch, and the jobless recovery, two of their byproducts. It is positive that some universities have discovered the plight of their long-suffering students now. Especially the ones that were bamboozled by a double whammy, the promised cheap student loan rates fixed at 3 percent, and then cheated by the ARM rate, that is now around 6-7 percent per annum. Moreover, the promised job market that was vaporous.

The student walked into the post Iraq-war jobless-recovery economy, worsened by the obstructions of the wrong political party, austerity and sequestration, and their belated post-wars deficit hawking. Do you think those students will discover they are blocked out of casting their legal votes without reading? Voting rights are rescinded, blocked, reduced, and ham-hugged, in monopolistic one political party system at states levels. There are valiant efforts by great lawmakers of both political parties. Yet, this fast but not too deep mathematical study of comparative averages is not kind to the corporatist view, which tends to cheat the badly needed academic content-makers, modern innovators, and the middle class and working educators, and poor, which go under the budget buses readily.

The cooperation minimum tax, social security tax for higher incomes were not adopted, they were not even on the menu, but everyone else goring-oxen were on the menu. They want something for nothing for cooperate profit maximization, but they never want or understand the overall economic relative-competitive sustainability that maintains the balances, and encourages the circulatory conditions of demands and supplies.

The average tuition in some public university is estimated about $7000 per annum in 2013, in 1970s it was around $1000 a year. A book of about 200 pages or less was around $20 in 1970s. The arithmetic calculation of the relative ratios is solved by this kind of formulation,

($7000x$20)/$1000 = $140. That is the estimated average cost of the same kind of books in 2013 dollars. Most textbooks of less than 200 pages are priced at or around $80-$120 a book, if you look at your university bookstore.

Nevertheless, let us look at the bigger arithmetic picture. The economy that cheated the old students then, and plagiarized their works, subjected them to xenophobic bigotry, and under paid their wages then, cheated itself. Now the same students may be the academics that are writing books. Because the same broken political machinery will accuse them of anger issues, greed, while cheating them out of good contracts, vanishing tenure systems, a livable level of living incomes and benefits, and let entropy eat out the infrastructural constructions beneath their feet and America.

Therefore, they will cheat the economy out of sustainable recoveries. Moreover, they will blame them for a decaying anachronistic criminal cooperate greed that aims and tends to rhetorical wealth-concentration, away from the wealth creation of modern teconomic sciences. That involves job-creation, too.

Arithmetic Holistic View

The bigger arithmetic pictures show the more holistic vision of these idiotic and reviled nightmares. Gasoline was $0.35 per gallon (in nominal terms), when I bought my first car, the blue jet, it is $3/gal, 2013. Now, that is 857 percent increase for the last 35 years, 22 percent a year.

Average U-CEO (a U. administer) salary was $100,000. It is about $1 million now. That is at the poor house-Us, state public universities. That is 1000 percent increase, 28.6 percent per annum.

The costs of cable connected big screen TV is $1000+$2400 is equal to $3400 per year. The cost of the TV was $200 the rest was free, 1975. That is 1700 percent cost of living adjustment. It is 48.6 percent per year. I will not further elucidate cooperate CEOs 500 plus times over the Americans' average incomes of $40,000 a year. However, let us face it. The $40,000 seems two times higher than most average salaries around your neighborhoods.

The Sponged-brain damaged sportsmen on the cable sport channels 24/7, some are sometime lucky in the shorter run. Only those lucky few will get million dollars contracts, and the unlucky many will parish in solitudes with damaged brains and mostly penniless. That is the human savagery of the last two millenniums, which continues unabated. It is one of most intellectually dishonest human right abuses for cooperate entertainments of our lifetimes, since the fall of blasted gladiators of Roma. Children, university players, and pros are all subjects of cooperate brain-sponge-making money-machine for profit. Yet, corporatist anti-educators will want to add the academic book writers to the bodies of these victims.

Things will really get ugly, if we raise the curtain and look under the table of the bombastic anger mongers, and bloviating blow hearts of modern cable-media. You know the $10 & $11 million dollars a year nabobs of negativities, and the 24/7 nothingness, the true masters of blubbering mental incertitude, and the squeaking windmills of their minds. The same corporatist-blue-dogs and their corporatist' charlatans that declared class warfare on the middle class, working poor, graduates, and absolute poor some 30 years ago, they are still at it, again. Trickle-down doubtful economic assertions became tinkle-down political spins a long time ago. The war on intellectuals and academic started with Nixon, not yesterday by a few rightwing nuts.

Teachers have been bamboozled like everyone else, with almost all of the middle class workers for a flat 2-4 percent per year cost of living adjustment, while the rest of economy has been pulling ahead, which is causing the slow recovery. Institutionally cheating your academics, educators, or book writers out of their share will damage the econmy where it really hurts, in your personal economy, aside from their rights to exercise of their legal options and remedies. You can always stay in the ocean of ignorance and 'curse the recondite darkness' you have created institutionally, without blame against the idiotic leaderships. The obsolete cooperation spinners hope you will be used to it, and become their cooperation intellectual and eye slaves. It is importunate you read the good books, even if it financially helps the intellectuals and the academics sometimes.

Harsh Historic Economic Lives of Others

The Great Millennial Legacy of Nelson Mandela (1918-2013) is a shared experience with other leaders of the civil right and nonviolent movement internationally.

The three continents none-violent political and economic movements advanced and learned from the life story of Madiba in the last two millenniums.[2] The great legacy of President Nelson Mandela contains many accomplishments. He was the modern leader of the nonviolent political movement for freedom, justice, and an egalitarian, peaceful, and finally and mostly productive co-existence political movement. He was also a freedom fighter, announced and denounced, and jailed terrorist, and finally the universally admired President of South Africa.

President Mandela shared his beloved country and Africa with India's Mohandas Mahatma Gandhi.[3] Their timelines and shared life story are amazingly similar.

Gandhi, Mandela, together with Dr. Martin Luther king Jr. they gifted three continents, of America, Africa, and Asia with the freedom, peace, and justice and the successful nonviolent co-existence. [4] These multicultural political civil right movements advanced humanitarian lives and the personal economies of all races on three continents.

The reviviscences of great human persons of last and this millennial history is a severe but required admonition of the long gallops away from democratic and constitutional jurisprudence, into the hate-lands of state militaristic-intrusions, or technology-intensive violence against privacy and property of citizens with massive collateral damages. States can fool the citizenry with false security, while they abolish their rights and humanities. The old media documented the three vanquished harangues in history extensively, if the commercial modern media wanted to do reality-exposition of facts of history.

The life and time of Mahatma Gandhi evolved from overt violence of South African Apartheid, colonial feudalistic repressions, mono-racial domination politics, to then India under colonial economic domination and overt racial-politics are enumerated conservatively in his memorial book.

These governments were using technological advancements of their times, not for economic advancements of their population, or the majority of their population, but for domination, political and economic objectification, and control of the majority of their populations, which happened to be black and brown. Utilizing technologies as paper please laws, individual monitoring for control. They would have immediately adopted E-verify, Cell phone tapping, computer implants, if they had the technology. They would have applied them for the profiling and subjugation rather than advancement of their population.

The moral of stories of lives and times of Mohandas Mahatma Gandhi, Dr. Martin Luther King Jr., and President Nelson Mandela are not the success or the whitewash of state terrorisms, feudal colonialism as public control policies. Since, the states would use jails, guns, bullets, and advanced technologies (drones & robotics), and violent terminations of privacies, and human dignities, against their population. Moreover, they did. It is the success and advancement of human causes of even marginalized people, their freedom, one-person one vote, economic and political rights, triumphs of justice, dignity of making a living, jobs, and working within humanitarian frameworks and laws that shines.

The exclusionary politics and policies they fought, and the 'inclusion' of politics and economics they advanced, all benefited more people. They employed more than one race or group economically. Some of the basic facts escaped then the President Ronald Regan administration, but not both houses of representatives, when they overturned the President Ronald Reagans White House veto on divestments from Apartheid-government of South Africa, (as W.H. shared sympathy with Europe, Israel, and some other nations).

We would all live smaller economic lives, if we forget their lives-lessons from their lifelong struggles internationally. It is astonishing how easily these lessons are lost on big and small, democratic or dictatorial modern governments. Perhaps great gatherings of leaders in his great memory will advance greater causes of peace, egalitarian job-income equities, more trades, and more job-creations.

Notes

[1] Millennial political economic issues, which none-functionality and obstructionisms have accumulated nationally and internationally. Realistic and educated configurations and new strategies out of the compound economic problems evolved, they were presented and they are studied. Dr. Bahman Fakhraie (Author), *POLITICAL MONOPOLISTIC CAPITALISM, WEALTH CONCENTRATION SCHEMA, UNITED STATES TECONOMIC ANALYSIS, 2014 The Haves, The Have-Nothings, And The Have-Less* , Paperback– January 21, 2014, http://www.amazon.com/Political-Monopolistic-Capitalism-Wealth-Concentration/dp/0989453995/ref=la_B00IKAR1CM_1_4/177-6617163-7755868?s=books&ie=UTF8&qid=1417192184&sr=1-4

[2] http://www.goodreads.com/author/list/367338.Nelson_Mandela http://www.npr.org/2013/12/06/191579391/the-man-the-myth-the-reading-list-3-books-on-nelson-mandela, Long Walk to Freedom: The Autobiography of Nelson Mandela, Conversations with Myself, By Nelson Mandela, http://www.usatoday.com/story/life/books/2013/12/06/nelson-mandela-reading-list/3890661/

[3] The Story of My Experiments With Truth, The Essential Gandhi: An Anthology of His Writings on His Life, Work, and Ideas by Mahatma Gandhi, Louis Fischer (Editor), etc. https://www.goodreads.com/author/list/5810891.Mahatma_Gandhi

[4] Stride Toward Freedom: The Montgomery Story. New York: Harper & Row Publishers, 1958. Dr. King's first book, The Trumpet of Conscience. New York: Harper & Row Publishers, 1968. (Foreword by Coretta Scott King.), Where Do We Go From Here: Chaos or Community? New York: Harper & Row Publishers, 1967, Why We Can't Wait. New York: Harper & Row Publishers, 1963, http://www.thekingcenter.org/books-bibliography#BookMLK http://www.thekingcenter.org/books-bibliography

CHAPTER 16

CONCENTRATION AND PERMANENT-WARS SCHEMA

Blame anything for the jobless economic recovery, but the bad policies that caused it. If you do not fully comprehend the powers of imperfect competition and the full implication of organization power in keeping wages low and disposable income flat for three decade, you will go blame something else (it can be technologies) for economic joblessness, you blame everything you do not understand.

Paddling plumping jobs, low wage jobs, and two-year college degrees when you have substantially kept DPI low, is a new intellectual lowbrow politics, slithers out of the failed supply-siders and our friends in that desperate political party, and their embedded journalistic companions, which deported the middle class job creators and jail-warehouses the unemployed youth and minorities.

However, they have clung to that new economic religion as readily as blame guns, or technology as if these entities can think and do thing for themselves, and they can dispossess massive populations, or keep wages and incomes increases flat as a percentage of GDP, for the middle class, labors, workers, graduates, since 1970s.

Perhaps, next we will hear that it is the technology that is pumping cooperate citizens (the other new entities') money into local, national, and presidential campaigns, for certain laws, while suppresses the voters rights, and fight reasonable health care for all citizen, or a functional comprehensive immigration bill. They will not represent efficiently, the majorities that are portrait as takers.

Yet, the do-nothing-congress persons still are paid, and they receive their universal healthcare, while they are not doing the citizens business.

Wealth-Concentrators

Wealth-Concentrators They sing free-enterprise economy, but they do not see anything wrong with massive shoveling of money, 500 time more than average incomes to one class as CEO wages. If you do not want to pay your taxes on that ill-gotten public money in your own private catchy, of course you will blame anything or anyone to disguise the facts. Therefore, instead of pushing for a functional constitutional democracy, more balanced sustainable fiscal policies, and monetary policies, you blame inanimate objects for wrecking the middle class economic conditions. Instead of cost of living raises, level of living wages for educators, workers, you blame them for what your underfunding urban and rural education has caused.

They pay for hack journalism, and backward embedded journalism, small-minded scholarship, and fake wars, which kill and dispose real people. I think American citizens already know who will wreck USA economy, because they are the same people who already wrecked the middle class USA, Detroit, Stockton, others. The American and people globally know it was not an IT.

The Teconometrics

It was not elderly measly pension fund contracts. The investor bankers, their political industrial complex, deregulated the laws and swindled them out of their IRA, stock funds, and pension benefits, and usurious student loans, and no-jobs recoveries, well before the new crew shown up for their shameful legacy banners.

Econometrics Relation of Employment and Disposable Personal Income Data

Av rg tot 7.2 slope of job/dspi 1959-2013 0.150135321
Av rg 3.66 slope of job/dspi 2003-2013 0.051169688
RSQ tot 1959-2013 0.871441531
Corr tot 1959-2013 0.933510327

Natural logarithm growth rates, and averages, and slope regression and RSQ, and Corr for correlation among employment and disposable personal income indices are used.

Beyond positive correlation, there is the magnitude of slopes. That is much higher for total data 1959-2013, monthly data of dpi, and total employment, when average growth rate of dpi was higher at 7.2 percent 1959-2013, versus the average growth rate of 3.66 percent for 2003-2013. That is also reconfirmed, by a positive relation and correlation 93 percent, and total data shown by RSQ 0.87 for total data 1959-2013. Some summation can note the higher growth rate 3-7 with much higher job growth slope. That overall job-creation performance was three time higher than the millennial recovery periods of job creation from the year 2003 to year 2013.

Job-Creation

Despite Jeers or Adulation, Job-Creation We Must! Europeans' political fascinations with extreme right, even after messianic terrorisms by far right individuals, are cause for further contemplations.[1] One prepends, is it rumination for economic enlightenments, or the unfortunate regurgitation of past nightmares. The suppositions, which blame multiculturalism (mostly Moslem emigrants this time, it was Jews a few generation back), in otherwise exclusionary and elitists' cultures, neither contributes or assists Islamic scholars in moderation of Islamic radicalism, nor can it curb the implosive peculations, which have increased joblessness and multicultural misfortunes equally.

They have the immorality of latent Machiavellianism, and the violence of Uncle Adolf's Menageries; nevertheless, they have no remedies for mass reemployment.

European governments chose expensive and failed but essential macroeconomic experimentalisms and joblessness, which encouraged the far rights' erroneous trite suppositions.

Great Leadership

Leaderships that fear the extreme right will again fail the Western world. In time of economic scarcities, which will test or prohibit "beg thy neighbors" dependencies, leadership is needed. Will the great leadership prevail? What economic destinations are in the leaderships' visions?

Thus, financing adventurousness without full benefit of free trades and enhanced commercial-international trades (otherwise, jobs creating and sustaining healthy economies) will only serve as determents to free commerce. These situations will only encourage prudence of diplomacy over carte blanche (blank checks) militarisms. Historically, this modesty of intend seem to have been imposed on the leaderships repeatedly. Even United State will have hard enough time, to shift from war footing into domestic economically enhanced job-creations.

It is amazing how imperceptibly, with a short skip from the haloed high halls of higher education to certain political catacombs Job-creationism retrogrades into theological creationism; alas, the echoes are trite, untrue, unconvincing, and displaced logical constructions and maintenances of sounders structures, and hypothesis, all available to functional democratic free market economies.

Deregulations can be more harmful than bad regulation. Deregulation of meat industry can lead to bacterial outbreaks. Deregulation of clean-coal industries can give us cave-ins in our numerous global coalmines and string of death, toxic streams and lake, acid rain, and the same old expedited carbon-over-loads. Relaxed regulation can unchain petroleum deep-water cowboy-drillings, which wasted Southeast food industry, and for years and billions of dollars, yet to be fully and economically studied.

The unhindered nuclear energy industries can shut down and radiate a third to half of another nation for years and trillion dollars, yet to be partially comprehended or researched. The unencumbered natural gas industries can proceed with their deep well fracturing, yet to be economically researched, or fully disclosed, which can duplicate the deep well spill disaster on land. Currently, we have to take the words of the industry in forms of commercial outtakes for the future of this great nation.

Deregulation of investment banking, the cowboy-securitization of mortgage-industries without the jeered consumer protection regulations, and the fought-regulations of derivative industries have done more than BenLadenism did, but they do it intentionally and internally.

Most of these alteration and objections to regulations came from oligopolistic or even monopolistic cooperate interest with only a veneer of pro-free enterprise spin from financiers. Mr. Madoff goes without roommates and poker hands, awaiting many global political and financial mega-Madoffs. The justice department can barely keep up with them. Yet, no one is droned Wall Street shenanigans, or all of these white-color crimes in USA, or Europe.

Political Deconstructions of Infrastructures, Immigration Law, and American Economy, 2014

Political deconstructions of infrastructures, immigration law manipulations, in 2014 did not help American economy to bloom. The policies of deconstructions of American infrastructures and economy have not been good for American middle class, or America. Why should we sugar code them now? However, the GOP has a chance to repair the deconstruction. Let us beware of anti-immigrant creeps, anti-minority, anti-elderly and anti-women, anti-democrat, anti-science, and anti-liberals deliberate bad-news-clustering by monopolists' media (YNN, farcical fixed news, and others) they use bad news clustering, and planted attack news, as political agenda for deconstructions. The xenophobic, bigoted southern strategists, fake rented-intellectuals, and token purchased-GOP energy experts are taking advantage of fake Democrats and dumping news on American viewers, while they insist on American deconstruction policies. The agenda has not been job creation, real disposable income adjustments, and functionality of governmental services, for middle income America.

It has been tax breaks for upper incomes and cooperate citizens, and income transfers, and wealth concentration for the upper income earners. The deconstructions have been a gradual and chronic sideshow. Health care industries, educational and higher learnings, incarcerations industries, and finally national security and privacy busting industries have used privatization and free enterprises cover for harmful deconstructions, with maneuvering, profiteering, revolving door shape shifting commonly reported occurrences.

Somehow a pipeline to export Canadian very dirty and polluted oil to other international markets, which will pump and dump that toxic pollution in the California, Oregon, Seattle and Alaskan air initially in less than four days, and the rest of America later, has become the end of all policy mantels of the vocal village idiots for cash.[2] It is important that proper expert-studies that would measure the huge and increasing negative externality costs of toxic pollution, underground aquifers' permanent pollution, children with asthma, adult pulmonary diseases went ignored, unpaid, and unstudied by the friend of industry research papers, and fake sciences of anti-science industry. However, those less than 100 permanent jobs are job creation, but the multimillion jobs for needed infrastructures-projects were not, and they were not job-creation in all states of United States. All these years the American infrastructures were to be ignored, because they help employ Americans, but tangentially they may help a black minority president.

The other ballyhoo screams these days has been that immigrants take jobs away.[3] These incompetent anti-science-jerks, sexists, xenophobic bigots refuse to acknowledge that they have obstructed job creation, for all these year that they have illegally derailed, usurped, tricked and cowed administrative enforcements, and blocked ethical, moral, or functional comprehensive immigration laws. All the While, they are calling the waiting victims of their institutional legalese, their political inactions, abusive politics, lawless banking and real estate economic plunders, and their familial deconstruction of immigrations-policies established laws, illegals.

Let us read the first sentence of Amendment XIV Section 1, "All persons born or naturalized in United States and subject to jurisdiction therefore, are citizen of United States and the state wherein they reside." Any of the three conditions are qualifiers despite the xenophobes' exclusionary interpretation. After all, the founding fathers did not write the constitution in a neo-Nazi camp. Abraham Lincoln was the 16th president of the United States.[4] He found the intellectual root and the immigration links to Declaration of Independence.

John F. Kennedy another great president of the other political party thought the subject of such importance that he wrote a book on immigration.[5] Nevertheless, the issue has been bipartisan among all Presidents. Because of its importance, any alterations must meet necessity, sufficient, and sustainability conditions.

Figure 31 shows unemployment since 1947.[6]

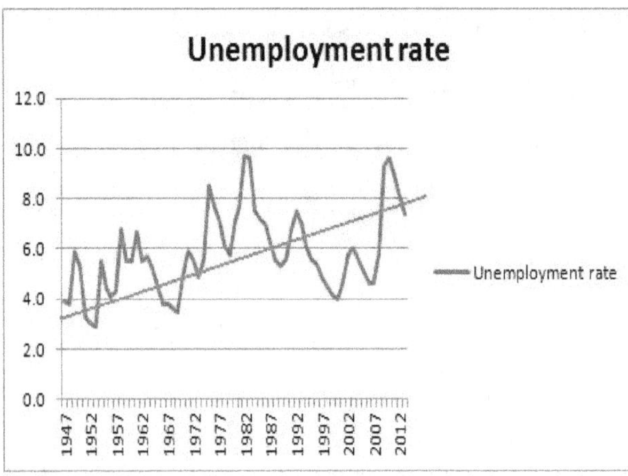

long term unemployment rate, and trend line

Figure 31, Unemployment rates and trend line 1947-2012.

Therefore, no president has left his or her constitutional purgative unexercised in fear of mouthy bigoted xenophobic bullies. So, a president going big and flying high and bold for America, easing and unclogging naturalization regulations maize and costs, is the only legal way to stop the odoriferous and odiously anti-constitutional intellectual-constipation of the GOP-anti Reagan and anti-immigrants' xenophobic hate agenda of the extremists.

Moreover, presidents expand the dwindling election fortunes of his or her political party, especially after the gerrymandering and vote blockages recently. We assume all of that gerrymandering is "legal," and it is not antithetical, corruptive, and coercive to concept of representative republic, relative free markets, and democratic representations.

All these years job creation has declined and data shows job per population ratios and trend lines have structurally declined, and unemployment rates have increased not because of immigration, but because of insufficient flow of immigration, human and other capital obstructions.

The ill impacts of wealth concentrations versus wealth creation had also been enumerated in multiple scholarly studies and books. The negative externalities of declining real disposable income and middle class Americans had been demonstrated as well. All of these occurred as they blocked immigrations, but followed bad policies of deconstruction of American infrastructures and economy by their own republican selves.

Figure 32 shows employment population ratios for gender and age in United States for 2004 to 2014.[7] The structural unemployment down ward shift is seen in all segments of the population. The youth has sustained 25-35 percent unemployment ratio levels.

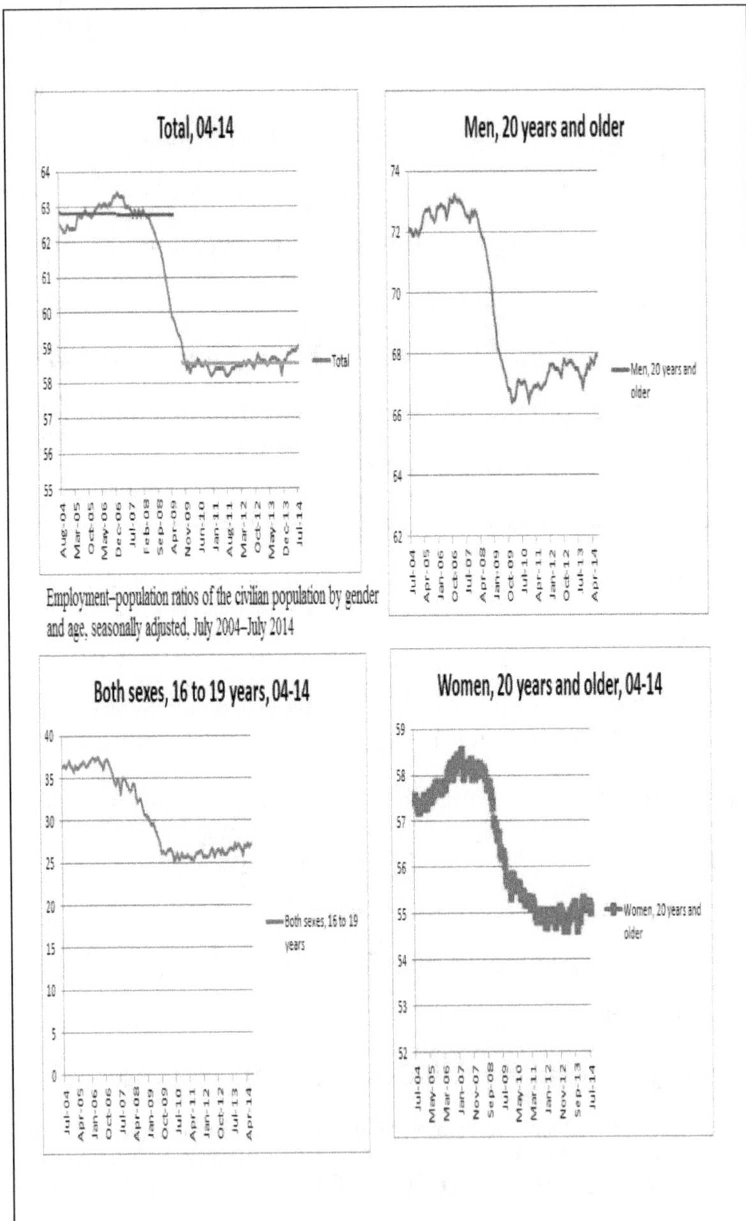

Figure 32, Employment population ratios for gender and age in United States for 2004 to 2014.

They have failed a simple grasp of the obvious economic model for dummies, if you give $17 trillion value of GDP to one American; you will still have a huge economic depression problem, as circular flow and redistributive aspect of relatively free market will shut down, un-sustainability and socioeconomic unrest will be probable and expected. If the one American employs up to 300 million Americans and gives them all jobs and livable salaries, those index show signs of economy activity, twice the normal indices. Since we do not like any entity (a government), take 55-80 percent, and redistributed it like a communist, or totalitarian government. Since, all 300 million people will need to live, be schooled, hospitalized, and drive on roads to markets here and there. There has to be enough low taxes 15-35 percent to build those infrastructures, in a functioning democracy.

They have been the job killers, since data shows the rate of unemployment has increase for all those years that they blocked the comprehensive immigration, a fact that presidents after president understood and said so, President Reagan expressed it. Those presidents used administrative enforcements to countermand xenophobic self-flagellations of grand wizards of temporary success, and short-term shenanigans, which victimized American job creation for all these years.

Talking about important presidents, that is why we have reached that point of constitutional and constructional-crisis, which a president can rightly tell the know-nothing and do-nothings: you have failed to do your constitutional duty for too long. Therefore, we will give you a full meal in form of a comprehensive immigration laws. Moreover, you tell Americans, while you are victimizing them, why you cannot tie your shoes running to cash your taxpayers paid big congressional checks for all of these years that you have done nothing.

There are no reason to use any internet portals, unless they respect Net-Neutrality, your privacy, and personal rights. Do not support or use browsers, politics, and businesses who do not respect your interests, your constitutional rights, and protection. Why feed business monopolies, and internet monsters that become monetizing animals, which will devour your legal rights. We have arrived at that fork in constitutional road. Choose very wisely, and support and encourage the right business behaviors, and commercial conducts among your internet links, consumptions, and web market choices. You are after all the 80 percent of American business, not the overpaid CEOs that would suffocate American job-creation economy for their personal wealth-creation strategies. Do not feed the xenophobic bigoted media monopolistic jerks, that victimize minorities, immigrants, and elderly for shyster new shakedowns, and objectification by sexists bamboozles of the week, or threaten violence, when they are breaking the law and committing human right crimes, class warfare, and cultural war crimes against poor, middle class, and elderly Americans for cooperate greed and profiteers.

The epochs of political mantras are past. The focus will have to be forward to the future, looking to 2016 and way past the election to appropriate future democratically elected governments. Because mostly stopping deconstruction of United States economy and meaningful job-creations cannot sadly wait for another election, and a republican president. Since the only road to higher office is a higher campaign road. Skillful opponents, self-inflected extreme obstinacy, and xenophobic hate language have reduced opposition's chances of successful victories. Unless the oppositions use undemocratic older techniques like gerrymandering, vote blockages, raise election ID card costs, voter intimidations, and dirty tricks are used to reduce voters. The construction should be dynamic regardless of peculiar politics of incumbents and minority party.

Notes

[1] Dr. Bahman Fakhraie SA on (9-20-2011).

[2] Dr. Bahman Fakhraie (Author), Teconomics of Dynamic Risks: All natural Disasters, And Energy Resource Production Disasters, and Some Financial Risks, Utah, FERDAT Publishing, 2013, https://www.createspace.com/4282704. For more reading try the book web pages links:

a-http://bahfecon.wix.com/bahfecon
b- http://www.amazon.com/Dr.-Bahman-Fakhraie/e/B00IKAR1CM/ref=ntt_athr_dp_pel_1
c- http://drbahfecon.wix.com/teconomics

[3] http://www.foxnews.com/…/source-obama-to-announce-10-point…/

[4] Patrick Young Esq., Lincoln, the Know Nothings and Immigrant America, http://www.longislandwins.com/…/lincoln_the_know_nothings_a

[5] John F. Kennedy, A Nation of Immigrants, 26-27, Jan 8, 1963, http://www.ontheissues.org/…/Nation_of_Immigrants_Immigrati

[6] http://www.bls.gov/ces/#tables

[7] Ibid, Dr. Bahman Fakhraie (Author), Teconomics of Dynamic Risks: All natural Disasters, And Energy Resource Production Disasters, and Some Financial Risks. Utah, FERDAT Publishing 2013, https://www.createspace.com/4282704.

CHAPTER 17

MISERLY SHEMA AND JOBLESS RECOVERY

Therefore, the suppositions of the executive suites and their paid lobbyists, that it is either Dodge City or full-unemployment, are manufactured manageress of dangerously unpatriotic greedy war-robots. It is astonishing how the self-defense of realm, has evolved and expanded into global dominations, and police action international, while the tax base of funding wars had devolved to the incomes of middle class and low income portion of the population.

The sententious absolutisms seeds to encumber job-creation for political misdeed will yield unfortunate shared harvests. It will only add to the other sins of union bashing, low-wage control, discernible capital mobility, defalcation of national wealth in the recent path for permanent-wars, and dishonest upward wealth-concentrations. It will add to the perceptual sins of domestic populism for greed and self-enrichments without the promised shared social benefits.

Figure 33 shows the gap between individual income taxes, and business taxes.[1]

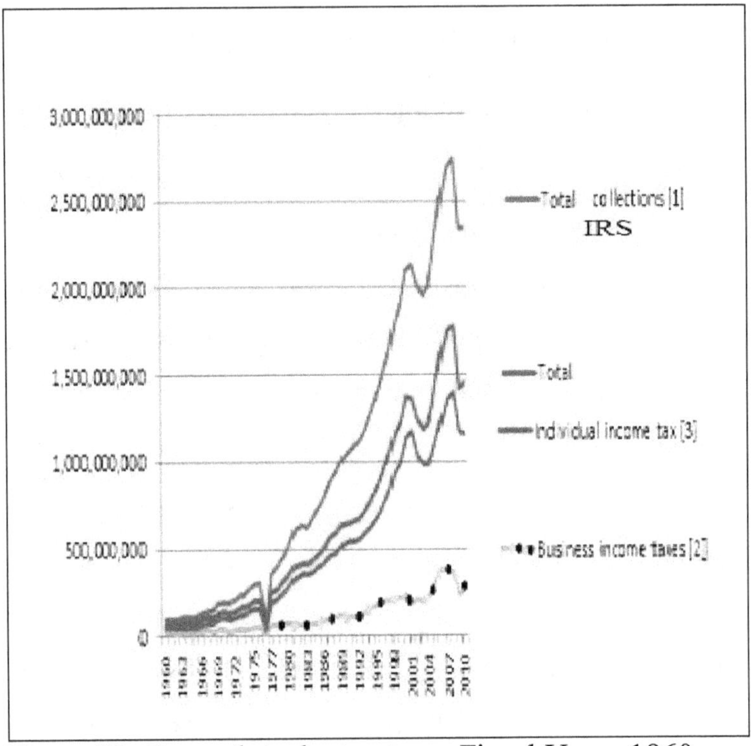

Figure 33, Gross data, by tax type, Fiscal Years 1960–2010

The econometrical analysis of the magnitude of slope of growth rates, show three important points.

∂ T∂ It≥Ω1

∂ T∂ Bt≥Ω2

One is the positive direction of increases. However, what is alarming, is not only the difference, largeness of omega one, over omega two, but the rate of taxation in omega one. It shows that more is extorted than received by individuals under the current system. That is what has been unsustainable for some time.

$\Omega 1 \asymp 1.02$

$\Omega 2 \asymp 0.77$

Therefore, the cogent solutions incognizance in these complex arithmetic of taxation rate analysis of statistical slope of growth rate of actual collection from different classifications by IRS are also yield adventitious answers.

Unfortunately, for the nescience political party, increasing fees and further taxes on the larger omega will prove counterproductive. Job-creation will increase the base, but the quality of the jobs, and take home real income is the determinant policy jolt.

Unfortunately, for the nescience political party, increasing fees and further taxes on the larger sigma will prove counterproductive. Job-creation will increase the base, but the quality of the jobs, and take home income is the determinant policy jolt.

Especially, it becomes hypocritical, when they have deemed the lower sigma a job killer repeatedly. That is why the insistence that immigration law modification had been urged incessantly away from the populous emotionalism nature of the 1996 alteration to that law.

Because simply halving sigma one will not be accomplished by nativist sentimentality. That is even after full employment policy implementation of government job for all PhDs including, liberal arts graduates. Figure 34 shows the annual growth rate of USA population.[2]

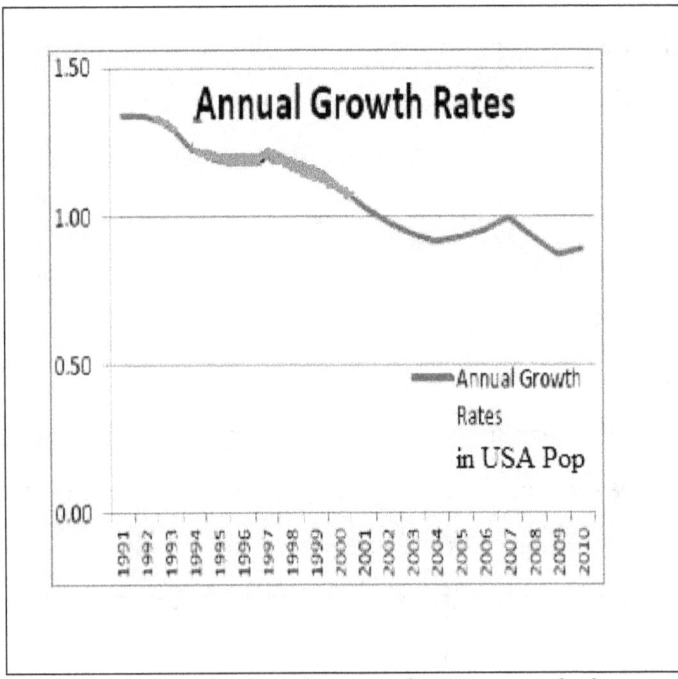

Figure 34 Annual growth rate of USA population.

The dynamic nature of population decline and the baby-boomers population-spikes are dynamic econometrics' composition certainties. Moreover, the CEO wages, bonuses, and looting fiascos are simply not sufficient to widen and deepen the base revenues.

There have been some Ponzi schemes and some Al Capone angles, and now we find out they will not even pay their fair tax shares to fix the country, which they get to enjoy more comparatively.

The lowest green graph shows how much the business paid versus the individual income taxes, total income taxes paid, and total revenue collated by IRS. Nevertheless, American middle class, elderlies, students and their mega student loans ($30 to $300 thousands), academics, teachers, firefighters, policepersons, and legal immigrants are the victims of these destabilizing peculations, as the political onionskins peel off these rotting-political party two-step shuffles.

Americans are discovering the real perpetrators of the heinous unpatriotic greed and cash-hording for the new millennium, the patriot acts I, II, FISA laws were not for them or their security.

They live on the hill, and they do not want to pay their fair share of taxes, which maintains the colored glassed cathedrals on those hills. Worst yet, they ignore sage consul. The few percentage adjustment in the mega billions will not harm but benefit the country, and the economy, if it goes toward true job-creation, and by money-velocity and commerce will come back in your tills, after the multiple sometimes global circulations.

It is an astonishment that this known abstract hypothesis escape leaders of industry and political hacks alike, easily. Since, it encroaches on their monopolistic cooperate share of national wealth, incrementally. Hence, they are the makers, and all other people are the takers. Figure 35 shows profits and wages as percentage of GDP.[3]

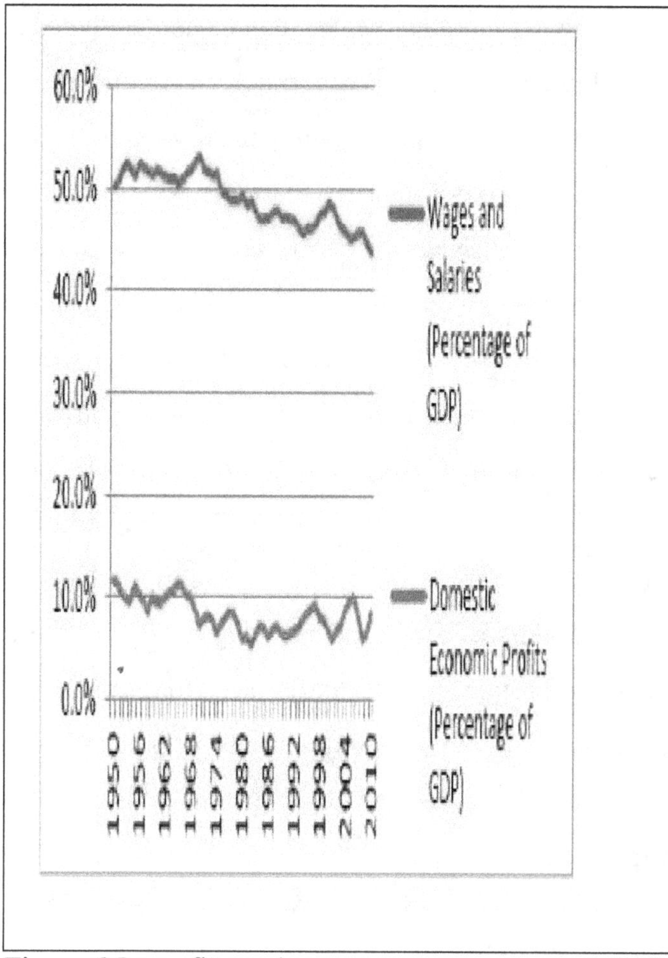

Figure 35, profits and wages as percentage of GDP.

Since 1970s, the declines in growth rate of population and wages, and profit as percent of economy are prominent. Moreover, math will tell us the 10 percent of the economy alone cannot master job-creation that the 55 percent of the economy did in the good old days, government is part of this deductive job-creation solution. However, paying their share is a good start.

This would have been much easier, if demand side technological injections were much larger and were aimed at domestic nondefense expansions, it went to tarp one (the save the investment bankers fund, the American version, and then the European version), and over the table defense and under the table defense, the mushrooming and unaccountable security concrete. So, we do not know other than the few people that touch your junks in airport, are there job-creations or criminal frauds under the security acts, or cash transfers in airports of Baghdad and Kabul? Even thou, they claim they did not see more than 2 or 3 million dollars in roads and buildings in these countries! However, certain political party has had ample times to play abstractionisms, abandonments, denial and blame, catcalls and jeers, along with their new “do-nothing religion absolutions.”

Therefore, we are supposed to shut off the 2.5 million-government job engines meekly in a bad prolonged recession, while cooperation hoarded profits and cash, and discernibly lumbered 1.5 million temp-type work and Mac-jobs, excluding the executive bonus bundles. All these time small businesses were snookered out of capital market, and the middle class are bamboozled out of the payroll tax breaks to boost aggregate demand temporarily.

Remember that social security number check

President Bush sent you 2001, that is that peak in 2002-2003 in the above graph. Why are they squabbling about another boost to the middle-class legitimate paychecks, and numbers of employed and adequately paid workers?

Figure 36 show the average growth rates of USA employment.[4]

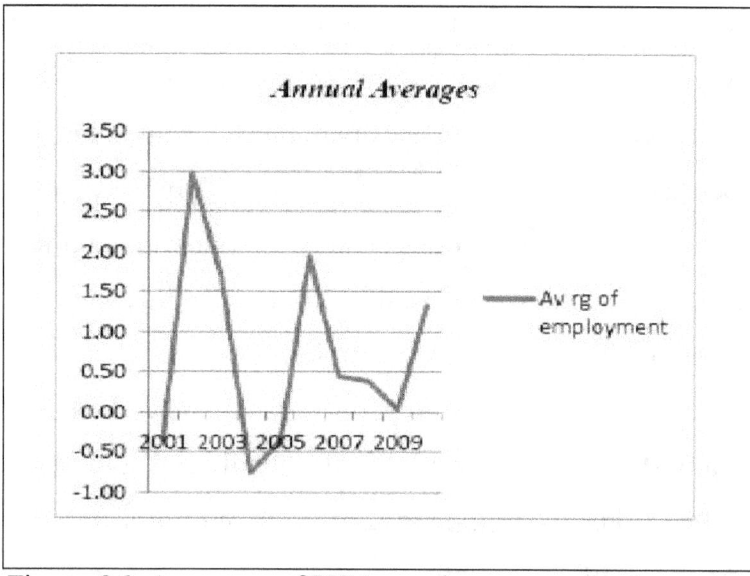

Figure 36, Averages of USA employment growth rates.

Why are they hauling deficit. This latent riotousness of reformed perennial deficit-spending sinners is cheap political theater for their well-coddled meal tickets and your passive votes.

Hence, we start over with another true job-creation plan amongst the jeers, instead of adulations. We have more economic tools to deal with inflations, but sparse few tools to deal with stagflations.

The American infrastructures, unlike the mushrooming security buildings, are fading away in neglect, pancaking roads and bridges, imploding-waterways undergrounds, and the disemboweled schools. These entire infrastructure and more, the employment of teachers and professors, they want the America to languish with quotidian joblessness, while they amass thirty more silver and gold coins! Here are domestic wolves and BenLadenism we can no longer effort. Moreover, the hypocrisy and the unintellectual contortions are painful to all constituencies, which suffer from the negligence of these parties "irreligious absolutions."

American people as people around the globe have too many shared lives, their familial, friendly and commerce connections to succumb to depression of efforts and smallness of bad intentions, and illiberal narrowness of mind. That is, that didactic poetry the madness of far rights cannot comprehend about legal immigration, about freedom that all people seek. The scientific wholeness and modernity of positivism seeded in the modern functional communities, which multiculturalism has cultivated even outside academic high halls.

People will know, not to trust the same power drunk, tax the poor and middle class crews, with their economic lives, again. Not unless, they are sure, they are well away from the depression ledges, that the political party led them there, and left them there, not long ago. You ought not to be able to fool all of the people, all of time. It is unnatural, and yes counter intellectual, unscientific, even illiberal. We sure have not seen signs of intellectual economic lives among the other political party, despite the full-time alien probing.

Especially, it becomes hypocritical, when they have deemed the lower omega as a job killer repeatedly. That is why the insistence that immigration law modification had been urged incessantly away from the emotionalism nature of the 1996 alterations to that law. The attainment of omega-one will not be accomplished by nativist sentimentality. That is even after full employment policy implementation of government job for all PhDs including, liberal arts graduates.

The dynamic nature of population decline and the baby-boomers population-spikes are dynamic econometrics' composition certainties. Moreover, the CEO wages, bonuses, and looting fiascos are simply not sufficient to widen and deepen the base revenues, and government revenues to do the jobs.

Tinkle-Down Spin Is Not Modern Economics

There have been some Ponzi schemes and some Al Capone angles, and now we find out they will not even pay their fair tax shares to fix the country. Nevertheless, American middle class, elderlies, students and their mega student loans ($30 to $300 thousands), academics, teachers, firefighters, policepersons, and legal immigrants are the victims of these destabilizing peculations, as the political onionskins peel off these rotting-political party two-step shuffles.

However, the monopolistic political advocacies own the system, wash out monopoly taxation and reduce taxes on cooperate citizens, reline and shift as higher taxes on the lower incomes and middle class, adjust the revenue and protect the cooperate welfare and spin it for the constituencies.

Americans are discovering the real perpetrators of the heinous unpatriotic greed and cash-hording for the new millennium, the PATRIOT Acts I, II, FISA laws were not for their securities. The golden goose laid the golden eggs for the insider of the security-military industrial complex. It was to pilfer business strategies, private records, phone calls and e-mails illegally, retrenchment of global commerce and global backlash are the accumulated results. The international security and cooperation have retrenched. Thus, they have opened business fields for the competition to flourish.

They live on the hills, high on the hogs, and they do not want to pay their fair share of taxes, which maintains the colored-glassed cathedrals on those higher hills. Worst yet, they ignore sage consul. The few percentage adjustment in your mega billions will not harm but benefit the country, and the economy, if it goes toward true job-creation, instead of miserly political jobs, or crony security-job creationism and in-house featherbeddings, and revolving door militarism of domestic economy.

Since 1970s, the declines in growth rate of population and wages, and profit as percent of economy are prominent. Moreover, math will tell us the 1 percent or even the 10 percent of the economy alone cannot master job-creation that the 55 percent of the economy did in the good old days, government is part of this deductive job-creation solution now.

Cooperate-Citizens' Minimum Tax Law

However, paying their share is a good start. This would have been much easier, if demand side technological injections were much larger and were aimed at domestic nondefense expansions, it went to tarp one (the save the investment bankers fund, the American version, and then the European version), and over the table defense and under the table defense, the mushrooming and unaccountable security concretes.[5] So, we do not know other than the few people that touch your junks in airport, are there job-creations or criminal frauds under the security acts, or cash transfers in airports of Baghdad and Kabul? Even thou, these countries claim they did not see more than 2 or 3 million dollars in roads and buildings in these countries, while American taxpayers are billed for 4-trillion dollars permanent wars!

However, certain political party has had ample times to play abstractionisms, abandonments, denial and blame, catcalls and jeers, along with their new "do-nothing religion absolutions."

Ethical and moral Cooperation, Ethical Governments

Therefore, we are supposed to shut off the 2.5 million-government job engines meekly in a bad prolonged recession in economic-lifesaving sequestrations and austerity plans.

Therefore, underfunding infrastructure rebuilding and national investments are disruptive to employments. While cooperation strategists have hoarded profits and cash, and discernibly lumbered 1.5 million temp-type work and Mac-jobs, excluding the executive bonus bundles, cash bundles offshores, thus reducing the multiplier effect. In the meantime, the political monopolistic cooperate machinery applies reelection-funds and law making organization power of political monopoly to reduce their taxes and government revenues. Therefore, they are shutting down the fiscal job-creation systems.

All these time small businesses were snookered out of capital market, and the middle class are bamboozled out of the payroll tax breaks, which boosted aggregate demand temporarily. In addition, the immigrant job-creators are jailed and deported systematically, with Machiavellian law manipulations, legalese, and disruptive none-functionalities.

United States job creation machine is still not making enough jobs to maintain employment levels positive. Remember that social security number check President Bush sent you 2001, that is that peak in 2002-2003 economy. Why are they squabbling about any boost to the middle-class, or job creation investments? Why are they hollering deficit at 7 to 25 percent unemployed of minorities, women, and older workers. This latent riotousness of reformed perennial deficit-spending sinners is cheap political theater for their well-coddled meal tickets and your votes 2014 and 2016. Especially, when sequestration is deconstruction of your infrastructures dynamically, decline in your real disposable income, chronic joblessness, and jobless economic recoveries. Are you fooled, yet?

Therefore, ethical and moral cooperation and businesses, ethical governments will be a new good starts toward the national and global improvements summit.

Hence, we start over with another true job-creation plan amongst the jeers, instead of adulations. We have more economic tools to deal with inflations, but sparse few tools to deal with stagflations. The American infrastructures, unlike the mushrooming security buildings, are fading away in neglect, pancaking roads and bridges, imploding-waterways undergrounds, and the disemboweled and closed schools.

These entire infrastructure and more, the employment of teachers and professors, they want the America to languish with quotidian joblessness, while they amass thirty more silver and gold coins! Here are domestic wolves and BenLadenism we can no longer effort. So, why do we vote them back in habitually, instead of weeding them out intellectually. Moreover, the hypocrisy and the unintellectual contortions are painful to all constituencies, which suffer from the negligence of these parties "irreligious absolutions." American people as people around the globe have too many shared lives, their familial, friendly and commerce connections to succumb to depression of efforts and smallness of bad intentions, and illiberal narrowness of mind, and multibillion dollars permanent war mongering machines.

That is, that didactic poetry, which the madness of far rights cannot comprehend about legal immigration, about freedom that all people seek, and exuberance that it injects in the job creation machinery of modern economies. The scientific wholeness and modernity of positivism seeded in the modern functional communities, which multiculturalism has cultivated even outside academic high halls, among clergies, business people, and job-creating communities with positive attitude about their futures.

Notes

[1] Calculation and graph by author Data source.
http://www.irs.gov/taxstats/article/0,,id=171960,00.html

[2]

Source: U.S. Census Bureau, International Data Base
(http://www.census.gov/ipc/www/idb/)
organized into ERS/USDA Baseline countries and regions
Historical Population and Growth Rates in Population for
Baseline Countries/Regions 1969-2010
Updated: July 20, 2010 based on June 2010
Census Bureau Update
http://www.ers.usda.gov/Data/Macroeconomics/

[3]

CBO's Year-by-Year Forecast and Projections
for Calendar Years 2011 to 2021, (and Actual Data for
Calendar Years 1950 to 2010).
Published in *The Budget and Economic Outlook: An Update August* 2011).

[4]

Growth rate of employment in United States.
Note: author calculation from,
source,http://data.bls.gov/timeseries/CES0000000001?output_view=net_1mth

[5] "Pepsi, IKEA, AIG, Coach, Deutsche Bank, Abbott Laboratories and nearly 340 other companies have secured secret deals from Luxembourg that allowed many of them to slash their global tax bills."
Leslie Wayne, Kelly Carr, Marina Walker Guevara, Mar

Cabra and Michael Hudson, LUXEMBOURG LEAKS: GLOBAL COMPANIES' SECRETS EXPOSED, November 5, 2014, 4:00 pm, http://www.icij.org/project/luxembourg-leaks/leaked-documents-expose-global-companies-secret-tax-deals-luxembourg

CHAPTER 18

ASSUMTIVE FORCASTS

It is important to look at the caliber of economic challenges, before setting or reassessing the economic journey ahead. The greedy intentions and miserliness of purposes have failed us measurably. The one percent upper income levels may have miscalculated the size and the impacts of the downsides, which would affect their interests that is above 80 percent, versus the 20 percent or less of accumulations of all others in this modern economy.

In those scholarly endeavors at macroeconomics and strategic levels, comparative studies of indices lends a valuable helping hand, to the educated-minds' eyes. The next figure shows a dismaying index, because it is the ten-year averages of growth rates of real Gross domestic product of United States. It has been declining since 1970s.

Rates of population decay, percentage of wage and profits from GDP dropping, declining averages rate of employment are indices with important forces, unless a true recovery is replacing the false jobless recoveries of the recent past. The employment index can easily increase quantitatively like a magic parlor statistic trick, with increasing numbers of wage earners with bellow living-wage salaries retaining two or even three jobs that are underpaying jobs. Those low quality jobs need doing. While nativists, often on multiple government stipends are claiming their employment opportunities and wages are kept low. Because "illegals" immigrants retain those low quality jobs and pay taxes and do not take out benefits. That last part is true.[1] The part that there are Americans in queues to go into the fields and do fields work, and hard factory works, low end housing and yard works is proven to be total fabrications. Historically, and factually they will not be caught dead doing those jobs. Vegas, or Atlanta, and hosts of other American hospitality industries, and fresh-agricultural businesses cannot rely on the nativists' sentimentality, nor can the budget of American middle class, small businesses can bankroll the higher costs of these once affordable infrastructures of commerce, often on the back of immigrants' workers.

Figure 37 studies the annual rate of growth calculated by the logarithmic formulations.[2] It shows a dismaying trend line for most of this millennium.

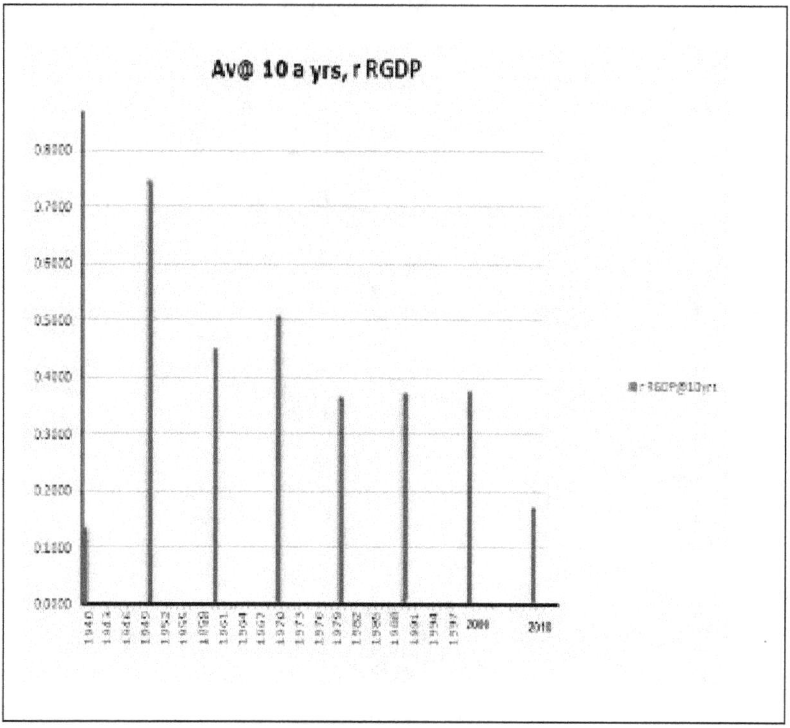

Figure 37, Ten years averages of GDP growth rates.

Figure 38 improves the odds by studying the antithetical proposition despite the size of the recovery and the miserliness of governmental investments in the economy. [3] There are positive indications of small upticks in the trend line in recent data.[4] Assuming that holds, the forecast can improve.

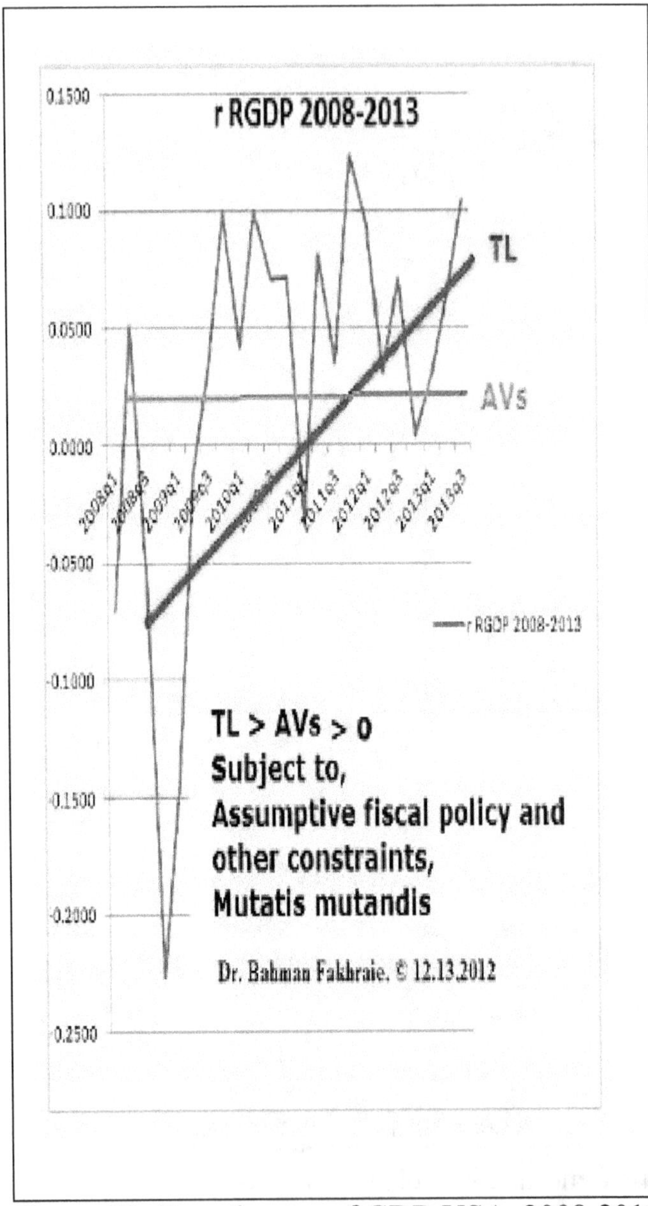

Figure 38, Growth rates of GDP-USA, 2008-2013

Nevertheless, onslaught of political mischiefs,

austerity and sequestration schema, incompetence in job creation strategies, government shutdown fevers, are numbers of ill winds that may not relent. Yet there is that good news forecasts for the next years, given the functionality assumptions hold, mutatis mutandis.

Given, TL > AVs > 0

The forecasts are subject to, assumptive fiscal policy, organizational strains of imperfect competition from duopolistic to monopolistic modus operandi, and other political constraints functionality versus games-returns expectations, Mutatis mutandis. This is a limited forecast, but it sets the logarithmic growth rate of chained-gross domestic product north of 2.4 to < 6.4, distributive rebalance, reasonable jobs, and value-exchange theories (livable wages) are also part of the nationally refocused economic scene. That will prove the engine of growth for the global economy, if peaceful diplomacy averts pitfalls induced or caused for the usual political suspects.

Hence, the short-term trend line chained Gross Domestic Product (RGDP) is larger than the averages growth rate of GDP, and they are both greater than zero and positive, the probability improves toward a positive trend in a growing economy subjects to the assumptive conditions imposed.

People will know, not to trust the same power drunk, tax the poor and middle class crews, with their economic lives, again. Not unless, they are sure, they are well away from the depression ledges, that the political party led them there, and left them there, not long ago. You ought not to be able to fool all of the people, all of time. It is unnatural, and yes counter intellectual, unscientific, even illiberal.

We sure have not seen signs of intellectual economic lives among the other political party, despite the full-time alien probing. In presence of intellectual candidates, they immediately retrograde to their designated underground cavities in search of new uninformed crews.

In a functioning democracy, the demonstrated infelicitousness of empathy will invite the luscious victory of the other party, unfortunately after some two years more languishing of real 10 to 25 percent unemployed and underemployed, and some 60 to 80 percent upset constituencies? We can even go back for the old fashion six month of nasty useless squabbling, called "election campaigns television seasons" to enrich the media Inc. Henceforth, for the betterment of America, and all good people, job-creation we must! Do not let them forget it. The elections are almost here, even without jobs, you are getting the donation bills already.

Nevertheless, wealth-concentration and permanent wars economic schema are not free enterprise, free market strategies to create jobs or save USA middle class economy.

There are political monopolistic organizational arrangements like the morphed security industrial complex, which they have become self-leaking financial ice creams and they have not served the American economy well. They have longed abandoned serving the American people qualitatively, while they will claimed it quantitatively. For the successful economic model of wealth creation strategy, which Americans and the free market have done well many times in the history of modern economics. Americans have to tend to the few main fundamental principles that served their constitutional democratic republic well, with relatively free markets principles.

Nations have to invest and even reinvent domestic job-creations, exchange and value theory and balanced distributions systems, infrastructures, education systems, investors (immigrants' investors, scholars, job-creators), and cultivate domestic job creators. In the democratic republic, the public can select new teams of representatives.

The new years are foundational for a positive, reasonable, balanced futuristic, exceptional, and successful American economy model, which is a global economic model, since everyone is reading the same books.

Summary

The magnitude and clausal nature of demands for seven billion people on earth replaces much of callosity of obsolete paradigms of extreme dogma for the newer and softer sciences (economics and social and behavioral economics among them), which allow resource utilizations favoring human capital and renewable resources.

Those combined with economic prudence in rate of entropy in utilization of finite and nonrenewable resources can light a newer longer path for such growing populations. In those endeavors and tasks, it not given that unemployment and idleness of different human capitals and skills levels, as much as presently bedevils our societies.

Ii is wonderment, if greed and politics of prejudices are at work, perhaps positive human capital interferences can improve and even remedy our futuristic conundrums. The accumulations of research and studies have shown that such a progressive path can exists with strong probabilities. The readers have to see if that optimism can guide their paths to the future.

TIME, THE HIT AND RUN OF YOUR AGE
YOUR GRACE

When time has aged you,
and your youth has fled.
Not even a mystic can divine you,
the mysteries of your age.

When your beauty has passed,
and grace is in your head,
but compassion has fled.

Not even a mystic can divine you,
the mysteries of your life.

Let stay human in your heart,
and let the nesciences head flee.

Then even a mystic can divine you,
the mysteries of love.

Let knowledge find you,
and let ignorance flee you.

Then, a mystic will divine you
the mysteries of your lives.

By Bahman Fakhraie, Phd. © 2014

TIME, THE HIT AND RUN OF YOUR AGE

By Bahman Fakhraie, Phd. © 2014, 12/ 4/ 2014

When time has aged you,

and your youth has fled.

Not even a mystic can divine you,
the mysteries of your age.

When your beauty has passed,
and grace is in your head, but compassion has fled.

Not even a mystic can divine you,
the mysteries of your life.

Let stay human in your heart,
and let the nesciences head flee.

Then even a mystic can divine you,
the mysteries of love.

Let knowledge find you,
and let ignorance flee you.

Then, a mystic will divine you
the mysteries of your lives.

Note

[1]From subsequent Native American migrations to Americas, to global transfer of technological injections for time immemorial the anti-science vehemence fighting an established scientific 'law' not just a theory. Recent London study only reconfirms strings of academic research about contributions and net positive benefits of such contributions.

*-Christian Dustmann and Tommaso Frattini, The Fiscal Effects of Immigration to the UK, November 2013, http://www.cream-migration.org/publ_uploads/CDP_22_13.pdf

*-"Recent immigrants to UK 'make net contribution", 5 November 2013 Last updated at 05:04 ET http://www.bbc.com/news/uk-24813467

2

Figure xii, Logarithmic annual growth rate of USA GDP, 1929-2012.
Notes, Dr. Bahman Fakhraie
http://www.bea.gov/National/Index.htm,
Current-dollar and "real" GDP (Excel)
Logarithmic analysis of growth rates and graph by
(LN (C80)-LN (C79))/LN (C79)

3

http://www.bea.gov/National/Index.htm,
Current-dollar and "real" GDP (Excel)
Logarithmic analysis of growth rates and graph by
(LN (C80)-LN (C79))/LN (C79) Dr. Bahman Fakhraie

[4] Dr. Bahman Fakhraie's books web page link, http://bahfecon.wix.com/bahfecon

CHAPTER 19

INFRASTRUCTURES AND MARKET ORGONISATIONS

There may be false assumptions that economic hypothesis are not tested, or they are not testable, so anything goes. In these next chapters, simple Popperian test is applied to nominal and real study of aggregate economic data. Since, subject attracted research, and this methodology was applied in mid 1970s, the result and conclusions have become more cemented. Therefore, the experience is shared with student of economic and political economics, to save the public from the negative consequences.[1] Market organization is another of those essential economic tools. They are studied in this book as infrastructures. They enhance market functionality and economic activities substantially, and measurably.

Policies advance untested, even on unsound intellectual foundations, gather negative externalities, and social costs, regardless of good or patriotic intentions of the political sources of those policies. If the original intentions are negative, these policies venture into unethical teconomics hinterlands. The negative externalities will still be higher.

MARKET INFRASTRUCTURES

The additive and cumulative of building roads, bridges, and market connection in advancement of human history have been expounded in details. The fact that tribal market to villages' formation and rural and urban development are always associated with links to market accessibilities. Therefore, it is important for growth and developmental theories that such market infrastructures are constructed and assisted.

In this study, the degree of sophistication, costs, and complexities that are associated with formation and expansions of markets International trade, and global flow of resources, and funds, are essential elements of market-infrastructures in economic growth and development. Therefore, it is important not to allow illegal activities, to harm other human endeavors, trades, and commerce globally. It is also doubly important not to interfere with those legal and ethically global transactions and economic development.

The sudden and disastrous destructions of the infrastructures have been illustrated vividly in Dr. Bahman Fakhraie's Risk and catastrophes books as well.[2] These books also illustrate that interference with ethical and legal flow of commerce, and formation of proper market-infrastructures in local economies, and international trade.

FREE MARKET ORGANIZATIONS

Since the advent of barter, whether tribal, or village-to-village bazars, to modern day garage sales to outdoor markets, or even the more complicated caravans to ocean going ships in big shipyards, and more complicated-global adventures, the exchange of goods have required some degree of organizational complexities.

In the digitized economies exchanges are multibillion exchanges (trades) organized by internet and intranet connectivity globally, between buyers' computers, cell phones, or mobile devices, with the sellers' mobile devices. Therefore, the implications for trade accommodations and job creations are obvious. Expansion in communication reflects increase in technological supplies associated with organizational development and communication technologies.[3] The expansion of digitized Persian bazaar will increase market-to-market connections and activities.

The manufactures of market exchanges requires human interventions at different degree of organizational complexities. In case of the suppliers of each modular production process, there is one or a group; therefore, there are supplier organizations. At firm level in economics the classification falls under numerous suppliers, and competitively lower prices. Agricultural smaller modular productions were identified in this competitive free market organizational classification. Even in perfectly competitive free market conditions, sellers, and supplier can join groups, trade unions, sellers' coops to effect pieces of their products higher.

In case of demands for the products or services, there may be individual consumers or tribe, city, or group demands, as buyers' clubs they will reflect the interests in lower costs or prices, (and culture) of the organization with the demand. Nevertheless, individuals can divide the products and consume them individually. An organizational collusion has influenced the exchanges.[4] Hence, the unusual chance for higher risk events in a group, as part of their organizational behaviors.

The general consensus of classic and neoclassic economists have been that under a theoretical and assumptive perfect market conditions, the economy will balance out equitably and remain sustainable over the long run. The long term is defined about 3-5 years.

The assumptive conditions of free market perfect competition organization are detailed. The mathematical discourses have been extensive. Assumptions are and for of perfect information, or perfect knowledge of prices, wages, interest, costs and rents. The discharges of all supplies and demands in equilibrium prices and wages, etc. will ashore probabilities of continuity of both. The fallacy of composition, in economics states what hold true for the part, must hold true for the whole, or there are consequential longer-term harms. Politically, even in democratic republics, to extend continuities, they may have replaced sustainability, utilizing game theory (as in disequilibrium) instead of assumptive equilibrium conditions. Hence, allowing for different market organizations, other than perfectly competitive market organizations to function in aggregations, and in the longer term, beyond the 5 years periods.

Practitioners in other fields and other economists, econometricians have grown concern that longer-term aggregate data has differed from the happy neoclassical propositions, and scenarios. For example at microeconomic level, wages are held low, and there are full employments at those low wages. Alas, in aggregation, there is not enough aggregate demand and income to sustain market activity. Another example is farmers discover a new technology that will exponentially increase their crops, and they shared it with other farmers. The assumption will be that more output more income. Except, the market organization will reduce price, income, and substantially, if they all stay with that product.

The highest risk events, like criminal activities are not usually clever to disguise for long, while some skims, investment frauds are hidden for some times.

The purely academic exercise of real life events studies the cases that sustainability is upheld, but equilibrium conditions have been waved. Therefore, especial cases of longer-term damages and harms are studied to show the harmful and extensive effects of negative externality cost, shadow costs, and imbalanced aggregations that can harm the economy accumulatively.

Notes

[1] Karl R. Popper, The Open Society and Its Enemies, Princeton University Press, 1950

[2] Bahman Fakhraie, PhD, Teconomics OF Dynamic Risks: All Natural Disasters, And Energy Resource, Ferdat Publishing, June 4, 2013
http://www.amazon.com/Teconomics-Dynamic-Risks-Disasters-Resource/dp/0985295856/ref=tmm_pap_swatch_0?_encoding=UTF8&qid=1460467933&sr=1-10
*- Bahman Fakhraie PhD, Teconomics Of Catastrophes: All natural Disasters, Dynamic risks & Energy Resource Production Disasters, Ferdat Publishing, July 20, 2015
http://www.amazon.com/Teconomics-Catastrophes-Disasters-Resource-Production/dp/0989453960/ref=la_B00IKAR1CM_1_9?s=books&ie=UTF8&qid=1460467933&sr=1-9

[3] Bahman Fakhraie, PhD, Politeconomics: Political Teconomics, Ferdat publishing, December 8, 2014
http://www.amazon.com/Politeconomics-Teconomics-Dr-Bahman-Fakhraie/dp/0989453944/ref=la_B00IKAR1CM_1_4?s=books&ie=UTF8&qid=1458577267&sr=1-4

[4] Dr. Bahman Fakhraie (Author), Political Monopolistic Capitalism, Wealth Concentration Schema : The Haves, The Have-Nothings, And The Have-Less, Ferdat Publishing, January 21, 2014
http://www.amazon.com/Political-Monopolistic-Capitalism-Wealth-Concentration/dp/0989453995/ref=la_B00IKAR1CM_1_5?s=books&ie=UTF8&qid=1460467933&sr=1-5

CHAPTER 20

HIDDDEN HANDS, INVISIBLE FINGERS IN FREE MARKET

Hidden fingers, invisible hands, and free markets assumed false idols status outside their academic paradigms. Hidden fingers, invisible hands, and assumptive perfectly competitive free markets have come up short in estimations of the crowds, now. Theologically, supply-siders, marketers, and student-economists were admonished to avoid market-money worship, as idolatry. Aside from a prayer for less inflated commodities prices and more inflated wages and salaries, do economics or social sciences have anything to illuminate in their field, philosophically or scientifically?

Since perfectly competitive markets are only hypothetical in capitalism, there are hidden hands in free markets, which cause negative externalities (shadow costs) to increase. These negative externalities, costs become astronomical in markets for goods and services with calculated inelastic demands and with the none-competitive organization power players, without the check and balance of the promised invisible hands. There are the Adam Smith invisible hand incentives, which added profit for entrepreneurial sprits, operational profits to small farms, livable wages to motivate workers, and value to products, and it is included in the costs of each item honestly, within his moral frameworks. Besides, the difficulties about prefect knowledge and competitions in real markets, some social scientists seem to ignore the assumptive conditions that Adam Smith established in his two books, and go for the easy steps, as I discovered in1970s.

There are world of difference between the two free markets capitalism-scenarios, this escapes the intellectual grasp of many amateur politicians, and student-economists. These at micro abstracts seem small; however, in dynamic macroeconomics, with the technological injections steroids, add up to be harmful to individuals and national budgets.

There were good sad examples at the start of this week. They are all over the media, but there are more examples, which they never see daylights, or media attention.

The first example is the negative externalities, of United States, football-games brain injuries, in the multibillion-dollar industry that affects lot of younger American lives, and it is equal parts, Apple pie, the flag, and Americana.

The hidden parts are enumerable in older ball players that fade and die in the darker corners of American anonymities, their families and younger ball players may have their career and future ended with cheers and dancing angles with pompoms bursting in the air around their heads, with permanent bodily injuries, and career ending disabilities. Perfect knowledge, information honestly shared will help the decision-making somewhat. If we let everyone and their moms know the costs and negative externalities upfront, the music may not stop, but the accounting may change, and society will get enough to pay for the brokenness left in the trail of this glory.

So far, only the families, American taxpayers, and small communities have internalized the costs, and the harsh lumps of life that came with those hidden hands. Perhaps, that is no longer possible.

DAMAGED BODIES, BRAINS, AND REPUTATIONS

Can free market fix brokenness, it does not see. The information and facts can be hidden from the markets, intentionally, criminally, or ignorantly. A physician discovers CTE in the donated brain tissue of a late great football player Mike Webster, applying well-established traditional medical science. There are long trails of damaged bodies, brains, and reputations left in the way to causation-linkage of CTE/brain damage and playing football.

In pro-players, when doctors were tested donated brains, the probabilities in at least two samples were 95 percent, and 97 percent. Watching boxers and fighters, the arguments and accepting the causation-linkage proposition had been around.

The new studies will become more conclusive, because brain-imaging technologies have advanced the pool of victims from the dead pro-players, to living victims' brain scans, like the high school and college players, and dropout-football players of all ages.

However, up to now, the new samples and tests have increased the probabilities of causation-linkage of CTE/brain damage and playing football, and the tests have not reduced them, that the causation-linkage of CTE/brain damage and playing football is a more substantiated hypothesis now than before.

There is a legal settlement for retired pro-players a laudable giant leap financially, but somehow the size of negative externalities and shadow costs of the games and lives of the younger players may never be recognized. There are series of reports that have kept up with some of these lives and the subject.[1] It is good journalism. The full sacrifices of all, before we arrive at the moment of Super Ball entertainment climax is a dynamic that will continue after the games, and after retirement of these great players, and with their families, and children. One way to mitigate these lives is to establish legacy externality funds to cover the damages of all involved, at high schools and colleges levels, too.

It will be greater for the games to do well in business ethics and for graceful sportsmanship to step over the greed, to acknowledge the full sacrifices of other people in this game of multi-billion dollars entertainments, so we can conceivably keep the games, and we can probably all be winners in the longer run.

Nevertheless, now we all know before we play, what are the full costs and the nature of this great game, to children and younger players, to our hero pro-players, to their family members, to an honorable society that will have to pick up the brokenness.

You can decide if a caveat emptor can do all these cases justice, or a set-aside fund is needed, may be government (tax and benefits) can do it, in these oceans of deceit, hidden fingers, megalomaniacal profiteering, and legal obstructionisms, organizational self-benefiting. Some entities need to guarantee that multimillion-dollar players as well younger-players have a chance at a living, if the worst happens to them.

The shut-down-government politics have in-house polemicists defeating their cases regularly, because hidden fingers of criminal conducts, dishonesties, and xenophobic, bigoted, sexists' ignorance undermine their arguments for good government.

DRUG WARS, DRUG-LEGALIZATION, CRIMINAL HIDDEN HANDS

What age of inhumanity thunders?
Wonderments and conundrums aplenty,
Opiates are well rewarding, and deadly to all innocence,
Wisdom is life giving, and punishingly unrewarded.

Other hidden costs will need sunlight, too. The negative externalities of drug wars, one on hard drugs (heroin, meth, cocaine) that fail, and we have young victims self-destroying themselves. Another one that was a waste of rare resources, and it will become an inelastic commodity (marijuana, Alcohol, tobacco), but still there will be victims like with the alcoholic road-kills and health problems, and tobacco cancerous sagas, on daily or nightly news, an at familial atomistic budget bases.

There are victims with high sugar, fat, and salt content processed food, when lab-tested manufactured food has replaced fresh food, combined with sedentary low-income life style of most Americans, and all others that join in the American life style, globally.

What is astonishingly irresponsible is that certain state governments blame these issues on the immigrants (or illegals) less than 0.033 percent of the population.

They have managed to parley these types of xenophobic unintellectual legalese into profiling reports full of index-illusions (biases), public policies, illegal immigrant profiling, self- deportations, administrative removals. Legal immigrants do not fear much better, multiple delays, blocks, and increasing fees toward citizenships' process of even legal immigrants and foreign-born American citizens, which are only 14 percent of the total population. The true American natives, in USA and Alaska, the indigenous American people there are 5.3 million, only 2 percent of the population. American citizens that they called 'native' with criminal records are estimated at 20 percent of population.

DHS yearbook data statistic show 267 percent higher total removal versus the criminal alien removal. Moreover, USA BAR had issued a warning on treatment and procedurals. Some of immigration judges themselves have complained about lack of legal representation, luck of translators, and alarming disparities of results among different judges and jurisdictions, thus red-flagging the inadequacy of the process.

It is understandable that infusion of cash brings results and a lot of big technologies, the quality of the result is another issues, and who, what, and how the wheels of the machinery grinds used to matter the American democracy, judiciary, and Justices in less prejudice times.

"(US-VISIT) program surpassed $17.9 billion in fiscal year (FY) 2012. This amount is nearly 15 times the spending level of the US Immigration and Naturalization Service (INS)"

And,

"In the ensuing 26 years, the nation has spent ($219.1 billion if adjusted to 2012 dollars) on immigration enforcement by INS and its successor agencies, CBP and ICE, and the US_VISIT program."

Nevertheless, the anti-immigration laws propose transfer of resources from fighting the hard drug crimes, and apply them to immigrations policing, instead of the real issues. Therefore, they are ham-hogging efficient commerce, and good policing, for modern day emotionalism and bad-labeling conservatism, in ignorance. National resources can be preoccupies with violations of three hundred million people citizens-constitutional rights.

The misapplications of resources can enrage at least around 2 billion Muslims worldwide, and alienate and insult seven billion potential cell-phones-customers globally, pre-emptively as probable terrorists, while less than 3000 or 300 people harbor ill-intends, and they are probably organized to carry it out, from known areas.

Making it even harder to identify or distinguish bad people from good. Nevertheless, we can increase the poll of dead-end makers by irresponsible intolerances, general warrants, and abuse by head cracking police squads domestically and internationally. United States of all nations have had the most vivid experiences of civil right social unrest under most abusive misuse of police force. It is very difficult to argue bigoted ill-intends and xenophobic mischiefs are not behind repetition of that particular history, and which institutions' hands are clean.

All these examples needed better (more efficient) federal governmental involvements, than jailhouse jubilees and monetization theatrics in extremists' states. Especially if xenophobia, discriminations, racial profiling, lazy or militarists' police-works pollute the data samples from states to states, which it will waste resources, and leave capitals and personals preoccupied with the wrong endeavors, while the hard drugs kill more people faster.

Aside from the more frequent recent videos of police illegal shootings at family vans, frequently deadly or improper use of Tasers, states have tampered with the evidences and DNA, charged, and executed innocent people, usually minorities with an alarming higher frequency.

Therefore, it is unusually alarming to hear states push both to militarize their police forces, and they want them to enforce immigration federal laws. Since, the classified hard drugs have such expansion of their supplies nationwide, and the body counts to confirm it. It is important to see where the concentration of resources, which is police work and money to hire police persons, can be realigned.

Anything but Public Service

Thefts, legalese malfeasance, criminal mischiefs are not public service. What are their public services? Thefts, legalese malfeasance, criminal mischiefs, and public service are not cafeteria-style choices for any government-employed public servants agencies. If they conjugate in any government employee-minds' eye criminal mischief is afoot. They pollute the pool of decency that true public servants and agencies engage in on daily bases, and all citizens require at all times. They do a disservice to good public servants. Such men and women exist in United States and globally. We all experience their services and excellence, their innate basic human dignities on daily bases. It is the taxpayers' savings funding these endeavors.

They have standing to ask for quality services from these greater people.[2]

"Who takes your money before they prove that you've done anything wrong with it?"
The federal government does. ... They're going after people who are really not criminals," said David Smith, a former federal prosecutor who is now a forfeiture expert and lawyer in Virginia. "They're middle-class citizens who have never had any trouble with the law."

This toxic and criminal practices are anti-free market concoctions, brewed in department of treasury by GOP-NEOCONs while ago, which has been on the sly passed on to other governmental agencies to hide their criminal and anti-constitutional natures, and to disguise their undemocratic and anti-commerce intends. While tortures of real terrorists, the ISIS, ISIL, WASEM, and regular innocent peoples have caught some public lights and were disclosed. These styles and practices against American Middle Class citizens and others were kept in the dark by and among the anti-constitutional-officious elitists. They inflected public harm on Americans on mass and on middle class Americans, unchecked. It will easily be pinned on the slow-witted liberals that fall for any governmental swindle as a taxing method of the middle class, or the spin experts will blame democrats for it readily. While the agencies were ignoring real mega cartels and drug-criminals that are awash in cash transfers as reported by ocean going ships, major transportation (trucks or trains), and multiple underground tunnels.

These illegal techniques were sharpened against immigrants and voiceless victims before, under different criminal and illegal disguises, fraud, ID-theft, phishing swindles, overt hackings are proof of some governmental criminality, and overt violation of constitutional rights, they do not need secondary court costs by mom and pop American victims of government-agencies. If it take agencies well over 50 billion dollars of taxpayers funds to supply computer security, and multinational hacking controls, and you are failing, you should hardly be trusted by new and endless hyper-constitutional powers. The government should be held to task for the toxic cleanup of their own officious creations, and pay for past due damages, harms, and remedies incurred by these small and financially victimized smaller Americans, and small job creating businesses since they have hidden their criminal misconducts in security and national emergency bills of tenders by NEOCONS and friends. The history of abuses by American institutions tells that government used the mob to set up more intrusive and abusive institutions that mob or any criminal organization could organize using, utilizing taxpayers own money. Bad practices were litigated, and convicted. If governmental agencies do not want to show up in a court and in front of a judge to show intend, chain of relevant events, proof of guilt, honest witnesses, and generate a warrant, they have defined the kind of government they prefer. They are droning, killing, and bombing incent victims to defend the wrong declared government style. Why should we let them destroy our financial systems without legal challenges?

Bankrupt banks, A local or state, or federal government (some are on edge of bankruptcies) can hide their bad intends and use any number of events, and use structuring as reason for theft of private property without proof of probable cause, in these misconducts illegality and financial harm of the innocent Americans looms larger now.

This is more dangerous than any plot socialism or communism could have skimmed against market economies, externally. Fast digital criminals from off shores can do lot of financial damages, while the keystone cops are busy paper cutting and bankrupting American mom and pops. Why add to the fifth column subversives, WASEM, ISIL lone wolves, when the termite-institutionalisms are undoing the faith and trust in the financial systems and collapsing it around our heads and pocket books.

Most of middle class America deposit their hard earned and under paid real incomes regularly in banks and financial institutions, even with these institutions checkered rules in housing and economic crashes in this millennium. Majority of upper middle class income workers earn under $10,000, the higher income individuals even more than that, some federal treasury bills legally require $10,000 to purchase. Criminal agents, bad agencies can criminally misuse structuring for ill-intends and even theft and mischiefs.

The full implications of such abuses are so detrimental to stability of financial systems and institutions, even more detrimental at time of global instabilities that may explain the resent risk-eversions of most none hedge fund investors, wealthy Americans vacating their citizenships to cash, and middle class diminishing real disposable incomes causing lower investing in USA. Thus, the slow responses of major economies to repeated unsuccessful-simulative-macroeconomic policies, as 70-80 percent of job-creation occurs by the lower smaller businesses and lower incomes individuals. All elements involved should find other non-governmental jobs, as some already have chased higher salaries out, under all administrations.

The magnitude and overtness of these millennial human and constitutional right violations are in the massive references, since they span over more governmental agencies and many years, like treasury, IRS, and more, these will sooner than later require honest American judges and courts, and some international courts interventions for remedies. Perhaps past vehemence and hate speech against UN and international courts by NEOCON should have raised a few alarm bells about the guilt and involvement of the NEOCONS. Those making American constitution the enemy, while the enemies thrive and inflected harms and damages. They have done it, and harmed out of malice afore thought, or ignorance, neither make good bases for logical defense, in modern laws, and law makings.[3] American people should know, from large and accumulated history of these matters, their votes are more detrimental than ever. That is why certain parties try so hard to obstruct and stop their voting. They are only waiting anxiously to be reelected, to reignite these kinds of passionate thefts of the middle class and private capitals, anew. Why should Americans help them with their bad or criminal intentions?

Caging the Hounds of Wars Again

Some days, it is enlightening to stay caffeinated and reread important signs, as they evolve faster than we like, or the faster than leaderships' usual rate of intellectual Osmoses.[4] Even though, no one can delight in the multitudes of misfortunes, massive displacements, and more failing forever mud-wars, unfortunately, in fanatical pursuits of nihilism, as one group leads and hides, others follow and die. Just look around, it is a hope observers can see any signs of cooperative peaceful coexistence, or international constructionism? Some days, we even would compromise for symbiotic-codependences' survivals and primal-instincts to co-exists as in two states solutions, to help the humanity.

When your dream is a nightmare for too many; perhaps, after idle blame games, sectorial totalitarianism long in brutal practice even by so-called allies, you either fight and disappear, or unite and rebuilt on a more coexistence paths. At least, intellectual curiosity requires it. That is a learned human habit, sometime displeasing, and of course to American Allies happy with their 5th Colum political infiltrations, and the infestation of pro-militant Israeli 'land grabbers', extremists 'GOP', the know-nothings, and the do-nothings militarists', and fanatical Sunni-Wahhabism and Sunni-Salafism extremists, Jihadi Al-Qaida (the ISIS version), and the universal nihilistic terrorists extremists. They are now lumped and tagged as Islamists or jihadists under a general heading by the most bigoted, ill-read, xenophobic, sexists, sub-educated agencies of modern media? There are overt beneficiaries of recent GOP and American GOP-Militarists contributions to Syrian conflicts, over or under the tables, by the Sunni rich minorities, blind outside funding, and arm transfers with generous idiotic cacophonies of anti-Iranian, anti-Shiite-Islam, and overt Islam-o-phobic media bashings.

These have resulted in multitudes of mass bombings, car explosions, mosques destructions, and general mas-murderous campaigns against moderate Muslims innocents, beside the others: Sunnis, Christens, Jews, Yezidism, etc. The worst of the miss-informed sub-intellectuals of modern media there or here contribute generously to the murderous rampages and overt Islam-o-phobic recitations against moderate Islam and Muslim, which are killed, beheaded, and executed, at much higher rates than all others children and families in the area. We suppose to buy into the idiotic notions that the victims' religion is to blame, and no one else here or there has feed, funded, and fueled the flames of wars, or the vicious (negasatha) hounds of war, all these years of imposed miseries.

Keep in mind, the only defense-wall between the ISIS, the crazy Al-Qhuaeda-rejects, and the decapitation of Western embassy workers were the Iranian and Iraqi Shiites, and Moderate Sunni Muslims, which were executed already. Who apparently do not exists to the imbedded modern fixed media and their masters, as they are being mass executed by ISIS-Sunnis in Iraq. One good reason for the madness of that crowd is the Shiites and moderates Muslims, Sunni and Shiites in Iraq interfered and stopped the main Sunni extremists agenda, the beheading of Western and other embassy workers on the American-Media, as ISIS and their Sunni-paid-interests take over Baghdad by pre-designs with the new GOP-militarists cheerleaders' assists or abject ignorance. That burka has been lifted the hard way. These American media plutocratic mongrels still may get their wish; unfortunately, without any blames for any of these mass executions, beheadings, and the morphing of megalomaniacs and plutocratic media moguls' greed and blood lasts. The executed victims are blamed, a religious is supposed to be the causal force by itself, and it gets the blames regularly. That will take a lot of Alpo out of crazies-wars-funds, and under the table war funds, the thefts, and the deficits, and the GOP patrimonial militarism, and naive nihilistic sequestrations. Any peace talk, or commerce or cooperation in general, or with Iran will send these mad dogs of wars up the flag pools or in front of the nearest TV-cameras in a second, as we have seen rapidly and repeatedly. The securities of USA or American people, protection of Americans' constitutional privacies and human dignities are the last thing on their greedy-plutocratic-war-pandering small minds. Nevertheless, the so-called Arab states allies funding these mad dogs, they are the self-destructive prays of the infanticide and these war parties, and these recent idiocy jamborees. They will all do better in cooperative reconstruction, economic and (youth) jobs recoveries and developmental assistances,

The politically failed honey wagons do another rerun, passing the inspection of the most imbecilic, and the moronic of modern media, the overpaid agencies, and the fallacious paragons of our constitutional first-amendment protections, our economy, and our national security interests. Once, again we see why we are in deep malarkey serenaded by their well-paid imbedded cacophonies. It has long past time for American voters, taxpayers, citizens, to tell these fudge-ups to fudge off, and take their 5th Colum the paragons of pomposity, their political failing war fallacies, with them. Old choices do not exist, and you cannot kill enough people to fit in those old Sunni-Saddam models again; or the old Stalin and associates models again. Those who are not 5th Colum allies know these already very well.

Wisdom remains in the depleting peaceful-diplomacy as its times arrive, and for coexistence constructionism and mutual respect for others and others religions, after caging the mad hounds of wars, again. That had been the hardest choices to the least sophistication, which will only become harder choices to the well-known and well-televised paragons of 5th-colum fantasy agendas, the junked Generals, and domestic masters of malarkeys, and their flunked failing wars dynamically. They have failed and they think themselves Americas' mental-media masters and mentors, they are not dark skinned or religious, uniquely.

Those intellectual hard choices in peace will become hardest in forever-wars, or disappear altogether. It is important not to follow their failed costly cacophonies. It is important to undo their war agendas for peaceful domestic constructionism, and actual jobs, it is important for all voters to vote, rather than allow people to cheat them out of voting.

Our humane intellectual constraints should apply to all extremists, and their co-conspirators political party, the extremists' war-dancers, and enablers.[5] As fresh history abides, they use the smoke and dusts of one extreme situation and use it to degenerate and dispense with human rights, and civil rights of innocence around us, while all the time they say they know who exactly has been doing harm. It is a good time for patriotism sakes to piggyback their civil right waving laws with multimillion-dollar punitive fines, when they screw up and victimize the innocence lives royally here or there.

Hence, wiser nations can cage the hounds of wars to contribute to economic reorganizations, and recovery and sustainable job creations, eventually. Caging the hounds of wars again, for true global jobs and Economic Progress may have to become voters' mandate.

THE GLOBAL INSECURITY AGENDAS

More experienced politicians are recalculating the economics of rare resource utilization and applications by making distinctions between true national security, and wasteful and harmful constitutional violations for monetizing and insiders' revolving doors agendas, and newer industrial complexes. Just how many billions in costs of negative externalities the nation would like to endure? How many international businesses and contracts will be lost with vanishing global trusts, internet data tribalism, World Wide Web security honeycombs, retaliatory demonization, and diminution of international trade and commerce?

What damages the United States enfant-technology industries will sustain? Can they survive the wave of national and international monopsony-competitions in the same product markets? In addition, how much will that affect sectorial unemployment? The actual walk backs enacted are important. However, the agencies must respect or follow the actual practices, or laws. Some of current divulged practices were deemed illegal under TALON, in the 2000s.

However, new political organization, and the same old institutional actors means, they get newbies to do their illegal deeds, and keep their multibillion contracts, or bend the laws, or enact new unconstitutional laws. The use of general warrants, have been constitutionally band, since the red coat war of American independence.

On more than one occasions, agencies have pushed for that en mass criminalization, phone-meta data and USA national license-plate data warehousing (private or government) are the just latest skinny-dipping in the muddy waters. Why and when did that become such a herculean efforts? At least by now, the complexities of <PATRIOTs ACTs> sunsets-requirements have enlightened the civilian honest monitors. They vanished. The answers are another wonderment of modern American politics.

It is only recently, the revolving door natures of intelligence super-duper financial constructs were exposed. The hand-offs and the hand-downs, and revolving doors, accommodative laws leave nothing to the imagination.

When did middle class and poor American taxpayers replace foreign terrorists and drug lords on the lists? On the other hand, were those the original clever-job-creation plans of the forever wars? How much money was transferred from domestic infrastructures job-creations into the crocodile war funds? Did our civilian representatives' monitors (house and senate) ever ask any hard questions? Moreover, why do you think they are trying very hard to stop your votes for 2014, 2016, as they did before, and will try it again later, with gerrymandering in any good old national or local elections? Because Mr. and Mrs. America, probably, it is your votes that possibly will stop the wrongs.

Cooperate-advocacies, and extreme-wealth concentrated political-interests will subvert any governmental styles.[6] The votes will induce the pushback, the checks, and the balances of a functioning democracy.

The appropriate dynamic economic systems and policies will flow from fully informed citizen involvement in the system and the process. Partially informed citizens with limited votes, discouraged from voting cannot do it.

Infrastructures, Deconstruction and Global Consequences

Quotidian practices in the face of this new viral spread may prove to be problematic, if not fatally failing! The fundamental logic tells us that the exponential expansion phases of Ebola are closely related to under investments in infrastructures globally. Innate infatuations with military investments, chronic multiyear divestment in education, health, food, and agribusinesses and sequestrations have yielded current unpleasant harvest of what we seeded globally. A pensive study is timely, before we venture in another costly dark right miss-adventure.

Ebola Infrastructures

Why would infrastructure matter in the life cycle of viral Ebola? The implosions of the tribal and familial infrastructure evolved in waves in recent regional history. Village and familial lives have been uprooted frequently, regional wars, famine, drought, disemboweled rural fragile systems, and lives. The normal villages to townships or cities intermigrations have met regional wars, major diseases like pandemic AID, and pandemic Malaria, and now epidemic Ebola, which kill adult-earners, educators, builders, and maintainers of their rudimentary infrastructures, and the producers of these rural families.[7] Therefore, the process destabilizes the structural adhesiveness of the tribal rural younger-aged societies. Hence, this process is making these sub-cultures unsustainable and vulnerable to predatory militarism, terrorism, unsuitable earnings at the urban centers, human trafficking (for modern illicit boiler room operations, drug cartels, and prostitution slavery), child soldering, etc. Even after studies, and United Nation study that presented the human right laws and covenants at international levels, the public comprehension of the problem is null.[8] If some think these problems are specific to certain poor nations, a few specific religions, one continent, they are not paying attention to the degree of recent global poverty, and the root and depth of the global socio-economic problems, and the evolution of real politics. Therefore, they will exacerbate the issues and add to more complexity of the problems, as well as the final total costs.

The rudimentary tribal infrastructures, I am defining here is a simple mud hut, or straw huts, without indoor bathroom or sewer systems, other than open ditches and shallow trenches connected to road side or field side ditches, in-between living quarters, where human an animal feces intermingle with normal children and other human traffics.[9] The chances of second and third stage Ebola-full infection bodily fluid, from vomiting, diarrhea, sneezing, blood with viral Ebola getting exposed to others, children, family, passers, or cleaners, removers, postmortems washers, healthcare workers, and soldiers in the same area increases accordingly and substantially. Hence, there is a regional Ebola epidemic crisis. The 7-1400-4000 known and reported global deaths are the current estimates. Dynamic numbers may not include all regional cases.[10]

Lack of access to back countries, and estimations in the rural areas will show underestimations of changing data.

Availability of cleaning supplies, Clorox, detergent solution, the educational skill of using 5 or 10 present solution for cleaning, healthcare hazmat suits and the funding for that level of infrastructures are additional hurdles. NGOs and large donors have had successes in Malaria control (30 to 40 percent), clean water projects, and even AID. The introduction of proper insurance and healthcare for bigger populations (Universal or Private) will also be constructive here, and in advanced economies, where large portions of the population are left uninsured. It will be foolish to run and hide from such a disastrously large global pandemic potential, in fear and loathing, greed and human ignorance.

In middle-income economies with different degree of urbanization and health infrastructures, the issues may be less lethal if proper care is applied. Nigeria presented and demonstrated that situation. They followed the initials patients and traced contacts, and monitored them for the 21 day very strictly. Alas, at this level and some advanced urban centers improper health care and market economies' blind spots loom larger now, especially in cases of viral epidemics. The Flu virus kills estimated 54000 American citizens annually. The initial release of the USA first Ebola case in Texas demonstrates this fact most vividly. Most urban healthcare facility in United States under current private insurance arrangements void of universal protections release their patients without proper insurance very regularly and much too casually into public places, bus stations, public streets, or missions. The lack of universal insurance options and these casual bad practices are deadly combination awaiting future events and deadly flash-epidemics.

In a more advanced economy, Ebola is the preoccupation of the do-nothing and know-nothing political machinery that fought the White House In transfer of funds away from domestic infrastructures (enough adequately paid domestic jobs, health and education infrastructures included) into expansive militarism, used for older failing agendas. But, now military may be the only tool left to reinvent a health infrastructure in most African nations, where demise of education and heath infrastructures have had fatalistic global consequences. Can you read any signs of latent enlightenments, or remorseful penitents in the ether of election hyperbolic talks, radio-hate tirades, bombastic political verbosities, or the anal attentive self-righteous pomposities and their overt poor and middle class hates? If you can, you are smarter than the rest of us mortal-scholars underpaid and under employed, while the

500 symbolic anti-sciences anti-evolutionary, the stunted monkeys first cash their government checks, then they have run amok with nihilistic budgetary policies, anti-emigration laws, anti-entrepreneurial and small business enforcement brutalities, a do-nothing de-constructive agenda.

Political Demagoguery

The examples of rudimentary infrastructures were used first to ease the hard blows. One of the biggest superpower economies with some heads-up warning time has demonstrated many handicaps in less than stellar initial performances in this war on Ebola. Thus, accordingly anxiety, fear, political fear mongering, hyperbolic, and opportunistic exaggerations are taking the hill.

Instead of checking their biases, bigotry, xenophobic spins pandering at the doors of hospitals, and morgues, they run with particularly bad old political idea of general sequestering of specific health and educational infrastructures in USA. Otherwise, the circumstance of no or inadequate infrastructures will become the next chapter of Sequestrations story of the right wing extremism in United States, as it is ubiquitous in Western Africa developing economies. The reality is that less than half of dozen Ebola trained specific healthcare facilities and hospitals can reportedly handle about 10 to 12 Ebola infected patients at this time. We have to remain mindful.

The relative mortality risks in advanced economies are lower. USA, 1 mortality relative to 1400 in West Africa has a 7 in10,000-probability risk at its initial time. Compare to flu virus death domestically, one Ebola death to 54,000 Flu deaths, is 1 in 100,000 comparative probability risks. Even though, the statistics can change dynamically, and it will give no respite or relief to the victims from the viral death penalty.

However, this epidemic is a dynamically changing situation and we are learning, changing, and adopting new solutions as fast as they evolve and we can understand them. The CDC is doing their best under sequestration budget cuts. The house held up, and Robert Bork<ed, verb> the USA Surgeon Generals confirmation.[11] [12] Therefore, the nationalization of Ebola patients care in all hospitals and nationally uniform care packages in all of these hospitals are unavoidable, initially at the points of contacts, and blood test. Alternative solutions have to be funded, reported, and followed, at least, for this early phases of the disease.[13] The guilty political party, while trying to ban global traffic and blame the minor-refugees, emigrants, and other minorities for the Ebola erroneously with other fear mongering, now they are trying to cover up their sins, like the guilty house pet that digs up the lawn to cover up their messy stinks.

That is why Texas hospital experiences both successful or failed ones are training and learning moments in this dynamic process.[14] There will are other moments, other hospitals, and other diseases and ailments, too.[15] We do best to keep those closed bigoted minds and ears open, and learn. There are many hero health-care providers, front line delivery doctors, and nurses, educators, cleaners, janitorial services that may fall victims to this or other scourges of our time. They along with soldiers, police persons, airport service and other people, and public transportation workers are the backbones of our modern infrastructures at all time, in all parts of the globe. Regardless, what Sequestrations-tablets of bad-wisdom the know-nothing and do-noting political operators misrepresent as economic book of wisdom to the gullible masses, anew? We will do well to appreciate the services these providers, educators, workers, nurses, and their unions supply to all of us, in some grace, and maintain the societal construct dynamically, instead of giving in to the mules that will kick down the barns constantly. Moreover, encourage the wider health insurance coverages, if not universal health coverages for viral and pandemics, as well.

Teconomics of Infrastructures

Holistic Teconomic Solutions

Ebola-Infrastructures global, and constructive economic strategy to deal with the Ebola Economic Risks and Holistic Teconomics Solutions are presented in this shortened applied study.

The positives are slowly reconstituting a general strategy, perhaps too slow to match the exponential rate of spread of the virus. Nevertheless, large donors are coming, where sequestrations were proven decisively harmful, even deadly. Moreover, military unites are building infrastructures. The mastery will be in increasing the rate of constructive improvements to surpass the catch-rates and get ahead of the rate of exponential spread of Ebola, again. The upgraded and newly constructed health and educational infrastructures cannot afford to make mistakes. If we know that, the 21-day lifecycles Ebola virus-incubation is true. The Ebola virus mode of infection is not airborne, but infections occur by specific contacts. We need to have soldiers, healthcare workers, public transportation users informed. If they are part of groups that contacted with suspected Ebola-victims. They need to respect that 21 day self-restrains, and cautionary isolation, unless symptoms appear sooner, or test results are negative, on the honor systems or by mandatory requirements, which will require prepaid facilities for travelers, or designated hospitals for the sick, and military facilities for the soldiers.

The 21-day issue and positive test for Ebola in first stage of the viral infection are important scientifically. However, people focus on medical staff and the military aid, but ignore more frequenters from Media, illegal game poachers, game and human smugglers, and illicit commerce, which can add to the risks, too. If there are uniform streamline procedures, we need to share them with all levels. Nevertheless, why give in to hyperbolic fear mongering, and the know nothing do nothing failed strategies of the political abstractionists, or aimless and blind furry of travel-bands, anti-commerce tirades, aimless victimizations of mass travelers.[16] These political hijackers of the medical and scientific processes by the anti-science nabobs of negative-actions, and the luddites-deniers are as dangerous as the viral afflictions.

Constructive Contributions

Keep a positive strategy ahead and let us catch up and surpass the rate of viral destruction by human constructive endowments. We have down it before many times, humanely. Ebola private and military healthcare assaults teams are an innovative solution, if the equipment, supply, health and education infrastructures, and skills are presented, and maintained dynamically at state and local levels. Therefore, those walk-in cases will be tested for Ebola on the spot In Los Angeles, New York, or Texas, or over sea, instead of releasing the sick to their own faith and misfortunes, if they test positive for it at the first stage. That uncharacteristic under investments in infrastructures will be the fatal flaw of the past health-ointment strategies, or falling bridges, gas and water pipe infrastructures erosions. Otherwise, and fear and loathing in politics of greed, ignorance, and fear. Mindless sequestration-deconstruction of infrastructures strategies will bring big infrastructural-mistakes on American populations. Why should we repeat such simpletons' mistakes, so inexpertly?

Millennial Competitive and Complex International Commerce

International Trade and more complex millennial competitive commerce are on the menu, if EU-USA-Middle East thought competitive international economics, commerce, peace and trade negotiations in Middle East would play second fiddles to their domestic security games, or any other arrangements and sophomoric agendas; they just received a proverbial 30 years shock to their system resets, which will not be deterred.[17] The Russia-China natural gas international trade deal can easily rearrange some international trade chessboards. It will demand some sustained attention, dynamically.

Some may be too busy to see the global tectonic plates are shifting on them, especially when one of their suppliers does not need them as much, and they have grown intolerant or even hostiles to other suppliers. The awful and unspeakable truth remains they are too busy with their political squabbles, sequestrations, anti-immigration, minority hate minutiae, and plutocracy pandering to comprehend that their international economic world just became a small fiat, if not a Yugo, instead of a four door Cad, Benz, or a Bentley.

They can wait and watch, or compete, readjust, reset, make new-old friends, and remain relevant. The treadmill of dynamic economic growth and development with technological injections will wait for no mortals. Let us hope, we can still keep it humane. You cannot kill your consumers and still survive and thrive financially. Apparently, these sustainable-balanced graces are in shorter supply these days, among terrors, unhinged terrorism, Islam-o-phobia, minority victimizations, ignorant and overt Muslim bashing, and militaristic institutionalizations.

Africa, and Middle East, can reset a global financial reality with manufacturing and energy sources of Millennial-Asiatic expansions. They can create a parallel world to Western monopolies and unsustainable monopolistic plutocracies, which cannot retain academic lessons of non-competitive systems of old, and their harsh backlashes, chronic joblessness, low and declining disposable real income of their larger middle-class-customers in their economies. Other developing fiscal voids, and trade give a ways to competitors may have added to these DRI declines. Assuming their bad habits and many under developments will not subsume these developing nations' resources along the trails.

Of modern commerce and international trade, our world just changed.[18] You will know it in 20-30 years hence.

NOTE

[1] PBS/frontline on this subject.

[2] SHAILA DEWAN , Law Lets I.R.S. Seize Accounts on Suspicion, No Crime Required, The New York Times, http://www.msn.com/…/law-lets-irs-seize-account…/ar-BBbbfW3…

[3]

https://archive.org/…/final…/finalreportofsel01unit_djvu.txt
http://www.pbs.org/…/f…/homefront/preemption/churchfisa.html
http://www.pbs.org/moyers/journal/10262007/profile2.html
http://www.salon.com/2012/04/21/e_2/
http://www.huffingtonpost.com/…/nsa-senate-church-committee…
http://www.nytimes.com/…/challenges-to-us-intelligence-agen…- senate-inquiry-of-70s.html?pagewanted=all&_r=0

[4] Rewrite of SA, By Dr. Bahman Fakhraie, Copyright 6/24/2014, 9:47 AM USA

[5] http://jurist.org/forum/2014/08/marjorie-cohn-israel-crimes.php

[6] http://drbahfecon.wix.com/teconomics

[7] Stefan Kirchner, "Ebola, Human Rights and Health Discrimination," JURIST - Academic, October 20, 2014, http://jurist.org/academic/2014/10/stefan-kirchner-health-rights.php.

[8] International Covenant on Economic, Social and Cultural Rights,
Adopted and opened for signature, ratification and accession by General Assembly resolution 2200A (XXI) of 16 December 1966, entry into force 3 January 1976, in accordance with article 27,
http://www.ohchr.org/en/professionalinterest/pages/cescr.aspx

[9] Ebola crisis: WHO focuses on preventing regional spread, 16 October 2014 Last updated at 11:43 ET,
http://www.bbc.com/news/world-africa-29648598

[10]

http://www.democracynow.org/2014/8/22/dr_paul_farmer_on_african_ebola
"Dr. Paul Farmer on African Ebola Outbreak: Growing Inequality in Global Healthcare at Root of Crisis As the death toll from the West African Ebola outbreak nears 1,400, two American missionaries who received experimental drugs and top-notch healthcare have been released from the hospital"

[11] http://en.wikipedia.org/wiki/Robert_Bork

[12] Hearing on the nomination of Surgeon General designate,
http://www.help.senate.gov/hearings/hearing/?id=7f4d5e03-5056-a032-5246-3fe3e2ebe224

[13] Ebola: Texas hospital says it's 'deeply sorry' - CNN.com: Ashley Fantz, Holly Yan and Catherine E. Shoichet, Sources: Nurse with Ebola will be sent from Texas to Maryland,CNN, updated 11:56 AM EDT, Thu October 16, 2014, http://www.cnn.com/2014/10/16/health/us-ebola/index.html?eref=rss_topstoriesomics

[14] Josephus Weeks, Ebola didn't have to kill my uncle, Thomas Eric Duncan, Chicago Tribune-Oct 16, 2014 http://www.chicagotribune.com/news/opinion/commentary/chi-ebola-thomas-eric-duncan-nephew-comment-20141016-story.html

[15] Jayne O'Donnell, Feds move to close no-hospital coverage loophole, USA TODAY 10:06 a.m. EST November 4, 2014, http://www.usatoday.com/story/news/nation/2014/11/04/cms-no-hospital-coverage-loophole-employer-coverage/18455871/

[16] Patrick Young Esq., Lincoln, the Know Nothings and Immigrant America, http://www.longislandwins.com/.../lincoln_the_know_nothings_a

[17] SA, Oct 7 2014, Dr. Bahman Fakhraie © 2014

[18] Picture and articles from, http://www.washingtonpost.com/.../map-what-the-epic-china-ru.../

CHAPTER 21

COMPETETIVE ORGANIZATIONS

Competitive market organization, in the case of suppliers of each modular production process, there is one or a group trying to sell their goods or services. Therefore, there are supplier organizations. In the case of demands for the products or services, there may be individual consumers or tribes, city, or groups' demand, which will be reflected in an organization with the demand. The minimum potential originations for perfectly competitive exchanges are at least three.

The supplier, the consumer, and the exchange market are three elements of each exchange, which is accomplished by a buyer and a seller, and the buyer can be the modular producer. Therefore, there are potential for at least two market organizations in a perfectly competitive market.

However, those familiar with stock exchanges, commodity barter or exchanges understand the complexity and numbers of intermediaries, and governmental agencies involved in each minute transactions.

Bahman Fakhraie, PhD. © 2015

THE SUPPLY-SIDERS' MODELS FAILED DATA TESTS

There has always been a diaspora between the ultra-wealthy and the rest of the economy, it is widening exponentially, while national structural unemployment has stayed high long after the recent economic recovery post-recession. The demagogues love to argue 'eat-the rich', Socialism, Marxism slogans in defense or offense. The gathering clouds of discontents far more important than their collective and limited vocabulary, at this time in history of aging modern technology-capitalism.

There are the violations of assumptive conditions, formulated by the perfectly competitive market models, which I presented as rarities in 1970s, they have become more pronounced in millennial economies. Then there are the more realistic models, of relative free markets, and natural or governmental oligopolies and monopolies. These form , the all shades of gray that is imperfect competition models, and more complex organizational involvements in multinational markets, which have gathered momentum, aggregate macroeconomics forces, and they affect policy, and sustainability conditions readily (you may have to read my first two books for more serious details).

In discussion of income inequalities, poverty, and dynamic models of wealth creation within the relatively free market models of capitalism it is very important to study the longer run implications of micro and macroeconomic balances and economic welfare theory. Economic-theorists may recall Joan Robinson (Cambridge, UK.), and Dr. Edward H. Chamberlin (Harvard, USA), '1933' to 1980s Microeconomic discourse, if they need to refresh their older theories. I had a short visit with Mrs. Robinson in late 1970s, early 1980.

Hence, the reason for democratic governments' attentions to the sustainability balances of wealth-creation, as a counter balance force to self-harm of raw-wealth and unchecked-political power concentrations, in political monopolistic capitalism.

Therefore, sound fiscal policies are not some demagogic loyalty oath to memory of Karl Marx, despite the anti-socialism cacophony of the millionaire media crowds. Recently, wealthy capitalists (nouveau riche) have realized their toolboxes of purchased political powers. They have used it too excessively. Nevertheless, they have not all realized their responsibilities, and the steroidal effects of technological injections, thus the consequential imbalances. Therefore, they have ignored the backlash powers, which are accumulative and unleash unexpectedly.

There are educated capitalists some old school, "let pay our share of taxes crowds (plus a minimum cooperate tax), for education, infrastructural, and reparative fiscal job-creation, so the economy uplifts all yachts and kayaks."

They also realized the government rule as a counterbalance to the negative forces that cause class poverties, as a force for sustainability instead of poverty creation at one extreme, and wealth creation at another, and accumulative forces of social Darwinism. The purchased gradual drift from the hard educations of 1930s history have harvested both momentum and claw backs.

We can name many of the one percent wealthy that are wise beyond their billions. They contribute to global health and welfares infrastructure immensely, by self-governing, self-motivational, and very effectually. They have greatly reduced global infant mortality rate. They have supplemented or supported willing local governments. They have supplemented commercial enterprises, and created many jobs, and their own eminence wealth, all laudable endeavors for detractors and admirers. Their wealth creation will not be problematic to job-creation, or to national wealth creation strategies.

However, the rate of zero-sum-game version of wealth concentrations, and its implications, its hostility to others livable wages, level of livings, direct impact on aggregate demand, economic activates, circularity and velocity of money in national and international economy are consequential accumulatively. They are massively influencing economic policies, political-policy. Their effort will affect employment, taxation, and rRDIPPC. These make them, their method of wealth concentration central to economic solutions, just by paying a reasonable tax rate, nothing confiscatory, as they fear initially. Histories tell of accumulative pent-up forces, which are not too kind to capital constructionists that dillydallied too long.

The immense diversion of incomes will meet the usual spin and forget treatment from the media. However, the exploding diversions have explosive social instabilities issues.

The usual spin-jobs or the one-party political maneuvering and push for re-election funds will not serve the systems well. The expansive issues of the American people and the need of educated wealthy patrons are not good justification for them to depart from their honestly earned hard cash, if all they get is none-functionality and hostile environments to commerce locally or globally.

Legacy Law, Ccooperate Citizens

The cooperation of the market organizations of the top one percent brackets for individuals and cooperate entities are reflected in their rate of economic benefits, which they are amassing at exponential rates to top one percent organizational groups.

The progress of all income and economic activates for all quintiles hide the fact that middle-income earners decreased, or their earnings remained flat, as their costs are, (COLA) inflated. That is the fallacy of index-illusions of economic, when a small number get large incomes, and large numbers get very little, the averages can falsely show a large average income for the sample population. We will see the important implications of wealth concentration instead of wealth creation as national policies.

Figure 39 shows top one percent and all other quintiles' income earners incomes, before and after taxes in United States, 1979-2010.

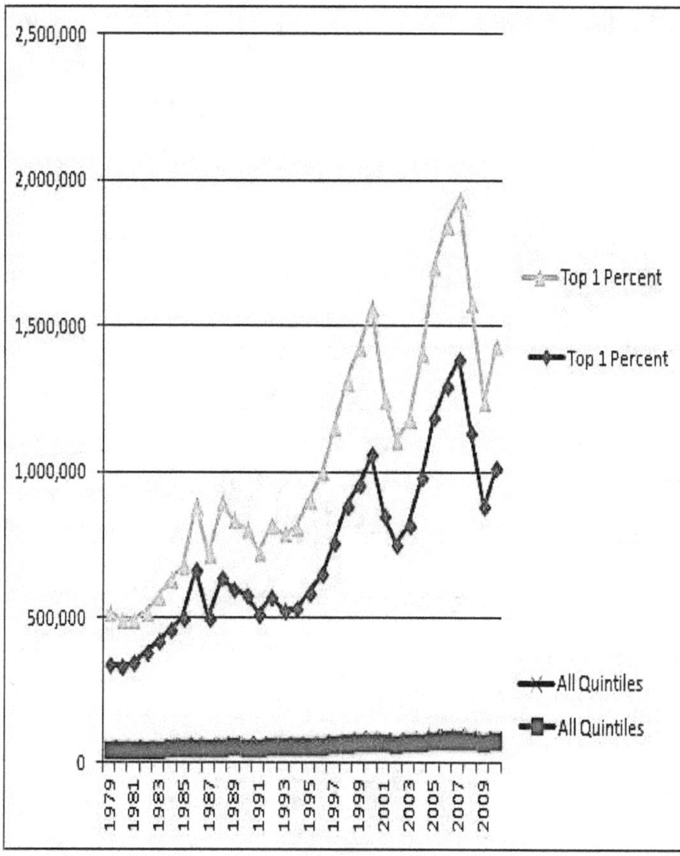

http://www.cbo.gov/publication/44604

Analysis and graph by Dr. Bahman Fakhraie © 2013

Figure 39, Top 1 % and other quintiles' incomes, before and after taxes.

The next two graphs show the cooperation's' wealth concentration that have followed the Supreme Court pro-cooperate, citizen decisions in USA.[1] Figure 40, shows income paid that has increase, for cooperation interests in Untied States in 2002-2010.

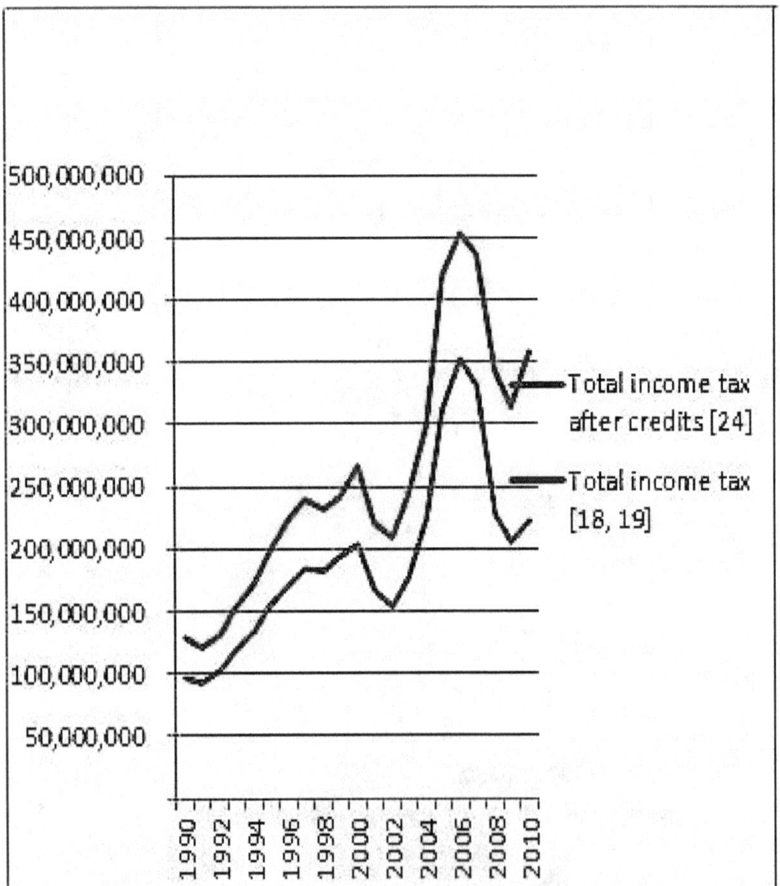

Figure 40, Cooperation income taxes data.

The good top 1 percent citizens even carry out infrastructural duties, when governments fail. The late industrialists' Henry Ford and the advocacy of late Senator Teddy Kennedy are vivid examples.

Figure 41shows cooperation profits and net income that have exploded in Untied States in 2002-2010.[2]

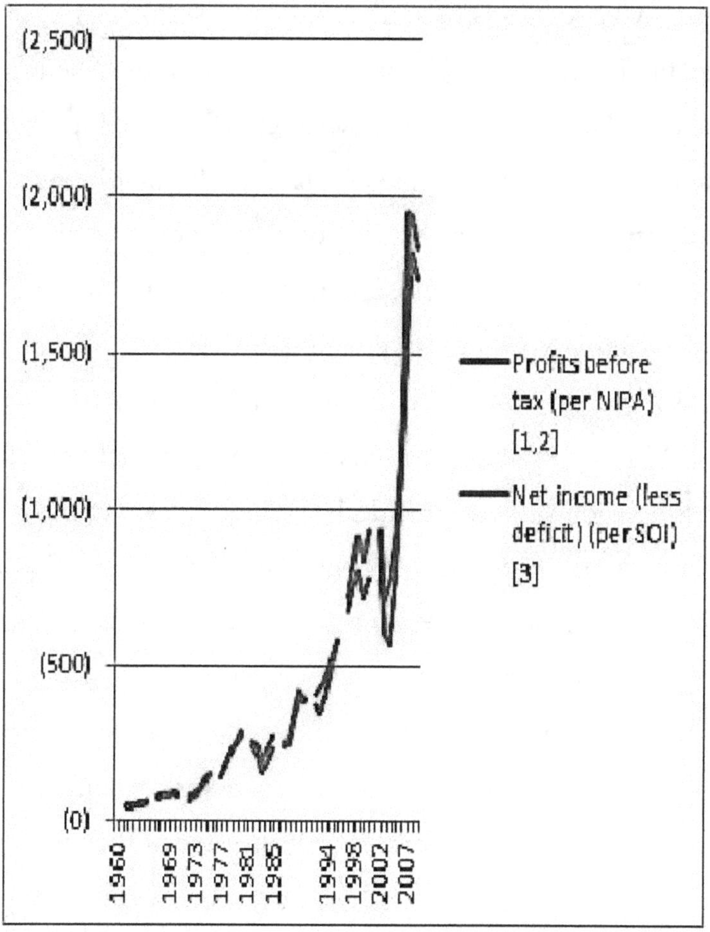

Figure 41, Cooperation net incomes and profits in Untied States in 2002-2010.

However, there are the uneducated nouveau riche capitalists, or more deliberate capitalists' mega rich. They carry politics and spins full of rhythmic bull, which means. What is mine, it is mine, what is the middle class, and poor is mine, too.

'The let them eat cake kinds, they need to pull up their own bootstraps. Tax the middle class takers, not the wealthy job makers.' Unfortunately, they are not the job-makers. They are deporting (self-deporting) the job-makers. Nevertheless, they purchase cash-hoarding wealth-concentrating policies. These policies nourish certain lower skilled practitioners, and none-functionality that adds to the accumulated negative externalities and unsustainability forces that histories tell us, they are very destabilizing. While the funds of the workers, and middle class pension savers, the elderly savings remain in the country and are recycled as consumer demands and up to 75 to 78 percent of GDP, and as producers- investments in real estate and job-creations domestically.

However, the transfer of government tax for revenues have shifted to individuals, to older workers that are retiring and need healthcare, Medicare, social security, and pension protection laws, and geriatric care, as the RDI declines, so will the economy decline. So does their pension, IRAs, and saving.

These legacy benefits are regularly under verbal attacks by the worst of the worst of cooperate criminals, riders, and their high salaried financial media minions. Their spins are against the rich elderlies, and the CEOs, the multibillionaires, the hedge funders, with the $ 300 million to billion dollars salaries, bonuses, and benefits get the media pass, and the rare admiration nibble. It is all fine, if they pay their minimum cooperate tax rate.

The CEOs have driven cooperation their operations overseas to monetize their productions (modular productions) for higher CEOs salaries and benefits. They hire the best professionals to under pay or not pay taxes. The top one percent pays less than 10 percent of taxes. They have avoided the flat minimum cooperate tax rate of 30 percent under the last three presidents, and both parties, and in both houses.

They are also wrecking immigration policies since President Reagan. In order to reduce competitions with their organizational operations in foreign-markets, where they can hire American university educated skilled workers, deported from America and American universities on the cheap.

The same graduates they denigrate as unskilled at home in USA, while equating and blaming unemployment on immigrants, they are deporting the job makers, too. The last two graphs showed their explosive revenue growth. There have not been any sufficient job creations or RDI increases to benefit the government revenue or aggregate demands, domestically.

The job-creations promised by both parties for large groups among the middle class have not appeared. The lack of a fixed immigration policy harms the elderly GOP most, since their pensions are deemed removable by the CEOs and the GOP politicians as bad legacy costs, too. Why would any honest American President buy their oppositions political lines and keep deporting Americans at thousand a day rates?

Figure 42 shows the reduction of cooperation taxes per total assets. That is 50 percent drop in cooperate tax obligations since 1995, 17 percent decline 1995-2006, and an additional 33 percent decline 2006-2010. This is at the same time that the middle class tax breaks were terminated during 2013 tax years.

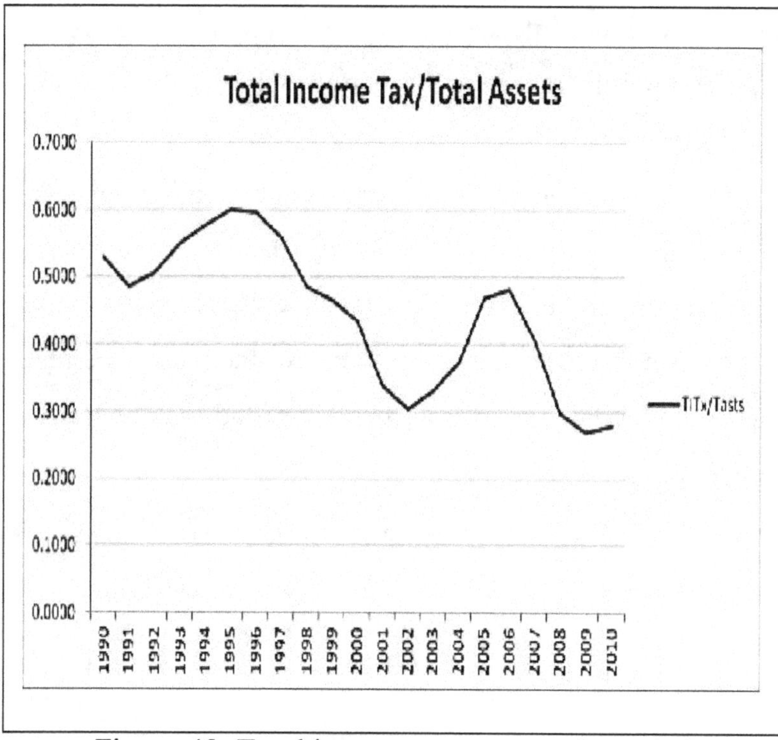

Figure 42, Total income tax over total assets for cooperation data.

It is difficult to accept the argument that only criminal elements are deported, while summary judgments and court cases have been reported as one-a-minute judgments. Indeed, these are their expressed-observed facts. Moreover, we have a history of general warrants against select population. In addition, The history of summery rash judgments against big groups, nationalities, colors, sexes, tribal nations, whether they are Asian,

Chinese, Japanese, American Indians, or Muslims, Jews, sick, and others. This has only recently improved marginally, under intense scrutiny and vigilance of a great American public. Less we forget our vigilance, bad things in history reoccur.

Figure 43, shows while wealth concentration have been in the one sector of the economy, the upper brackets tax revenues has declined, like it declined for the cooperation interests in aggregation. All the while, the real disposable incomes of over 80 percent of individuals have declined.

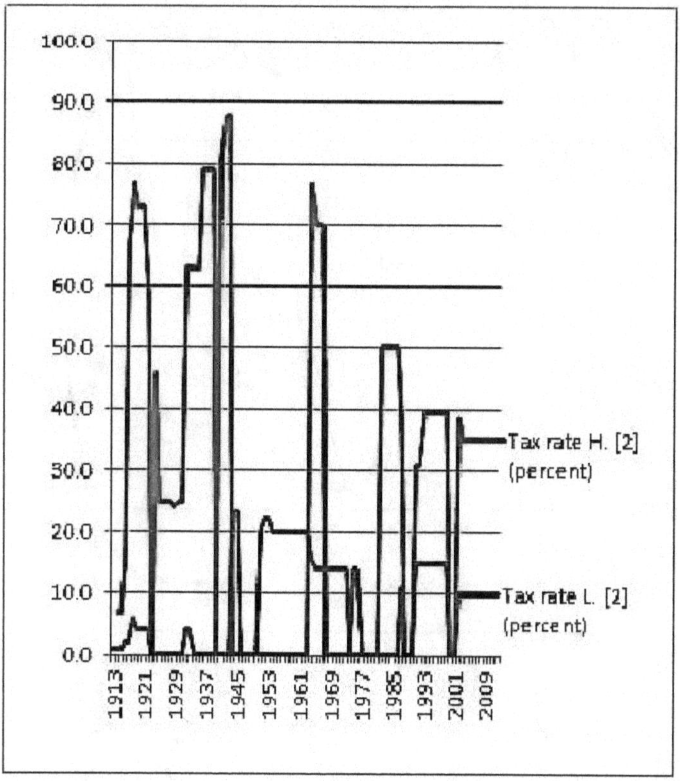

Figure 43, highest and lowest tax brackets tax rates 1913-2009.

Figure 44 shows the federal revenues from selected major tax-sources.[3]

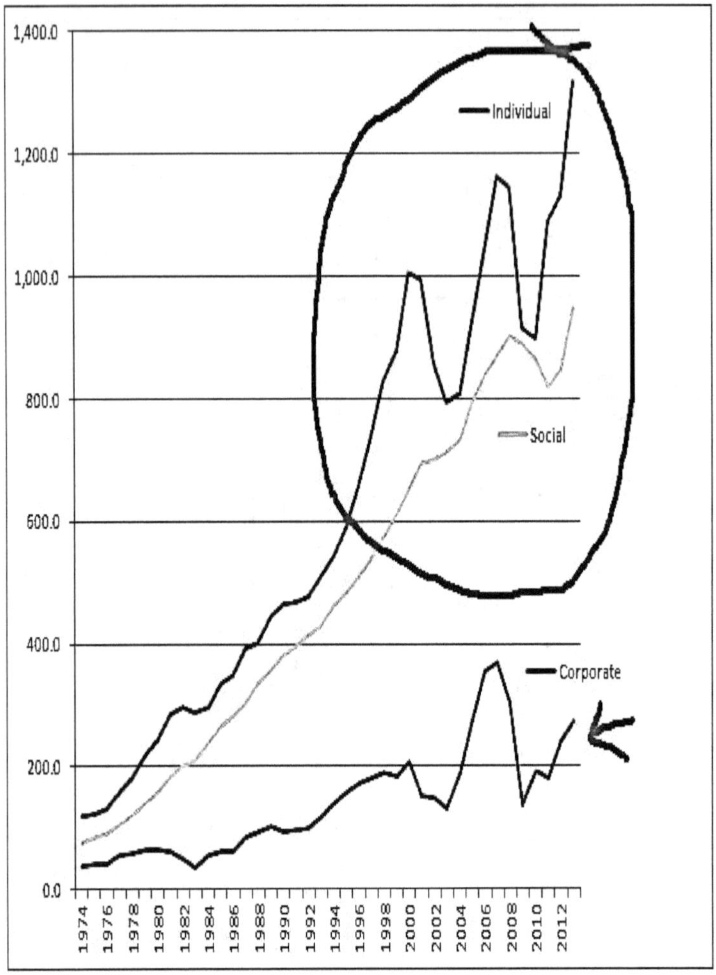

Figure 44 shows federal revenues from selected major tax-sources.

Figure 44 shows within a few recent decades the federal revenues, which were lower and closely shared in 1970s, have exponentially exploded at the expense of individuals in this millennium. Figure 43 shows that it took 80-90 percent taxes rates 1920s to1940s, it may take 30 percent cooperate-minimum flat tax now to repair their harms. Even optimistically, it will take 40 percent later, and 55 percent by 2025 to repair their damages, if these jobless-recoveries remain as our economic norms. They are hoping their organizational control of the political machinery and both parties will suffice to get those taxes from the middle class and working poor. That reality may prove much harsher, as the financial margins in other classes, the percentiles of the taxpayers do not exists to cover their extravagance wealth concentrations and all societal expenses.

TAX BURDEN SHIFT AND DECISION MATRIX

History tells a different story, 1920s their firm grasps of mantels of power was much firmer than it is now, Hoovers' supply-siders were serious about their remedies, and they were resolute adamantly. Yet, they had to pay up to 90 percent in taxes to repair the damages to the societal infrastructure, structural implosions, and resuscitation of the employments systems. Even if their political control nightmare scenario is succeeding now, the money, the cash flow, based on the trends of RDI, and their inabilities to create jobs, or pass a job creation bill will not generate revenue from (declining population of) individual taxpayers to compensate this historic cooperate ride on the treasury.

This has occurred with the blessing of their representatives in both political party, but mainly by the GOP. Everyone needs to recalculate the balance of his or her greed with the functionality in the economic system anew, in a way that improves others economic condition as well.

Those obstruction-mindsets cause paranoiac policies, against everyone except the one percent, which causes backlash. Their represented media, and journals, their purchased-political monopolistic spins and attack-machines push these policies for the failed supply-siders. They push the "Nazis-Kristallnacht" economic-models not objective news, or sciences. Therefore, their ignorance is harmful to national security, beyond intentional harming of a black president and his legacy agenda, or legal immigrants, or middle class economics. Moreover, it will cost more to fix their damages to the economy.

Figure 45 shows Federal revenues major sources as percentage of gross national products (GDP, 1974-2013).[4]

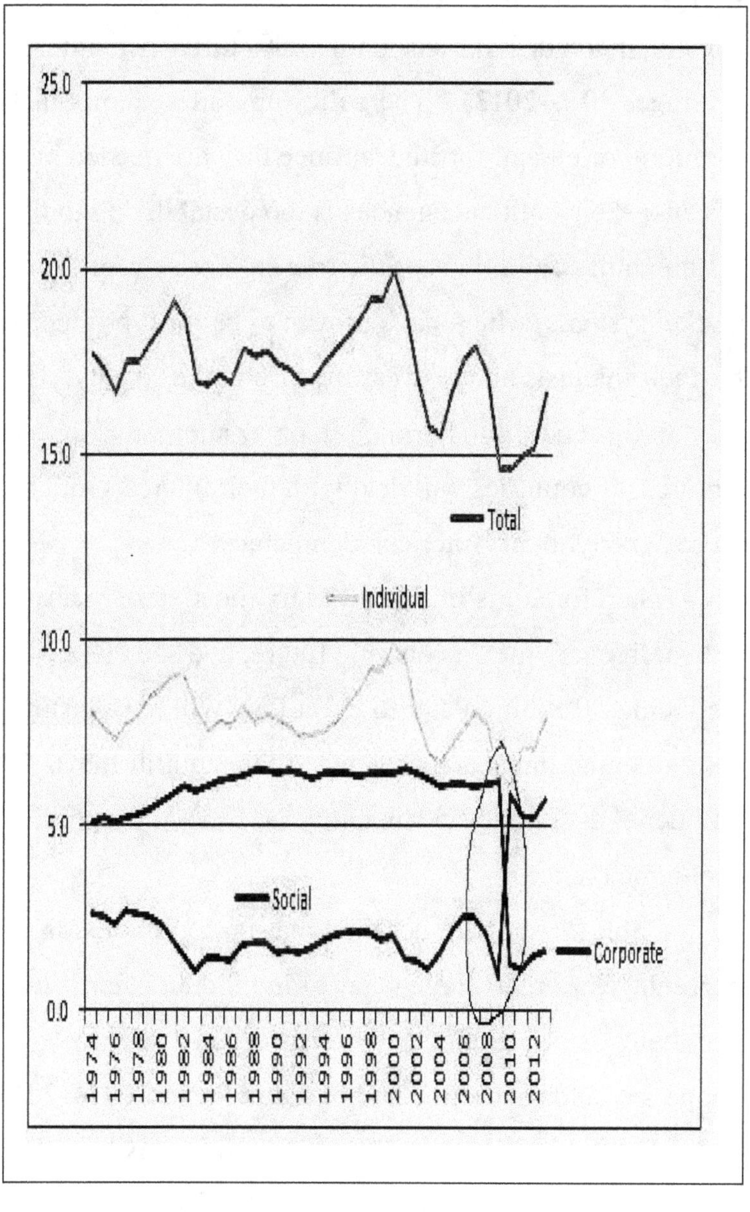
25.0
20.0
15.0
10.0
5.0
0.0
Total
Individual
Social
Corporate
1974
1976
1978
1980
1982
1984
1986
1988
1990
1992
1994
1996
1998
2000
2002
2004
2006
2008
2010
2012

Figure 45, Federal revenues as percentage of GDP, 1974-2013.

Cooperation taxes have dropped already, the average-cooperation tax rate as a percentage of GDP has dropped from 6.5 percent (averages until 2009) to 1.4 percent, (averages 2010-2013). The policy upgrades are not just for moral or ethical fortitudes, since they are needed badly. Because their political agendas is too destabilizing to the sustainability conditions of the free enterprise capitalist market systems, which have proven to be most productive for their interests above everyone else in the society. If they really succeed in harming it, other alternative systems, cultures, or countries will deal with their interests much more harshly, than American democracy.

Therefore, it is important to fix the system in a way to benefit everyone's' economic future, and societal wellbeing. Robbing Peter to cheat Paul will have lasting consequential impacts on social welfare equilibriums. It will derail economic sustainability. It is a poorer political economic choice.

Table 27 shows a decision matrix, formulated in percentages from average taxes of individual income taxes and their social benefit taxes overtime and average of cooperate taxes over time and over total taxes, 1974-2013.

This table 27, tax shift matrix shows a tax burden shuffle from cooperation to individual taxes and social benefit taxes of individuals. This reconfirms, what the last few figure 4, and figures, 43,44,45 represented about the taxes. That cooperate taxes per total cooperate assets have declined. The upper bracket taxes have also declined. Only taxes for the lower brackets have increased.

Table 27, Tax shifts in matrix percentages, USA 1974-2013.

Matrix of Tax Shifts, as Percant of GDP		
Avgs/yrs	Individual & Social Taxes	Cooperate Taxes
1974-09	57	35
2009-13	82	9

Nevertheless, there is an attempt made to shift all of the economic burdens to middle class and working poor, without giving them an income increase that matched COLA, or regular raises.

There has been a lot of political money paid to arrange elections, and hide this simple tax shuffle among other agendas. Most of government revenues are collected from the individual income taxes with flat or declining DPI. In the worst case of hiding the trick-hands, the right wing media have attacked the democratic administration for IRS tax targeting of the wealthy and c-nonprofits, while the big news is the need for a minimum-cooperation-tax rate, and the tax loud shuffle to the middle class 47 percent, and the other 99 percent. Yet, we see the opposite is true by the USA aggregate data that it is the middle class and working poor have been burdened for cost of government, while tax burden has been shifted away from the cooperation and the mega wealthy, for the fake promise of job-creations. The promised they signed in blood oath their saint President Ronald Reagan of all thing good and angelic in economic growth and free markets miracles, which it only tepidly and occasionally materialized, but not in the series of recent jobless recoveries, when the fund went for wealth concentration among the very oligarchical few.

Figure 46 shows nominal federal social benefit outlays.[5]

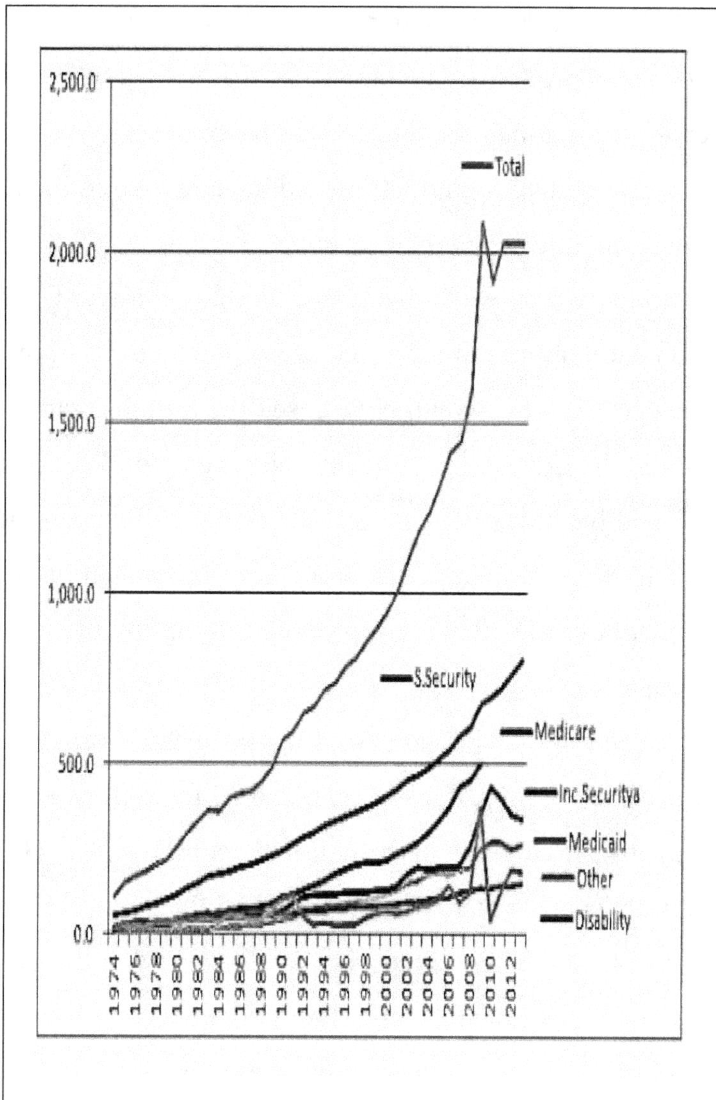

Figure 46, Federal social benefits outlays, 1974-2012.

The fix in the fixed news is the attacks on legacy benefits, social security, pension, medical benefits have been coming from the megabanks, and ultra-wealthy takers, cooperate welfare kings and queens, megacorporation and all of the other demagogic nonsense that comes out of mega-international-cooperation media spins.

The ethical high roads would have increased jobs, real income, governmental revenues, reparative solutions, immediately after the down turns. Perhaps a lower CEO bonus path, a more modest rate of wealth accumulation for the mega-wealthy, would have eased the troughs, and repaired the down turn damages. Now, they will feel the fixes and the adjustments more. They are still screaming at the nation for cooperate comprehensive tax reduction for jobs, without the 30 percent cooperation minimum tax mandate.

The middle class and working poor had deserved the tax breaks, the jobs, the wages, and RDI increases to raise the aggregate demand in the national economy. The GOP forgot their taxes were 80 percent when President Kennedy reduced them. Their taxes were 60 percent when President Reagan reduced them, again. Each time we had post-recession increase in employment and increase in RDI.

Figure 47 shows federal social benefit outlay as percentage of GDP.[6]

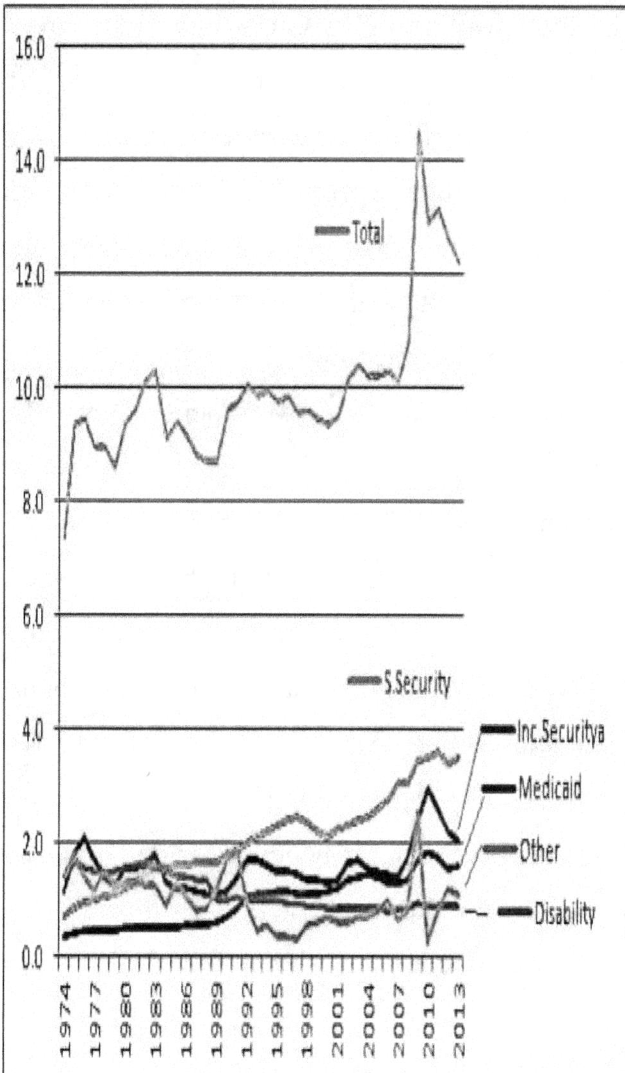

Figure 47, Federal social benefit outlay as percentage of GDP.

Figure 47, Federal social benefit outlay as percentage of GDP. The increase in the curve shows the time of major economic downturn in USA economy. Since the same cooperate interests and representatives have become the vocal advocates of least taxes and much less government, and hence less government jobs; therefore, a rational conclusion and expectation is why these cooperate profiteers have not created jobs out of the jobless recoveries for this millennium.

Those increased the government revenues from income increases at all level of incomes. It is also important to note, before 2007, total federal social benefits stayed around 10 percent. Despite the permanent wars, and long GOP wars, and their damages to the economy, the social costs of mandatory outlays remained around 14 percent and declined. This is after, they caped the social security tax for people making over $100,000 a year salaries, without capping benefits. They also voted and removed the middle class brackets tax breaks. This is after the soldiers came home with multiple disabling issues. Moreover, the wealth concentration went to the few at the top, and RDI of middle class and working poor stayed flat, or declined.

Blaming the matter on the legacy benefits, low productivities, unions, workers-skill sets, under prepared graduates, and underfunded education systems are malicious purchased-spins to stop ethical contributions to job creations, and the future of this great nation. Clear sign adjustments have to be rectifying promptly. The check and balance have increase more prominently in operational functionalities of governmental, political, and economic organizations.

NOTE

1 -

http://www.cbo.gov/publication/44604
Analysis and graph by Dr. Bahman Fakhraie © 2013

2 Ibid. Analysis and graph by Dr. Bahman Fakhraie © 2014.

3 -

Gov. revenues, by Major Source, Since 1974-2013

Sources: Congressional Budget Office; Office of Management and Budget.

www.cbo.gov/publication/45010

Analysis and graph by Dr. Bahman Fakhraie © 2014

4 -

Gov. revenues, by Major Source, Since 1974-2013,
as a Percentage of Gross Domestic Product
Sources: Congressional Budget Office; Office of Management and Budget.
www.cbo.gov/publication/45010
Analysis and graph by Dr. Bahman Fakhraie © 2014

5 -

In Billions of Dollars
Sources: Congressional Budget Office; Office of Management and Budget.
Mandatory Gov. Outlays Since 1974_2013
www.cbo.gov/publication/45010
Selected data
a. Includes unemployment compensation, Supplemental Security Income, the refundable portion of the earned income and child tax
Graphed and Analysis by Dr. Bahman Fakhraie from sources data
Analysis and graph by Dr. Bahman Fakhraie © 2014

6

Sources: Congressional Budget Office; Office of Management and Budget.
Mandatory Gov. Outlays Since 1974_2013
As a Percentage of Gross Domestic Product
www.cbo.gov/publication/45010
Selected data
a. Includes unemployment compensation, Supplemental Security Income, the refundable portion of the earned income and child tax
Graphed and Analysis by Dr. Bahman Fakhraie from sources data.
Analysis and graph by Dr. Bahman Fakhraie © 2014

CHAPTER 22

GOVERNANCE INFRASTRUCRES POLITICAL TECONMICS AND PROGRESS

The importance of legal institutions in inducements about ownership, capital use, and protection of private rights of ownership and conduct of business activities also play an important part in the process of technological progress, and capital formation. The infrastructures of good governances are to maintain functionality, and good rights of ownership, and relative free market functionalities to induce dynamic participation and continuity. The following were some fundamentals about legal rights and returns on capital, which also have current implications for use of capital,

1. Ownership and use rights were absolute.
2. The relative market price of capital, return, or interest reflects the scarcity of capital.
3. Risk of losses of different capital made their returns different.
4. Interest on funds are the minimum, bellow that the return of other capital cannot go, in order to remain an investment opportunity.

Austrian economists (L. V. Misses, and F.V. Hayak) paid much attention to the system-implication of such institutions and further progress, which aided progress. In light of Soviet Union (now Russia) and Eastern Europeans' economic systems and institutional changes in 1980s, the work of L. V. Misses, and F.V. Hayak attracted renewed interests. The importance of such infrastructure and the impact of technological-changes have been over looked, or miss-applied. Thus, slowing construction to correct the repeated dangerous past experiences. United State depression and WWII experience found two solutions after the historical globalizations of early misapplications of "laissez faire" of Adam Smith. So the Hayak solution out of Hayak and Keynes roof top paradoxical solutions to the only alternative of Marxism let to the Keynes-ism, since the Hayak solutions had been assumed tried and failed in the " laissez faire" era of pre-depression. F. D. Roosevelt and others tried Keynes, were either pulled to the Statists' extreme in the post-depression and WWII experiences of United States, or they were propagandized as much. It is not surprising that the less informed students of economic, and political economics now mistake swing to Hayak solution as repudiation of Keynes, when they mean repudiation of Statists' extremism, the Stalinism's branch of Marx, which has made a comeback in some regulatory and policy circles. The following graph in Figure 48 shows political economic systems and market dependencies.

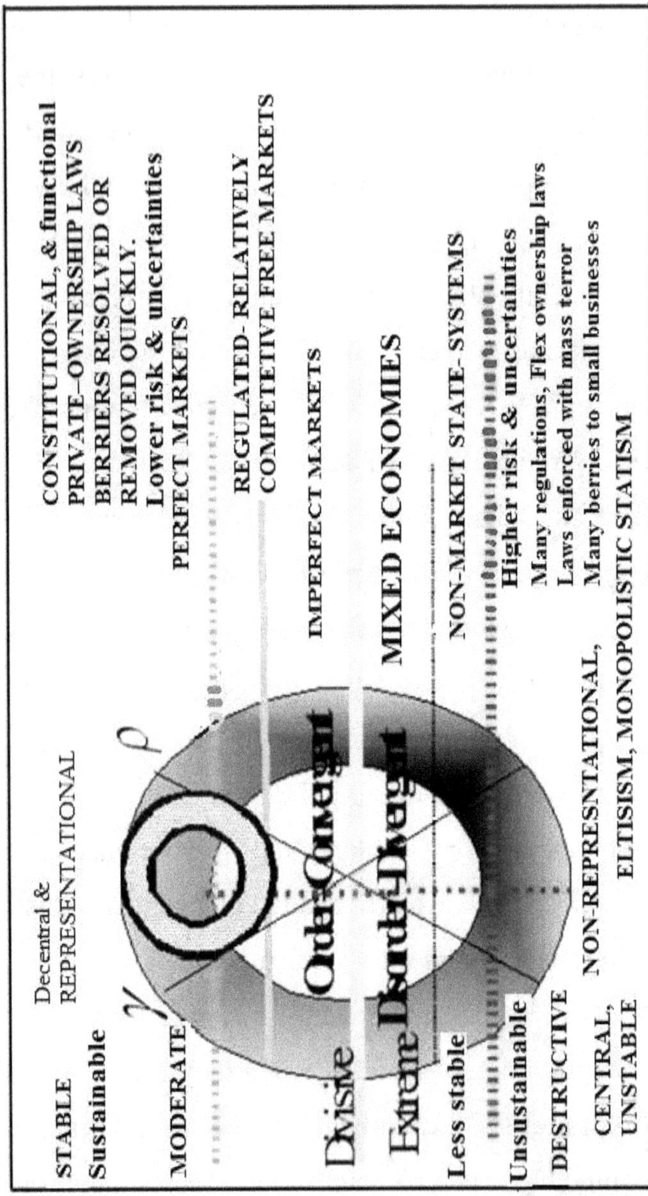

Figure 48. Dr. B.Fakhraie's Political-Teconmics system analysis for innovation.

It is an over view of some infrastructure links. The

impact of regulatory risk to free capital flow, or human capital alone can influence most if not all international investors.

In one hand, with the aid of old-fusions political centralism, in another hand, by inducement and encouragements of financial capitalism in cooperate centralism and distributive misallocations of both political power and funds, they have tested other dark dead ends of political monopoly economic miss-models.

That is not the reputation of evermore-ubiquitous mixed economies, taxes, and fees on one side, jobs, and reasonable higher real wages (especially reasonable lower executive pay packages) on the other. Governments will still misapply "laissez fair" again, even with global consent, which will result in equally sad consequences. Only enhanced by technology of "mass and immediate" communications will expound the potency of the past failures. Therefore, "buyers be aware" gets a global refurbishing in political economics, macro-economic and international economic, in finance and trade, again! All academics can do is to forewarn the alerted, well read, and educated proactive constituencies.

Argentina, South East Asia, Mexico 1990-2002 ought to be yet other alerts to "Laissez fair" Monetarism from guarded scholarly branches of Monetarism, which are alluded to later.

Governments globally spend political and financial capital on inappropriate technological transfers. Which have no infrastructural-foundations in their political system or regulatory systems? Some of the most recent examples are reflected in the totality of what is explained as Arab spring.[1] The 2008-2010 Islamic countries closely allied with the West and United States, initiated a series of political economic alterations, which will reverberated globally, as much as the 1980s Russian system alteration had affected the global realignments. A small individual business owners' reaction to extreme diversions from economic equilibrium at his expense reverberates in Tunisia set off a chain reaction of predated events that had implication for governments of Tunisia, Egypt, Libya, and Yemen, and all other states, which are in transitions or will follow.[2]

They readily adopt regulation neutralizing what they spend inordinate amount of national capital to obtain and operate, in a rigid political system, which will expunge itself of newness of others, thoughts, technological knowhow, and commercial actions. Moreover, most tragically, are the political leaderships, whom will loud innovations total metamorphism readily, and wage war on its elemental parts' adoptions mercilessly. One-step forward for profit maximization, and two steps back for optimization and sustainability. Figure 48 non-market state-systems are illuminated by thee examples from Tunisia, Egypt, Libya, and Yemenis, and others to come.

The longevity and sustainability of the governmental leadership is not a matter of historicism, the propagandists' militarism, or media-led triumphalism, they will remain a matter of importance for future academic research. The special contribution of technological progress will play a prominent factor in these futuristic advancements phenomena. Practically, no style of governments will be free from these meddlesome aspects of technological injections, and its intrusive consequences. The best results will be possible if stratagems for adoptions of new technologies are studied, then adopted to harvest social and private benefits of these technologies. Then, it will be easier to counter balance the negative externalities of these technological injections.

FREE MARKET IMPERFECTIONS

Imperfections in market competition are endogenous to self-inducements of the markets. The imperfections of perfect competitive assumptions will influence final costs, price, wage, rent, and interest depending on the market organizations of the modular production, and the organization of the buyer groups. These are classified under three general cases. That is, imperfections of competitive assumptions, oligopoly, duopoly, and monopoly versus monopsony. The effects on the markets are as follows.

Qc < Qd,o < Qm

Pm > Pd,o > Pc

The presence of any barriers to modular production process, like new technology or skill, or barrier to entry to the market place, or litigious blockages to production or entry initiates upward price alterations, and reduction in quantity presented to the markets. The clear implications at the value theory microeconomic levels are that quantities supplied reduce, and price of differentiated or rare items increase.

One the most modern example of technological duopoly is MS-PC with MS operating system, and Apple-PC, which have had parallel development for differentiated products, but there are older technologies and mature products. They influenced higher than normal prices of PCs until recently, when prices went below $400 ranges.

They have reduced number of workers in each operational facility comparative to manufacturing facilities, and they have formulated policies. In some cases, they have kept their taxes lower for entrepreneurial purgative and enfant industry portion far too long. There are newer technological clusters that have challenged the uniqueness nature of computer industry duopoly.

The digitalization, mobile-technologies, and wireless internet connectivity, and larger number of modular producers in the newer nanotechnologies, therefore the technological industries have pushed quantity of products higher, and their prices of product-packages below $200. This trend will continue for sometimes.

The manufactured the financial market disasters of this millennium at one hand, and the garnished political forces behind the taxpayers bail out at the other hand, inquire what kind of governance allowed them to flourish unattended, and then mushroom globally. All events require honest holistic teconomic analysis.

PLUTOCRACY, TECHNOCRACY

The organizational drifts from the pull of competitive incentives to imperfect competitions enticements of wealth concentration of oligopoly and plutocracy, and further to monopolistic market forces and oligarchies have dominated the last few decades.

The Substantial social and private costs leveled at free enterprise economic systems taxpayers. Financial market crash, institutional bankruptcy, and governmental interventionism with jobless-recovery seem to be fading memories in wait for the reappearing of undiscovered-unrepentant sinners.

Yet, there are no limits to their greed agenda, and their attempts to victimize the unemployed, structurally unemployed graduates, the middle class, and working poor. Do you remember, when they said cooperation limitless money in election is free speech and it will not affect your financial conditions, or your economy? All the while, their GOP representatives, Democratic Party helpers, media enablers have arranged the tax codes differently.

They arranged the social costs to come out of diminishing lower tax brackets and income of individual-taxpayers, not cooperation minimum taxes. These individuals have had flat or declining real incomes due to the nature of economic down turn.

Figure 49 shows millennial nominal private fixed investments in major economic sectors.[3] The digital and software enfant industries show more sustained private fixed investment than the residential sector of the economy.

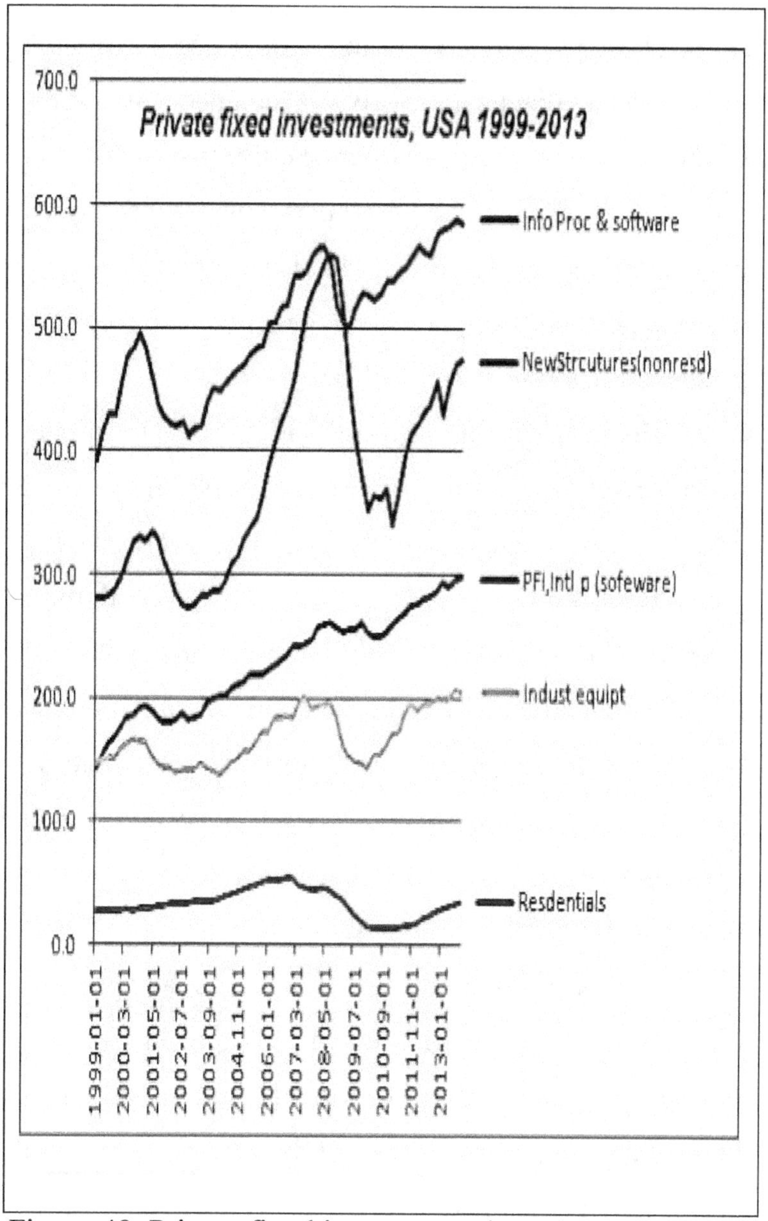

Figure 49, Private fixed investments in major sectors.

MINIMUM COOPERATE TAXATION

Those purchased laws and class warfare on majority of American citizens internally, by the uneducated ultra-wealthy, and their mega cooperate citizens have affected government revenue and your taxes, your benefits, and still have not made enough jobs. That is their plutocracy and technocracies, and oligarchies have failed, and these next three provisos prove their failures.

The trends for nominal private investments in all major sectors are positive after main recession cycles. The one exception in the graph is the residential structures, which has been flat. There are three provisos with these otherwise bright and supposedly illuminating pictures. One is residential structures, flat or declining nominal private investment in that sector is bad for overall jobs indices. Two is the nominal numbers increases have to be verified or falsified by the real increases in the indices for a scientific affirmation or hypothesis-rejection.

The third provisory condition has already proven difficult, too. That is the balancing comprehensive immigration fixes. After breaking the system, it will cost them even more. Even if they pulled a fast one to make taxpayers pay the megabank miss-investments. It is getting harder to fool all of the people, even in the off year's elections.

Nevertheless, a scientific presentation can simplify the conundrums. Indeed, if real private investment have declined, despite the nominal increase, and real disposable income per population have declined, the cooperate tax revenues have dropped, the national economy will suffer. Because aggregate demand will dissipate, and logarithmic real growth rate of GDP will decline. Moreover, all cooperate manipulation will not remedy the events, expo facto. Hence, their plutocratic economic models have failed.

Their answer will be to cut the social security, and social safety nets, Medicare, legacy private contracts, increase full time hours, and cut government jobs and all. That will compound the problem form cyclical recessions into major economic down turn, jobless recoveries, and into 1933 type of a depression. Given, we are in none-functionality phase of our political cycles, the probabilities of the worst event occurrences due to fiscal policies none-functionality increases, regardless of monetary policies.

NOTE

[1] Bob Simon, *How a slap sparked Tunisia's revolution*, CBS News, February 20, 2011 7:58 PM, http://www.cbsnews.com/2102-18560_162-20033404.html, "Bob Simon reports from Tunisia, where protests against the repressive government not only toppled its autocratic ruler, but sparked the uprising in Egypt that forced President Hosni Mubarak to resign."

[2] Yasmine Ryan, *Tunisian revolution yet to solve inequality*, Al Jazeera, April 11 2011, http://www.aljazeera.com/indepth/features/2011/03/2011331172249350413.html, "Hassine Dimassi, an economics professor, wants fairer distribution of wealth in new Tunisia."

[3]

FRED Graph Observations
Federal Reserve Economic Data
Link: http://research.stlouisfed.org/fred2
Help: http://research.stlouisfed.org/fred2/help-faq
Economic Research Division
Federal Reserve Bank of St. Louis

CHAPTER 23

MARKETS AND POLITICAL SYSTEMS

Market organizations and political systems have long interdependent coexistence that at times may go out of balance, if unchecked. These producers and CEOs, in technological oligopoly fields, and mega investment banks, and mega-internationals have garnished wealth concentration. The organizational development has advanced around self-serving pay structures, the unethical version of X-managements techniques, and wealth concentrations. Thus, an atmospheric change in governance, which have benefited from technological and governmental regulations forms of oligopoly and monopoly organizational controls and blocks have been garnished toward those tasks.

Therefore, they have utilized both market and political organizational-technologies to monetize their strategies around the X-managerial and operational systems. In the past when we studied mathematical multivariable optimization, Sheppard Lemma, the assumptions were that market forces acted alone, however, in Dr. Bahman Fakhraie's Sustainability Lemma new dimensions are studied that influence, complement or extend duration of market forces. The extensive utilization of political organization influences, and market influences have monetized and extended the duration of market activities. They have influenced wages, prices, and shareholders pay at (value theory for the firms' operational level).

The removal of Glass Steagle act, modifications of cooperate tax rate, nullifications, burden-transference, transparency controls, and manipulations of tax rates of the upper tax brackets will constitute the vigorous existences of these adjunct-organizational powers. These economic organizations are targeting economic policies, instead of traditional, complementary, managerial efficiencies and functional fiscal policies. They are acting collectively in a harmful manner. They have been successful enough to induce funding. It will not be difficult to assume they will mushroom in form of political organizations to influence elections, votes, voting regulations, and policies in other directions than free democratic public votes, or free flow of public opinions. They will ultimately introduce malleability to democratic principles toward wealth concentration mechanism, than wealth creation sustainability of free market systems.

That will make them (plutocracy or oligarchy) extremisms in some cases. Therefore, they act counterproductive to the competitive free market economics principles. They have affected workers and national income at the aggregate data level, too. Hence, they have reduced employment nationally by increasing unemployment rates and in reducing re-employment rates structurally.

The harming of domestic housing industry had a great impact on domestic economic growth, income inequalities, and jobs creations, in the millennium down turn. They did this at the supply side, by harming domestic mortgage industries, and at the demand side, by inflicting real disposable income depression, and promotion of jobless recoveries.

The computerization, digitization, and smart robotics have introduced structural adjustment in re-employment rates, in most cases with substantial tax-breaks and subsidies, which do not go to benefit the structurally unemployed, but they are offered to the new factories, or industrial arrangements with more knowledge-capital intensive-technologies at state and federal levels.

Therefore, economic recovery will require specific monetary and fiscal remedies tailored for the events that are an essential aspect of economic recovery, which will encourage job creationism, temporarily.

The cultural adjustments can replace the obsolete an outdated X-Techniques with a managerial Y-Matrix strategy, which will remain accommodative and foundational to modern technological paradigm. Thus, the core values of tasks are accomplished with self-fulfillments, and satisfaction of invisible hands. Moreover, the matrix allows for multiple disciplinary participations, for more complex collective tasks, which will include profits, and optimizations. Therefore, the strategies for organizational development will accommodate planned changes flexible to internal and external factors.

The organizations will need to comply, and be accommodative to the recovery. Especial taxes on such organizational activities may be required to educate public of their rules and policy intends, and to comply with the transparency of democracy. The least active fiscal policy side, will need to raise taxes of the cooperate entities at the top one percent highest brackets from 10 percent or lower (zero, or negative rates) to 30 percent minimum cooperate tax rate (MCTR).

A portion of that government revenue will have to go to retaining and job-creation, if we adopt the Y-Matrix managerial teconomic strategies advanced here. The job-creation involves state and federal infrastructural replacement projects, with retraining for secondary positions, placements, or vertical job placements. The cooperation and free enterprise employment with living wages will increase in such recoveries as they arrive cyclically.

A good portion of that government-revenue have to be transferred to an standalone earned income tax credit (EITC) for middle class and lower income earners, especially in jobless recovery counter cycle epochs. Even, if we still insist to follow the supply sides' obsolete model of X-managerial (CEOs-self-promotion) arrangements.

MULTICULTURALISM AND LEGAL IMMIGRANTS

Political discrimination, anti-multiculturalism, and anti-legal immigrants' laws are visceral emotionalism ascribed, thus they are not helpful to the progress of an economic recovery, and the longevity of this constitutional experiment in democratic republic.[1] They have garnished organizational supports from neo-Nazis, skinheads, Southern Strategist, xenophobes, and anti-multicultural international terrorist gangs. Those negative political organizations have influenced harmful laws to American economic, and they are influencing lawmakers to detriment of better economic optimality conditions and economic jobless recoveries.

The implications of these two major impacts of organizational forces on economic optimizations and recovery efforts are their negative counter cyclical natures. That will make them important to economic policy and national economic wellbeing in a difficult economic time.

One can opine constitutionally that the reason ultra-wealthy Americans are concerned about policy so much, it is because they paid for so much of it to be ignored. Perhaps, they do not want to be treated, as the immigrants and legal immigrant-Americans, by the hate-agenda they (some of them) have financed so much. For one, I do not blame or dismiss their concerns; however, they paid and are paying for these anti-immigrants' monstrosity laws among other bad laws. Why would terrorizing 14th amendment American children and youth get a pass from xenophobes and new laws? Americans have to check these negative organizational tendencies for their own economic self-interests, beside the constructive positive ethics, or the ignored morality sakes.

Laws to monetize or criminalize immigrants' productivities, and legal immigrants daily lives are pushed in many states and DC. Laws that tear up families, and familial links and financial lives, are not unlike the Federal Reserve policies that extended duration of the 1930 depression. They have to be filtered and checked regularly.

The millennial cyclical economic activities have had down turns in the employment numbers, too. Nevertheless, the upturns have not had increase in the employment typical of their history.

In the book (Teconomics*), the complex population-age components were discussed more substantially. The complexity and components of millennial private investments have also been detailed. Therefore, it is more alarming that updating our fiscal policy formulations devolved into ideological mud fields, into dangerous extremes and none-functionality.

Indeed, did external-terrorism inflict so much harm, to derail the national economic resolve to advance welfare and income of all workers and citizens? Did someone there spend our national accumulated wealth, deteriorating our advanced educated systems, and stopping fiscal policy responses exogenously? Taxpayers spent 17 trillion dollars over a decade. That is divide among the 7 billion estimate of global population is $2,428 per soul globally. Still, it takes a few pennies a day to feed most hungry masses. Alas, we have hungry population globally. Are we spending our resources wisely?

Internally, a system reboot will require readjustments of some ethical mishandlings, in politics, business, finance, mega-wealthy lobbyism, their cash in politics, and economics organizations.

Figure 11 does not show a validation of the hypothesis that unemployment rate fluctuations and cyclical upturns are substantial and normal. Therefore, the hypothesis is rejected.

The Popperian falsification of the same hypothesis is shown in the civilian labor-force-participation rate. It has been declining since 1999. The rejection of hypothesis is reconfirmed in the decrease in the employments per population rate, which has paralleled the decline in the unemployment rates in the same graph.

The proposition was presented that structural unemployment has been confirmed among the working population 25 year and older. That will require intervention by public initially, but by both public and private organizational market forces.

The explanation for the multiple confirmation of structural unemployment are three folds, one is the retirement of baby boomers. Two is the implosions of legal immigration regulations since 1996 act, and organization obsceneness to reparatory fixes. Three, is the decline of real minimum wage, and its substantial diversion from the living wage.

Figure 50 shows labor participation and unemployment per capita rates, of college graduate over age 25, employment per population, and civilian unemployment rate.

Laws tax immigrant families of their pennies and dims, while their children, American children are in stress of law violations in going to colleges, and face the student loan heavy burdens, and graduate joblessness and inadequate wages. Laws that violate the 1st, 4th, 14th amendments of the United State constitution regularly, and other amendments frequently, laws that separate families forcibly, laws to e-verify and segregate, and miss treat large segment of the society anti-constitutionally, without probable cause, or legal foundations. The "Nazis-Kristallnacht" ultra-wealthy people know best, they can become these laws, or these organizations and vicious political parties' new victims. They will be called names, like ultra-wealthy RINOs on new petitions, too. Their wealth can be targeted readily. Government can countermand their private-contracts.

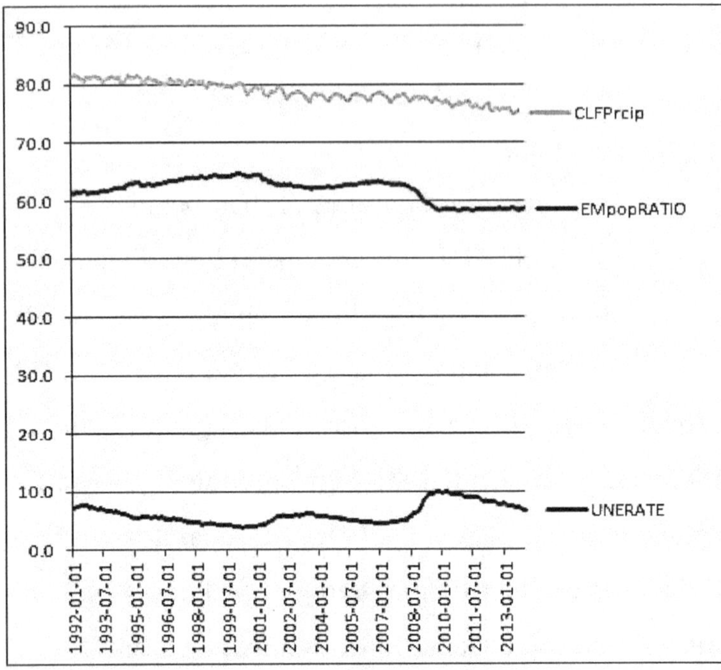

Civilian Labor Force Participation Rate - Bachelor's Degree and Higher, 25 years and over, (LNU01327662), Percent, Monthly, Not Seasonally Adjusted
Civilian Employment-Population Ratio (EMRATIO), Percent, Monthly, Seasonally Adjusted
Civilian Unemployment Rate (UNRATE), Percent, Monthly, Seasonally Adjusted
FRED Graph Observations
Federal Reserve Economic Data
Link: http://research.stlouisfed.org/fred2
Help: http://research.stlouisfed.org/fred2/help-faq
Economic Research Division
Federal Reserve Bank of St. Louis
Analysis and graph of data by Dr Bahman Fakhraie

Figure 50, Civilian labor-force participation-rates.

Quick laws can resent their social contracts with America, too. While constructional economic mobility could have remedied most of the class warfare divisive post-recession ailments. The fixed immigration laws could have increased government revenues, jobs, economic conditions, and velocity of money in increased circulation, and aggregate-demand, nationally and internationally, too.

POLITE, FUNCTIONAL, AND HUMANE POLITICS

There are no close comparative equivalences. The certain political party machinery turned hate on immigrants, women, minority, elderly middle class, young students, and poor Americans, for their 2014 campaign-agendas, they betrayed their own political principles. Abraham Lincoln was the 16th president of the United States, serving from March 1861 until his assassination in April 1865.[2] He found the intellectual root and the immigration links to Decoration of Independence. John F. Kenney another great president of the other political party before President Obama thought the subject of such importance that he wrote a book on immigration.[3] Deconstructions make apolitical party self-destructively negative and not futuristically sound.

They have utilized the newness of citizens-united-cooperation laws into new negative political organizations, knowing the legal diversions of free speech and hate speech. They are doing it knowing the bad results, which are turning the 80 to 90 percent of all groups against them.

Americans do not vote for hate group into office, they vote to get them out of their political offices.

Turning anti-science has consequences. Ask the politicians in those states that were not proactive to winter snow, before and after the last perfectly unhappy January 2014 snow and ice storm, and the last few tsunamis. Did their spin save them? The weather-persons-scientific defense will hurt their politics even more, in places they have not yet conjured.

Therefore, voters please tell them again to stay human, real, and functional Americans (as much as possible) on all issues and immigration-issues, because 2014 and 2016 are here and now.

Moreover, Americans usually do not vote for hate groups, or their chicken hawks into office. Just do not let them slow your logic down, by blocking your voting, they will charge you more for a voter-ID, you will use for few votes rarely. You stay in voting-queues more than others in their voting-districts do. Hoping you will go home. Vote your votes anyway. Make a special day to vote, and vote them out of office, if they are betraying the constitutional laws, find others who follow the constitution.

FOREIGN POLICY, SUPERIORITY PSYCHOSIS

The gestalt of our foreign policy toward Islamic nations, in Asia and Africa cannot be a Hopson choice between psychosis and schadenfreude. It has to be based on foundational of diplomacy and truth telling, potentially contradictory matters.

Otherwise, extremists, abstractionists, war profiteers, destructionists, international monopolists will drive our policy off and away from the progressive roads that help sustain our economy most.

The people of these nations like our middle classes have to see a positive drive and an agenda of peace and prosperity, a constructionists' plan ahead for themselves and their children.

American voters cannot be mollified for long, by xenophobic, racists, sexist, and hate-speech derangements syndromes (HDS, and other psychosis ailments), which have afflicted the right wing-nuts, and the hate radio and multimedia dim-lights. The voters do not vote hate.

It is all too much, too much to ask a broken political party not to morph into another hate-group, while it is fading away from polite politics, and joining the free market purchased monetization of politics, and lobbyists industrial complexes, and negative organizations. The anti-immigrant degeneration of modern politics, the anti-science fervor, these are all accumulative and destructive negative economic externalities.

The technological enhancements of such skill sets have hastened devolutionary forces, which will leave an indelible mark on exceptionalness of any philosophically advanced and thinking culture. It has ended many powerful hate groups of history. At 100 to 400 million-dollar tickets, purchased democracies, politicians, and laws are no longer representative democratic republics, but agenda organizations, and some hate and negative-agenda organizations. Unless there are traces of truthful dictum (of the people, by the people, and for the people) in the vestige-nature of such organization, it will be hard to see them as patriotic tools.

American people like people around the globe, they do not give up on themselves, when they discover the differences between the hidden fingers, instead of the invisible relative free market hands, the costs are too dear to us all and to the democratic republics.

Otherwise, how will a society countermand the impacts of accumulative inequalities and powerful destabilizing forces unlocked by profiteering of imperfect-competition economics, and political monopolistic capitalism accumulatively? The logic is not there.

The Nazis (no disrespect intended to great and kind German people) among others were never convinced, of the imperfections of their implosive economic philosophy or the inevitabilities of global complications after their savage colonial dirt-wars. Yet, like other cultures north and south, east and west, the scholar did learn fanatical delusions make harmful companions for time travelers of history.

Some assumed mistakenly, that technologies would compensate for foundational terminal logics, fiscal policy nonexistence, deliberate financial crimes, organizational mischief-makers, and governmental nihilistic paralysis. It has been a mistake, to ignore corrective constructional relatively-perfectly competitive-free-market signals, which do fall short ominously faster outside democratic functionalities.

Therefore, polite, functional, constructional, bipartisan, diplomatic, domestically intensive economic policies and humane politics are good models that pay positive dividends for the holistic teconomics models of the future, in time.

American people and democratic nations generally have corrective instincts, which are capable of correcting mistaken side trips, for shared economic growth and developmental steps. Therefore, in the light of better paradigms, the future looks optimistically bright, considering all other alternatives.

NOTE

[1] The Nihilistic Self- flagellations, Political Tango of the Unwise: Recent restudy of immigration contributions redefines their contributions, as net benefit; tax revenue minus benefits from migrants is estimated at 25 billion pounds 2001-2011, versus negative 600 billion pounds for native net benefits over the same time. The same study and results were presented and hold true for USA economy. As it was suspected, this will make no deference to neo Nazi, skinheads, Neocons, xenophobes, bigots, GOP extremists, week and scared liberals, and wobbly democrats and EU riffraff fearing competition and workers supplying their diminishing funds, supplies, and retirements of aging populations, and declining real disposable income over time.
New EU migrants add £5bn to UK, report says, November 2014 Last updated at 10:11 ET, http://www.bbc.com/news/business-29910497,

[2] Patrick Young, Esq., Lincoln, the Know Nothings, and Immigrant America, http://www.longislandwins.com/news/detail/lincoln_the_know_nothings_and_immigrant_america

[3] John F. Kennedy, A Nation of Immigrants, p. 26-27 Jan 8, 1963, http://www.ontheissues.org/Archive/Nation_of_Immigrants_Immigration.htm

CHAPTER 24

POLITICAL INFRSTRCUTRES

Constructive political infrastructures are and additional remainder that free market economies are not for free, there are costs to proper market structures, for coming and going to the market places, and maintenances of the markets, and dynamic continuation of the markets. That also includes adequate and balanced but not over bearing governments that assure legal and proper functionality of the market places.

Extremism Dangers

The signs of extremism dangers have become glairing. Especially where the voids of constructive political infrastructures are prominently demonstrated. It is getting harder to swallow that the White Trash Television, KKK-cable cabal takeovers of the visual universe, and the diminished intellectual content of our daily habitual media are the phantoms of the viewers' creations, or the byproducts of fertile minds of social media and the unemployed-clickers in their under garments. Yet, the shared-economic and sociopolitical externality-costs will be real, if not exponentially expanding. It is difficult to fathom ways that they will not harm that political party, or the two party political systems. Therefore, they will harm the infrastructures of the democratic systems.

USA-Great-ism may be a new screen, and the global extremism may be the new screams, but Racism, Islamophobia, Xenophobia, anti-education, anti-academia, Ageism, and Sexism among other sociopolitical and economic ills may have found their home and their welcome openings on certain southern strategists' morning shows and in certain cable cabals, and more amply among the hate radio hosts. Moreover, they have found an all media push to dominate the election coverage<s> for a certain political party.

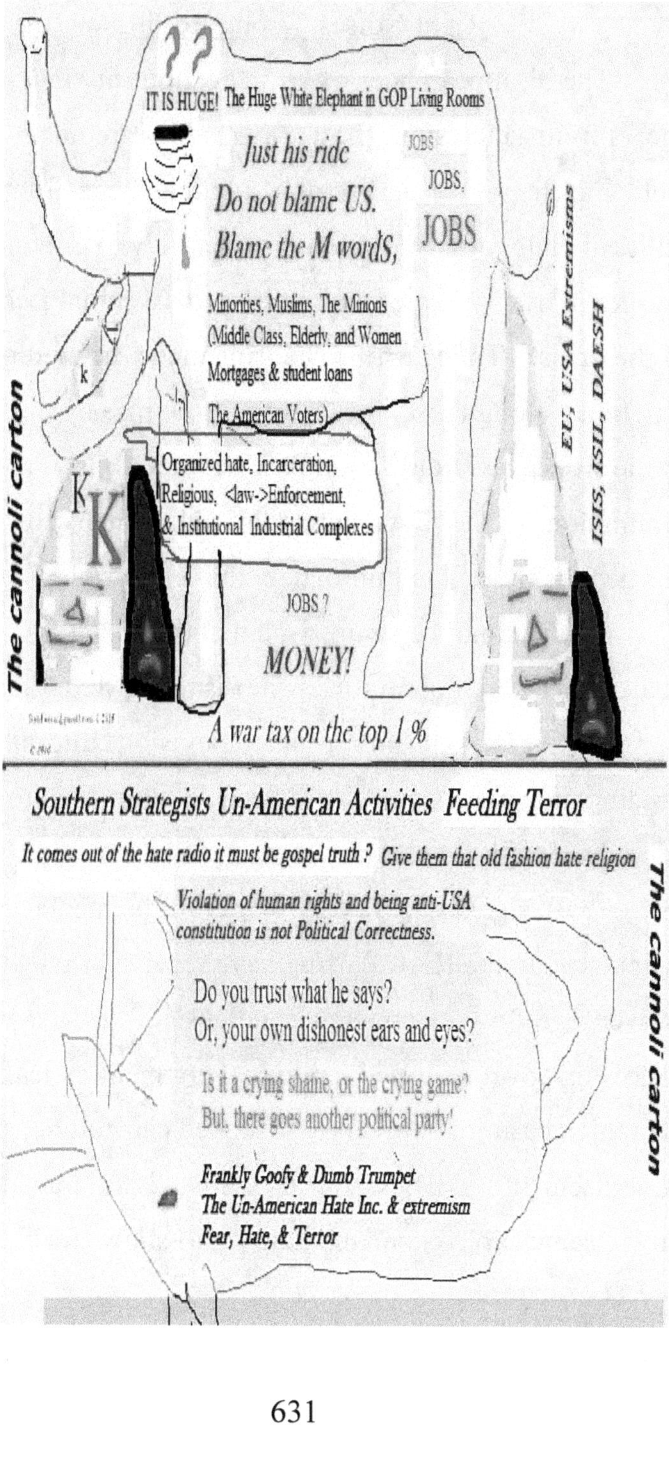
IT IS HUGE! The Huge White Elephant in GOP Living Rooms
Just his ride
Do not blame US.
Blame the M wordS,
JOBS
JOBS,
JOBS
Minorities, Muslims, The Minions
(Middle Class, Elderly, and Women
Mortgages & student loans
The American Voters)
Organized hate, Incarceration,
Religious, <law->Enforcement,
& Institutional Industrial Complexes
JOBS ?
MONEY!
A war tax on the top 1 %
The cannoli carton
EU, USA Extremisms
ISIS, ISIL, DAESH
Southern Strategists Un-American Activities Feeding Terror
It comes out of the hate radio it must be gospel truth ? Give them that old fashion hate religion
Violation of human rights and being anti-USA
constitution is not Political Correctness.
Do you trust what he says?
Or, your own dishonest ears and eyes?
Is it a crying shame, or the crying game?
But, there goes another political party!
Frankly Goofy & Dumb Trumpet
The Un-American Hate Inc. & extremism
Fear, Hate, & Terror
The cannoli carton

Bahman Fakhraie, PhD. © 2015

Right Noises Wrong Results

The disappearances of very few minority faces, and shows from Television, shows, and cables are not a welcome change for democratic, adult, and constructive political dialogues, free discussions, or advancement of political parties' greater real politics, or eventual freedom of the press.[1] The Fairness Doctrine made the media functional along those lines before its demise by the hand of the worst intentions among us; with its vanishing, are diminutions of the first amendment rights, inclusive political intellects, and ultimately the bill of rights.

It should not be a surprised that the southern strategists are all hog in for Trump-ism, or white-only shows, but it is astonishing, cable television editorials and funding money machines have been so brain dead to it, if it is not by design for one last hora.

By-design means, every twitter of the media-Frankenstein, the KKK darling have received first converge, follow-up coverages, defense of the first and follow up coverages, while political competitors leaked campaign cash for "we do exist funded campaign advertisement". They were ridiculed and disparaged 24/7, on the same cable-cabal and hate-radio-shows for free.

NEHELESITIC HATE-PROVOVTEURS INTERNATIONAL

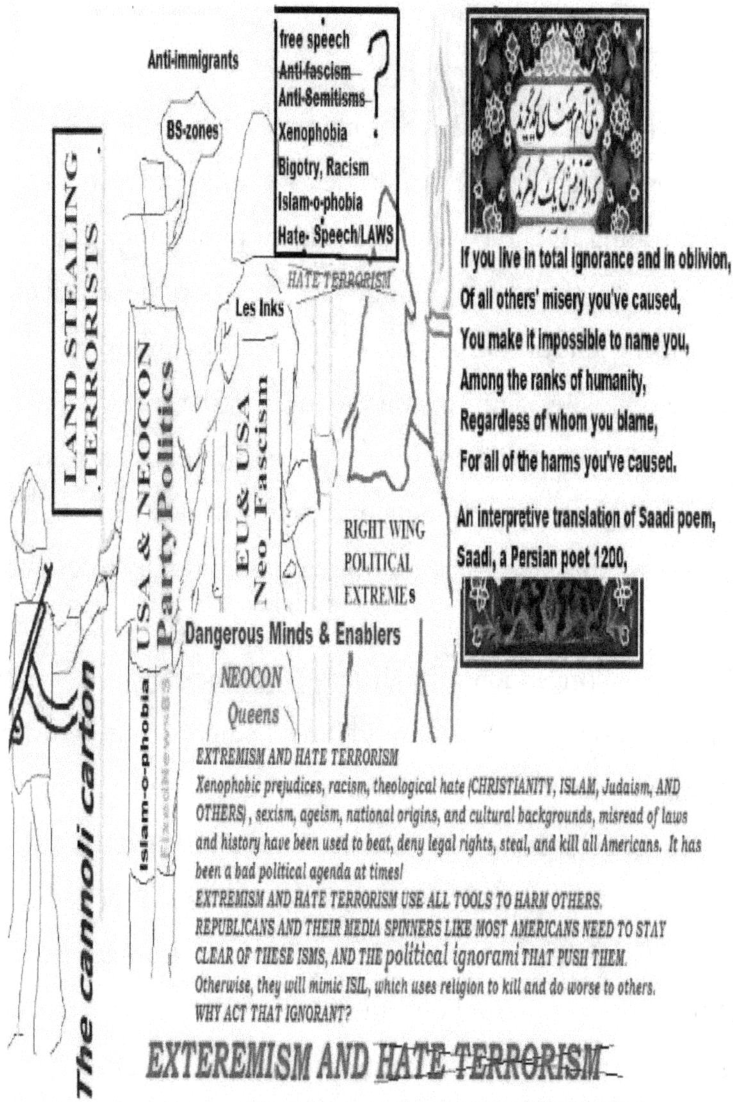

EXTEREMISM AND ~~HATE TERRORISM~~

BUT VIVA LA FREEDOM FOR A DAY ANYWAY.

The force of establishment republican party and the usual barking dogs eating under their food tables abolished the fairness doctrine. It "required that TV and radio stations (especially the hate propagators) holding FCC-issued broadcast licenses to (a) devote some of their programming to controversial issues of public importance and (b) allow the airing of opposing views on those issues. This meant that programs on politics were required to include opposing opinions on the topic under discussion." This was a minimalist competitive condition imposed, on lawless and hate speech, hate and political monopolists of the opinion markets. The fact that it could not be tolerated should have been telling in abundance of logic.

Consequential Fairness Doctrine Law

The consequences should have been obvious, as soon as, (the fairness doctrine) the balance- coverage-Act for political speech-laws were targeted and abolished a few years ago.[2] The rightists targeted and abolished those laws like the Glass Steagall law. Thus, Glass Steagall act was not the only push with consequential results. There was a design behind their madness, and we see the resulting madness and hate speech of their design on our democracy. I wrote about the implosive result of the Glass-Steagall act in the capitalist markets; where wealth concentration and billionaires broke the competitive markets system and the infrastructures by under investments, when they were given a free hand. Now we see where the billionaires can break the political system as easily by a push for triumph of wealth concentration over wealth creation strategies, the traditional education, jobs, and wages/income routs.

The crowd behind those movements have been well compensated and monetarily rewarded; in order, to break up the traditional wealth creation rout, functional educational systems, and the competitive democratic politics.

They will fight for their money now, thus they will fight rather than relinquish our democracy to voters. For the same reasons the cooperate-monopolists (regional and digital) will not submit to lower competitive market prices/profits for the longer and sustainable benefit of all, without the full force of the law.

Bahman Fakhraie, PhD. © 2015

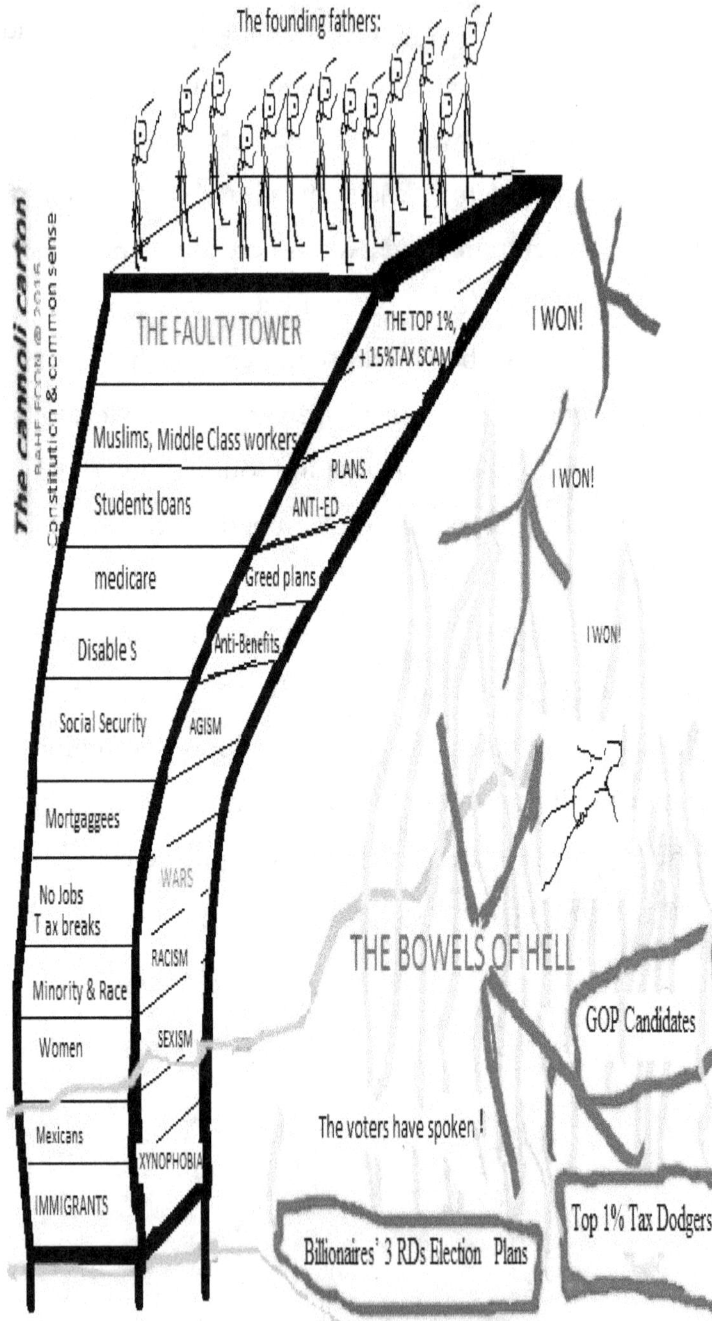

Metastasizing Malignant Extremists Ideology

Therefore, the usual suspect, the one, the most extremes, the outrageous carnival acts have received the most coverage. These were based on the vacuous assumptions that there will be no economic or sociopolitical backlashes to the overt current media Trumpism, vacuous bombastic bloviating Fake-Great-ism, political cabals, and the white-only extremism.[3] American political, economics, and democratic institutions have paid with blood and treasures for their retro- subrogation of Abraham Lincoln republicanism. Those pushing the essentials of the anti-civil -war ugly arguments anew are in violation of the constitution, and the laws. They do mean to harm the American society for greed and averse, they have chosen to wage political war on theological freedoms, and all notion of liberty and freedom, the theological prefix they use hardly shall cover their ugly and demented intentions and deeds.

Those bridges for free press profiteering and defense of democratic principles are burning faster than multimedia can equivocate among the white-trash cable politics, white only retrogrades, neo-fascism, EU-neo-Nazis regenerations, xenophobia, Islamophobia, Southern Strategists, the KKK and Trumpism. Make America great again and make white-America-only great again are not the same propositions, and one of them has already failed miserably and repeatedly, It has left the fields of Virginia to southern lands of Georgia, and most southern states washed in blood of Americans gray and blue. It is in fact in violations of the written and voiced state and federal and international laws. So excuse us if we do not fallow the new political mules over the edge again. Greater lawmakers, global Scholars, and American and international intellectuals, and the constitution of United States have not been reticent on the subject, even when ignored.[4] Those that are putting the country in the deadly roads to those failed Valhalla are worse than the outside Terrorists are to law and order, and democratic principles. They are the inside dangerous but modern Benedict Arnold<s> to the modern functioning democracies. Caveat Emptor before you vote is much less costly than the shared costly day after implosive failures.

The Utah academic premier knowledge center and Governor Mitt Romney ought to be congratulated for their valiant attempt to reintroduce dignity and decorum back to the selection of the presidency, among a long and growing list of national and international leaders and scholars that have finally faced the conclusion. That a political party drifts short of intellectual skeletal infrastructures is often moribund for disaster and subject to extremism takeovers, before the voters have chance to even vote their primary votes. Since, that democratic process had been left unattended and has since been abundant to the least of intellects among us, which will lead to unfavorable results with enhanced certainty.

It did not take long for the hate groups, and the <Vulgarizer-Maximus> to establish their links and support for the presidency of the least qualified incompetent, most bigoted, and the xenophobic ignominious marketers to go to kkk-robots-calls in Utah and some other states to attack anti-TRUMP disclosures and truth telling.[5] The lingering reticence led to assumption of acceptance, while this last Thursday night (before the super Tuesday-vote) GOP-debate-melee established all of the anti-law, and anti-norm, anti-military and the constitutional degeneracy, and affront to good sense that one could stand. The media flies that gather on this mess do not have the intellect to make distinction between honey and turd, let alone defend the first amendment or the constitution. They ought to know joining the fixed news implants in annunciating him El-President, the monarch, or king will not make him so, or make them journalists.

Deconstructive Strategies

There are no constructions in these deconstruction-strategies. Insults, fistfights, the xenophobic and religious hate, and all of the vulgarisms are smoke screens and hiding places from the hard questions, when they do not have any viable plans. What are you going to do better and different from all these past mistakes? Why would doing the same mistakes over again get us to a better economic place, or a better sociopolitical place? Minorities, Muslims, the Minions (Middle Class, Elderly, Educators, Students, and Women, (the American Voters), Vulgar-isms Maximum Billionaires are asking for your 2016 Election-Votes, they have another tax break/economic growth plan for USA economy. Should you abide them another tax break? Do you trust what they say? Do you trust your own dishonest ears and eyes? You should wonder, too.

Vulgarisms Maximum Billionaires have shifted the tax burdens to the Middle Class, working poor in low relative wages, students in high student loans without jobs, and elderly pensioners in reduced pensions, confused benefits, and diminishing healthcare fights. While they have amassed, tax breaks on their extreme high incomes, so much so that the CEOs joined them in carving special tax heaven and tax credit to shelter their hundred millions dollar salaries.[6] This election in 2016 is about reducing the American standard of living to protect the tax breaks and the benefits of the multi-billionaires.[7] Are you voting your own minds and your living conditions, or are you voting somebody else dictate, bells, and vessels? Freedom and democracy come with immense responsibly of thinking for your selves. Furthermore, it involves the hard job of truthfully educating your own state of mind. I know you can do it.

Organized hate, Incarceration, Religious, <law>Enforcement, & Institutional Industrial Complexes seem to fall short. Is it a crying shame, or the crying game? However, there goes another political party! We live in interesting times, in the Peter rabbit tune times! In case, you wake up in this dreamland, too far down in the dark rabbit-hole.[8] Europeans' headaches are also related, but they are victims of flex democracies and functional governance that became easy prey to hate groups' pull, but they have been slow upgrading to modern anti-terror and anti-crime fighting lessons. They were quick in use of war technologies to destroys homes, countries, and economies, but they have proven clueless, about the consequential what next. President Eisenhower followed the four years of war, with more than half of millennium of reconstructive economics, investments, and balanced trade. NATO may be inadequate as a cure all, because its task was military and defense-centric. Europeans' (EU) bigger problems are now sociopolitical, and require Federal-EU focus solutions that deal with bigger more costly socioeconomic dynamic problems, economic sustainability, and post-militaristic short-term solutions that unleash their current sustained plights.

Refugees have become the multiple victims of the terror groups, hate groups, and lethargically responsive states to techno-media monsters and anti-social extremists of these times. Nevertheless, the screams at emigrants, victimizing the refuges have been to hide the evil intend of these dark forces death trashing, hiding among and behind them, while criminal killing of the innocence among humanity is proposed to cure humanity, or kill us.[9] They are surprised when they are completely rejected on all intellectual sides, with the exception of self-eliminating followers, theological fanatical extremists, and the forced suicidal head zombies. What remain most disconcerting, is the plight of modern societies with the political idiotism that love to milk these bulls of hate for the essence of humanity, and the bull kicks back hard, and we are all surprised when they fail us.

Voters Infrastructures Matter

The voters must cast their own best-mind interpretations of these cabalism and coronation of least qualified moneyed interest to the highest democratic office in the land, since it shall be at their expenses.

Democracies have passed through dark nights of bigotry, xenophobia, greed, howling wolfs and barking dogs before. Decency, diplomacy, democracy, and people once aware of their own self-interests and their self-preservation, we shall prevail again. Our votes' infrastructures matter sometimes, because it sustains the republics at times.

Dr. Bahman Fakhraie, © 2016: Notes and Books to read,

*- http://www.amazon.com/Teconomics-Elections-Extremisms-Bahman-Fakhraie/dp/0996633499/ref=la_B00IKAR1CM_1_11?s=books&ie=UTF8&qid=1458577267&sr=1-11

*- http://www.amazon.com/Analytical-Remedies-Millennial-Cascading-Economic/dp/0985295864/ref=la_B00IKAR1CM_1_2?s=books&ie=UTF8&qid=1458577176&sr=1-2

*- http://www.amazon.com/Teconomic-Verbalism-Bahman-Fakhraie-PhD/dp/0985295848/ref=la_B00IKAR1CM_1_1?s=books&ie=UTF8&qid=1458577267&sr=1-1

*- http://www.amazon.com/Politeconomics-Teconomics-Dr-Bahman-Fakhraie/dp/0989453944/ref=la_B00IKAR1CM_1_4?s=books&ie=UTF8&qid=1458577267&sr=1-4

*- http://www.amazon.com/Political-Monopolistic-Capitalism-Wealth-Concentration/dp/0989453995/ref=la_B00IKAR1CM_1_5?s=books&ie=UTF8&qid=1458577267&sr=1-5

*- http://www.amazon.com/Dr.-Bahman-Fakhraie/e/B00IKAR1CM/ref=ntt_athr_dp_pel_1

NOTES

[1] http://www.nytimes.com/…/melissa-harris-perry-is-out-at-msn…

[2] A brief history fairness Doctrine:
http://content.time.com/time/nation/article/0,8599,1880786,00.html
Kathleen Ann Ruane, Legislative Attorney, Fairness Doctrine: History and Constitutional
Issues, July 13, 2011,
http://fas.org/sgp/crs/misc/R40009.pdf

[3] The country-list of EU white-right extremisms groups politically active and vocal at this time.
http://content.time.com/time/specials/packages/completelist/0,29569,2085728,00.html

[4] Nick Robins-Early
Associate World Editor, The Huffington Post, and BERGGRUEN Inst.,
A Field Guide To Europe's Radical Right Political Parties
02/12/2015 09:30 am ET | Updated Feb 12, 2015
http://www.huffingtonpost.com/2015/02/12/europe-far-right_n_6511022.html

[5] http://www.newyorker.com/…/donald-trump-and-the-ku-klux-kla…
*- http://www.sltrib.com/…/sit…/sltrib/pages/printfriendly.csp…

[6] Some alien-probing<s> are more massive and telling than others are to the real VICTIMS!
Lawyer At Center Of Panama Papers Data Leak Says Firm Suffered 'Limited Hack'
The head of Mossack Fonseca said his firm had fallen victim to "an international campaign against privacy.",

04/04/2016 06:10 am ET
http://www.huffingtonpost.com/entry/panama-papers-mossack-fonseca-hacked_us_57023b52e4b083f5c6080913?utm_hp_ref=world

[7] There are always more bad pickles in the pickle jars: What You Need To Know About The Panama Papers Leak
The documents have implicated several world leaders.
04/04/2016 03:58 pm ET | Updated 18 hours ago
*-http://www.huffingtonpost.com/entry/panama-papers-leak_us_57027188e4b0daf53af010d1?utm_hp_ref=world&utm_hp_ref=world
*Inside the Secretive World of Tax-Avoidance Experts
Sergey Nivens / Shutterstock / Fotolia / Paul Spella / The Atlantic
Brook Harrington, Oct 26, 2015,
http://www.theatlantic.com/business/archive/2015/10/elite-wealth-management/410842/

[8] A little reading list at following link for these expensive times:
http://www.amazon.com/Dr.-Bahman-Fa…/…/ref=ntt_athr_dp_pel_1

[9] http://www.spiegel.de/…/how-the-refugee-crisis-has-change-g

CHAPTER 25

INFRASTRUCTURES, SUMMERY AND CONCLUSIONS

Certain economic systems accommodate economic recoveries better than others do. The free enterprise capitalist economies in general are assumed more accommodative to this notion. However, in this book there are documented reasons, why these systems have not performed well in this last recovery cycle. The existences of expansive and growing interrelated infrastructures play important and connective mechanisms in the advanced economies that cannot be ignored.

SUMMERY AND POPERIAN TEST

In summary condition for test of the hypothesis about nominal and real investments, for verification and falsifications were enumerated. The result is double-checked by the natural logarithmic measurement of growth rate of certain indices. The nominal private investments in major industries were discussed previously. It was noted that nominal graphs were looking positive in number of areas. The industries showing promises were information-processing software, new nonresidential structures, industrial equipment all favored an upward trend line, all but housing industries (residential). That has declining trend line, and investment in mines that is flat or increased slightly. This graph is important in the Popperian test we established in this study.

The test of this hypothesis was to check the real privet investment for a more detailed trend line over time, which either confirmed and verified the positive trends, or falsified and reject the hypothesis, by negative trend line. The rejection of the hypothesis would require long-term trend-line of real private fixed investments to be negatively sloped. It will mean a decline in real investment overtime at aggregate economic level.

Figure 51 shows the real private fixed investment, USA 1999-2013.[1]

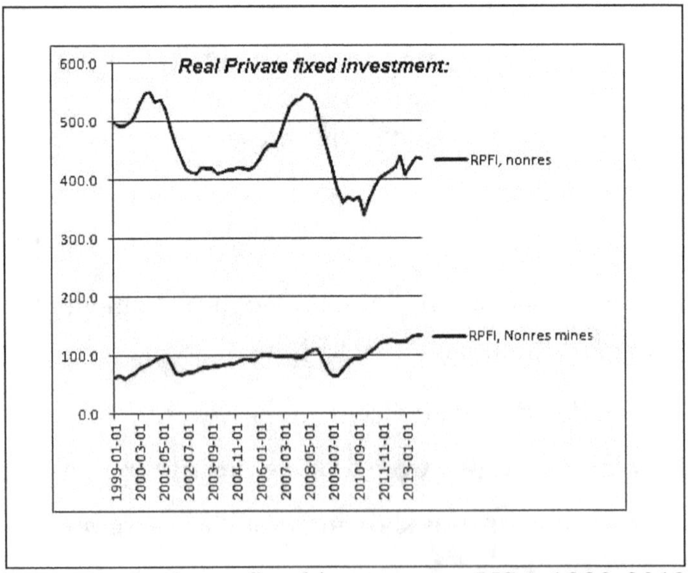

Figure 51, Real private fixed investment, USA 1999-2013.

Even if there are positive nominal investments in software, robotic modular manufacturing production processes, and digital sectors, the real fixed private investments are declining. That is, when and why aggregate governmental involvements in job-creation make the difference.

The constructive population age mix of workers and taxpayers have been harmed by bad anti-family and xenophobic immigration policies, too.

Unfortunately, even after reading the research, they are hoping some STEM-policy will pay off in 8-11 future years. Just how many more deep recessions they want the American economy to experience, knowing it will not affect their income brackets, or job status. How long, how many years is it rational for the structurally unemployed to pull themselves up by their own bootstraps?

Science tells us; hopefully, the opposition supply-siders are evolving too, whether they believe in it or not. Polite, Functional, and Humane Politics mean do not self-destruct your political party or national economic models for your private greed. Cultivations and rebuilding of infrastructures, physical, organizational, political, are facing dynamic entropy laws and they are constantly deteriorating over time. Therefore, in the face of entropy law, population increases, market advancements, and economic growth appropriate aggregate investments in the infrastructures cannot depend on the inflections of policy. Weather public or private investments are assigned the task, they have to be maintained at an appropriate rate sufficient for the rate of rebuild that matches or exceeds the current and future continual needs for infrastructures in the economies. Aggregate data trend-lines for rRDI (Growth Rate of Real Disposable Income), rRDIPC, (Real Disposable Income Per Capita) and population growth rates stay flat or decline.

Figure 52 shows growth rate for RDPI, RDPIPC, and population. While the wealth concentration of the top 1 percent or 0.01 percent occurs, in a Jobless-recovery cycle over time, distribution index illusion (DII) is formed. The mathematics and the books may have been too complicated. In using aggregate data, rRDI, rRDIPC (Growth Rates of Real Disposable Personal Incomes per capita) indices have been used in my books for certain logical necessities. Because when Nash-disequilibrium game theory is used in policy, system tolerance allows sustainability to hold up to a threshold limit. There are specific preconditions that allow for systems tolerances. However, sustained reduction in aggregate demand will have consequences for joblessness.

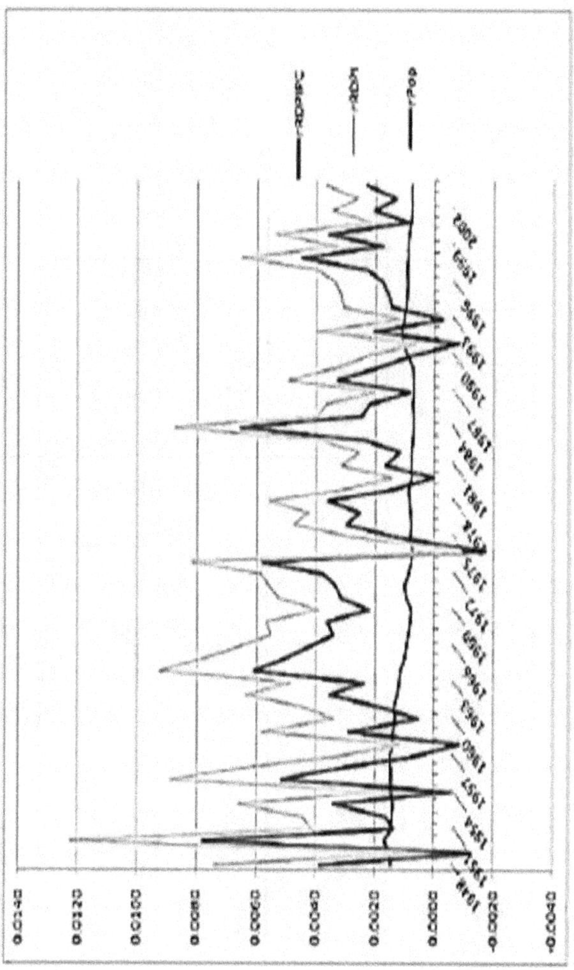

Figure 52, growth rate of Population, real disposable income (RDI), RDI per capita.

Table 2 show a decision matrix formulated to study patterns of income distribution in a dynamically functional economy, and the risks associated with a few case studies of income distributions, expo facto.

Table 28, Distributions plus risks matrix.

Sustainability, Distributions, and risk-decisions Matrix (SDRM)				
Pop%, income brackets / Cases	50P/L	40P/M	10P/H	Total 100 %
A - ur	30/0.06	25/0.625	45/4.5	100 %
B +	35/0.7	45/1.1	20/2	100 %
C - prv	10/0.2	10/0.25	80/8	100 %
D -- prv	80/1.6	10/0.25	10/1.6	100 %

In this hypothetical example, there are 4 cases (A, B, C, D,). Potential for social unrest (ur), and pre-revolution thresholds (prv) are so designated. Fifty percent of population is low-income brackets, 40 percent is medium, and 10 percent are high-income brackets. Percent of national income going to each of three brackets groups and fractions going to per capital individual in the group designate are in inside cells. While cases C and D represent extremes, they are only approximate estimations and distributional estimations.

This is not a preset income distribution by governments, utopians Socialism, or Marxism Valhalla, but a warning and risks of social unrest matrix, which should alert the governments or the society to know, they have chosen unwisely and they will need to reassess their employment arrangements, rather than confiscatory redistributions.

Demagogues can scream, from a hysterical perspective, two extremes come to mind, French and Russian revolutions.

In modern time, the private contractors, job-creators may have to be supplemented or be induced to rectify their ways back on the more competitive relatively free market path. Fuller employments with living wages are part of that temporary fiscal arrangement.

Therefore, it is important that cooperate taxes reflect cooperate and business ethical contributions to the societal good. Their taxes should also reflect their extensive uses of roads, market accesses, financial and product exchange connections, and modern electronic and digital infrastructures and connections that modern markets sustain.

The directional redistributions can bring unsustainability and social unrest as false redistributions did, if it derailed, off the narrow path of job creation with livable real wages. Older economists hear redistributions and distributions theory and they think Marx, or Milton Friedman. The updated economists know you cut out employment and exchange theory, and job-creation, and livable salaries, and government counter-balancing acts out of the equations for directional redistribution to top income earners, you are asking for implosives or explosives deconstructions. Taking the money and running out of the economy to off-shore tax-heavens is still a bad idea.[2] They cannot take taxpayers incomes at time of distress, which they mostly caused, and after their crisis, the cooperate (citizens) entities revoked their own social contracts unilaterally, ex post.

Figure 53 shows average federal tax for total, individual, and cooperate rates at top 1 percent, 1979-2010.[3]

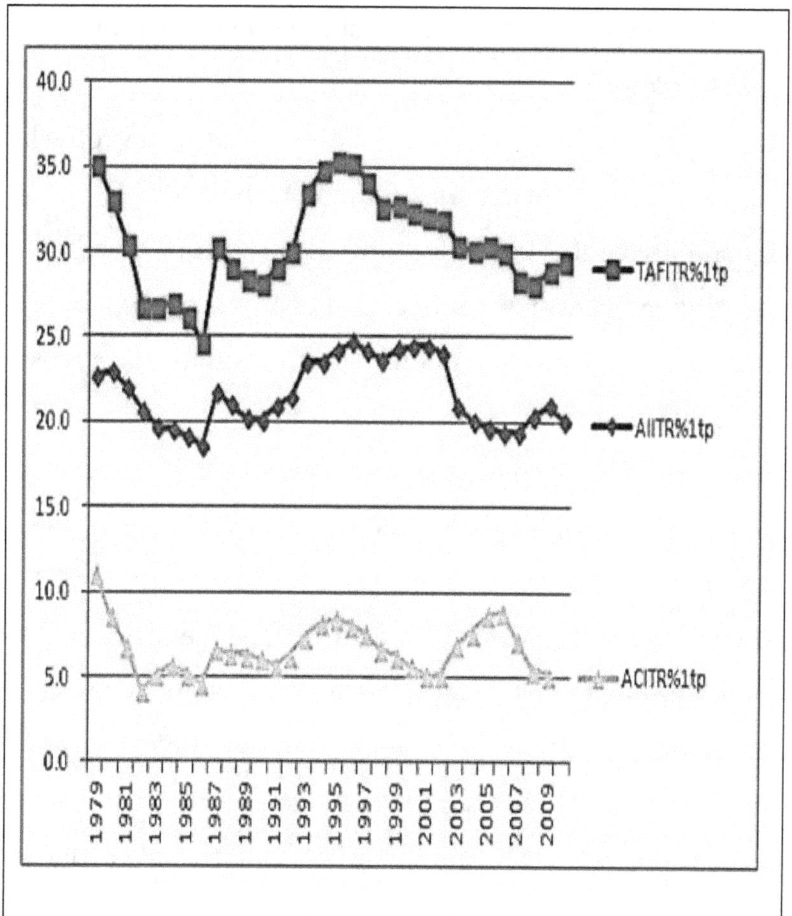

Figure 53, Average Federal Tax for total, individuals, and cooperate rates.

Especially, at the top one percent level, there should be cooperate-minimum-tax rates that maintain fiscal policy sustainability, somewhat at the level of average federal tax rates of top one percent individual-taxpayers. So, the uneducated mega-wealthy will not feel so victimized by their paid-cruel system!

There will be a definite revisiting of tax rates for the upper brackets, for tax and job-creation in full force. Perhaps another look at the USA-CBO tax rates will refresh your memories. The tax rates for top one percent cooperation are the lowest for one reason and one reason only. When they cannot deliver that task, and fulfill the wealth creation by job-creations, when they turn risk-averse do not invest, their tax rates will need to be adjusted quickly, or indexed to increase the governmental revenue that will generate jobs for the recovering economics.

They will need to pay the same amount as the individuals, the teachers, the firepersons, police officers, professors, and the working secretaries, or the lucky few at the top one percent tax and income brackets levels, so government can finish their tasks and to ensure a sufficient aggregate demand. The minimum 30 percent flat tax sound just perfect for cooperation over two million dollar gross incomes.

The federal government (fiscal economic policy) must make sure that the increased government revenues goes to job-creation and not crony-capitalism, reelection crocodile-funds at state or federal levels, or any other purposes, or return it to small businesses that do create most of jobs, even with the mandatory level of living wages.

However ignoring a wrong path will cause more problems. One can read 1920s-1930s United Sates economic history, or more recent structural unemployment shortcomings and wealth concentration. The economic wisdom fall short of mark, when imperfect competition, monopolies, oligopolies tweak the economy into the wealth concentration path, by greed or criminal crony capitalism. Adam Smith invisible hand or economic sciences have nothing to do with the oligopoly and monopoly greed shuffles and the cooperation-tax-dodging, other than the self-interests run amok unchecked, and without competitive forces to balances them.

Therefore, in that logical light, wealth concentration, and negative private fixed investment, and collusions among monopolistic and other imperfect comparative organization forces in aggregate economy are rearrangements that add to deteriorations of sustainability conditions enough to imply system reactions, negative or positive. The mindset of "what is mine is mine, and what the rest of societies produce, are mine too," are conflict-intensive mindsets, it is not diplomatic, or cooperative, nor is it a constructively productive policy. It is true that after tax revenue and private contracts must hold firmly and honestly in a free market, for it to exist.

Even mildly restated, the accumulation of negative forces gathers momentums, under certain conditions. Human history of conflicts and social discontents should be enough to pick our interest.

It is important for the top one percent to internalize that the economy is a shared free market, or relatively free market economic system, especially if they are paying the most taxes for its continuums, to rephrase Churchill, it is the best system given the relative conditions of all other economic systems. Purchase and replacement of these systems by different political economic systems will have definite unproductive results, contrary to their best welfare and interests of all classes. The top class will always have the most benefit in protecting the sustainability of just, employed, and productive economy.

Optimistically, in order to change the vector of a falling star, the further away from the event (earth) you start the better is chances for successful result. That is the star bypassing the earth instead of a collision with it. In social condition and societal order, the sooner we know of gathering problems, with the loud presumptions of functionality, the wiser and less costly will be our remedy-decisions.

It is optimistically a better wiser economic path, than the none-functionality path of devolution. It will be little gained, from revisiting the 1920s, 1930s economic mistakes, but higher risks, hardened competitors, and tougher opponents. Since the engine of economic advancement have gathered some steams, it is important to make sure ethical lapses do not harm the economic advancements, and all goes well with both the supply and demand sides gradual stepping upwards, optimistically.

Wealth and Infrastructures

Wealth can be a touchy subject in the wrong context, or if you are given to idiotic bloviating and boastful tantrums in your speech. Lately, some have used it as marketing and political marketing hooks, but it has negative backlashes. Wealth concertation cannot long exist, without its twin the wealth creation. Those are little people: almost the 90 percent of any economy, the working poor, and the middle class, minority, and the elderly pensioners are all included.

In any economic system, especially in capitalist systems, or the defined free market versions, these are the customers, supplier of money to the wealth concentrators and wealth creators alike.

There are many shipwrecks of cultural and societal empires and adventurers that have chosen the trills of wealth constriction and elitism that have rendered their ship of states wrecked on the shoreline of human history. If you are theology oriented, as far as I know, there is only one maker, and he or she does not admit its own ubiquitous existence. Aside from the organized theologies, there have been groups, tribes, and followers that have manufactured close resemblances, and idols, all the way back to the twilit of human history, in order, to cash in on the house. All knowing that he wills settle accounts, when you check out/in! Therefore, when a big gambling bear or another politician is verbally trapped in the election cycle verbosity.[4] [5] He or she is in bad news, even if he is not running for the dogcatcher office.[6] At least, two out of three books should enlighten wealth inheritors that have skipped the class education they need, in or out of politics. In order, to buy them a spot of educated peace, by not insulting their customers, the poor idiots that are parting with their hard earned cash in the wrong house.

Just remember, the billionaires will not run your house, built it, supply it, and tend to the customers, guests, built the roads and airports that bring the customers, or fly them around.[7] They will not staff the banks, hospitals and hospitality services, schools, libraries, utilities, security and defense services, factories, and food services.[8] Those are all the points in the infrastructures between your demand and the supply you need and want in a functioning market economy.[9] The more advances the market economy is the more points of infrastructures exit between the customers and the suppliers, more infrastructures- jobs are created.

Therefore, it is important to understand the deconstructive strategies of people attempting to divest in the advanced economies.[10] They engage in short term maximizations maneuverings, but unsustainable strategies, to save or enhance profit margins and boosts executive pay, at the expense of social benefits, livable salaries, sustainable long-term benefits, and the adequate real income of the society.

Whenever, the economy has cheated groups, by joblessness, lowered social benefits and healthcare, reduced real wages and incomes, the aggregate economy has suffered for it by many folds. The few billionaires you see helping with financial services, wealth and job creation, and as important and protected as they are in market economies, they are the odd ants on the massive ant farm of societal infrastructures that sustain them. We are all in the survival communal societal boat, regardless how much of the boat we occupy now, or in our different life stages.

NOTE

1

Real Private fixed investment:
Real private fixed investment in new structures: Nonresidential
Billions of Chained 2009 Dollars, Quarterly, Seasonally
FRED Graph Observations
Federal Reserve Economic Data
Link: http://research.stlouisfed.org/fred2
Help: http://research.stlouisfed.org/fred2/help-faq
Economic Research Division
Federal Reserve Bank of St. Louis

[2] "...340 other international companies have secured secret deals from Luxembourg, allowing many of them to slash their global tax bills while maintaining little presence in the tiny European duchy, leaked documents show.
These companies appear to have channeled hundreds of billions of dollars through Luxembourg and saved billions of dollars in taxes, according to a review of nearly 28,000 pages of confidential documents conducted by the International Consortium of Investigative Journalists and a team of more than 80 journalists from 26 countries."
Leslie Wayne, Kelly Carr, Marina Walker Guevara, Mar Cabra and Michael Hudson, LUXEMBOURG LEAKS: GLOBAL COMPANIES' SECRETS EXPOSED, November 5, 2014, 4:00 pm, http://www.icij.org/project/luxembourg-leaks/leaked-documents-expose-global-companies-secret-tax-deals-luxembourg

3

http://www.cbo.gov/publication/44604
Total Average Federal Tax Rate, top 1 Percent, TAFITRs
Average Individual Income Tax Rate, top 1 Percent, AIITR
Average Corporate Income Tax Rate, top 1 Percent, ACITR
Analysis and graph by Dr. Bahman Fakhraie

[4] http://nypost.com/2016/04/08/casino-mogul-steve-wynn-nobody-likes-being-around-poor-people/?link=mktw

[5] http://www.marketwatch.com/story/casino-mogul-steve-wynn-says-nobody-wants-to-be-around-poor-people-2016-04-08

[6] http://www.amazon.com/Politeconomics-Teconomics-Dr-Bahman-Fakhraie/dp/0989453944/ref=la_B00IKAR1CM_1_4/183-7614428-6691826?s=books&ie=UTF8&qid=1460388739&sr=1-4

[7] David Masciotra, We let the idiots take the wheel, Apr 11, 2016, 04:00 AM MDT http://www.salon.com/2016/04/11/we_let_the_idiots_take_the_wheel_donald_trump_fox_news_and_how_we_let_our_democracy_rot/

[8] http://www.amazon.com/Politeconomics-Teconomics-Dr-Bahman-Fakhraie/dp/0989453944/ref=la_B00IKAR1CM_1_4/183-7614428-6691826?s=books&ie=UTF8&qid=1460388739&sr=1-4

[9] http://www.amazon.com/Political-Monopolistic-Capitalism-Wealth-Concentration/dp/0989453995/ref=la_B00IKAR1CM_1_5/183-7614428-6691826?s=books&ie=UTF8&qid=1460388739&sr=1-5

[10] The Book-Web pages are at these links:
a-http://bahfecon.wix.com/bahfecon
b- http://www.amazon.com/Dr.-Bahman-Fakhraie/e/B00IKAR1CM/ref=ntt_athr_dp_pel_1
c- http://drbahfecon.wix.com/teconomics

THE END

Appendix

In Memorial to two economic greats,

The advanced student of economic doctrine should know, I shared my thought with great Mrs. Robinson (Joan Robins, 1903-1983, Theory of Imperfect Competition, 1033). She was more than gracious and kind. She was very generous with her time and memories of post Keynes and Cambridge, United Kingdom, during her visit to University of Utah, Salt lake city, Utah, USA, in last millennium. She thought that the theoretical differences with Edward Chamberlin, 1966-1899 (Monopolistic Competition, 1933) were overworked. I like to acknowledge both of their contributions to economic science in memorial, (and social and behavioral sciences) and my thanks, and see here, she received more pen time. I hope that will irritate people in Harvard, but not too much.

Joan Robinson, Economist

Joan Violet Robinson FBA was a post-Keynesian economist who was well known for her work on monetary economics and wide-ranging contributions to economic theory. Wikipedia

Born, October 31, 1903, Surrey, United Kingdom

Died: August 5, 1983, Cambridge, United Kingdom

Education: Girton College, Cambridge, University of Cambridge

Dr. Edward Chamberlin, Economist

Edward Hastings Chamberlin was an American economist. He was born in La Conner, Washington, and died in Cambridge, Massachusetts. Wikipedia

Born, May 18, 1899, La Conner, WA. Died: July 16, 1967

Books: Towards a More General Theory of Value

Education: University of Michigan, Harvard University, University of Iowa

A

ARITHMATIC OF OPTIMIZATION

The series of mathematical analysis are presented henceforth, to study utility optimization and demand side, and production optimization and the supply side analysis. The traditional mathematical evaluation for optimization analysis is as follows:

Traditional productions function,

$$o = f(v_i^{\varepsilon})$$

Necessary condition, it is also known as the first order condition (FOC):

$$f'(v_i^{\varepsilon}) > 0$$

Sufficient condition, it is also known as secondary condition (SOC):

$$f''(v_i^{\varepsilon}) > 0$$

The traditional production function is with mathematical evaluation for optimization analysis.

Conditions in Case of Growth

$$o = f(v_i^{\varepsilon})$$

Necessary condition:

$$f'(v_i^{\varepsilon}) > 0$$

Sufficient condition:

$$f''(v_i^{\varepsilon}) > 0$$

Implication: the function is positive and increasing at the increasing rate.

Condition in Case of Decay

$$o = f(v_i^{\varepsilon})$$

Necessary condition:

$$f'(v_i^{\varepsilon}) > 0$$

Sufficient condition:

$$f''(v_i^{\varepsilon}) < 0$$

Implication: the function is positive and increasing at the decreasing rate.

B

ARITHMATIC OF ENTREPRENEURIAL TIME

Lagrange analysis of n-variables and multi-constraints Lagrange multipliers the following is the mathematical analysis of productive use of available entrepreneurial times, on daily bases. Individuals have to make decision in time-use management, between productive choices they have to make in use of the fixed 24 hours given.

They make assumptive choices about their time uses, for required sleep, and time lot spent on education, and required work for income, as the following relations show. However, in post emergency, disaster, jobless times, other arrangements have to be made to replace the collateral plus time losses, and the income earned of time. Churches Mosques, Temples, and governmental and none governmental (NGOs) entities have had a historical rule.

$$f(X_S X_E X_W) = Q_i$$

$$g(X_S X_E X_W) = 24$$

$$h(X_S X_E X_W) = y_0$$

$$Z = f(X_S X_E X_W) + \mu[(24 - g(X_S X_E X_W)] + \gamma[(y_0 - h(X_S X_E X_W)] = 0$$

$$Qi = f(Xi)$$

$$g(Xi) = 24$$

$$h(Xi) = y_0$$

$$Z\mu = 24 - g(Xi) = 0$$

$$Z\gamma = y_0 - h(Xi) = 0$$

$$Zi = fi - \mu\, gi - \gamma\, hi = 0$$

Arithmetical Proof:

FOC

$$\vartheta Z^1 = 0$$

SOC

$$\vartheta Z^2 < 0$$

All constants are great than zero.

C

MAXIMIZATION OF GAINS, OPTIMIZATION OF VALUE

Budget determines expenditure on costs of production of X, and Y. Y can be designated governmental, or NGO injection in new innovational capital, while X, is some local productions still operational, which must be encouraged to keep the level of economic activities high to accommodate the post technological-injection economy. 81 is unit costs.

$$B = 81\ X1 + 82Y2$$

S denotes level of skills, technological injections required. In this example, 82 denote the skill level of NGOs, or governmental units presented at the scene of disasters. In some nations, local skill or technologies are not able to present the type of presence, which the post disaster conditions demand. Geographically isolated areas require naval assets, which are not present in most countries to meet the logistic demands of post disaster conditions.

$$S = s1\ X2 + s2\ Y2$$

Education and retraining required in use capital productively.

$$E_k = e1\, k_X + e2\, k_Y$$

Production function is,

$$Q = f(X, Y : \dot{B}, \dot{S}, \dot{E})$$

The Lagrange equation is,

$$Z_Q = f(Vi) + \mu i\, [(\dot{B} - \lambda i\, Vi)] + \mu j\, [(\dot{S} - \lambda j\, Vj)] + \mu l\, [(\dot{E}_k - \lambda l\, Vl)]$$

FOC

$$d\, Z_Q/dt = 0$$

SOC

$$d^2 Z_Q / d^2 t < 0$$

More assumptive conditions are as follows,

All constants > 0

Optimization of Value Θ is a function of maximization of profit, minimization of costs, and optimization of social welfare function of Vi.

$$\Theta = f\,(\max B, \min C, \text{opt } Ui)$$

$$Ui = f\,(qxi, qyi : Cvi : Bi, \ -/+?)$$

And

$$Ui = f\,(+, 0, -/+?)$$

COMPENSATORY SUSTAINABILITY CONDITIONS

Individual Utility Function

$$Ui = f\,(+, 0, -/+?)$$

The utility of individual Vi is improved in consumption of Qxi, while the consumption of Qyi stays the same, and the budget line can improve, stay the same, or become negative, thus also influencing the utility function.

Social Welfare Function of Group Utilities

$$\text{Opt } SWFvi, \ SWFvi = f\,(Ui, Uj, Ul, -/+?)$$

Majority of group utility will be better off at a new position A, therefore, they will agree to the project. The utility of some of group utility will stay the same. They stay either satisfy or join the last groups at position B. The utility of some of group will be worst off, there has to be tradeoffs, as in exchanges, higher remunerations, or tax-transfer strategies to optimize the experiences of all involved for them to agree to move to the better position A. This is another clause added to the arguments for sustainability conditions in all economic system orthodox or unorthodox, holistically.

SUSTIANABILITY CONDITIONS OF TECHNOLOGICAL INJECTIONS

Let us take a little time to study some of the sustainability conditions of investment in innovational new capital, with respect to social welfare functions for the group utility functions, for all individual in the group.

Two positions are A, and B, such that A is better than B.

$$A > B$$

Therefore, A is preferred to B,

$$\therefore A \ P \ B$$

$$SWFvi = f\,(Ui, Uj, Ul, -/+?)$$

The benefits sustainability conditions are as follows,

1. Sustainably condition universal criteria, it is if at least one individual utility function improves at A, others feel no change, then → A, A > B.

2. Sustainably condition Kaldorian criteria, this is when those in position A, pay, bribe, exchange with losers for the move to A, since A P B, then A > B. Alternatively, they offer to aid at their time of need.

3. Sustainably condition Hicks criteria, those losing from move to A, cannot bribe the groups to keep them from moving to A, therefore

   APB, → A, A > B.

4. Sustainably condition Scitovsky criteria, if the gainers can compensate (promise to help later) some of the losers. Moreover, some of the losers cannot bribe any of the winners from the move to A. The move will take place. Such that A P B, hence, →A, A>B.

5. Sustainably condition Dr. Bahman Fakhraie criteria, or the dynamic sustainably universal criteria, (NGOs or Gs assist production to operational levels) that technological injection will improve all utilities positions proportionally, such that [∀ Ui at A] P B, then →A, A>B. For some future post-functionality arrangements, (as tax and transfers).

There are more studies under welfare economic theory, and potential economic dissertational works.

D

RATES OF GROWTH AND DECAY

$$r^* = (Xt2 - Xt1)/Xt1$$

$$r = \frac{\ln Xt2 - \ln Xt1}{lnXt1}$$

$$Ey, ms = \frac{\frac{\delta y}{\delta t}}{\frac{\delta ms}{\delta t}}$$

SELECTED BIBLIOGRAPHY

Bailey, Martin J. National Income and the Price Level: A Study in Macroeconomic Theory, New York: McGraw-Hill, 1971.

Baumol, William J. Economic Theory and Operational Analysis, 4th ed., New Jersey: Prentice-Hall, 1977.

Blaug, Mark, Economic Theory in Retrospect, 3rd Ed., London: The Cambridge University Press, 1978.

Böhn_Bawerk, Eugen Von., Capital and Interest: Positive Theory of Capital, vol. II, Trans. G. D. Hunt & H. F. Sennholz, Chicago: Libertarian Press, 1959.

Boulding, Kenneth E., Economics As A science, New York: McGraw-Hill Book Company, 1970.

Byers, Lloyd L., Concept of Strategic Management: Planning and Implementation, New York: Harper & Row Publishers.

Caves, Richard E. and Jones, R. W., World Trade and Payments: An Introduction, 2nd ed., Boston: Little, Brown and Company, 1977.

Chiang, Alpha C., Fundamental Methods of Mathematical Economics, 2nd ed., New York: McGraw-Hill Book Company, 1974.

Coombs, Philip H., The World Educational Crisis: A System Analysis, London: Oxford University Press, 1968.

Domar, Evsey D., Essays in the Theory of Economic Growth, New York: Oxford University Press, 1957, 154-167, 168, 181.

Druker, Peter F., Innovation and Entrepreneurship, New York: Harper & Row Publishers, 1985.

Eisner, R. "Depreciation Allowances, Replacement Requirement, and Growth," The American Economic Review, XLII, December 1952.

Dr. Bahman Fakhraie, Teconomic of Verbalism, Utah, FERDAT publishing 2012, and
Paperback link is at, https://www.createspace.com/4121720
The EBook Link is at,
http://www.amazon.com/dp/B00B1LO7UQ
Books web page at, http://bahfecon.wix.com/bahfecon

—. The Demand and Supply Sides of Appropriate Technological Advancement. (Research paper at University of Utah Economics Dept. 2003),

—. Teconomics: the microeconomic analysis, Utah, FERDAT publishing 2012, and,
https://www.createspace.com/4196760, Books web page at,
http://bahfecon.wix.com/bahfecon

—. Demand and supply Sides of Technological Injections, Utah, FERDAT Publishing, 2004, And at,
http://www.amazon.com/dp/098529583X/ref=rdr_ext_tmb
#reader_098529583X

—. Technological injection, dynamic new capital measurements, and Production Theory in Economics, (Michigan: ProQuest LLC, 2010) and, https://order.proquest.com/OA_HTML/pqdtibeCCtpItmDspRte.jsp
Books web page at, http://bahfecon.wix.com/bahfecon

—. Teconomics of Verbalism, Utah FERDAT Publishing 2012, and at, https://www.createspace.com/4121720,
Books web page at, http://bahfecon.wix.com/bahfecon

—. Analytical Remedies for The Millennial Cascading Economic Declines, Utah FERDAT Publishing 2012, and at, https://www.createspace.com/4187823,
Books web page at, http://bahfecon.wix.com/bahfecon,
Author books, http://www.amazon.com/Dr.-Bahman-Fakhraie/e/B00IKAR1CM/ref=ntt_athr_dp_pel_1

—. Teconomics of Dynamic Risks: All Natural Disasters, And Energy resource Production Disasters, Utah FERDAT Publishing 2013,
, http://www.amazon.com/Teconomics-Dynamic-Risks-Disasters-Resource/dp/0985295856/ref=la_B00IKAR1CM_1_4/175-7073716-3994312?s=books&ie=UTF8&qid=1394043193&sr=1-4

—. Teconomics of Dynamic Sustainable Budgets, Utah FERDAT Publishing 2013,

Bahman Fakhraie, PhD. © 2015
http://www.amazon.com/Teconomics-Dynamic-Sustainable-Budgets-Teconomic/dp/098945391X/ref=la_B00IKAR1CM_1_5/175-7073716-3994312?s=books&ie=UTF8&qid=1394043193&sr=1-5#reader_098945391X
Book Webpages are at these links:
a-http://bahfecon.wix.com/bahfecon
b- http://www.amazon.com/Dr.-Bahman-Fakhraie/e/B00IKAR1CM/ref=ntt_athr_dp_pel_1
c- http://drbahfecon.wix.com/teconomics

—. POLITICAL MONOPOLISTIC CAPITALISM, WEALTH CONCENTRATION SCHEMA, UNITED STATES TECONOMIC ANALYSIS, 2014, Utah FERDAT Publishing 2014, http://www.amazon.com/Political-Monopolistic-Capitalism-Wealth-Concentration/dp/0989453995/ref=la_B00IKAR1CM_1_3_title_0_main/175-7073716-3994312?s=books&ie=UTF8&qid=1394043193&sr=1-3#reader_0989453995

—. "Economic Theories and Practices in Technological Changes, capital measures, and Production." (Research paper at University of Utah Economics Dept. 1988)

—. “Hallowing headless nations: the need to invest on public education under the 1980s international economic conditions,” (Research paper at University of Utah Economics Dept. 1988)

—. “Transfer of Technologies and Socioeconomic Theories of Dualism,” (Research paper at University of Utah Economics Dept. 1983)

Friedman, Milton and Schwartz, Anna Jacobson, The Great Contraction 1929-1933, vol.2, 2nd ed., New Jersey: Princeton University Press, 1973

Gander, James Patrick., Technological Change and Raw Materials, Salt Lake City: Bureau of Economic and Business Research, University of Utah, 1977.

Gardner, Ackley., Macroeconomics: Theory and Policy, New York: Macmillan Publishing Co., 1978.

Girton, Lance and Roper Don, “Theory and Implication of Currency Substitution,” Journal of Money, Credit, and Banking, 13, no. 1 (February 1981): 12-30.

Hayek, Friedrich August Von., "Kapitalaufzehrung." Weltwirtschaftliches Archive 36, 1932, II, 86-108.

Heilbroner, Robert L., The Worldly Philosophers, New York: Time Inc., Special Ed., 1962.

Hicks, Sir John, The Crisis in Keynesian Economics, New York: Basic Books, Inc. 1974.

Hirshleifer, Jack, Investment, Interest, and Capital, New Jersey: Prentice-Hall, 1970.

—. Time, Uncertainty, and Information, New York: Basil Blackwell, 1989.

—. Price Theory and Applications, New Jersey: Prentice-Hall, 1976.

Henderson, J. M. and Quandt, R. E., Microeconomic Theory; A Mathematical Approach, 2nd ed., New York: McGraw-Hill, 1972. 191-199, 280

Hunt, E. K. and Howard J. Sherman, Economics: An Introduction to Traditional and Radical Views, 2nd Ed., San Francisco: Harper and Row Publishers, 1975.

Intriligator, Michael D., Econometric Models, Techniques, and Applications, New Jersey: Prentice-Hall, 1978.

Johnson, J., Econometric Methods. New York: McGraw-Hill, 1972.

Kant, Immanuel, Critique of Judgment, Trans. J. H. Bernard, New York: Hafner, 1951.

Kennedy Charles and Thirlwall, A.P., "Surveys in Applied Economics: Technological Progress," The Economic Journal, March 1972: 12.

Keynes, John Maynard, Essays in Biography, London: The Cambridge University Printing House for Royal Economic Society, 1972.

—. The General Theory of Employment, Interest and Money, 1st ed. 1936, London: The Cambridge University Printing House for Royal Economic Society, Reprint 1973.

Kindleberger, Charles P., The World in Depression 1929-1939, Los Angeles: University of California Press, 1973.

Kirzner, I.M., Discovery and the Capitalist Process, Chicago: University of Chicago Press, 1985.

Klein, P. A. and Moore, G. H., Monitoring Growth Cycles in Market-Oriented Countries, (Mass.: published for N. B. E. R., by Ballinger publishing Co., 1985).

Knight, Farnk H., Risk, Uncertainty and Profit, Chicago: University of Chicago Press, 1985.

Landes, David S., The wealth and poverty of nations: Why Some are So Rich and Some are So Poor, (New York: W.W. Norton & Company, 1998).

Lindert, Peter H. and Kindleberger Charles P., International Economics, 7th Ed., Illinois: Richard Irwin, 1982.

Mansfield, Edwin, Technological Change, New York: W. W. Norton & Co., 1971.

Mark, Blaug, Economic Theory in Retrospect, 3rd Ed. London: The Cambridge University Press, 1978.

Marx, K. (In a letter he wrote to Engel, dated 20 August, 1862, London), (handout by Professor Randa, 2004)

McKinnon, Ronald I., Money and Capital in Economic Development, Washington D. C.: The Brookings Institution, 1973.

Mensch, Gerhard, Das technilogische Patt., Frankfurt: Umschau Verlag, 1975.

—, Stalemate in Technology: innovation overcome the Depression, (Massachusetts: Ballinger Publishing Company, 1979).

Miles, T.R., "Gestalt Theory," in The Encyclopedia of Philosophy, New York: Macmillan Publishing Co., vols. 3 and 4, 1967.

Mishan, Edward Joshua, Cost-Benefit Analysis, 4th Ed. London: Unwin Hyman, 1988.

Moran, Michael. "New England Transcendentalism," in The Encyclopedia of Philosophy, (New York: Macmillan Publishing Co., Vols. 3 and 4, 1967).

Mundell, Robert A. , "Growth, Stability, and Inflationary Finance," Journal of Political Economy, 73, 1963.

Pindyck, R.S., and Rubinfeld, D.L., Econometric Models and Econometric, 2nd ed., New York: McGraw-Hills, 1981.

Ott, J. Steven, The Organizational Culture Perspectives, (Pacific Grove, California: Brooks/Cole Publishing Company, 1989).

Quirk, James and Saposnik, Rubin, Introduction to General Equilibrium Theory and Welfare Economics, New York: McGraw-Hill, 1968.

Rima, Ingrid, Development of Economic Analysis, 7th ed., New York: Routledge, 2009.

Rodinson, M. Islam and Capitalism, Trans. B. Pearce, Austin: University of Texas, 1981.

Rosenberg, Nathan, Technology and American Economic Growth, New York: M. E. Sharp, 1972.

Ruttan, V. W. "Usher and Schumpeter on Invention, and Technological Change," Quarterly Journal of Economics, 1960, 602.

Ruttan, Vernon W. "Usher and Schumpeter on Invention, Innovation, and Technological change," Quarterly Journal of Economics, 1960, 73.

Samuelson, Anthony Paul. Economics, 11th Ed., New York: McGraw-Hill, 1980.

Savich, R.S., and Thomson, L. A., Resource Allocation within the Product Life Cycles, Business Topic, MSU: MSU, fall 1978.

Schmooker, Jacob, Invention and Economic Growth, Massachusetts: Harvard University Press, 1966.

Schultz, Theodore W. Investing in People: The Economics of Population Quality, Berkley, University of California Press, 1982.

Schumpeter, Joseph A. Business Cycles, vol. 1. New York: McGraw Hill Book Company, 1939.

—. Business Cycles: A Theoretical, Historical, and Statistical Analysis of the Capitalists Process, vol. I, New York: McGraw Hill Book Company, 1938.

—. The Theory of Economic Development: An Inquiry into Profits, Capital, Credit, Interest, and Business Cycle, Trans., Redvers Opie, London: Oxford University Press, Reprint 1980.

Smith, Adam., An Inquiry into the Nature and Cause of Wealth of Nations, Edited by E. Cannon, Chicago: University of Chicago Press, 1976.

—. An Inquiry into the Nature and Causes of Wealth of Nations, vol. 2, 2nd ed., Oxford: the Clarendon Press, 1988.

—. The Theory of Moral Sentiments, London, 1st ed., 1757.

Smith, E.J. Chambers, R.H. Scott and R.S., National Income Analysis and Forecasting, Glenview: Scott, Foresman and Company, 1975.

Spiegle, Henry William., The Growth of Economic thought, North Carolina: Duke University Press, 1983.

Stigler, George J., The Theory of Price, 3rd ed., New York: The Macmillan Company, 1966.

Takaki, Ronald., A Different Mirror: A History of Multicultural America, London: Little Brown and Company, 1993.

Taylor, John R., An Introduction to Error Analysis, Mill Valley: University Science Books, 1982.

Thirtle, Colin G. and Ruttan V. W., The Role of Demand and Supply in the Generation of Diffusion of Technological Change, Switzerland, 1987.

U. S. President, Economic Report of the President, (Washington, D.C.: Government printing office, 1990)

Usher, Abbot Payson, A History of Mechanical Inventions, London: Oxford University Press, 1954.

Usher, Abbot Payson, A History of Mechanical Inventions, Revised ed., London: Oxford University Press, 1954.

Viner, Jacob, Studies in the Theories of International Trade, New York: Harper and Brothers publishers, 1937.

Wainwright, A. C. Chiang and K., Fundamental Methods of Mathematical Economics, 4th ed., Boston: McGraw-Hill Irwin, 2005.

Webster, Merriam, Merriam-Webster's Collegiate Dictionary, 9th ed., Springfield: M.W. Inc., 1985.

Young, Hugh D., Statistical Treatment of Experimental Data, New York: McGraw-Hill, 1962.

FERDAT AND LEGALS

FAKHRAIE EDUCATION RESEARCH
DEVELOPMENT
AND TRUST

Budgetary, Managerial Directive and Legal Clauses

Legal letter and charges for unauthorized information use.

Section 1, Mission Statement

Section 2, Budgetary Clause

Section 3, Managerial Clause

Section 4, Legal Clause

Section 5, Organization Chart

Section 6, Data Management

Section 7, Vita

Legal letter is in cases of e-fraud, misuse of firms' information, or harm under sec. G. All linked and relaying entities, institutions, governmental agencies are accountable no exception.

Dear Sirs, persons, INC., (illegal use of firms' info), your current bill is **$10,000, ≤Ceiling $60 mils.** On behalf of Dr. Bahman Fakhraie, FERDAT, and the firm, family trusts.
These are the current charges related to illegal e-fraud and all harmful misuse of firms information, after the first time we asked you to terminate all contract and remove our name, firms' name etc. on this date.

1-Illegal use, the unapproved initial use of firm's name, contact name, duns #, any and all information supplied to USA government for the soul purpose of firm doing business with USA government, grant.gov, and NSF, Universities, other governmental and tribal entities, and all grantors. Minimum charges are $10,000.00, up to the ceiling of $ 60 million.

2-Use of firm contacts, names, address phone #, TIN/#s, and any information related to that.

Minimum charges are $10,000.00, up to the ceiling of $60 mils.

3- Continuation after repeated formal request to terminate illegal actions, sending junk e-mail, junk mail, forcing this firm to send back, by mail and certified mail. Legal costs related to that.

Minimum charges are $10,000.00 per each event, up to the ceiling of $60 mils.

4- Interference with firm soul business, time sensitive writing of government and private grants, at grant.gov, and NSF, universities, private foundations, NGOs and all grantors, with 4.5 million dollars floor. The Minimum charges are 4.5 million dollars, up to the ceiling of $60 mils.

4- Absolut or required non-disclosures by the firm or Dr. Fakhraie will require pre-paid plan with minimum flooring pay. Flex-legalism targeted at the firm, or Dr. B. Fakhraie will be due cause for nonpaid termination by the same, and harm-terms of Sec G of private contracts.

6- Punitive damages are up to 60 million dollars, if you do not stop, after the first notification.

Please make an effort to pay your bill. There will be additional charges added and sent to you for each time you try to contact the same entities, after the same dated termination notices.

Dr. BF, this is part of the legal notices under sec G, or formal termination notice dates.

Section 1, Mission Statement

To formulate optimum functionality in management teams, in order to make profitable and beneficial contributions, and create opportunity for merited advancements, **to advance research** in my fields of study. Utilizing rare combination of theory and empiricism, cultivated in multi-cultural inclusive settings in academic and private enterprises, I enhance the management in productivity and completion of productive projects, or suggest corrective recursive evaluation and total quality control improvements.

Experiences, among fields of International Trade, Managerial, and Production theories in Economics, Finance, Personal Finance management, and Businesses, which modern business and academic institutions find very expensive to employ and too costly not to employ. My extensive backgrounds help me advance research in my fields of study.

Biography and Books,

Dr. Bahman Fakhraie, PhD in Economics, University of Utah, and his dissertation added to the influences of the Unorthodox Holistic Economic doctrine and complemented the modern orthodox economic theories, in the millennial age of technological paradigm shifts. He applies analytical skills with gestalt study of history, mathematics, and econometrics to economic analysis, with scientific background. He is a Published Economist, Author, Researcher, Investor, and Private Contractor. His skills are in international trade and finance, economic production (theory and application), growth and development theory, econometrics, agriculture economics, and agronomy. These are greatly valued skills combinations to employ.

Bahman married Kay Davis 1976, a master in Speech Pathology. His daughter, Lara Fatemeh Fakhraie, earned her Master's degree from Oregon State University. She is a published author. She resides in Oregon. His son, Anayat Fakhraie, a screenwriter earned his Master from the American Film Institute. Fakhraie families have endured revolutions, death of family, and hardships. The sui generis caravan of joy de vive continues merrily. Dr. Bahman Fakhraie was invited by Senator Frank M. Browning to attend Utah State University, when Senator visited his family. He received two degrees from Utah State University; he attended University of Utah for his PhD in Economics. He has published books, eBooks. He is presenting a few in Amazon.com. He has met most of modern day science and economic opinion leaders.

Dr. Bahman Fakhraie's books web page is at,

1- http://bahfecon.wix.com/bahfecon#

2- http://www.amazon.com/Dr.-Bahman-Fakhraie/e/B00IKAR1CM/ref=ntt_athr_dp_pel_1

Section 2, Budgetary Clause

* All initial dedicated deposits (inflows) will be transferred to a FREDT, or FREDAT business account.

* No allotments or contracts activity will take place, until full transfer of funds has taken place per contracts. The cash-accounting method is used for tax purposes.

* Alteration to submit to requirements and regulations will fully transfer all risks, fees, and penalties, and legal responsibilities, to the source of the requirements.

* There will be a minimum product list, or writing, or proposal-output for further research, which will be presented and agreed to at the initial phases.

* This will be the only output legally required at the end of contract, or at the end of grant periods.

* There is a managerial flow chart enclosed to enhance comprehensions of cash flow, read after the legal notes section.

Section 3, Managerial Clause

* Dr Bahman Fakhraie will act as agent, manger, and soul administrator, Executives director, Principle Investigator PI for FERDT, FERDAT, Fakhraie Bahman Organization, with full rights to take legal action and make final settlement on its accounts.

* Dr Bahman Fakhraie will act as agent, manger, and soul administrator for Fakhraie Bahman Organization, with full right to take legal action on its accounts.

* A general electronic bookkeeping is followed, on periodical bases, as grants require it. Current standard is quarterly, post full disbursements of grant funding. (FRR is required quarterly)

* Details, information, managerial technologies are legally protected, and no such disclosure will be made of the

Organization, administrator, assignees, or representatives of FERDT, FERDAT, or Fakhraie Bahman Organization. All copyright materials are marketable, or further developed by Mr. Fakhraie. All existing rights are reserved.

* All informal and formal requests can be made by mail, or email.

* There is forfeiture of all advances, in cases of mortality, health, or attempt at disbarment, legal action, harm, against soul administrator, Fakhraie Bahman Organization, with full right to take legal action on its accounts.

* Any and all such request will have to forward additional funding for legal representations and undue imposition of costs or harm, please read the legal note and sec. G. It will always apply.

* Alteration to submit to requirements and regulations will fully transfer all risks, fees, and penalties, and legal responsibilities, to the source of the requirements.

* The reviewers will have access to a portion of the progress.

* Full transparencies are practiced for authorized agents only, mostly through the internet, after proper signatures are obtained.

Teconomics of Infrastructures

* PI, FERDAT; Fakhraie, Bahman

  Dr. Bahman Fakhraie, PhD, UOU, UT, USA

* Position Classification, Executive level I,

* Salary exceeds Fed Cap for private contracts.

* NSF ID, 000586796, Organizational ID Code, P 269878425

* Private for Profit Business:

* DUNS Number D&B # 966689684,

* CAGE/NCAGE: 692S3, Congressional Districts, UT_001

* Sec G of private contract always applies

* For institutional DUNS, etc. Please, check cover letter, or contact PI. Thanks

* UOU PI Information

□ Federal Interagency Committee on Education (FICE) Code for the U: **003675**
□ EIN. TAX ID/TIN: **87-600**
□ DUNS Num: **D & B #009**

□ Cage Code: **3T**
□ NSF Institutional Code: **367**
□ NIH Institutional Code: **514**
□ Congressional District: **UT-002**
□ Type of Organization: **State Institution of Higher Education**
□ AAALAC Accreditation: **8 March 2000 - (Animal Resource Center Facilities and Programs Accreditation)**
□ USDA Registration Number (Animal Subject):
□ PHS Animal Welfare Assurance ID Number: **-01**
□ Human Subjects Federal Wide Assurance:
□ Effective Date of Cost Accounting Statement: **Disclosure Statement submitted**

Section 4, Legal Clause, All Right Reserved & Other Legal Notes

E. Speech, Lecture Tours, and Research Papers & Follow Up:

All publications or Grant-products are commonly published on completion, USA Library of Congress, Trade Journals, Or Author's websites, etc.

Contact for individualized contracts

F. For Time Donation, And Charity Events: 1. 5% of Net contracts paid 2. Time by Appointments Only.3. Write Donations Checks to Fakhraie Trust fund / Bahman Fakhraie

G. Any and All Risks or Harms invokes these legal clauses. The Following legal clauses are base minimums, and will not limit all rights and legal protections, with uniform constitutional rights they are implied and accorded. Contractually all rights are implied and accorded. Please, read all the legal notes before using any materials.

G1. In Cases of misuse of these materials, plagiarisms, use to put at risk of harm, or to harm, (Legal, or Etc.) the firm, CEO, FERDT, president: Mr. Bahman Fakhraie, His family members, it will result in $60 million legal action per each event in United States Courts/ any Jurisdictions determined or set by author or a trust set up by Mr. Bahman Fakhraie. Also, use of creative ideas and intellectual properties for any commerce direct or indirect or by proxy, expansions of outlines, attempts to defraud, over charge, harm with illegal acts, misuse of private and confidential materials, information, and properties, letters, checks, e-mails, faxes, any and all communications, and any electronically stored materials and pictures, or false claims against the above entities will be an agreement with and subject to all elements of this contract, and as a user license, without nullifying further and ensuing legal actions or collections, or as directed by the same or authorities. All other contracts are one-time contracts and s. t. this contract. Please, notify firm, Mr. Bahman Fakhraie, of all infractions, transactions, or transfer to individuals or to private or government entities in accord with current laws.

G2a. All Costs due to inquiries, related or required business licenses, legal paper works, and hours, all costs related to corrective or reparation publicity, bonding and insurances costs, stock related activities, all costs related to any harm (financial & legal) will be charges to the sources and inquirers, and none to the firm or Bahman Fakhraie, his family, or any and all of their related assets. All attempts to harm, engagements, cashing checks or accepting cash from the same entities is an agreement with all elements of this contract.

G2b. All copy rights associated with written works and further development of all works remains with the author Bahman Fakhraie or his trusts. All development rights are reserved by the same entities.

G3. Any and all unsolicited commercial phone calls, to Mr. Bahman Fakhraie and, his family will result to a minimum of $ 500 per call charged to the source, due and payable in the same month the call is made, all other elements of this contract also apply, all contracts remain subservient to this contract, all costs of collection and legal actions also are added to the bill payable by source and not Bahman Fakhraie and these entities.

G4.All Consultation and coaching involves risks due to market, business, political, etc. costs and damages related to all such risk are paid by individuals or business entities involved and none is implied or taken by Bahman Fakhraie, his family, or any related assets, under any and all conditions. These entities' court fees are $10,000, at minimum.

G5.Uncomfortable conditions, misapplications of any law to harm, harassment, odd-hour calls, etc will be due cause for termination of services without refund, and are actionable per this contract.

§§§§

All Right Reserved & Other Legal Notes

All publications or Grant-products are published on completion, USA Library of Congress, Trade Journals, Or Author's websites, etc.

E. Speech, Lecture Tours, Research Papers & Follow Up:

1. Per Each Event-$ 350,000 +.
2. with Foreign Travel-$ 3,000,000
3. Book/Cash Advance $6,000,000; Net Royalties ~40%
4. Scripts: /Starting from.....................$ 300,000
5. Movie Script (120+Pages).................$ 3,000,000
6. Or Cash Advance Plus 2% of All Gross paid annually
7. Consultations Fee/Initial charge non-refunded $ 10,000, & ...10 %
8. Business limited ventures, partnerships, etc. .... ∃ 30%
9. Salary executive level I

F. For Time Donation, And Charity Events: 1. 5% of Net contracts paid 2. Time by Appointments Only.3. Write Donations Checks to Fakhraie Trust fund / Bahman Fakhraie. G. Any and All Risks or Harms invokes these legal clauses. The Following legal clauses are base minimums, and will not limit all rights and legal protection, with uniform constitutional rights they are implied and accorded. Contractually all rights are implied and accorded. Please, read all the legal notes before using any materials. G1. In Cases of misuse of these materials, plagiarisms, use to put at risk of harm, or to harm, (Legal, or Etc.) the firm, CEO: Mr. Bahman Fakhraie, His family members, will result in $60 million legal action per each event in United States Courts/Jurisdictions determine by author or a trust set up by Mr. Bahman Fakhraie. Also, use of creative ideas intellectual properties, expansions of outlines, attempts to defraud, over charge, harm with illegal acts, misuse of private and confidential materials and properties, letters, e-mails, faxes, any and all communications, and any electronically stored materials and pictures, or false claims against the above entities will be an agreement with all elements of this contract, and as a use license, without nullifying ensuing legal actions or collections, or as directed by the same or authorities. Please, notify firm, Mr. Bahman Fakhraie, of all infractions, transactions, or transfer to individuals or to private or government entities. G2a. All Costs due to inquiries, related or required business licenses, legal paper works and hours, all costs related to corrective or reparation publicity, bonding and insurances costs, stock related activities, all costs related to any harm (financial & legal) will be charges to the sources and inquirers, and none to the firm or Bahman Fakhraie, his family, or any and all of their related assets. All attempts to harm, engagements, cashing checks or accepting cash from the same entities is an agreement with all elements of this contract. G2b. All copy rights associated with written works and further development of all works remains with the author Bahman Fakhraie or his trusts. All development rights are reserved by the same entities. G3. Any and all unsolicited commercial phone calls to Mr. Bahman Fakhraie, his family will result to a minimum of $ 500 per call charged to the source, due and payable in the same month the call is made, all other elements of this contract also apply, all contracts remain subservient to this contract, all costs of collection and legal actions also are added to the bill payable by source and not Bahman Fakhraie and these entities. G4.All Consultation and coaching involves risks due to market, business, political, etc. costs and damages related to all such risk are paid by individuals or business entities involved and none is implied or taken by Bahman Fakhraie, his family, or any related assets, under any and all conditions. These entities' court fees are $10,000, at minimum. G5.Uncomfortable conditions, misapplications of any law to harm, harassment, odd-hour calls, etc will be due cause for termination of services without refund, and are actionable per this contract.

§§§§

Letter of Agreement with FRDET and DR. Fakhraie Bahman

I/We (Ms, Mrs., Mr.): ....

Business Name: ....

Social Security numbers: ..../......./................ ..../......./................

Tax ID Numbers: ....

Driver License Numbers: ....

Passport (Birth Certificate) Numbers: ....

Have read all the information supplied by Mr. Bahman Fakhraie, and /or FRDET (Trust, LLP). Agree to supply all correct financial and related information and select the following services by marking (X), or Letter a b c, Or Number 1 2 3, or write and specify. Agree to the power of attorney required to confirm or acquire financial and related information. Plus a check for $3000, for preliminary registrations, legal and financial inquiries, and licensing fees.

1: □ 2: □ 3: □ 4: □ 5: □ 6: □ 7: □ 8: □

Specify which kinds of the following accounts you will require:

Individual/Gov. □ Joints □ Joint with survival rights □ Trusts □

Details: ....

Business types:

Ltd Partnership (LLP, LLC) □ Soul Owner □ Inc/Gov □ Firm □

Details: ....

I/We agree to pay the fees and costs as they accrue, after 30 days a charge of %10 per annum is added to past due amounts until they are settled or paid in full. That at least 75% charges and expenses are paid no later than six month after initial reports or outlines are examined. That all travel lodgings and phone charges, legal research, and research hours, I/We request are fully paid. I/We have read and understand the nature of business, business cycles, market price fluctuation risks, currency fluctuation risks, social and political risks, natural and climatic risks, and all other risks herewith not itemized; therefore, I/we accept all financial losses, responsibilities, all punitive or compensatory damages that occur for all activities that are undertaken based on or claimed related to the report or reports, advise and etc., generated by Money Wise Firm, Bahman Fakhraie or all the entities named, agents, and associates. I/We understand in cases of any false, misleading, or withholding information the Money Wise Firm and all entities named above will not be held accountable, responsible, financially or otherwise, and will be refunded for any damages fully. I/We release all others associated with Money Wise Firm, and Bahman Fakhraie from financial losses, responsibilities, all compensatory and punitive charges concerning activities I/We undertake.

Sign (full name, titles, and address)

Business (Name, Address; Agents' title):

Section 5, Organization Chart

⇔Requests for grants, grant and contract proposals and Minimums contracted output Grant Funds,

⇓ Organization DUNS, University DUNS ⇓

Administrator ⇒FRDAT

⇓

FERDAT

Publishing and Production

President, Administrator, Executive level 1

⇓

Bahman Fakhraie, PhD, © 2011, UOU, UT, USA ®, ™

⇓

Tasks and controls, TQC, and Redo, Recycles

⇔Tax and expense disbursements

⇓

Completed project Vs. Minimums contracted output

⇔ Informal notification of source of funds, with future project proposal if any,

⇒Formal and final notification from FRDET, FERDAT

⇔ Final confirmation of conclusion from Administrators

⇒ Final confirmation of conclusion from Organization Fakhraie

⇔ Keeping communication and network open to future project.

Section 6, DATA MANAGEMENT:

Relevant data will be managed, and stored.

Moreover, the data and the progression of data used will be stored post completion.

As a common practice, Dr Bahman Fakhraie will, also preserve a historical over view of data for legal purposes, for future use. A portion of that will be shared if requested in written form, post settlement of all expenses.

The ethical requirements will be followed in accordance with the applied law established.

The final product will be shared with the grantors, after all the financial settlements have been met. The reviewers will have access to a portion of the progress.

All publications or Grant-products are published on completion, USA Library of Congress, Trade Journals, FERDAT Publishing, Or Author's websites, etc.

Labor laws and benefit distribution will be according to the institutional Fed Cap limits, private contracts; vendors are responsible for their own legal obligations. (Publication Ink, FedExx, kinkcos, vendors etc.)

CPA and Legal establishment, outside to this entity will be contracted to handle more complex issues when they arise, all cost are due, prior to any such required actions are requested.

Full transparencies are practiced for authorized agents only, mostly through the internet, after proper signatures are obtained. All copyrights and proprietary rights are granted, accorded and reserved to Dr Bahman Fakhraie,

All future development, educational development will have to be contracted, or signed out temporarily, they will revert to Dr. Bahman Fakhraie, in case of all legal issues.

These and other clauses will be amended and upgraded as required over time. They all apply.

Absolut or required non-disclosures by the firm or Dr. Fakhraie will require pre-paid plan with minimum flooring pay. Flex-legalism targeted at the firm, or Dr. B. Fakhraie will be due cause for nonpaid termination by the same.

G. Any and All Risks or Harms invokes these legal clauses. The Following legal clauses are base minimum, and will not limit all rights and legal protection, with uniform constitutional rights they are implied and accorded. Contractually all rights are implied and accorded. Please, read all the legal notes before using any materials.

Section 7, Vita

Bahman Fakhraie, PH.D. University Of Utah

Economic Dept., Salt Lake City, Utah USA, 84112

Permanent Address: c/o 1120 Canyon Rd #29; Ogden Utah 84404-7663

E-Mail: bf9@utah.edu , dr.bahf.econ@gmail.com

Honors and Awards: Omicron Delta Epsilon Honor Society

Student leadership positions: President of International Student Association

Bachelor of Science: Utah State University

Master of Science: Utah State University

PhD, University of Utah University of Utah

Dr. Bahman Fakhraie's book web pages are at these links:

1- http://bahfecon.wix.com/bahfecon#

2- http://www.amazon.com/Dr.-Bahman-Fakhraie/e/B00IKAR1CM/ref=ntt_athr_dp_pel_1

Mission Statement:

To formulate optimum functionality in management teams, in order to make profitable and beneficial contributions, and create opportunity for merited advancements.

Utilizing rare combination of theory and empiricism, cultivated in multi-cultural inclusive settings in academic and private enterprise, I enhance the management in productivity and completion of productive projects, or suggest corrective recursive evaluation and total quality control improvements.

Experiences, among fields of International Trade, Managerial, and Production theories in Economics, Finance, Personal Finance and Business, which modern business and academic institutions find very expensive to employ and too costly not to employ. The extensive background helps advance research in my fields of study.

Goals:

I have initiated, passed, and funded many constructive projects --goals by committees--, where it has been value enhancing and mutually beneficial individually, and by team assists.
Private Senior Economist: Research Positions with Contracts, Teaching, Research, Books, with contract.
Short Term Private Contracts are for economic and financial educational consultations.
Academic Preparatory Continuum:
PhD, University of Utah

Dissertation:

TECHNOLOGICAL INJECTION, DYNAMIC NEW CAPITAL MEASUREMENTS, AND PRODUCTION THEORY IN ECONOMICS

Dr. Bahman Fakhraie's Book-link is at,
https://order.proquest.com/OA_HTML/pqdtibeCCtpItmDspRte.jsp

Thesis statement:

The dynamic influences of technology and elemental factors of production --defined and measured in this dissertation-- are greater than commonly have been calculated or expected. The impacts of different measurements of capital stocks (traditional and new adjusted capital) on embodied and disembodied technological variables, on productivity, and economic growth of national social products are tested. The econometric effects of two new capital stock measures introduced in the writing of Friedrich August Von Hayek, John Maynard Keynes, and further developed by Evsey D. Domar, and ignored by most modern economists are examined. Therefore, we focus on the demand and supply side of technological embodied in capital, in human skill and produced goods and services, and the economy.

Post-Doctoral Goals:

1. Updating the econometrics of the dissertation to most recent available data and dates. (per available grants)

2. Include, countries, with acceptable data in the study, set up formulaic development in excel etc for use.(per grants)

3. Focus on the theoretical advancement in production processes for systemic innovational additive methodologies, in Movie production, Agriculture, and other creative industries, using existing or newly hired faculties, in anchored and linked institutions. This is a great serious work in shadows of Adam Smith, Schumpeter, Hayak, and Keynes.

4. Stream line methodologies, and project for PhD Students, master students, and introductory fields' level, an extension of the dissertation and current copyrighted writings.

5. Of course, this will be under Sec G of private contract and without infringing on rights of marketing, publishing, and distribution of the same. Certain contracts will be more restrictive, including specific names.

Production theory in Agriculture

Agro-production, Sheep production in Iran (an onsite research project 1975)

Monetary Macroeconomic Specialization (Milton Freedman,)

International Monetary macroeconomic Specializations (Robert Mundell)

Fiscal Analysis of oscillatory modifications

Applied Agricultural production in developing economies

Inappropriate Technology Transfers by Corporations

and dualistic induced instabilities in a pre-democratic economies.

Book Webpages are at these links:

a-http://bahfecon.wix.com/bahfecon

b- http://www.amazon.com/Dr.-Bahman-Fakhraie/e/B00IKAR1CM/ref=ntt_athr_dp_pel_1

c- http://drbahfecon.wix.com/teconomics

Dr. Bahman Fakhraie Published-books as of 3/20/2014 are,

1- Dr. Bahman Fakhraie, Teconomic Analysis of Cascading Millennial Economies, https://www.createspace.com/4187823

2- Bahman Fakhraie, PhD., TECONOMICS OF VERBALISM

3- Bahman Fakhraie, PhD., DEMAND AND SUPPLY SIDES OF TECHNOLOGICAL INJECTIONS,

4- Bahman Fakhraie, PhD., TECONOMICS, Utah FERDAT Publishing 2012, https://www.createspace.com/4196760

5- Dr. Bahman Fakhraie, Teconomics of Dynamic Risks All Natural Disasters, And Energy Resource...,

6-Dr. Bahman Fakhraie, Technological injection, dynamic new capital measurements, and Production Theory in Economics,

7- Dr. Bahman Fakhraie, TECONOMICS OF DYNAMIC SUSTAINABLE BUDGETS, Utah, Ferdat Publishing, 8- Dr. Bahman Fakhraie, Teconomics of Dynamic Risks, Utah, Ferdat Publishing, 2013,

9- Dr. Bahman Fakhraie, POLITICAL MONOPOLISTIC CAPITALISM,

WEALTH CONCENTRATION SCHEMA, UNITED STATES TECONOMIC ANALYSIS, 2014, Utah, Ferdat Publishing, 2013, EBooks,

10- Dr. Bahman Fakhraie, TECONOMIC OF VERBALISM,

12- Bahman Fakhraie, PhD, TECONOMICS OF DYNAMIC SUSTAINABLE BUDGETS, Teconomic of Dynamic Sustainable Strategic Budgeting in X, From Small to Large Operational Modular-Production growth Models.

13- Dr. Bahman Fakhraie, POLITICAL MONOPOLISTIC CAPITALISM, WEALTH CONCENTRATION SCHEMA, UNITED STATES TECONOMIC ANALYSIS, 2014, Utah, Ferdat Publishing, 2013

14- Dr. Bahman Fakhraie, Teconomics of the Budget Ethics: Hidden Figures or Invisible Hands of Free market capitalism, Utah, Ferdat Publishing, 2014

VITA

Bahman Fakhraie, PH.D. University Of Utah

Economic Dept., Salt Lake City, Utah USA, 84112

Permanent Address: c/o 1120 Canyon Rd #29; Ogden Utah 84404-7663

E-Mail: bf9@utah.edu, bahf.econ@gmail.com, dr.bahf.econ@gmail.com

Honors and Awards:

Omicron Delta Epsilon Honor Society,

At University of Utah

Certificate in

"KEYS TO AGRICULTURAL DEVELOPMENTAT LOCAL LEVEL"

At Utah State University

Student leadership positions:

President of International Student Association

Bachelor of Science:	Utah State University
Master of Science:	Utah State University
PhD, University of Utah	University of Utah

Mission Statement:

To formulate optimum functionality in management teams, in order to make profitable and beneficial contributions, and create opportunity for merited advancements.

Bahman Fakhraie, PhD. © 2015

Utilizing rare combination of theory and empiricism, cultivated in multi-cultural inclusive settings in academic and private enterprise, I enhance the management in productivity and completion of productive projects, or suggest corrective recursive evaluation and total quality control improvements.

Experiences, among fields of International Trade, Managerial, and Production theories in Economics, Finance, Personal Finance and Business, which modern business and academic institutions find very expensive to employ and too costly not to employ. The extensive background helps advance research in my fields of study.

Goals:

I have initiated, passed, and funded many constructive projects --goals by committees--, where it has been value enhancing and mutually beneficial individually, and by team assists.

Private Senior Economist: Research Positions with Contracts, Teaching, Research, Books, with contract. Short Term Private Contracts are for economic and financial educational consultations.

Academic Preparatory Continuum:

PhD, University of Utah

Dissertation:

Teconomics of Infrastructures

TECHNOLOGICAL INJECTION, DYNAMIC NEW CAPITAL MEASUREMENTS, AND PRODUCTION THEORY IN ECONOMICS

Thesis statement:

The dynamic influences of technology and elemental factors of production --defined and measured in this dissertation-- are greater than commonly have been calculated or expected. The impacts of different measurements of capital stocks (traditional and new adjusted capital) on embodied and disembodied technological variables, on productivity, and economic growth of national social products are tested. The econometric effects of two new capital stock measures introduced in the writing of Friedrich August Von Hayek, John Maynard Keynes, and further developed by Evsey D. Domar, and ignored by most modern economists are examined. Therefore, we focus on the demand and supply side of technological embodied in capital, in human skill and produced goods and services, and the economy.

Post-Doctoral Goals:

6. Updating the econometrics of the dissertation to most recent available data and dates. (per available grants)

7. Include, countries, with acceptable data in the study, set up formulaic development in excel etc for use.(per grants)

8. Focus on the theoretical advancement in production processes for systemic innovational additive methodologies, in Movie production, Agriculture, and other creative industries, using existing or newly hired faculties, in anchored and linked institutions. This is a great serious work in shadows of Adam Smith, Schumpeter, Hayak, and Keynes.

9. Stream line methodologies, and project for PhD Students, master students, and introductory fields' level, an extension of the dissertation and current copyrighted writings.

10. Of course, this will be under Sec G of private contract and without infringing on rights of marketing, publishing, and distribution of the same. Certain contracts will be more restrictive, including specific names.

Production theory in Agriculture

Agro-production, Sheep production in Iran (an onsite research project 1975)

Monetary Macroeconomic Specialization (Milton Freedman,)

International Monetary macroeconomic Specializations (Robert Mundell)

Teconomics of Infrastructures

Fiscal Analysis of oscillatory modifications

Applied Agricultural production in developing economies

Inappropriate Technology Transfers by Corporations and dualistic induced instabilities in a pre-democratic economies.

Certificate in Rural Development from Utah State University

Research Skills:

Statistical packages, data selection, analysis, and formulations.

Computer Languages, Spread Sheet Data Analysis, Writings

Multimedia and Creative Skills: Film and video production, CD: audio and video works

Languages: Fluent in English and Farsi, I can read and write some French, and Arabic.

Fluent in Dezfili Dari dialectic [One of the earliest spoken languages]

Teaching Experiences:

University of Utah: macroeconomic and microeconomic: introductory course, and related mathematics.

Utah State University: Economic Department, Persian language, and cultural studies to faculty and students, and teaching assistance for Agricultural economics.

Volunteer Helping of other students

Student leadership positions AUSU, as an undergraduate

PROFESSIONAL EXPERIENCE:

Founder and Management of Money Wise Firm (A Private Financial Education Foundation for Personal Financial studies), 1970 to date.

Volunteer work: President; V.P., and Treasurer of Cherrywood Association Inc., multimillion dollars project. (Different 3 year cycles 1980 to 1999)

Real Estate Investor and Renovations, General Manger, to date.

Agribusiness management, owner manager

Auto Agency sale manager/sold

Auto shop management/sold

Numerous Volunteer Projects: planning, budgeting, contracting, and finishing.

Beside educational publications, and digital multi-media, DVD, CDS, copyrighted at USA the library of congress.

Other Experience:

Budget Analysis, Budget Setting, Budget Forecasting, Asset Allocation Studies, Portfolio Analysis Studies, Saving (Goal Setting) Plan, Tax Management Studies, Risk/Reward Management and studies, Economic Condition risk Analysis, Managerial Goal Setting and Project Production Process and Enactments.

Economic Topics of Research and Lectures:

Teconomics of Infrastructures

Non-Marxist Revolutions in Middle East (Iran).

Economic and Indices (Measurement Issues).

Economic Theories of Technological Changes and Capital Measures.

Technological Change, Growth Rate, and Capital Formations with US Data.

Education and Taxation

Hollowing Headless Nations! Education Crisis

Technological Parameters Statistical Measurements.

New Econometric Measurements of Capital in Production Theory.

Reading (Economic, Science, mystery, ancients), Films (art, industry), Jazz, Fly-fishing

BOOK PROMOTIONS

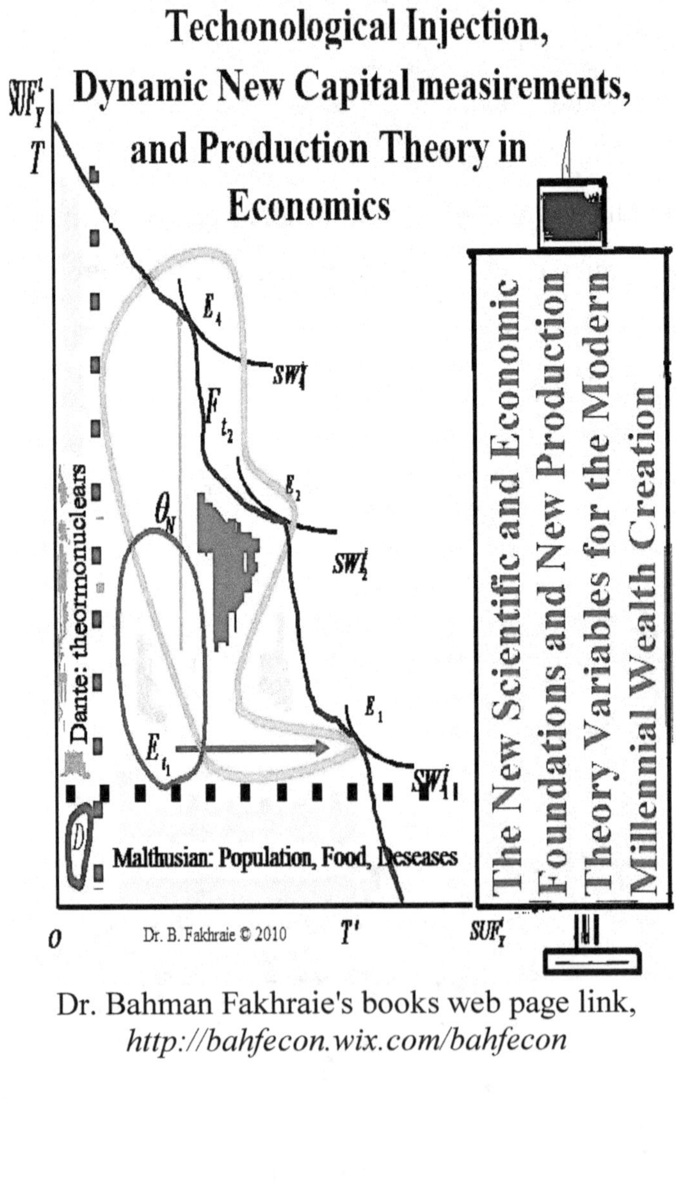

Dr. Bahman Fakhraie's books web page link,
http://bahfecon.wix.com/bahfecon

DEMAND & SUPPLY SIDES OF TECHNOLOGICAL INJECTIONS

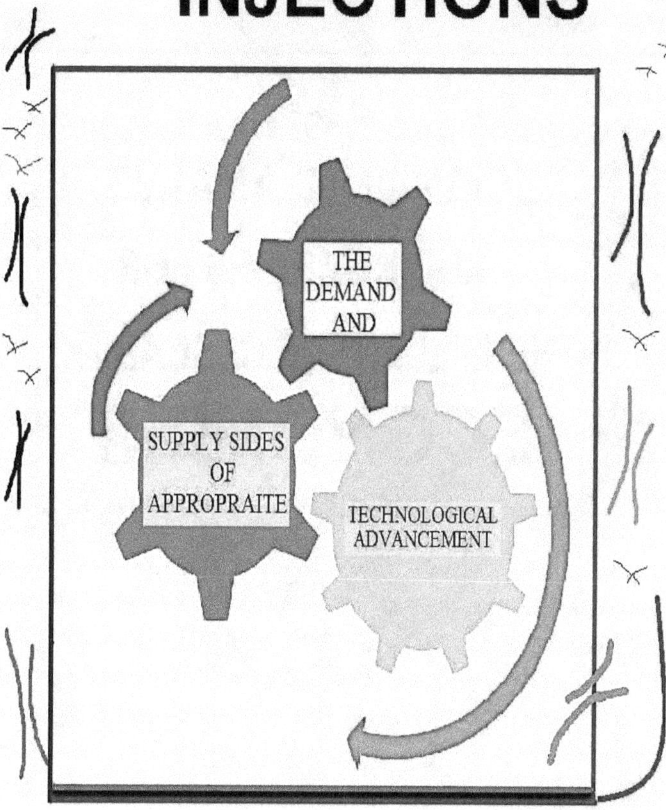

Dr. Bahman Fakhraie's books web page link,
http://bahfecon.wix.com/bahfecon

Supply
Demand
Technological injections
TECONOMIC ANALYSIS
AND REMEDIES FOR
THE MILLENNIALCASCADING
ECONOMIES
Micro
Macro
Policy
Solutions, beside repeating past mistakes.

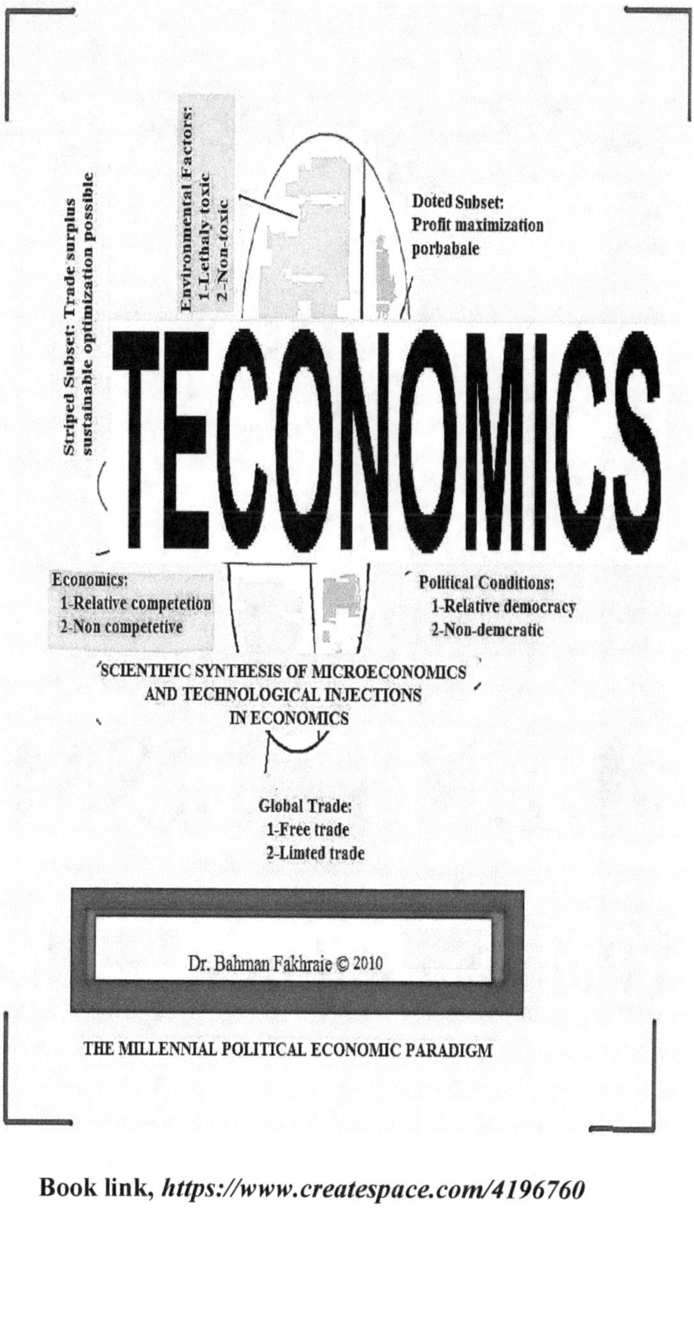

Book link, ***https://www.createspace.com/4196760***

https://www.createspace.com/4121720

TREATISE ON TECONOMICS ØF DYNAMIC RISKS

ALL NATURAL DISASTERS,

&

ENERGY RESOURCES PRODCUTION DISASTERS

Bahman Fakhraie, Ph.D.

https://www.createspace.com/4187823

EBook, http://www.amazon.com/POLITICAL-MONOPOLISTIC-CAPITALISM-WEALTH-CONCENTRATION-ebook/dp/B00HQPBZBK/ref=sr_1_1/180-8302534-5503723?s=digital-text&ie=UTF8&qid=1389203920&sr=1-1#reader_B00HQPBZBK

Print Books link, ***http://bahfecon.wix.com/bahfecon***

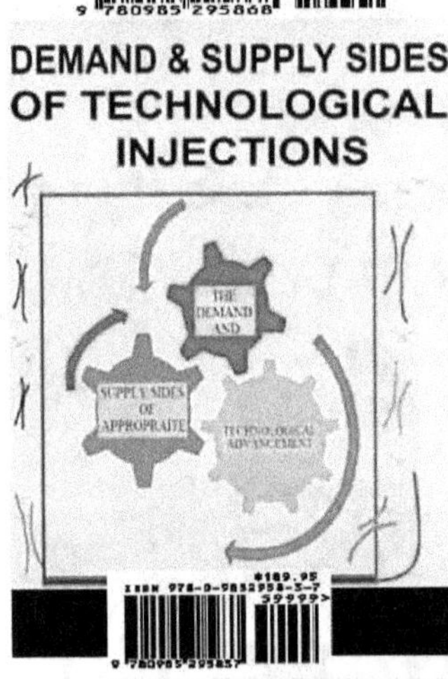

Price in United StatesDollar 389.99
Bar Code Price Tag $389.99
Library of Congress 1688472
ISBN: 978-0-98529558-9-9

Please contact FERDAT PUBLISHING C/O dr.bahf.econ@gmail.com with your DISCOVER, VISA, OR MASTER CARD. All sales are final (no refunds), postages, FEDEX, UPS, grounds with trace will be added. (All costs or legal costs will also be added). There is a temporary promotional, first four books for $999. Sorry, all unrelated communications will be spammed, without replay.

Dr. Bahman Fakhraie's books,

http://bahfecon.wix.com/bahfecon

http://www.amazon.com/Politeconomics-Teconomics-Dr-Bahman-Fakhraie/dp/0989453944/ref=asap_bc?ie=UTF8

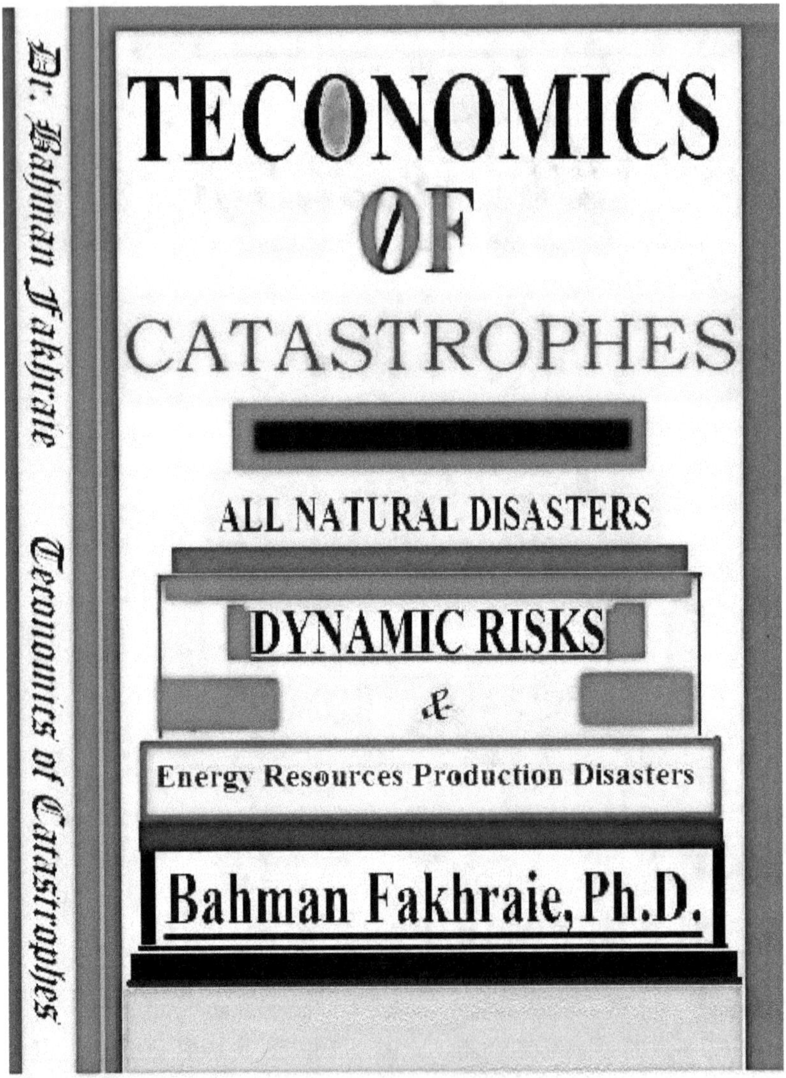

http://www.amazon.com/Teconomics-Catastrophes-Disasters-Resource-Production/dp/0989453960/ref=la_B00IKAR1CM_1_9?s=books&ie=UTF8&qid=1460135054&sr=1-9&refinements=p_82%3AB00IKAR1CM

To All Lives

Dr. Bahman Fakhraie, PhD in Economics, University of Utah, and his dissertation added to the influences of the Unorthodox Holistic Economic doctrine and complemented the modern orthodox economic theories, in the millennial age of technological paradigm shifts. He applies analytical skills with gestalt study of history, mathematics, and econometrics to economic analysis, with scientific background. He is a Published Economist, Author, Researcher, Investor, and Private Contractor. His skills are in international trade and finance, economic production (theory and application), growth and development theory, econometrics, agriculture economics, and agronomy. These are valued skills combinations to employ. Books links, http://bahfecon.wix.com/bahfecon

ISBN-10: 0-9894539-8-7
ISBN-13: 978-0-9894539-8-1

$125.00
ISBN 978-0-9894539-8-1
59999>
9 780989 453981

www.ingramcontent.com/pod-product-compliance
Lightning Source LLC
LaVergne TN
LVHW052203200926
848481LV00001B/22